Chinese Marriage and Social Change

Max WL Wong

Chinese Marriage and Social Change

The Legal Abolition of Concubinage in Hong Kong

Springer

Max WL Wong
University of Hong Kong
Hong Kong, Hong Kong Island, Hong Kong

ISBN 978-981-15-1646-7 ISBN 978-981-15-1644-3 (eBook)
https://doi.org/10.1007/978-981-15-1644-3

This Springer imprint is published by the registered company Springer Nature Singapore Pte Ltd.
The registered company address is: 152 Beach Road, #21-01/04 Gateway East, Singapore 189721, Singapore

Preface

This book originated from research work of a potential litigation a decade ago, which would have hopefully helped to clarify a woman's status as a wife or concubine in a family dispute. However, my research work had to be halted because, like many such family disputes in the Chinese community, this case was settled privately by mediation. Nonetheless, the materials gathered during that period laid down a good foundation for further study. I decided to go forward by conducting further research on the legal status of the concubine in Hong Kong. Since then, the academic journey of this research has taken me into the uncharted waters of traditional Chinese family law in the Qing period and the application of Chinese customary laws and practices in Hong Kong. This journey is never-ending, even after this book, because traditional Chinese family law is still under-researched.

I soon realised the difficulties in researching traditional Chinese laws after I started to research the legal status of the concubine in the Qing period. The relevant elements of Qing law included statutory laws (such as *Da Qing Lü Li*), regulations in palace (such as *Da Qing Huai Dian*), judgments and precedents (such as *Xin An Hui Lan*), provincial laws and regulations, judgments by local magistrates (such as archives in Ba County at Sichuan or Tan Hsin at Taiwan), personal memoirs of local magistrates and other related materials on the rules and regulations at local levels, not to mention that there were special laws which governed different ethnic groups such as Mongolians. I analyse the status of the concubine in Qing laws in the Hong Kong context. Then, I attempt to investigate the ways in which these laws were transplanted into the common law system in Hong Kong after 1843 and, in a wider context, the common law systems in other East Asian jurisdictions.

This journey also led me to study government records in the National Archives in the United Kingdom and the Public Records Office in Hong Kong. With the support of research assistants, I got a clearer picture of the policy developments in both governments that led to the abolition of concubinage and the promulgation of the Marriage Reform Ordinance in Hong Kong in 1971.

This book could not have been finished without the support of many scholars, friends and research assistants. I would like to thank Prof. Michael Palmer and Dr. Dixon Wong for their continuous support and encouragement. I would also like to thank Harry Tse, Melissa Leung, Billy Fung, Samuel Lai, Eric Lai, Janice Lee and Dr. Amy Kellam for their assistance and support in this journey. Finally, I would like to thank my wife, Vivian, and my daughters, Frances and Agnes. As always, their patience and support have been my greatest motivation to finish this monograph. All in all, any errors in this book are mine alone.

Hong Kong, Hong Kong Island, Hong Kong Max WL Wong
October 2019

Contents

Part I
The Issues

Chapter 1
Introduction

Abstract This chapter introduces and explores academic discourse about the marriage law reform in Hong Kong with particular reference to the abolition of concubinage in 1971. The discussion places the Hong Kong case in the comparative sociolegal discourse of family law reforms in colonial contexts. It is also focused on the determining factors which contributed to the end of the recognition of concubinage in law: the pressure from the government of the UK, several reports on marriage reforms proposed by Hong Kong government and the pressure from local social organisations.

Keywords Abolition of concubinage · Hong Kong · Marriage reform · Chinese customary law and practice · Da Qing Lü Li (Great Qing Code)

1.1 Introduction

On 17 June 1970, the Legislative Council of the colonial Hong Kong Government debated the abolition of concubinage, as stipulated in the Marriage Reform Bill 1970. One Chinese Unofficial member of the Legislative Council, Oswald Cheung, was recorded as saying that:

> I do not propose to argue whether monogamy or the traditional Chinese marriage is the better institution. Any such argument, to my mind, is fruitless and would never end and, what is more important, would completely miss the point…the question is, is monogamy so manifestly a superior institution to the traditional Chinese institution of marriage that we should completely deny the right to people to opt out of it if they so wish? Are we right to force this institution upon the people who do not believe in it and who do not want it? (Official Report of Proceedings of the Hong Kong Legislative Council, 17 June 1970, p. 735)

Even though the colonial government had been consulting the Chinese Unofficial members of the Legislative Council on the abolition of concubinage before submitting the legislative proposal to the Legislative Council, such an unapologetic speech in support of the concubinage system was nonetheless shocking.

M. WL Wong, *Chinese Marriage and Social Change*,
https://doi.org/10.1007/978-981-15-1644-3_1

Another Legislative Councillor, Ellen Li, had been advocating the abolition of concubinage since the 1950s. She stood up for the approval of such legislation, arguing that the legislation had been long overdue for at least 20 years:

> Still some people may ask why the Chinese in Hong Kong cannot still be given a choice of the form of marriage they wish to follow. This is of course can only be construed to mean the dying struggle of a few selfish males who would have liked to retain their right to polygamy. If a choice would be given at all, it would have to be the choice between the registry marriage and the modern marriage, which is the law, or customs prevailing in mainland China and in Taiwan. (Official Report of Proceedings of the Hong Kong Legislative Council, 17 June 1970, p. 732–733)

In 1931, the Republic of China did not recognise the institution of concubinage in its new Civil Code (Hsia et al. 1930–1931, bk. IV).[1] In 1950, the Marriage Law of the People's Republic of China re-affirmed the abolition of concubinage policy.[2] And, Taiwan authorities abolished the institution after the end of the Japanese period following the adoption of the laws of the Republic of China. Singapore abolished the institution of concubinage after the passage of the Women's Charter in 1961.[3] This book examines the following question: why did the Hong Kong Government decide to abolish the institution of concubinage in 1971 and not earlier? This leads to another question: what factors contributed to the legal abolition of concubinage in Hong Kong in 1971? So, for example, did the global development of the notion of equality of men and women contribute to the abolition of concubinage in Hong Kong? Or, to what extent did social movements in Hong Kong, championed by women's organisations, bring about an end to the institution? Or, how far did political pressure from the Colonial Office contribute to the Hong Kong Government's proposal to abolish concubinage in Hong Kong? The key issue is: why not sooner?

---

[1] However, according to Chao Fengchich (a legal scholar in the Republican period), the institution of concubinage in the Republic of China was first recognised under the Provisional New Criminal Code 1914 and Supplementary Provisions of the New Criminal Code 1914. Chao mentioned that, in accordance with article 12 of the later law, any reference to "wife"—as appeared in article 82(2), article 82(3)(1) (relating to the hierarchical order of a family) and article 289 (offence of fornication with consent) of the Provisional New Criminal Code 1914—should also apply to "*tsip*". Chao considered that these articles constituted a legal recognition of the institution of concubinage. But since the Provisional Criminal Code 1914 and the Supplementary Provisions of the New Criminal Code 1914 were repealed by the promulgation of the Criminal Code on 1 July 1928, so Chao concluded that starting from this day, the institution of concubinage was abolished (Chao 1993/1928, p. 202). The relevant legal provisions can be found in Huang (2010, p. 513).

[2] Article 1 (Valk 1957, p.347).

[3] This law was enacted in 1961 to provide for the registered monogamous marriage system in Singapore (Singapore Statutes Online, 2019).

1.2 From Strickland Report 1953 to Marriage Reform Ordinance 1971

The journey to the abolition of concubinage in Hong Kong was first started with the Strickland Report—submitted to the Governor of Hong Kong in 1948 but published in 1953 (Committee on Chinese Law and Custom in Hong Kong 1953). At that time, the Hong Kong Government only recognised one form of Chinese marriage, Chinese customary marriage, and not Chinese modern marriage as developed in Mainland China. After the Revolution in China in 1911, there were two major changes in the form of marriage in Mainland China.

Firstly, there was a rise of a modern system of marriage. This was characterised by the reduction of rites in the Chinese marriage system, which departed from the traditional ones—the requirement of the rites including *Three Books and Six Rites*.[4] The new system was regarded as "Chinese modern marriage" in Hong Kong under the Marriage Reform Ordinance 1971. This modern system had become popular in Hong Kong before and after the Second World War.[5] Strictly speaking, the changes in Mainland China to Chinese modern marriages were not regarded as part and parcel of Chinese customary marriages in Hong Kong. At that time, the Hong Kong Government only recognised traditional Chinese customary marriages as effective on 3 April 1843. In other words, marriages contracted according to the *Three Books and Six Rites*, which therefore included potentially polygamous marriage. Since the Hong Kong Government did not recognise Chinese modern marriages, many couples in Hong Kong who contracted Chinese modern marriages went on to have difficulties over issues such as the validity of their marriage, and the inheritance and succession rights of their sons and daughters.

Secondly, under pressure from women's organisations in China, the Government of the Republic of China decided not to recognise the institution of concubinage in the Civil Code as promulgated in 1931. In 1950, the People's Republic of China promulgated the Marriage Law, affirming the principle of monogamous marriage. Meanwhile, in Hong Kong, the continued recognition of Chinese customary marriage meant that the institution of concubinage remained legal. Chinese customary marriage was the institution of "one man and one woman" as stipulated in the Great Qing Code (GQC).[6] Nevertheless, Chinese customary practices also allowed the husband to institute a union of concubinage, which meant that the Chinese marriage system was not monogamous but was potentially polygamous. In this system, the

[4] There had been a reduction in full compliance with the ceremony of *Three Books and Six Rites* in the Chinese marriage system after the establishment of Republic of China in 1911 (Tran, 2015, pp. 104–106).

[5] "Chinese modern marriage" was defined in Hong Kong as the marriage contracted in Hong Kong in supposed conformity with Articles 980–988 of the Civil Code of the Republic of China 1931 (Ridehalgh and McDouall 1961).

[6] Articles 101 and 103 of the GQC provided a "one man and one woman" marriage in the traditional Chinese marriage system. Any woman instituted other than a wife would be regarded as a concubine.

status of a concubine was not equal to a wife. A concubine was inferior to a wife in the Chinese family, though she might enjoy limited benefits, such as the right to maintenance, as stipulated in the GQC. The offspring of a concubine were considered legitimate, and the sons of a concubine had the equal share of the estates of the husband, as stipulated in the GQC. The institution of concubinage was unfair to women and incompatible with the notion of the equality of men and women. Consequently, while Hong Kong still allowed the institution of concubinage, Mainland China had abolished this discriminatory institution that could only do injustice to women. Since women in Hong Kong were treated unfairly in the name of "Chinese customary marriage", social organisations in Hong Kong had been advocating strongly for the abolition of concubinage following the legal changes in Mainland China.

A committee chaired by the Attorney General, Strickland, was appointed to review the above issues in Hong Kong in October 1948 (Minute from D.C.S, 6 October 1948). The Strickland Report, as published in 1953, attempted to deal with the issues of the validity of Chinese customary marriages, Chinese modern marriages and the abolition of concubinage in one package (Committee on Chinese Law and Custom in Hong Kong 1953). One key recommendation was the end of the recognition of Chinese customary marriage, which was to be replaced by a registered monogamous marriage system for the Chinese community. Other than that, the Strickland Report recommended that, after an appointed date, no Chinese customary marriages or modern marriages would be recognised in Hong Kong (Committee on Chinese Law and Custom in Hong Kong 1953, Appendix 18). The institution of concubinage would be abolished. The rights of the concubine and their offspring would be protected by various new laws as recommended in the Strickland Report. In sum, the issue of the abolition of concubinage was the focal point of the discussion in the Strickland Report. Once the issue of the abolition of concubinage had been decided in the Strickland Report, other changes in Chinese law and custom were inevitable.

However, the Strickland Report 1953 was strongly opposed by the senior Chinese Unofficial members of the Executive and Legislative Councils, as represented by Sir Man Kam Lo. He defended the institution of concubinage in his comments attached to the Strickland Report:

> They may even be persuasive arguments for the decreasing popularity in Hong Kong of the *tsip* as an institution. But I cannot see how they can be held to justify the statutory abolition of this institution against the express provisions of the successive Supreme Court Ordinances from the time when Hong Kong has had a Legislature. (Lo 1953, p.11, para. 28(9))

He instead emphasised the role of a concubine in supporting the family and commented that, "I know many a respected man of the old school who, because of his old age and the old age of his wife, or of his infirmity or health, has taken a *tsip* at the express request of his wife, so that the *tsip* could look after him in a way in which only a wife or a *tsip* can do" (Lo 1953, p.12, para. 28(14)). His comments, though controversial, marked the end of the road for the Strickland Report. The Hong Kong Government decided not to adopt the Strickland Report in 1956.

However, the proposal to abolish concubinage was only put on the shelf for a moment. Social organisations, especially women's organisations such as the Hong Kong Council of Women, were frustrated by the comments made by Sir Man Kam Lo. They kept on pressing the Hong Kong Government for the abolition of concubinage. Additionally, social organisations asked members of parliament in London to table parliamentary questions on the issue of concubinage in Hong Kong. This strategy worked effectively. The Colonial Office was forced by the parliamentary questions to review the position of the Hong Kong Government on the abolition of concubinage. The Hong Kong Government, however, was not subdued by the actions taken by social organisations. The principal government officer in Hong Kong, the Secretary for Chinese Affairs, considered that since the Chinese community—as represented by Sir Man Kam Lo—was opposed to such abolition, the government did not want to interfere with the community and create unnecessary conflicts between the colonial government and major colonial Chinese collaborators (Memorandum for Executive Council, 27 August, 1956, para. 5).

Nevertheless, due to social pressure from social organisations for the abolition of concubinage, the government decided to conduct another round of public consultation, now not on the Chinese law and custom as discussed in the Strickland Report, but focused on Chinese marriages in Hong Kong. After soliciting public opinions, the Ridehalgh/McDouall Report 1960 did not favour the legal abolition of concubinage; it recommended retaining such institutions and letting the custom die naturally, though the government proposed a review after 5 years (Letter from Colonial Office, 17 December, 1964). This time, the Colonial Office decided to actively become involved in the policy of abolishing concubinage in Hong Kong.

Internal discussion within the Colonial Office reveals that they were frustrated by the approach taken by the Hong Kong Government and the delay in abolition. The Colonial Office forced the Hong Kong Government to abolish concubinage based on two grounds. Firstly, the Colonial Office directed the Hong Kong Government to consider the its treaty obligations under the United Nations, wherein the Hong Kong Government must subscribe to the principle of equality of men and women—notably the United Nations' Convention on Consent to Marriage, Minimum Age for Marriage and Registration of Marriages signed by the UK in 1962. Secondly, the Hong Kong Government had to accept the fact that there was strong public demand from social organisations for the abolition the concubinage. Given the political pressure from the Colonial Office, in 1965 the Hong Kong Government decided to produce another report, the McDouall/Heenan Report, and decided to propose the abolition of concubinage. A draft of this report was given to the Colonial Office before submission to the Executive Council in 1965. The Colonial Office approved this report generally. After the approval of the Colonial Office, in 1967 the Hong Kong Government published this report in part, with a White Paper on Chinese Marriages in Hong Kong, seeking the public's views on the abolition of concubinage and other subsequent amendments to existing laws relating to Chinese law and custom. In general, there was not much resentment from the Chinese community at this time (Hong Kong Government 1967). In 1969, the Hong Kong Government published a White Bill for soliciting public opinions (Marriage

Reform Bill 1969). At this juncture, however, the Chinese Unofficial members of the Executive and Legislative Councils expressed frustration at the legislation.

The focal point of the argument between the government and the Chinese Unofficial members of the Executive and Legislative Councils was not the abolition of the concubinage, but the definition of a concubine. The Chinese Unofficial members of both Councils argued that in order to not let a mistress slip through the laws and inherit the estate of the husband, a definition of concubine should be given that was not based on the GQC, or traditional Chinese laws and customs, but on the local situation in Hong Kong. Given the pressure from the Chinese Unofficial members, a definition of concubine was added to the legislation. Contrary to traditional Chinese laws, the status of a concubine required the recognition of the wife, or the acceptance of the family generally, as a condition to being a concubine in Hong Kong law. In 1970, the principal legislative bill—the Marriage Reform Bill—was passed in the Legislative Council. Coupled with another seven ordinances, these laws were promulgated on 7 October 1971, and a new marriage system was put in place.[7] Thus, after nearly 20 years of discussion, the Hong Kong Government finally stamped out the institution of concubinage. In sum, without direct intervention from the Colonial Office in the UK, the abolition of concubinage would not have been proposed and passed in the Hong Kong Legislative Council.

This book is significant in the following areas. Firstly, the notion of "equality of men and women" as promoted by social organisations in Hong Kong played a pivotal role in making the abolition of concubinage a success. Social organisations in Hong Kong actively petitioned the UK and Hong Kong Governments urging for an earlier abolition of concubinage. Such social pressure had cornered the Hong Kong Government into facing the hard fact: either accept the petitions to abolish concubinage or keep colonial collaborators satisfied by retaining such practice. By listening to the call of social organisations to abolish concubinage, the Hong Kong Government might risk fierce resistance from Chinese political figures in the Executive and Legislative Councils who were going to defend the Chinese traditional family order without compromise. Ultimately, the Hong Kong Government bowed to social pressure and waved the flag of upholding the universal value of equality between men and women by abolishing concubinage.

Secondly, the Colonial Office was determined to abolish concubinage not out of a strategy to replace or erase Chinese customs: the Colonial Office did not have a master plan to reform the Chinese family order. The reason for the Colonial Office's support for the abolition of concubinage was primarily due to the responsible officer's distaste for the existence of such an institution in Hong Kong. As seen in the archives of the Colonial Office, the officials in the Colonial Office did not intend to overhaul Chinese customary marriage and replace it with a registered monogamous system. They did not ask the Hong Kong Government to erase or overhaul Chinese

[7] The other seven Ordinances are: Intestates' Estates Ordinance, Deceased's Family Maintenance Ordinance, Legitimacy Ordinance, Affiliation Proceedings Ordinance, Married Persons Status Ordinance, Matrimonial Causes (Amendment) Ordinance and Law Reform (Miscellaneous Provisions) Ordinance.

customary marriage or modern marriage in the colony. They did not even comment on the steps taken by the Hong Kong Government to deal with the issues of Chinese customary or modern marriage. So, once the goal of the abolition of concubinage was achieved in 1965, the Colonial Office let the Hong Kong Government deal with the details of legislation and consequential amendments. This experience showed that, at least on the issue of the abolition of concubinage, the Colonial Office did not have a plan or strategy to totally erase Chinese customary marriage, or invent a new tradition, or redefine the status of a concubine. It is important to note that it was the Chinese Unofficial members of the Executive and Legislative Councils in Hong Kong who demanded a redefinition of the meaning of concubine in the new laws, by altering traditional Chinese laws and customs, not the Colonial Office in the UK.

Thirdly, the Hong Kong Government was the main culprit for the delay in abolishing the institution of concubinage. To the Hong Kong Government, the issue of the abolition of concubinage was not just a question of the equality of men and women, but was a question of governance. Even though there was strong public support for such changes, the main collaborators of the colonial regime were Chinese senior political figures strongly opposed to such reform. The Hong Kong Government attempted to propose a *delay* approach on the question of concubinage because that might create tension between the colonial government and its major collaborators such as Sir Man Kam Lo. This shows that, at least as far as the Hong Kong Government was concerned, there was not a strong political will to put forward a drastic social reform programme that might wipe out Chinese customary marriage. They did that only after the intervention of the Colonial Office, and they did that reluctantly—for example, a legislative bill on the abolition of concubinage was only submitted to the Legislative Council in 1969, 4 years after the decision of the abolition of concubinage was approved by the Colonial Office in 1965.

1.3 Literature Review

To date there have been only a few publications directly related to the institution of concubinage and the abolition of concubinage in Hong Kong. Maria Jaschok (1988) in her book *Concubines and Bond Servants: The Social History of a Chinese Customs* gave an account of her interviews on a Chinese family regarding the *Mui Tsai* system in Hong Kong. There was no reference to the concubine system nor to the abolition of concubinage in Hong Kong.

Another book, by Hu Hung-lick—*Hong Kong Marriage and Inheritance Law*, which was originally published in 1957—had a chapter on the institution of concubinage. In it, he criticised Sir Man Kam Lo's comments on the Strickland Report on three grounds. Firstly, Hu considered that, in principle, the development of laws should follow social development and needs. Secondly, he strongly opposed a man taking a concubine in order to continue his patrilineal lineage. Thirdly, he opposed the use of a concubine to take care of an elderly husband. Hu (2009/1957, p.145) advocated for monogamous marriage because he considered that polygamous marriage was irrational and could not bring any benefits to society and, most importantly, that it would destroy the normal life of a husband and wife. However, this book did not discuss the social movements organised by some social organisations that led to the end of the institution of concubinage in Hong Kong.

An article written by Evans (1971, p.27) discussed the issue of the abolition of concubinage in the context of the application of Chinese customary law in the common law system of Hong Kong. He considered that because of social and economic changes in Hong Kong, the courts in Hong Kong began to apply customary law as part of the laws that were binding on the courts and parties, "binding in a way in which customary law had never conceived to be" Evans (1971, p.27). Evans (1971, p.28) considered that the judges changed the nature of customary law: "they made it susceptible not to localized and particularized control and interpretation but to the modus operandi of the common law with all that entailed". Evans considered that the Chinese form of marriage, which was forced to compete against the principles of the English law system, was still recognised in the Hong Kong courts as affecting the legal status of the parties concerned. To Evans, the institution of concubinage was even more problematic because "it raised moral objections in the minds of the judges". Nevertheless, Evans stated that the judges had put their moral attitudes aside and treated the institution of concubinage as a practical matter: "it was an established custom which affected the life and status of a good many people and, accordingly, the position of a concubine was recognised not as that of a 'wife' in the western sense, but as that of a person who had entered into a family with a relationship implying rights and duties on both sides". Given the abolition of concubinage in the Marriage Reform Ordinance 1971, Evans (1971, p.31) foresaw that the role of customary law as a living element in the law of Hong Kong would be virtually over. But his prediction of the role of the customary law was not fully materialised, because the New Territories Ordinance still required the application of the Chinese customary laws and there were some judicial cases relating to the arguments on the status of concubine even after the promulgation of the Marriage Reform Ordinance in 1971 (see Chap. 2, Sect. 2.2). In his article Evans did not discuss the reasons for the abolition of concubinage in Hong Kong.

Another scholar, Su Yigong (2007, p.186), agreed in general with the comments of Evans, but he considered that the issue of the status of a concubine in a Chinese family was more than just the legal principles as seen in the judicial cases in Hong Kong. Su (2007, p.190) considered that, firstly, the main difference between a wife and a concubine in a traditional Chinese family rested on the status of "names" (*ming feng*) and not on the inheritance of properties. Such distinction was found to be difficult for Westerners to understand. Secondly, Su (2007, p.191) considered that the core values of the traditional Chinese family order were Confucian values and *ren lun* (human relationship), the latter referring to the moral relationship between people. Although in Chinese customary law, women's right to inheritance of property was unclear, family members and especially the men in the traditional family system had an inescapable moral obligation to support and maintain the women. He considered that the Hong Kong courts were too restrictive to follow the legal rules literally without consideration of the cultural values enshrined in the Chinese community. Su's comments might be valid since the principal concerns of the judicial cases in traditional Chinese law were to promote and entrench the traditional family order. But in Hong Kong, the status of a concubine was highly related to the rights of inheritance of a wife and concubine to a husband's estates.[8] Nevertheless, Su did not discuss the reasons for the abolition of concubinage in 1971. He also did not comment on the ways in which the Hong Kong Government might attempt to legally reform Chinese customary marriage according to the notion of the "Western" concept of the equality of men and women. Finally, he did not discuss the impact of such a notion on the discussion of judicial cases relating to the status of a concubine in Hong Kong courts.

A scholar, Leonard Pegg (1994), discussed the two essential elements for the taking of a concubine as revealed in the judicial cases. He discussed how, in the case of In *Ng Ying Ho v Tam Suen Yu*, the court agreed that two essential elements were identified as the elements of a concubine: firstly, the intention on the part of man to take the woman as a *tsip* and, secondly, the public holding out of the woman as his *tsip* (Pegg 1994, p.31). However, Pegg (1994, p.31) considered that in the later cases of *Wong Kam Ying v Man Chi Tai* and *Re Wong Choi Ho & Another*, the judges had put more emphasis on the importance of the acceptance of the wife and family in the reception of a concubine into the family. Pegg considered that after the statutory definition of the "union of concubinage" was given in 1971,[9] which placed the emphasis on the acceptance of concubinage by the wife and recognition by the family, the number of women who could claim for to be a valid concubine in future cases would be reduced. Pegg's work questioned the definition of the union of concubinage but did not discuss the origins of, and the reasons for, the abolition of concubinage, nor did it mention the reasons for the marriage reform in 1971.

Another scholar, Athena Liu (1999), in her book *Family Law for the HKSAR*, discussed the nature of Chinese customary marriage and the Marriage Reform Ordinance. She considered that the purpose of the Marriage Reform Ordinance was to abolish Chinese customary marriage prospectively. On the discussion of the union of concubinage, she commented that the Marriage Reform Ordinance did not resolve the conflicting requirements, as given in the case law, regarding the taking of a concubine: for instance, whether a ceremony was required for taking

[8] This will be discussed later in Chap. 3.

[9] See Legitimacy Ordinance, s 14(2); Intestates' Estate Ordinance, section 13(2) and Deceased's Family Maintenance Ordinance, section 17 (2). The definitions of these three ordnances are identical. For instance, section 14(2) of the Legitimacy Ordinance section specifies that:

> In this section, 'union of concubinage' (夫妾關係) means a union of concubinage, entered by a male partner and a female partner before 7 October 1971, under which union the female partner has, during the lifetime of the male partner, been accepted by his wife as his concubine and recognized as such by his family generally.

a concubine.[10] She also commented that this Ordinance does not define the status and rights of existing concubines and their children (Liu 1999, p. 36). Although the author was correct in questioning the issues on the judicial interpretation of the status of a concubine in Hong Kong, she might not realise that the true intention of the Marriage Reform Ordinance was to abolish the institution of concubinage, not to reform Chinese customary marriage.

A dissertation written by Wong Pik-wan (2000) traced the women's movement for legal reform in Hong Kong. One of the chapters discussed the development of the abolition of concubinage movement in Hong Kong. She considered that the success of such abolition was mainly due to some domestic and external factors. These included the work and pressure exerted by local women's groups and the first female Legislative Councillor in Hong Kong, Mrs. Ellen Li (Wong 2000, p.160). Firstly, Wong (2000, p.161) considered that Ellen Li not only exerted pressure on the government to pass the abolition of concubinage by threatening to resign from the Legislative Council, Li had also conducted a lot of lobbying work to convince the male members of the Legislative Council and the leaders of different organisations, such as the New Territories' rural committees, to accept the abolition of concubinage. Secondly, Wong (2000, p.162) considered that the gradual process of modernisation (Westernisation) contributed to provide a favourable environment for the reform of marriage law in Hong Kong, since this helped to shape the government elite and the public regarding polygamy and other family laws. Wong argued that the perceptions of the public had been changed in the late 1960s. On the one hand, young women in Hong Kong began to feel that it was "shameful" to be a concubine and they preferred to work to earn their money rather than becoming a concubine for the sake of money. Wong also stated that modern Chinese men in Hong Kong gradually considered that taking a concubine or mistress was both "disgraceful and disgusting". Because of this change of attitude, women could gain more male support for the monogamy legislation.

Thirdly, Wong (2000, p.164) considered that the United Nations also played an important role in catalysing the marriage law reform in Hong Kong, since the UK had subscribed to the UN Charter and the Universal Declaration of Human Rights that emphasised the principle of the equal rights of men and women. And, the United Nations' Conventions, such as the Supplementary Convention on the Abolition of Slavery and the Convention on Consent to Marriage, Minimum Age for Marriage and Registration of Marriages signed in 1962, also showed that Hong Kong had begun to realise the necessity of complying with the international standard as required by the United Nations, which was reported in the McDouall/Heenan Report in 1965. Wong's thesis rightly analysed the movement for the abolition of concubinage

[10]The author quoted the case of Wong Kam-Ying v Man Chi-tai (1967) in which the judge Higgins J considered that the lack of any ceremony was not crucial (Liu 1999, p. 34). But the author considered that the case of Kwan Chui Kwok-ying v Tao Wai-chun (1995) attempted to clarify the requirement by stating that almost all unions of concubines would be evident by the requirement of Yap Kung ceremony— a tea serving the principal wife as a representation of the acceptance of a concubine in a family (Liu 1999, p. 36).

in the context of the socio-economic environments in Hong Kong—that the notion of the equality of men and women had been widely accepted in the society meant that the men found it difficult to support the institution of concubinage. Wong emphasised the efforts of the female Legislative Councillor, Ellen Li, in her advocacy of the abolition of concubinage. Wong also found that the UN conventions and resolutions contributed to the end of concubinage in Hong Kong. But her thesis did not extensively research archives in Hong Kong and the UK in order to investigate the underlying reasons for the sudden change of attitude of the Hong Kong Government regarding the institution of concubinage—that is, the Colonial Office's imposition upon the Hong Kong Government to make a final decision to end the institution in 1965.

The most relevant work of the abolition of concubinage in Hong Kong is the thesis written by Yip Ka-yan in 2014. Yip traced the historical development of the reform of Chinese law and custom in Hong Kong from the Strickland Report in 1953. She emphasised the role of social organisations, notably women's organisations, to press for such reforms in Hong Kong. On the decision to abolish concubinage in 1965, Yip (2014, p.153) suggested two possible reasons. First, since the UK Government had signed the human rights treaties of the United Nations, the UK Government was obliged to press for the Hong Kong Government to amend the laws to fulfil the requirements in such treaties. The second reason was that, after the appointment of Ellen Li—a famous women rights' advocate—as the Legislative Councillor, the Hong Kong Government expected Li to mobilise support for the abolition of concubinage inside the Legislative Council. Yip (2014, p.160) concluded that Li, encouraged by McDouall, put a lot of effort into lobbying for support from the Chinese Unofficial members of the Legislative Council and the senior figures of the New Territories. These efforts paved the way for the abolition of concubinage. Yip concluded her work by giving other reasons for the abolition of concubinage in Hong Kong in 1971. Firstly, it was the endless efforts of the women's organisations which put pressure on the Hong Kong Government to abolish the institution of concubinage (Yip 2014, p.176). Secondly, the notion of monogamous marriage had been widely accepted by the Chinese community after the Second World War (Yip 2014, p.179). Thirdly, there was a successful birth control policy and a rise in women's education and economic status in Hong Kong, which made the members of the community feel that there was no need to retain the institution of concubinage (Yip 2014, p.182).

Relying upon the archives from the Hong Kong Government, Yip gave a comprehensive review on the development of the reforms as proposed by the Strickland Committee since 1953. But Yip's thesis did not research the archives in the UK, resulting in a lack of discussion on the issue of the political pressure from the Colonial Office in London. The Hong Kong Government's sudden change of attitude in 1965, as shown in the public records in the National Archives in the UK, was due mainly to the political pressure applied by the Colonial Office. It is shown in the UK archives that, after the Raleigh/McDouall Report in 1960, the Colonial Office felt that because of the principle of the equality of men and women the existence of the institution of concubinage in Hong Kong was intolerable. In addition to parliamentary questions about the status of women in Hong Kong, officers in the Colonial Office who were strongly against the existence of concubinage put pressure on the Hong Kong Government to make a change as early as possible. It is argued that while social organisations, especially women's organisations, did put a lot of pressure on the Hong Kong Government to change its mind in 1965, the last straw that broke the deadlock of introducing reform on the abolition of concubinage came from the Colonial Office.

1.4 Outline of Chapters

This book is divided into four parts. The first part, Chap. 1, introduces the issues relating to the institution of concubinage. Part II, Chaps. 2 and 3, provide the social and legal framework which define the context of the book. Chapter 2 discusses the legal provisions relating to a concubine as specified in *Da Qing Lü Li* or the GQC—the legal code that governed Qing imperial society and a source of law on concubinage in Hong Kong. Apart from the analysis of the written laws, this chapter also investigates the application of the relevant laws by Qing authorities, such as the cases adjudicated by the Board of Punishments as reported in *Xin An Hui Lan*, *Bo An Hui Bian* and in memoirs written by retired local magistrates. This chapter shows that the GQC is not the only source that contains provisions relating to the status of concubine. It is important to note that since mediation played a pivotal role in resolving the domestic disputes at local levels, cases adjudicated by the local magistrate regarding concubines were often mixed process, with the use, or misuse, of the GQC being combined with local customary practices.

Chapter 3 discusses the application of GQC in East Asian jurisdictions. Because of the difficulties in identifying the sources of Qing laws, judges in other jurisdictions had to rely on expert evidence and gradually constructed the elements of the valid legal status of a concubine, taking into account legal development in Mainland China. The focus of this chapter is the judicial interpretations of the relevant laws in the GQC and, in particular, the impact of the development of the Chinese modern marriage system in China and the legal abolition of concubinage in the Civil Code of Republic of China in 1931. The case law in East Asian jurisdictions shows that, firstly, judges were willing to give more rights to the concubine in domestic disputes, especially relating to the status and the right to a husband's estates. Secondly, judges were also willing to depart from the provisions of the GQC and customary practice in Mainland China, grounding their decisions on the rights of the concubine in the Chinese family in the local environment. This departure paved the way to different interpretations of the status of the concubine in different jurisdictions. This leads to the question: did they invent, or re-create, Chinese customs to preserve a system of concubinage outside Mainland China?

Part III of the book discusses the legislative history of the Marriage Reform Ordinance (1971) in Hong Kong. Chapter 4 discusses the pressure placed by the UK Government on the Hong Kong Government for the abolition of concubinage in the territory. Based on the available archives from the UK and Hong Kong, pressure from the UK Government played a significant role in eradicating this customary practice. This chapter discusses the reasons for the formation of the Strickland Committee in 1948. This committee was established due to the issues arising from the recognition of Chinese customary marriages and the proliferation of the new and invalid Chinese modern marriages in Hong Kong. In addition, the Strickland Committee also investigated issues of Chinese law and custom such as the abolition of concubinage, the adoption of children and the succession and inheritance rights of the offspring in the traditional Chinese marriage system. This chapter ends with the refusal of the Hong Kong Government to adopt the recommendations of the Strickland Committee, due mainly to the opposition from the Chinese Unofficial members of the Executive and Legislative Councils—the colonial collaborators responsible for Hong Kong governance.

Chapter 5 discusses the interactions between the Hong Kong Government and social organisations on the issue of the abolition of concubinage. This chapter first discusses the background leading to the Ridehalgh/McDouall report in 1960. Despite strong political pressure from social organisations, the report recommended not abolishing concubinage in one stroke and instead letting it die down naturally. The continuous petitions from social groups to the UK and Hong Kong governments had generated strong social pressure for the abolition of concubinage. On the other hand, the Colonial Office was very critical of the proposals provided in the Ridehalgh/McDouall Report 1960 and urged the Hong Kong Government to abolish such institution as soon as possible. This chapter examines the internal discussions in the Colonial Office and how the views of officers in the Colonial Office contributed to the abandonment of the Ridehalgh/McDouall Report 1960 in Hong Kong and reignited the policy of the abolition of concubinage in the new report of McDouall/Heenan Report 1965 submitted by the Hong Kong Government.

Chapter 6 discusses the aftermath of the McDouall/Heenan Report in Hong Kong in two areas. First, this chapter traces the development of the McDouall/Heenan Report 1965 and the subsequent legal changes relating to the status of a concubine as given in the White Paper 1967 and the Marriage Reform Bill 1969. The most notable development was the discussion of the definition of the "union of concubinage". The Chinese Unofficial members of the Executive and Legislative Councils pressed for a definition of the union of concubinage in the new legislation that included the requirements that a concubine must be recognised by the principal wife and have the acceptance of the family generally. After much delay in the legislative process, the Marriage Reform Ordinance was finally passed in 1970 and promulgated in 1971. This chapter also examines the administrative responses to the Marriage Reform Ordinance. Firstly, the government introduced new laws to give more rights to the wife married according to Chinese customary marriage; for instance, the wife could have the same rights to divorce as a wife married under the Marriage Ordinance. Secondly, the Hong Kong Government introduced new laws with a view to abolishing the use of Chinese customs in the areas of succession and adoption. All in all, after 1971, a monogamous and registered marriage system has been applied in the Chinese community.

Part IV is the conclusion of the book. Chapter 7 concludes the book by examining the historical and social developments which led to the abolition of concubinage in 1971. Before 1971, although concubinage had become illegal in Republic of China in 1931 and the People's Republic of China in 1950, the existence of the discriminatory institution of concubinage was retained in Hong Kong (probably being re-interpreted in Hong Kong by the colonial courts), and was regarded as an obstacle to Hong Kong moving towards being a modern and industrialised society. In essence, given the rise in education levels and the general acceptance of the notion of the equality between men and women in Hong Kong, the final eradication of the institution of concubinage was unavoidable. The Colonial Office, though it did not have any systematic or strategic plan to abrogate Chinese customary marriage in Hong Kong, had played a decisive role to put an end to the institution of concubinage in Hong Kong. Finally, the chapter ends with the judicial responses to the Marriage Reform Ordinance 1971, with the cases of *Leung May Ling and Others v Leung Sai Lun Robert and Others* (1999) and *Suen Toi Lee v Yau Yee Ping* (2001), decided by the Court of Final Appeal. It is important to note that the courts in Hong Kong are generally receptive of the provisions given in the Marriage Reform Ordinance.

1.5 The Sources

Firstly, for the discussion of Qing law relating to the institution of concubinage, apart from the statutory laws of Qing authorities, the case reports from the Board of Punishments as published in various sources such as *Xin An Hui Lan*, *Xin An Hui Lan Xu Bian* and *Xu Zeng Xin An Hui Lan* will be studied. In addition, cases at the local level, as recorded by the archival records of the Tan-Hsin Archive in Taiwan and the Huangyan Litigation Archives in Mainland China, will be studied in order to examine the approach taken by magistrates when adjudicating family disputes. The personal records and memoirs of the local government officials will also be examined.

Secondly, for the discussion of judicial cases in courts and for conducting comparative study on issues relating to the institution of concubinage as applied in the courts, the following sources are used: law reports from Hong Kong, Straits Settlements, Malaya, Singapore and Burma; the *Da Li Yuan* of the Republic of China; and the Review High Court of Taiwan during the Japanese occupation period.

Thirdly, in relation to the legislative development of the abolition of concubinage in Hong Kong, the archival records of the Public Records Office in Hong Kong and the National Archives in the UK will be studied. Together these records point the way to how the decisions of the Colonial Office might have applied pressure on the Hong Kong Government to abolish concubinage in 1965. In addition, the records of the Legislative Council of Hong Kong and the reports and petitions of social organisations and women's organisations will be examined.

Finally, any attempt to unify the romanisation of Chinese characters used in East Asian jurisdictions would create more problems than solutions for the reader, because the same character will be romanised differently in different jurisdictions, depending on their respective use of the Chinese language. This book will retain the original romanisation of the Chinese characters as shown in the official records and documents. So, for example, the terms *tsip* or *t'sip* (Cantonese pronunciation), *qie* (*pinyin*) and *concubine* are used interchangeably in this book, but in fact all terms refer to the Chinese word 妾. Readers are strongly advised to check the glossary of this book if the Chinese characters are not romanised by *pinyin*.

References

Chao, F. (1993). *Zhonggou funu zai falu shang de diwei* [The legal status of women in China]. Taipei: Daw Shiang Publishing. (Original work published 1928).

Committee on Chinese Law and Custom in Hong Kong. (1953). *Chinese law and custom in Hong Kong: Report of a Committee appointed by the Governor in October, 1948*. Hong Kong: Government Printer.

Da Qing lü li. (1993). (Zhang R., Liu Y. & Jin M, Punctuators). Tianjin: Tianjin Guji Chubenshe.

Evans, D. M. E. (1971). Common law in a Chinese setting—The kernel or the nut? *Hong Kong Law Journal, 1*, 9.

Hong Kong Colonial Secretariat. (1967). *White paper on chinese marriages in Hong Kong*. Hong Kong: Government Press.

Hong Kong Legislative Council. (1970). Official report of proceedings of the Hong Kong Legislative Council, 17 June 1970.

Hsia, C., Chow, J. L. E., Liu, C. & Chang, Y. (Trans.). (1930–1931). *Book IV "Marriage", The civil code of the Republic of China* (Vol. 2). Shanghai: Kelly & Walsh.

Hu, H. (2009). *Xianggang de hun yin yu ji cheng fa* [The Marriage and Inheritance Laws in Hong Kong]. Hong Kong: Red-Publish. (Original work published 1957).

Huang, Y. (2010). *A Compilation of Penal Laws from the Late Qing to Republic of China (1905–2010)* (Vol. 1). Taipei: Angle Publishing.

Jaschok, M. (1988). *Concubines and bond servants: The social history of a Chinese customs*. Hong Kong: Oxford University Press.

Letter from Colonial Office. (1964, 17 December). *Chinese Law and Custom, Letter from Colonial Office, J. D. Higham to Colonial Secretariat, E. B. Teesdale, 17 December 1964* (HKRS 41-1-3106-10). The Hong Kong Record Series, Hong Kong.

Liu, N. C. A. (1999). *Family law for the HKSAR*. Hong Kong: Hong Kong University Press.

Lo, M. K. (1953). *Comments on the report of the Committee on Chinese Law and Custom in Hong Kong*. Hong Kong: Government Printer.

Minute from D.C.S. (1948, 6 October). *Chinese Law and Custom, Minute from D.C.S. to Hon. A.G., 6 October 1948*, (HKRS 41-1-3106-1). The Hong Kong Record Series, Hong Kong.

Memorandum for Executive Council. (1965, 27 August). *Chinese Law and Custom, Memorandum for Executive Council: Report of Committee on Chinese Law and Custom, 27 August 1956* (HKRS 41-1-3106-5). The Hong Kong Record Series, Hong Kong.

Pegg, L. (1994). *Family Law in Hong Kong* (3rd ed.). Singapore: Butterworths Asia.

Ridehalgh, A., & McDouall, J. C. (1961). *Chinese marriages in Hong Kong*. Hong Kong: Government Printer.

Singapore Statutes Online. (2019). Women's Charter. https://sso.agc.gov.sg/Act/WC1961. Accessed 12 Mar 2019.

Su, Y. (2007). *Chinese Law Applied by Westerners: Traditional Chinese Law and Custom in Hong Kong* (2nd ed.). Beijing: Social Sciences Academic Press.
Tran, L. (2015). *Concubines in courts: Marriage and monogamy in twentieth-century China*. Lanham: Rowan and Littlefield.
van der Valk, M. H. (1957). The registration of marriage in communist China. *Monumenta Serica, 16*(1/2), 347–259.
Wong, P. (2000). *Negotiating gender: The women's movement for legal reform in colonial Hong Kong*. Ph.D. thesis. University of California, Los Angeles.
Yip, K. (2014). *The abolishment of concubinage in Hong Kong: An analysis of its process and opinions on the issue (1948–1971)*. Ph.D. thesis. Chinese University of Hong Kong.

Statutes

Marriage Reform Bill, July 1969.

Cases

Kwan Chui Kwok Ying v Tao Wai Chun. (1995). 1 HKC 371.
Leung May Ling and Others v Leung Sai Lun Robert and Others. (1999). 2 HKCFAR 94.
Ng Ying Ho v Tam Suen Yu. (1963). *HKLR*, 923.
Re Wong Choi Ho & Another. (1969). *HKLR*, 391.
Suen Toi Lee v Yau Yee Ping. (2001). 4 HKCFAR 474.
Wong Kam Ying v Man Chi Tai. (1967). *HKLR*, 201.

Part II
Concubinage in Chinese Law and Society

Chapter 2
The Meaning of T'sip in Qing Law

Abstract This chapter discusses the legal provisions relating to concubines as specified in *Da Qing Lü Li* (The Great Qing Code)—the legal code that governed Qing imperial society. The *Da Qing Lü Li* was a source of law on the institution of concubinage in Hong Kong. Cases reported in *Xin An Hui Lan* and *Bo An Hui Bian*, local archives at Ba County and Tan Hsin from the Qing period, and some personal memoirs written by retired local Qing magistrates could all assist in understanding the interpretations of *t'sip*—who had an inferior status than wife in the Chinese family and could only have maintenance after the death of the husband.

Keywords Da Qing Lü Li (Great Qing Code) · Magistrates · Avoid litigation (Xisong) · Fu Ching · Inferiority and dissolution of concubinage

2.1 Introduction

In January 1841, after the defeat of the Qing military forces at Bogue Port in the Pearl River Delta, the representative of the Qing authority, Qi Shan, concluded a truce with the representative of the Great Britain, Captain Elliot—The Convention of Chuanbi. This peace treaty aimed to end the war between these two countries but failed to obtain approval from either government. Nonetheless, Captain Elliot proceeded to announce the terms in the Convention, in which the Qing authorities agreed to cede Hong Kong Island to the Great Britain (Endacott 1973, p. 17). Eager to occupy Hong Kong Island, despite the disapproval from both governments on the truce, on 16 January 1841, a naval force under Commander-in-Chief Bremer landed on Hong Kong Island. After declaring that Great Britain had sovereignty in Hong Kong on 26 January 1841, two proclamations were issued by Captain Elliot. The first proclamation, made on 2 February 1841, announced that "all natives of the island and all natives of China resorting thereto, were to be governed according to the laws of China, every description of torture excepted" (Norton-Kyshe 1971, p. 5). Another proclamation was made by Captain Elliot, together with Commander-in-Chief Bremer, on 1 February 1941 addressed specifically to the Chinese inhabit-

M. WL Wong, *Chinese Marriage and Social Change*,
https://doi.org/10.1007/978-981-15-1644-3_2

ants. This proclamation specified that the Chinese inhabitants would be governed, pending Her Majesty's further pleasure, according to the laws, customs and usages of the Chinese (every description of torture excepted) by the elders of villages, subject to the control of a British magistrate (Norton-Kyshe 1971, pp. 5–6). In this role, the Hong Kong magistrate would apply Chinese laws and customs to cases relating to the Chinese inhabitants in Hong Kong.

In March 1898, the Hong Kong Governor undertook to occupy the New Territories. Subsequently, after the Convention Between Great Britain and China Respecting an Extension of Hong Kong Territory was signed 9 June 1898, an announcement to the people of the New Territories gave the assurance that: "your commercial and land interest will be safeguarded and your usages and good customs will not in any way be interfered with" (Despatches 1898, p. 678, 1899, p. 21). This promise was later confirmed in the statute book, in the New Territories Ordinance of 1910. Section 20 of the said Ordinance stated that: "In any proceedings in the supreme court in relation to land in the new territories, the court shall have power to recognise and enforce any Chinese custom or customary right affecting such land" (Translation of the Chinese proclamation 1899, p. 1367). Therefore, Chinese law and custom which, in the eyes of Hong Kong judges and the legal profession at that time, were represented mainly by the GQC became part of Hong Kong law. Family law as specified in the GQC, and Chinese customary law and practice in China, became the main legal principles regulating Chinese customary marriage in Hong Kong before the abolition of concubinage in the Marriage Reform Ordinance of 1971. It is therefore important to investigate the principles of the Qing laws relating to the concubine that were applied to Hong Kong soon after the proclamations in 1841.

This chapter will first detail the relevant legal provisions of the concubine in the GQC. Then the supplementary customary practices of the rules relating to concubine will be discussed in order to investigate how laws or customs applied to specific local situations. All in all, the legal principles relating to the concubine were a mixture of legal rules and customary practices.

2.2 The Reception of Chinese Law in Hong Kong

The reception of Chinese law in Hong Kong was the result of the establishment of Hong Kong as a Crown Colony after the Opium War. The first question is, in what ways did jurisdictions other than Mainland China, such as Hong Kong, apply Chinese customary law?[1] This concerns legislation in some jurisdictions that contained special provisions requiring the courts to apply Chinese laws and customs in certain cases, normally those relating to civil matters such as matrimonial relation-

[1] It is worth noting that in some domestic disputes, such as divorce, courts applied foreign personal law under private international law.

ships within Chinese communities. In determining whether Chinese customary law could be applied, the judge would look at the domicile of both parties in the legal proceedings. The reason for the application of Chinese law and custom in the common law system was a practical one, as vividly explained by Lord Millett NPJ:

> It was a basic principle of British imperial policy to bring the benefits of English law to Britain's colonial subjects, while at the same time disturbing their traditional beliefs and practices as little as possible. This policy was not based on altruism but on practical considerations. British Governments were anxious to avoid causing unnecessary civil unrest among their subject peoples, and nothing could be more calculated to provoke unrest than interference with local customs and traditions, particularly in relation to marriage and land holding. (*Suen Toi Lee v Yau Yee Ping* 2001, p. 501)

Because of this policy, aimed at avoiding civil unrest, common law courts such as those in Hong Kong had to consider whether the personal laws of the parties should be applied in cases relating to matrimonial relationships. It is important here to give a brief account of the way Chinese customary law was applied in Hong Kong. Before 1997, section 3 of the Application of the English Law Ordinance (Cap. 88) in Hong Kong specified that:

> The common law and the rules of equity shall be in force in Hong Kong–

(a) so far as they are applicable to the circumstances of Hong Kong or its inhabitants;
(b) subject to such modifications as such circumstances may require.

Section 3(b) was significant because it laid down the principle that there would be modifications of the common law and the rules of equity "as such circumstances may require". That might be interpreted as the reception of Chinese customary law—with adaptations when necessary—since the precursor of section 3 was section 5 of the old Supreme Court Ordinance, promulgated in October 1873:

> Such of the laws of England as existed when the Colony obtained a local legislature, that is to say, on the 5th day of April 1843, shall be in force in the Colony, except so far as the said laws are inapplicable to the local circumstances of the Colony or of its inhabitants, and except so far as they have been modified by laws passed by the said legislature.[2]

The use of Chinese customary law in Hong Kong came from the relevant provision of Captain Elliot's Proclamation of 2 February 1841 when Hong Kong was ceded to Britain by the Qing government:

> And I do hereby declare and proclaim, that, pending Her Majesty's further pleasure, the natives of the island of Hong Kong, and all natives of China thereto resorting shall be governed according to the laws and customs of China, every description of torture excepted. (Norton-Kyshe 1971, p. 5)

[2] For the discussion of the year 1843 as the year of the reception of Chinese law, see Haydon (1962) and Evans (1971). Peter Wesley-Smith suggested that a specific date was required in order to prevent Hong Kong being subject to Chinese law after the cession of Hong Kong to the UK in the Treaty of Nanjing, so it might possibly be the date of the signature of the Treaty of Nanjing—29 August 1842. As Wesley-Smith (1994, p. 219) admitted, this discussion is an academic one par excellence.

In Ordinance No. 15 of 1844, establishing the Supreme Court in Hong Kong, the third section specified that:

> the law of England shall be in force in the said Colony of Hong Kong, except where the same shall be inapplicable to the local circumstances of the said Colony or of its inhabitants.

This enactment was renewed by Ordinance No. 6 of 1845, the relevant part of which was amended by another ordinance, Ordinance No. 2 of 1846, which provided that:

> only such of the laws of England as existed when the Colony obtained a local legislature, that is to say, on the 5th April 1843, should be of force therein. (Supreme Court Ordinance No.2, 1846, s. 3)

This provision extended the laws of England to Hong Kong on 5 April 1843. From the above provisions, it can be seen that a "dual" system existed in the Hong Kong legal system, whereby English common law and Chinese law applied to Hong Kong concurrently (*Chan Hing-cheung & others v R* 1897, pp. 209–210).

Such a "dual" system still exists today. After the transfer of sovereignty on 1 July 1997, the use of Chinese customary law was protected by two provisions in the Hong Kong Basic Law. Firstly, Article 8 of the Hong Kong Basic Law which specified that "The laws previously in force in Hong Kong, that is, the common law, rules of equity, ordinances, subordinate legislation and customary law shall be maintained". Secondly, Article 40 provided that "The lawful traditional rights and interests of the indigenous inhabitants of the 'New Territories' shall be protected by the Hong Kong Special Administrative Region." These articles provide the legal basis of the enforcement of the Chinese customary law in Hong Kong after 1997 and are exemplified in the New Territories Ordinance (cap. 91). Enacted in 1910, the ordinance provided that the court should have the power to recognise and enforce any Chinese customs or customary rights in proceedings related to land in the New Territories.[3] In *Tang Kai-chung v Tang Chik-sang* (1970, per Mills-Owens, p. 295), the High Court held that such provisions in the New Territories Ordinance relating to the use of the Chinese law and custom were mandatory in litigation. Therefore, for litigation regarding land and related disputes in the New Territories, the court must apply customary Chinese law and practice. In most cases, the court will apply the provisions of the GQC and the relevant Chinese customary practices.

However, the above rules and ordinances do not mean that there was a wholesale transplantation or direct application of Qing law in Hong Kong after the establishment of the colonial government. The general legal principle is that, for a ceded colony like Hong Kong, "pre-cessional law remains in force until replaced by the new sovereign, unless repugnant to fundamental principle of English Law" (Wesley-Smith 1994, p. 209). In this respect, the legislature generally applied English law in Hong Kong. Only if the circumstances of Hong Kong or of its inhabitants made the application of English law inapplicable, was Chinese law and custom applied

[3] Section 13 (1): "…in any proceedings in the Court of First Instance or the District Court in relation to land in the New Territories, the court shall have power to recognise and enforce any Chinese custom or customary right affecting such land".

(Wesley-Smith 1994, p. 209). And, some statutory laws, such as the New Territories Ordinance as mentioned above, also specified that Chinese law and custom would be applied in certain circumstances.

The above principle suggests that not all provisions relating to the concubine in the GQC, nor the customary practices relating to the concubine, necessarily applied to Hong Kong. Indeed, legislative and judicial experiences show that only those Chinese laws and customs relating to the status of the concubine and her offspring were applied in Hong Kong courts. Specifically, Qing dynasty laws were applied in Hong Kong in three areas: Firstly, the status of concubine was not only relevant to the succession of, or receiving maintenance from, family estates after the decease of a husband but also related to the right of a concubine to appoint an heir and the inheritance and succession of the family estates of the heir after his appointment. Secondly, Qing laws are relevant because of the status of the sons of a concubine in a family. According to Chinese law and custom, the son of a concubine would have an equal share of the household properties when the husband decided to do "household division" (*fengjia*). In addition, the son of a concubine would have an equal share of the estates when the husband died intestate. Thirdly, apart from the succession of properties by the son, the daughter of a concubine might also have the right to be supported (*yang shan*) by the family until her marriage, when she left the family.

To conclude, since not all Qing law relating to the concubine was applied to Hong Kong, there were only limited areas relating to the status of concubine or her offspring that were relevant. These were applied to Hong Kong through the legislature or judicial cases, which will be discussed later in this chapter.

2.3 Difficulties in Identifying Qing Family Law Relating to a Concubine

2.3.1 The Meaning of Concubine in Qing Law

Before the discussion of the meaning of concubine in Qing law, it is important to note that the legal meaning of concubine under the Qing law was a mixture of laws and customs. Firstly, there was the main statutory law—GQC—which defined the family relationship in the relevant provisions, especially the laws on households. Secondly, other legal instruments such as the *Da Qing Hui Dian* (which included all rules and procedures in the palace) and the Rules of the Six Boards, such as the Rules of the Board of Revenue and Population, also contained certain legal provisions regulating family disputes, especially on legal matters relating to ethnic groups such as the Mongolians. Thirdly, there were provincial laws which regulated local civil, criminal, economic, and social issues that were not covered by the statutory laws at the central level (Wang 2017, p. 19). Fourthly, case reports from the Board of Punishments provided additional sources to government officials such as local magistrates on the proper approach of applying the provisions of the GQC when adjudicating cases. The case reports offered precedents to the government officials for references. One famous set of case reports was *Xin An Hui Lan* (1840/1968; Chen 2017, pp. 29–30).

The local magistrates were expected to strictly follow the rules and precedents as provided by the GQC and developed from the cases decided by the Board of Punishments. However, a successful and career-minded local magistrate was expected by the Qing authorities to maintain social harmony. So, to a local magistrate, maintaining family and social order became more paramount than using laws for resolving family disputes. The personal memoirs of local magistrates reveal that, from time to time, magistrates would make use of their discretion to resolve the family disputes by other methods, such as mediation, rather than allowing cases for litigation. "Avoiding litigation" (*xisong*) was the guiding principle. The sole purpose was to dissuade people from initiating litigation. A retired magistrate Huang Liuhung stated in his memoir in 1694 that:

> All he can do is to advise people to avoid such actions as much as possible. The best way to persuade people to avoid litigation is to teach them to control their emotions and practice forbearance…What magistrate can do is express his exhortations in his actions by conducting trials in the most scrupulous way. Then two parties confront each other the magistrate will uphold the party in the right and repress the party in the wrong. Thus no one will dare to file unsubstantiated claims. (Huang 1984, pp. 258–259)

Another magistrate at Guangdong in the mid-nineteenth century, Nie Yifeng, also shared the similar principle in local administration. In his personal memoir, he said that during his tenure as magistrate at Shi Cheng county, he had published a public notice urging the public to avoid litigation and in support of mediation:

> The disputes (between two parties) would happen just out of frustration. After a while, both parties would be less antagonistic. Or, after the mediation by the relatives and the neighbours, both parties would become peaceful and their dispute would be reconciled. Then, there would not be any conflict again. (Nie 2012, p. 8)

It is important to note that most family provisions in the GQC fell under the jurisdiction of the magistrate due to the principle of "self-management of the districts level" (*zhouxianzili*).[4] The GQC specified that magistrates must adjudicate cases concerning offences such as affray, battery, fields and houses and marriage, with punishments ranging from below *chi* (flogging with a light bamboo) up to *zhang* (beating with a heavy bamboo).[5] In addition, with regard to cases that carried the penalty of 100 strokes of heavy bamboo or below, these cases had to be adjudicated by the local magistrate. Since most of the family provisions under the GQC normally carried the penalty of 100 strokes of heavy bamboo or below, the magistrates could not escape this responsibility.

---

[4] In *Da Qing Hui Dian*, it was specified that: "all cases relating to the family, land, homicide and theft must be adjudicated by the magistrates" (Board of Punishments 1886, p. 25). The role of the magistrate in cases of domestic disputes are discussed in Zheng (1988, pp. 37–38). See also Li (2012, pp. 55–57); Na (1992, pp. 137–138) and Wei (2013, pp. 51–53).

[5] Article 335, *tiaoli* 4 and 5 (*Da Qing Lü Li* 1993, p. 514).

Nevertheless, the discretionary power of the local magistrate in litigation was so wide that he had almost full jurisdiction to make a final decision in family disputes. But the ultimate goal of his local governance was to maintain social harmony. Commenting on the interpretation of Qing Law in cases relating to the interpretation of chastity in the GQC, Shen Jianben (1985, p. 2205) concluded the legal interpretation of the GQC was that "the GQC established the laws, the rites followed the human feelings" (*lüshedafa lishunrenqing*), which suggests the ways in which the local magistrate might interpret the provisions in the GQC on adjudicating domestic disputes.

In addition to the written laws and case reports, the local magistrate might rely upon local customary practices to resolve family issues. Five cases help to understand the approach taken by the local magistrate. The first case relates to the use of mediation: an approach that the local magistrates would normally use to deal with family disputes. Specifically, the local magistrates would ask senior figures in the clan or village (such as the heads of the clans or villages) to resolve the disputes. In the Zhang Rulong case at Huang Yan County in 1875, Zhang Rulong had repeatedly asked the magistrate to intervene in his family dispute after his wife ran away with a neighbour. However, the magistrate asked him to discuss the matter with the village heads and undertake mediation before making a formal submission to the court (Tian et al. 2004, p. 238).

The second case illustrates how a local magistrate could resolve family disputes by customary practices or even his own judicial experiences, rather through reliance on the GQC. For example, while he was the Provincial Administration Commissioner at Shanxi in early twentieth century, the government official Fan Zengxiang had adjudicated a case concerning physical abuse in Ding Xiaoyi's family. Ding Xiaoyi was the Education Officer (*Xue Guan*) in the local government. In this case, nee Xue, the concubine to Ding Xiaoyi, was accused of abusing the wife, Mrs. Ding nee Li. After the death of Ding Xiaoyi's first wife, Ding Xiaoyi married another woman, Mrs. Ding nee Li. But his concubine did not respect the new wife and physically abused Mrs. Ding nee Li. The case was brought to the local magistrate and subsequently appealed at the next level—where Fan Zengxiang had to review the case. Fan first had to deal with the dissolution of marriage proposed by Mrs. Ding nee Li. Since both parties agreed to divorce, Li Fan agreed to make this order (Fan 2007, p. 532).[6] After that, Fan considered that since the husband, Ding Xiaoyi, had allowed the concubine to physically abuse the wife, Ding must pay a penalty of 500 strings of cash coins. Feng warned that, if Ding failed to pay the penalty, he would be expelled from his job as Education Officer and would be punished by carrying the lock for 3 years and hard labour. With regard to the concubine, Fan ordered that if she confessed the crime (though no specific offence was given), she would not be

[6] Fan Zengxiang might possibly refer to the dissolution of marriage by mutual consent as specified in Article 116 of GQC that "If the two spouses do not get along together, but wish to divorce, there is no punishment".

punished by whipping her back for 100 lashes and carrying the cangue for 3 months (Fan 2007, p. 532).[7]

The third case, which happened in Hsinchu, demonstrates the importance of mediation with the local magistrate in family disputes. In a case at Hsinchu in 1884, Lin Laichang asked the magistrate to order the return of his wife Mrs. Lin nee Zhou who—as accused by Lin Laichang—had fornicated with his nephew in the same clan, Lin Ronghe (Case no. 35402, Tan-Hsin Archive 2009b, pp. 150–164). Mrs. Lin nee Zhou's elder brother Zhou Chenyang counterclaimed that Lin Laichang took a concubine then forced his sister to leave home. The local magistrate first ordered Mrs. Lin nee Zhou to go home and live with the husband. Ultimately, however, Mrs. Lin nee Zhou did not return to Lin Laichang. In light of this failure, the local magistrate ordered the military officer (*yayi*) to escort Mrs. Lin nee Zhou back to live with Lin Laichang. Finally, after conciliation and mediation undertaken by the relatives of both Lin and Zhou's family, bonds were signed by Lin and Zhou's relatives to resolve the dispute. In addition, the husband Lin Laichang and his wife Mrs. Lin nee Zhou promised to the magistrate that they would end the dispute and never return to court. Mrs. Lin nee Zhou returned home and lived with Lin Laichang (Case no. 35402, Tan-Hsin Archive 2009b, pp. 163–164).

The fourth case was reported at Hsinchu in 1883. In this case, the magistrate criticised the husband and wife for taking family disputes to court. The wife, Mrs. Xu nee Chen accused the concubine Xu Caixia of physically abusing her and trying to starve her to death. Mrs. Xu nee Chen's elder brother also made a submission to the magistrate, asking the magistrate to arrest the husband and the concubine for criminal investigation. The magistrate commented that this case was a family dispute which should not be taken to court. He ordered that the relatives of both the husband and wife should undertake mediation to resolve the dispute. The magistrate also disallowed further submission of the case for litigation (Case No. 21203, Tan-Hsin Archive 2009a, pp. 29–31).

Finally, a case at Ba County showed the importance of conciliation and mediation in resolving local disputes. In 1844 at Ba County in Sichuan, there was a case concerning a dispute between Tang Dengrang and Wang Fusheng ("Petition of Li Hongfa" 1996, p. 484). It was the neighbour of Wang Fusheng—Li Hongfa and others who submitted the dispute to the magistrate for resolution through mediation. In this case, because of poverty Tang Dengrang sold his wife, Mrs. Tang nee Zhong, to Wang Fusheng. With the arrangement of a go-between, Tang Dengrang signed a contract to sell his wife and received a dowry of 32 teals of silver. Some time later Tang Dengrang borrowed money from Wang Fusheng. Knowing that Mrs. Wang nee Zhang was pregnant, Tang Dengrang pressed Wang Fusheng to lend him more money. Met with refusal, Tang Dengrang retaliated by accusing Wang Fusheng of using trickery to deceive him into selling Mrs. Wong nee Zhang, and he submitted the case to the local magistrate. Wang Fusheng made a counter-submission accusing

[7]Fan Zengxiang explained that, based on his previous experiences, for such money-grubbing person, it would be more painful to him to pay the money than taking physical punishments.

Tang Dengrang of making a false allegation ("Petition of Wang Fusheng" 1996, p. 484).[8] Ultimately, the neighbour of Tang Dengrang, Li Hongfa, stepped in. Li Hongfa and others submitted to the magistrate that they had resolved the case on the following grounds. Firstly, Tang Dengrang was persuaded by other people that in making a case before the magistrate, he would get more money from Wang Fusheng. Now Tang Dengrang knew that this was wrong and he felt guilty. Secondly, Wang Fusheng's concubine was going to give birth, so Wang did not want litigation. Li Hongfa submitted that both parties wanted to end the dispute. The magistrate commented that since nee Zhang was pregnant and had separated from Tang Dengrang, she was pardoned from attending the court. But Tang Dengrang should be taken to court for punishment. Unfortunately, there was no follow-up reported in the archives. However, this case illustrates that the local magistrate was willing to accept the result of external mediation in family disputes.

In sum, magistrates were generally required to rely upon statutory law when dealing with family disputes, especially when the case was undergoing litigation. But commonly magistrates dealt with such cases using customary practices and resolved disputes through mediation. Such a conciliatory and flexible approach created some problems for judges in other jurisdictions, such as Hong Kong, when applying Qing law. Firstly, the legal materials were not easily accessible to normal people, apart from the written laws such as the GQC. Secondly, there was no proper legal reporting system at the local level, which meant that the application of the GQC by a magistrate was neither reported nor retained for application by other magistrates. Thirdly, even in high-profile cases such as homicide, which had to be reviewed by the Board of Punishments, case records and reports were normally kept by the relevant authorities but might not be distributed to the magistrates at the local level. Also, such cases normally referred to offences with the maximum penalty of capital punishments and not to family disputes, which could be resolved at the local level. Consequentially, the application of Chinese customary practice in litigation could normally only be found in the personal memoirs of the local magistrates or in archival records retained by the local magistrates such as the records at Ba County and Hsinchu.

2.4 The Institution of Concubinage: Qing Laws and Practices

2.4.1 Monogamous or Polygamous?

As discussed earlier, the application of Qing laws at the local level by magistrates was often a mixture of statutory law and local customary practice. In addition, old Chinese classical texts aided the magistrates in their interpretation of the law.

[8] There was no record of the submission of Tang Dengrang on his allegation against Wang Fusheng. This petition was the counterclaim against the original allegation submitted by Tang Dengrang.

This section will first briefly discuss the historical development of the status of concubine in the Chinese family system, followed by a discussion of the nature of the traditional Chinese marriage system and whether it is monogamous or polygamous.

The status of a concubine in the Chinese family system can be traced back to the Spring and Autumn period and the Warring States period. During these periods, in the Chinese noble class marriage normally entailed the wife bringing an entourage with her, which included female relatives such as sisters and cousins as well as maids. The wife was called *qi*. The sisters and cousins of the wife were called *ying* and were regarded as ranking lower than *qi* but higher than *qie*—the lower rank of concubine (Hsieh 2014, pp. 42–43). After the Song dynasty, a *ying* was called a "secondary wife" (Shih 1987, p. 132). When a husband married, he could take concubines from the wife's entourage: this was one way in which a husband could institute concubinage.

Apart from that, a man could also buy a concubine. In the *Book of Rites* (*Li Ji*), there is a proverb which states that "[H]ence in buying a concubine if he does not know her surname, he must consult the tortoise-shell about it". The nineteenth-century scholar, James Legge (1885, p. 78) explains that the purpose of consulting the tortoise shell was not to find out the surname of the concubine but to determine whether the surname of the woman was the same as that of the gentlemen or not. Another possible interpretation is that if he did not know her surname, a man could purchase a concubine by performing divination, as according to the *Book of Rites* a man could not marry a wife with the same surname (Legge 1885, p. 78). This might help the man make the final decision on whether he would take the concubine or not. A book written by Ban Gu (32–92 A.D.) in the Han period, *The Comprehensive Discussions in the White Tiger Hall*, gave the meaning of *qie* as "to connect", which meant that the concubine "at regular times meets the man for connection". In comparison with the wife, who "forms whole body with her husband", this phrase suggests that the concubine could only meet the husband from time to time and could not be regarded as the "whole body" (*heti*) of husband (Ban 1949, p. 261). Nevertheless, the distinction of *ying* and *qie* disappeared in the Ming Code. Since then, in the Qing law as exemplified in the GQC, all concubines were called *qie* (Chen 2017, pp. 29–30).

Accordingly, it is very important to discuss the nature of Chinese marriage in Qing law—whether it is a form of monogamy or polygamy or whether it is *potentially* polygamous. Without a knowledge of the traditional Chinese marriage system, it would be difficult to understand the status of a concubine in the Chinese family and whether a concubine had an equal or inferior status to a wife.

First, the ideas and principles behind Chinese marriage are essential to understanding the status of a concubine in a Chinese family. To some scholars, the essence of the husband and wife relationship in traditional China was called a "husband and wife unit" (Shiga 1978, pp. 119–120)[9] or "a union of husband and wife as one body" (*yiti*) (Chen 1992, p. 177). The word "yiti", denoted "a rule whereby during the

[9] See also Shiga (2003, pp. 104–136).

husband's lifetime the wife's personality is absorbed in the husband's body, whereas after the latter's death his personality is represented by his wife" (Shiga 1978, pp. 119–120).[10] However, there was no such idea of "yiti" in the husband and concubine relationship. The GQC only described the institution of a concubinage as the relationship between a head of family (*jiazang*) and a concubine.[11]

These principles were enshrined in the Qing legal system. The GQC specified some important elements for a valid form of marriage, which reflected the principle of *yiti*. Article 101 specified that a valid marriage was one that was arranged by the heads of the families, in other words, the parents of the man and woman.[12] Also, a valid marriage was required to follow the "rites". The rites were not specified in law but referred to customary practices and the rites and ceremonies as specified in the *Book of Rites* (*Li Ji*). The procedure of a typical traditional marriage was called "Three Letters" and "Six Rites", which could be simplified as follows: *nacai*, the sending of a go-between to offer a present to the girl's family, which was regarded as a formal proposal; *wenming*, which referred to the giving of the girl's name and date of birth to the boy's family; *naji*, which referred to the matching of the names and the dates of birth of the boy and girl; *nazheng*, the paying of money from the boy's family to the girl's family; *qingqi* which was the selection of the wedding date; and, finally, *Chan ying*, which referred to the wedding ceremony and the coming of the bride to the bridegroom at his home (Chiu 1966, pp. 5–6).

In contrast, the GQC did not specify the elements for a valid form of the institution of concubinage. Furthermore, the husband was not required to perform any rites or ceremonies in order to take a concubine (Chu 1961, p. 125). No classical texts could provide authoritative references and different clans or villages might adopt different rites or ceremonies. In Fujian, the customary practice at Jian Yang County was that the concubine could not sit on the "flower sedan chair" (*huajiao*) in the ceremony so as to distinguish the state of concubinage from formal marriage. An offender would be fined by the members of the clan (Judicial Administration Department of the Former Nanjing Nationalist Government 2005, p. 747). In Shouguang county at Shandong, the concubine was called "equal wife" (*ping chi*) in a family. Such practice denoted that the concubine had an equal status with the wife. The reason behind the use of *ping chi* was that the parents of the concubine did not want their daughter to be called "concubine". So, the concubine was called "equal wife". Furthermore, the parents would demand for the ceremonies of the institution of the concubinage to be the same as those of a normal marriage between a husband and a wife (Judicial Administration Department of the Former Nanjing Nationalist Government 2005, p. 660).

To protect the principle of *yiti*, Article 101 of the GQC punished the head of a woman's family who married off the woman again to another man. And, Article 101

---

[10]Chen Guyuan (1992, p. 177) explained this as an absorption of the wife's personality to the husband's personality.

[11]To avoid confusion, this book will use husband to denote a man's relationship with his wife and concubine.

[12]Article 101 of the GQC (Jones 1994, p. 123; *Da Qing Lü Li* 1993, p. 217).

also punished the man who knowingly agreed to take a woman in such circumstances and the person who was in charge of arranging such a marriage. This provision in effect prohibited bigamy, which further proved that the nature of the form of marriage in GQC was monogamy (Jones 1994, p. 123; *Da Qing Lü Li* 1993, p. 217).

In addition, Article 103 of the GQC made bigamy an offence: "If, while he has a wife, he marries another wife, he will also receive 90 strokes of the heavy bamboo. (The woman who is married subsequently) will be divorced (and returned to her clan)" (Jones 1994, pp. 125–126; *Da Qing Lü Li* 1993, pp. 218–219). This provision was originally provided in Article 177 of the Tang Code: "All cases of taking a second wife are punished by one year of penal servitude" (Johnson 1997, p. 154). The GQC clearly gave lesser penalty than the Tang dynasty for the same offence. In sum, both Articles 101 and 103 in the GQC provided the legal basis of a "one husband and one wife" relationship in a family—a system which resembles monogamy in the eyes of Western legal experts.

On the other hand, the GQC did not prohibit concubinage or place any limit upon the number of concubines in a family. Although the GQC did not specify the hierarchical order of the wife and concubine in the family, customary practice was that the first woman that the husband married was called the wife, while the second or latter was regarded as a concubine. One determining factor of valid marriage was whether the man and woman had concluded the formal marriage ceremony, in other words, the "Six Rites". However, would it be possible to have a husband institute a concubinage without a principal wife? As one scholar suggested, there was a possibility that if the contract of marriage was concluded, but the rites and ceremonies had not been conducted, a man could technically institute a concubinage without a formal wife (Shiga 2003, p. 449). However, the case law in Taiwan suggests that a concubine was sometimes customarily called the "second wife", in which case it is doubtful that the concubine could be called "second" without a principal wife (Ministry of Law 2004, p. 111).

Having said that, some Western scholars in the nineteenth and early twentieth centuries considered the traditional Chinese marriage system to be polygamous. Staunton (1810/2012, p. 110) was the first to reach such a conclusion in his 1810 book on the GQC. Later, Möllendorff (1878, p. 103) considered that: "[C]oncubinage is, however, at the same time permitted, and marriage with several concubines is allowed. The number of these, besides the one wife, is not limited by law, but only one wife is permitted". Möllendorff (1896, p. 165–166) stated that this marriage system was polygamous: "[I]n ancient times we find no people strictly monogamous. Polygamy was universally practised, generally without distinction between the wives, but sometimes a kind of monogamy existed side by side with permitted polygamy, i.e. one wife and several concubines…In China the case stands similarly. If the first wife is barren, a concubine is purchased, but almost always with the consent of the wife".

Another scholar, Parker (1879, pp. 79–80), considered that in the marriage ceremony, *kuo-men* (passing door) was important: "If a man has no wife, and lives openly with a mistress, or even with a prostitute, in his own house, and has children by her, these children are his, and the woman is his wife, and cannot be readily superseded by another wife wedded 'with red chair and music'; if he is already married to a *ch'i*, or wife, the woman becomes his *ch'ieh*, or concubine". Meanwhile, Jernigan (1905, p. 114), did not identify whether the marriage system was monogamous or polygamous. He described the traditional Chinese marriage system as follows: "after the marriage the husband may proceed, if he has not already done so, to fill his house with as many concubines as he feels competent to support; but there can be but one wife in the house, and she is the superior female in rank and authority". Jamieson, in his published work in 1921, used "second wife" to describe a concubine, but he clearly saw the term "second wife" as a "misnomer": "The Chinese do not call her *Ch'i*, wife at all, but *Ch'ieh*, concubine. There can only one *Ch'i* at the time. In event of the death of the wife a concubine may be raised to that rank, but a *Ch'i* can never be made a *Ch'ieh*" (Jamieson 1921, pp. 45–46).

From the above, Parker, Jernigan and Jamieson only described the relationship between a wife and a concubine; they did not define the marriage system as polygamous. In conclusion, judging from the provisions of the GQC and Chinese customary practice, if a man decided not to institute any concubinage after marriage, such marriage was monogamous in nature. Only if a man decided to take a concubine could such a monogamous marriage then become polygamous.[13] Consequently, contemporary scholars such as Carol Tan have considered that the traditional Chinese marriage system was "potentially polygamous" and that a husband could have as many concubines as he wished.

2.4.2 The Sources of a Concubine

Unlike formal marriage, the GQC did not specify the rites or ceremonies of a man who wanted to take a concubine. In the Tang Code, Article 182 specified that "[A] contract of marriage is still required for taking a concubine" (Yue 2015, p. 219), which suggests that a contract of marriage (*hunshu*) was the necessary element for a valid institution of concubinage during the eighth to ninth centuries. However, this provision disappeared in the law codes of Song and later dynasties. And, the GQC did not contain this provision.

If a man wanted to take a concubine, he might purchase a woman through a go-between. Therefore, in the customary practice of Hunan, if a man wished to take a concubine, he could ask a go-between to make such an arrangement and purchase a concubine, and he would follow the usual formality (similar to marrying a wife) to form the union of concubinage (Judicial Administration Department of the Former

[13] There is a record of a customary practice at Gansu where a Muslim husband can have four wives. The fifth "wife" was called a concubine (Judicial Administration Department of the Former Nanjing Nationalist Government 2005, p. 841).

Nanjing Nationalist Government 2005, p. 791).[14] In Ba County at Sichuan in 1851,[15] nee Peng Cheng sold her daughter to Li Shizhai due to poverty. Li Shizhai promised to give the sum of 30 teals to Yu Chuansheng as go-between. In the contract of selling her daughter, nee Peng Cheng promised not to stop Li Shizhai from taking her daughter away and declared that no go-between had used coercion or trickery to force her to enter into the contract ("Contract of selling daughter" 1996, p. 502). In Taiwan, a man could get a concubine from three sources: by taking a concubine from the domestic servants, by arranging a concubine through a go-between and by purchasing a concubine through contract (Provisional Taiwan Traditional Customs Investigation Committee 1993, p. 607). Apart from arranging for a contract or a go-between, a man could also get a concubine from other sources, such as snatching a woman from other families, receiving a woman as a gift, instituting a concubinage after fornication, taking lost or stray women, taking a concubine from his wife's sisters and taking a concubine by deceiving a woman (Cheng 2006, pp. 102–110).

However, the GQC prohibited the sale of woman as a wife or a concubine and the taking of a concubine in other specific circumstances. Article 110 prohibited a government official from taking a wife or concubine while administering his own local area (Jones 1994, p. 130; *Da Qing Lü Li* 1993, p. 110). In the Sun Huaifen case of 1798 ("Xin an hui lan" 2006, p. 504), the defendant was a sub-prefectural magistrate (*tong pan*) responsible for food and horse support in Shuentian prefecture. He bought a concubine from a go-between, who falsely told him that the woman was a widow. The Board of Personnel ordered that Article 110 should be applied to the case, but since the ranking of sub-prefectural magistrate was lower than the local magistrate, Sun Huaifen was punished with one lesser degree and was assigned to another post.

Another provision in the GQC punished a person who forcibly took the wife or daughter of another family as his wife or concubine. Article 112 specified that: "In all cases where a person who is influential and strong (who is in possession of force) forcibly takes the wife or daughter of an honourable family, and wrongfully makes her his wife or concubine, he will be punished with strangulation (with delay)" (Jones 1994, p. 132; *Da Qing Lü Li* 1993, p. 222). In this article, *tiaoli* 1 prohibited the taking of a good commoner by an offender as a man's wife or concubine. The offender would be punished with strangulation (with delay) (*Da Qing Lü Li* 1993, p. 222).

In the Zhao Fu case at Henan in 1829 ("Xin an hui lan" 2006, p. 557), the defendant Zhao Fu forced his uncle's concubine, nee Li, to remarry by first arranging a go-between and then inducing her to leave home. Nee Li refused to leave home

[14] In a customary investigation at the Shajin Village, Sunyi County at Hebei (now Sunyi District of Beijing) in 1941, it was recorded that a man would take a concubine at the age of 40. A go-between would help to arrange for the institution of concubinage (*Mantie nongcu diaocha* 2016, p. 516). The husband had to pay, from 300 to 500 dollars (*Mantie nongcu diaocha* 2016, p. 554).

[15] This contract was concluded in the 31st year of Daoguang Emperor. However, Daoguang died in the 30th year of his reign. It is possible that the paper was referring to the year of 1851 ("Contract of selling daughter" 1996, p. 502).

because she wanted to keep her chastity and take care of her daughter. Afterwards, nee Li committed suicide. The Board of Punishments firstly considered that there was no family relationship between the nephew and uncle's concubine in accordance with the mourning apparel (*fuji*); in other words, there was no formal family relationship between nee Li and his uncle under the GQC. Secondly, the Board of Punishments considered that there was no provision in the GQC regulating and punishing the offender (in other words, Zhao Fu) in this situation. Therefore, the Board of Punishments ordered Henan authorities to conduct further investigation and to recommend the appropriate form of punishments. In the final note to the records, the Board of Punishments commented that Article 105—punishment of the forced remarriage of a wife and concubine during the mourning period—could be applied in this case.

Furthermore, the GQC prohibited the sale of a woman by other means, such as trickery and enticement. Article 275 of the GQC specified that

> Anyone who devises tricks and entices and gets hold of honourable persons (to make slaves of them), or who kidnaps and sells honourable persons (to others) as slaves, will (without distinction between the principal and accessory and regardless of whether the person has been sold) be sentenced to 100 strokes of the heavy bamboo and exile to 3000 li. If he makes [the person kidnapped] a wife or concubine, a son, or son's son, then (the offender) is given 100 strokes of the heavy bamboo and penal servitude of three years. (Jones 1994, pp. 257–258; *Da Qing Lü Li* 1993, p. 415)

In addition, Article 375, *tiaoli* 1 of the GQC provided that anyone who purchased a woman from an honourable family to be the concubine and allowed her to commit fornication would be punished by cangue (*jiahao*) for 3 months and 100 strokes of heavy bamboo and exiled to the remote areas of Yunnan, Guizhou, Guangdong and Guangxi (*Da Qing Lü Li* 1993, p. 558).

In the Ding Rong case at Shanxi in 1819 ("Xin an hui lan" 2006, p. 1130), the defendant Ding Rong was a dismissed government official. He first induced his niece, Zhang, to pretend to be his servant and then sold Zhang to the doorman as a concubine. The Shanxi Governor submitted this case to the Board of Punishments. The Shanxi Governor commented that Ding's behaviour was despicable because, first, Ding was used to be a government official and, second, Ding lied about Zhang's status. Further, Ding sold Zhang to the doorman as a concubine. The Board of Punishments ordered Ding to be exiled to Xinjiang for hard labour. The woman, Zhang, was ordered to find another partner for marriage.

In the Xu Jingui case at Shangdong in 1810 ("Xin an hui lan" 2006, p. 1132), the defendant Xu Jingui kidnapped and induced nee Zhang to live with him, pretending to be husband and wife. However, nee Zhang could not live in poverty and fled to Dong Yuan's house. Dong Yuan asked nee Zhang to pretend to be Sun Yu's servant. Then, Dong Yuan sold nee Zhang to Ma Zhongjiao as a concubine. Nee Zhang later committed suicide. The Board of Punishments commented that, Dong Yuan should be given a penalty of penal servitude for 3 years, and Sun Yu was sentenced to imprisonment for 2 and a half years.

In another Article 367, the GQC prohibited anyone from facilitating and tolerating a wife's or concubine's fornication:

> In the case of anyone who facilitates and tolerates his wife or concubine engaging in fornication with another, the husband, the adulterous lover, and the adulterous wife will each receive 90 strokes of the heavy bamboo. If someone forces his wife, concubine, or adopted daughter to engage in fornication with another, the husband or the adoptive father will each receive 100 strokes of the heavy bamboo. The male fornicator will receive 80 strokes of the heavy bamboo. The wife or the daughter will not be punished. Moreover, her relationship [with the husband or father] is terminated. She is returned to her clan... If consideration is used to buy a divorce (*mǎixiu*) or to sell a divorce (*màixiu*) [i.e. someone gives the husband money to cause him to get rid of his wife] (in order) that [the one giving it] may marry another man's wife (by agreement), the husband and the wife and the one who is buying the divorce, will each be punished with 100 strokes of the heavy bamboo. (Johnson 1997, p. 348; *Da Qing Lü Li* 1993, pp. 555–556)[16]

In the Qiu Gui case at Sichuan in 1839 (Xin an hui lan 2006, p. 2716), the defendant Qiu Gui was the wife of Wang Bao. Because of poverty, Wang Bao planned with his father-in-law to sell his wife, Qiu Gui, to Pan Shouli as a concubine. Pan Shouli was told that Qiu Gui's husband had died. Pan Shouli's wife disapproved of the reception of the concubine and interrogated Pan Shouli for details. Then, Pan Shouli's wife assaulted Qiu Gui and forced her to leave the house. The Board of Punishments ordered that Qiu Gui, Wang Bao and Pan Shouli had violated the laws prohibiting buying a divorce and selling a woman by divorce and issued a punishment of 100 strokes with heavy bamboo.

It is worth noting that, from the cases above, the GQC did not prohibit the selling of a woman to a man as a concubine, and did not prohibit a man from buying a woman to be his concubine, provided that such buying and selling had received real and genuine consent from the man and woman. The GQC and cases from the Board of Punishments prohibited the use of trickery and enticement (Article 275) and the buying and selling of women (including wife and concubine) by divorce (Article 367) through inducement or kidnapping.

2.4.3 The Inferiority of a Concubine

The GQC criminalised the husband who failed to observe the order of a wife and a concubine. The second part of Article 103 specified that:

> Everyone who makes his wife a concubine will receive 100 strokes of the heavy bamboo. If, while the wife is living, he makes his concubine a wife, he will receive 90 stroke of the heavy bamboo. Moreover, his action will be corrected. (Jones 1994, pp. 125–126; *Da Qing Lü Li* 1993, p. 219)

This provision originated from the law of the Tang dynasty. In the Tang Code, Article 178 had a similar provision: "All cases of making the wife a concubine or

[16] However, the Qing scholar Shen Jiaben considered that if a husband was so poor that he could not afford to keep his wife and divorced his wife by selling her, that situation was regrettable. Shen Jiaben thought that this law might be difficult for the magistrate to apply and that it would be better to investigate the situation before delivering final judgement (Shen 1985, p. 2182).

making a slave the wife are punished by two years of penal servitude" (Johnson 1997, p. 155). The GQC specified a lesser penalty compared to the Tang Code. This provision proved that the status of a concubine was inferior to a wife in a family. It is worth noting that the GQC did not put a limit on the number of concubines in a family. In practice, a husband could have a wife and an unlimited number of concubines.

The Board of Punishments had a case relating to this provision. In the Hou Yongfu case at Zhili in 1789 ("Xin an hui lan" 2006, p. 489–490; *Xin An Hui Lan* 1840/1968. p. 637), the defendant Hou Yongfu was originally married to a woman in his clan. However, he pretended to be single and married another woman through a go-between when he moved to Beijing. The second "wife" and the mother of his second "wife" were deceived by the defendant. The Board of Punishments gave a memoranda (*shuitia*) that Hou Yongfu had violated the law by using fraud and deceit (*wangmao*) to institute the second marriage and that the wedding presents would not be returned.

2.4.3.1 Legality of Fu Ching

Another case relating to this provision referred to the legality of a customary practice called *Fu Ching*. The GQC did not have any provision relating to *Fu Ching*. In customary practice, *Fu Ching* referred to the situation when a husband uplifted the status of a concubine to his new wife after the wife died. But the GQC did not have any provision validating such practice. In the Mrs. Yang nee Zhang case at Fengtian in 1802 ("Xin an hui lan" 2006, p. 2716; *Xin An Hui Lan* 1840/1968, p. 2465), the defendant Mrs. Yang nee Zhang attacked her employee nee Wong with a heavy stick out of frustration. Nee Wong died after the attack. The defendant Mrs. Yang nee Zhang was originally a concubine to a bannerman of the Chinese Army (*Hanjun*) Assistant Caption (*zuoling*) Yang Yujue. After his wife died, the status of Mrs. Yang nee Zhang was promoted from that of concubine to wife. The Board of Punishments ruled that since there was no *Fu Ching* provision in the GQC, the status of Mrs. Yang nee Zhang could not be "uplifted". Therefore, Mrs. Yang nee Zhang's status as a concubine should be restored.

However, despite the prohibition from the Board of Punishments, this customary practice still existed in many provinces. In Shangdong, there was a customary practice that if the principal wife died with no son, the "side room" (*ceshi*) who had the son could be regarded as the formal wife. But this practice must be agreed by the relatives. Or, the son of the concubine, upon the consent of the relatives, could call his mother the principal mother (Judicial Administration Department of the Former Nanjing Nationalist Government 2005, p. 635). In Jiangxi, the customary practice was that, if a concubine wanted to be promoted to the formal wife by way of *Fu Ching*, she must be recognised by the relatives. Without such recognition, she could not be regarded as the formal wife in the lineage genealogy (Judicial Administration Department of the Former Nanjing Nationalist Government 2005, p. 712). In Hunan, such customary practice happened when the wife died with no son or the wife died earlier with a young son. Then, if the concubine gave birth to a son (which meant that she had brought good fortune to the family), the husband could "uplift" the concubine to be the formal wife. This practice was called "uplift to the formal house" (*shengzheng*), but it was *Fu Ching* in practice (Judicial Administration Department of the Former Nanjing Nationalist Government 2005, p. 793).

2.4.3.2 Mourning Obligations of the Concubine

Other provisions also illustrated the inferior status of a concubine in the family. Firstly, some provisions in the GQC relating to the rites on mourning showed the different treatments for a concubine and a wife. Secondly, some provisions on homicide in the GQC provided that the concubine would receive lighter penalty than a wife.

The mourning obligations and rights are important to the understanding of family order in the Chinese family. The husband, wife and concubine owed obligations in mourning as defined by their relationship. In general, the closer the relationship, the longer the time spent in the mourning period. In addition, the mourning obligations in a family were arranged by the five degree of mourning clothes (*wufu*). The time of the mourning period was also tied to the degree of mourning clothes. These were defined in the GQC in *juan* 3 (*Da Qing Lü Li* 1993, pp. 80–85). In general, the five degrees of mourning clothes were:

1. The first degree of mourning apparel was 3 years in untrimmed sackcloth with a mourning stick and a mourning hood, which was called *zhanchui*.
2. The second degree of mourning apparel was called *zicui*. It contained three different apparels. The first one was 3 years in even sackcloth; the second one was 1 year with a mourning stick; and the third one was 1 year without a mourning stick.
3. The third degree of mourning apparel was called *dagong*. It referred to the mourning period of 9 months with greater processed cloth.
4. The fourth degree of mourning apparel was called *xiaogong*. This referred to the mourning period of 9 months but with lesser processed cloth.
5. The fifth degree of mourning apparel was called *sima*. This referred to the mourning period of 3 months in fine sackcloth.

There were different mourning obligations which showed the inferiority of a concubine in a family. *Juan* 3 of the GQC gave detailed requirements for the mourning period for each member of the family. For the husband of a deceased wife, the husband was required to take the mourning obligation of the second degree, in other words, *zicui*, but the mourning period was 1 year with a mourning stick. However, the husband was not required to take on mourning obligations for his deceased concubine. Moreover, a wife was required to take the mourning obligation of the first degree, in other words, *zhanchui*, for her deceased husband. But a wife was not required to take any mourning obligation for a deceased concubine, although a concubine had to take the mourning obligation of the second degree for a deceased wife. So, broadly speaking, to the concubine, the principal wife could be regarded as one of the "superior or older relatives of the second mourning" (*qiqin zunzhang*) in the family relationship as specified in the GQC. And, to the principal wife, the concubine could be regarded as one of the "inferior or younger relatives of the second mourning" (*qiqin beiyou*) in the family relationship.

2.4.3.3 Differentiation of Punishments

Another example is that for some offences, particularly homicide in a family, the punishment of a concubine was harsher than a wife. For example, in Article 315, the punishment for striking husband is different for a wife and a concubine. This article first provides that, "whenever a wife or concubine strikes a husband…she will receive 100 strokes of the heavy bamboo" (Jones 1994, p. 299; *Da Qing Lü Li* 1993, pp. 488–489). It then stipulates that if a wife struck her husband leading to a fracture or worse, then in each case, "add three degrees to the penalty for injuring in ordinary affray as specified in Article 302" (Jones 1994, p. 299; *Da Qing Lü Li* 1993, pp. 488–489.) The same provision provided that "if it results in critical disability, then the penalty is strangulation (to be executed [immediately]). If there is death, then the penalty is beheading (to be executed [immediately]). If there is intentional killing, then the penalty is death by slicing" (Jones 1994, p. 299; *Da Qing Lü Li* 1993, pp. 488–489.

However, the penalty issued to a concubine is different. Article 315, *tiaoli* 2, states that "if the concubine strikes the husband or the principal wife, then add (to the penalty for a wife striking a husband) one degree. The augmentation may increase even if it amounts to death" (*Da Qing Lü Li* 1993, p. 489). In the same provision, some examples were given that, "if the injury was to the head of the household (husband), then there will be immediate execution. If [the injury is to] the wife, then there will be [execution] with delay. If it is critical disability or death or intentional killing, then it is the same as the wife striking a husband" (*Da Qing Lü Li* 1993, p. 489). So, if a concubine struck her husband, she received a harsher punishment than the wife by one degree. The punishment did not refer to the seriousness of the offence. The punishment was based on the "proper status" (*mingfen*) of wife and concubine in a family.

In the Mrs. Que nee Li case at Guangdong in 1766 (*Bo'an xinbian* 1781/1968, pp. 2049–2053), the defendant Mrs. Que nee Li was a concubine to the husband, Que Jinglin, who criticised the clan's younger brother—also his employee—of laziness at work. Que Jinglin was attacked by the employee so he counter-attacked by taking a knife. Mrs. Que nee Li tried to grab the knife, but Que Jinglin withdrew his hand and then wounded himself, dying 10 days later. The Guangdong governor proposed to punish Mrs. Qee nee Li under Article 302, meaning that she would be executed immediately by beheading. But the Board of Punishments disagreed with this proposal. The Guangdong governor later resubmitted that, after careful investigation, he considered that Mrs. Que nee Li did not intend to kill her husband, because the purpose of such act was not to protect the employee but to stop her husband from fighting. The Guangdong governor considered that Mrs. Que nee Li could not foresee that her husband would subsequently sustain a wound. The Guangdong governor proposed to punish Mrs. Que nee Li under the law regulating cases where "initially there was no intention to harm or kill another but [caused] death subsequently". The Board of Punishments agreed with this submission and sentenced Mrs. Que nee Li of 100 strokes of heavy bamboo and exiled to 3000 miles (*li*) (*Bo'an xinbian* 1781/1968, p. 2053).

Article 315 *tiaoli* 3, provides another example of such differentiation of penalty between a concubine and a wife. This part relates to the different penalties given to a husband who struck his wife or concubine. If the husband struck his wife, and if no fracture was found, there would be no punishment. But, "if it amounts to fracturing or worse, then reduce the penalty for an ordinary person two degrees" (Jones 1994, pp. 299–300; *Da Qing Lü Li* 1993, p. 489). In addition, if the injury amounts to death, then the penalty was strangulation (with delay). If there was intentional killing, the penalty was also strangulation.

But, in the same provision, if the husband struck his concubine, the penalty was more lenient. The provision provides that "if there is striking and injuring of a concubine amounting to fracture or worse, then reduce the penalty for striking and injuring the wife two degrees". However, "if [the injury] amounts to death, then punish with 100 strokes of the heavy bamboo and penal servitude of three years" (*Da Qing Lü Li* 1993, p. 489). Such difference in penalty can also be seen in the penalty relating to the wife who struck the concubine. In the same provision, "if the wife strikes and injures the concubine, this is the same as the husband striking the wife" (*Da Qing Lü Li* 1993, p. 489). In these examples, differences in penalty further show the inferior status of a concubine in the family.

How about the situation where a concubine attempted to murder the wife but failed? There was no such offence in the GQC. In the nee Tang case at Guangdong Shunde County in 1819 (Zhu 1828, p. 21), the defendant nee Tang disliked the principal wife Mrs. You nee Tan, because the latter often criticised her harshly. The defendant asked her relatives to help murder Mrs. You nee Tan but failed. The defendant was later arrested by the magistrate. The problem was that there was no specific offence in the GQC under which to punish a concubine for the attempted murder of a wife. The Guangdong Governor submitted—with the approval of the Board of Punishments—that since the wife was the "superior or older relatives of the second mourning" (*qiqin zunzhang*) to the concubine, punishment should take reference to the offence of murdering a "superior or older relatives of the second mourning". So, nee Tang, the defendant was sentenced to beheaded (Zhu 1828, p. 23).

There was a unique case which specified the penalty given to a grandson who murdered his grandfather's concubine. Article 319 of the GQC made the striking of paternal grandparents or parents an offence. It specified that, "every child or son's child who strikes his paternal grandparents or parents, or a wife or concubine who strikes her husband's paternal grandparents or parents will be beheaded. If he kills them, he will be sentenced to death by slicing" (Jones 1994, pp. 304–305; *Da Qing Lü Li* 1993, pp. 496–497). However, this provision did not specify the offence of a grandson killing the concubine of his paternal grandparents. Would it be a lesser penalty if the victim was a concubine? In the case which was submitted to the Autumn Assizes, the Board of Punishments had to recommend whether the emperor should pardon the defendant, who had been given the death sentence (Ying 1873, p. 31; Song 2009, pp. 322–323).[17] The critical points, as laid out by the Board of Punishments, were, firstly, whether the concubine to the grandparents or parents had any children; secondly, whether the concubine was an elderly woman; and, thirdly, the seriousness of the case. In the Gan Yanfa case at Jianxi in 1846, the Board of Punishments recommended that the defendant should be pardoned by delaying the death sentence. The reasons were that, firstly, the concubine of Gan Yanfa's father had frequently instituted quarrels with his father. Secondly, the death of the concubine of the defendant's father was a result of the defendant acting in self-defence. Therefore, the Board of Punishments recommended a delay in the death sentence, which was accepted by the emperor.

In another provision in the GQC, the punishment given to a concubine was harsher than the punishment given to a wife for the offence of scolding a husband. Article 330 specified that, "if the concubine curses the husband, she will receive 80 strokes of the heavy bamboo. If the concubine curses the wife, the penalty is the same" (Jones 1994, p. 312; *Da Qing Lü Li* 1993, p. 504). However, there was no such offence in the GQC for a wife cursing a husband; as explained in the same article, domestic disputes had to be resolved by forgiveness. However, if the situation of a wife cursing her husband did arise, Article 330 stipulated that Article 386 should be applied. Article 386 provided that: "everyone who does that which ought not to be done will receive 40 strokes of light bamboo" (Jones 1994, p. 359; *Da Qing Lü Li* 1993, pp. 569–57). Comparing the penalty of the concubine and the wife on cursing the husband, the penalty of the concubine was heavier than the wife.

Article 315, *tiaoli* 3 specified that if a wife intentionally killed the concubine (*gusha*),[18] or a concubine intentionally killed the husband, the penalty would be strangulation without delay (*Da Qing Lü Li* 1993, pp. 489. But in the Autumn Assizes, the wife might receive a pardon from the emperor, reducing the punishment in some circumstances (Song 2009, pp. 186–187). The rule as developed in the Autumn Assizes was that, in the case of a wife who committed murder or intentionally killed a concubine, if there was no intention to defraud, or to put the blame on others, and if there was no killing out of jealousy or frustration and the whole case was not very serious (as in, e.g. killing the husband and nephew at the same time),

[17] The Autumn Assizes handled all capital cases submitted by the provincial governors and endorsed by the Board of Punishments. The final decision was made by the emperor. The defendants would receive any one of these four final decisions: (1) defer the execution (*huanjue*), (2) worthy of compassion (*kejin*), (3) remain at home to care for parents or to perpetuate the ancestral scarifies (*liuyang chengsi*) and (4) facts are verified (*qingshi*) (Bodde and Morris 1971, p. 186). See also Article 411, *tiaoli* 1 on the procedure of Autumn Assize (*Da Qing Lü Li* 1993, pp. 629–630); Na 1992, pp. 144–149).

[18] "Intention to kill" (*gusha*) was referring to the homicide when the killing was taken place and the criminal did not have the plan to make such killing, in other words, an ad hoc killing (Shen 1751/1999, p. 681).

the penalty dealt to the wife could be reduced from immediate to delayed strangulation (Song 2009, pp. 186–187). However, there was no such reduction of punishment when a concubine intentionally killed a wife.

2.4.3.4 Prohibition on Remarriage of Concubine

The QQC prohibited the remarriage of a wife or concubine during the mourning period. But there was differentiation in punishment between a wife and a concubine who committed this offence. Article 105 specified that "[W]henever (a man or a woman) during mourning for his or her parents and (a wife or concubine during) mourning for her husband, himself or herself (as the person in charge of the marriage) marries or takes in marriage, he or she will receive 100 strokes of the heavy bamboo. If a son is in mourning (for his father and mother and) takes a concubine, or if a wife (while in mourning for her husband) or a daughter (while in mourning for her parents) marries a man as a concubine, the punishment for each will be reduced two degrees" (Jones 1994, pp. 126–127; *Da Qing Lü Li* 1993, p. 219).

In the Mrs. Zhang nee Liang case at Sichuan in 1801, the Board of Punishments had to review whether Mrs. Zhang nee Liang had violated Article 105 since she remarried another man during the mourning period. In this case, Mrs. Zhang nee Liang remarried Li Chaogui as a concubine, bringing with her 1400 dollars (*wen*) and her daughter. The elder brother of her former husband, Zhang Yunzhen, came to Li Chaogui asking for the money back. Li Chaogui then had a quarrel with Zhang Yunzhen and killed Zhang Yunzhen. The Board of Punishments agreed that Li Chaogui had violated Article 290, which provided for cases where an offender "during an affray, strikes and kills another, regardless of whether he has struck with the hand, or the feet, or with another object, or with a metal knife", and he was punished with strangulation (with delay) (Jones 1994, p. 276; *Da Qing Lü Li* 1993, p. 453). For Mrs. Zhang nee Liang, the Board of Punishments agreed that she had violated Article 105 of GQC and sentenced her to 80 strokes of the heavy bamboo (because she had remarried as a concubine, her penalty would be reduced by two degrees) (Du 2008, p. 523).

In the Wu Shihua case at Guizhou in 1834, the defendant Wu Shihua forced his father's concubine, nee Zhang, to remarry because he was living in poverty and could not afford to maintain her. Since there was no relevant offence in the GQC, the Censorate (which was responsible to review the case submitted by the magistrate) first ordered that Wu Shihua should be punished in accordance with Article 105 by analogy. However, considering that Wu Shihua had forced his *Shu Mu* to remarry, and had not considered her "face" by making false allegation out of frustration (*xiefenniekong*), the Censorate declared that he should be additionally punished by one more degree, in other words, 100 strokes of heavy bamboo and the cangue for 1 month. Nee Zhang would be sent back to her own clan.

2.4.3.5 The Killing of Adulterous Concubine

The previous provisions showed the differentiation of the punishments given to a wife or a concubine, where the women were the offenders. But one notable exception was that, in offences relating to the killing of an adulterous wife or concubine, the penalty given to the adulterous man and to the husband was the same. In other words, there was no differentiation of punishment whether the victim of the homicide was an adulterous wife or concubine.

The offence relating to fornication was provided in Article 285 of the GQC which specified that:

> Whenever a wife or concubine commits adultery with another, and (her own husband) catches the adulterous wife and the adulterer at the place [in the very act of] adultery and immediately kills [both of] them, there is no punishment. If he merely kills the adulterous lover, the adulterous wife will be punished in accordance with the law (on consensual adultery [Art. 366]). The official having jurisdiction will remarry or sell her, and the price will be forfeit to the government. (Jones 1994, p. 271; *Da Qing Lü Li* 1993, p. 441)

The Qing scholar, Shen Zhiqi explained that timing was the essence in determining the offence. In other words, the husband must kill immediately his adulterous wife or concubine and the adulterous man, at the place of committing adultery. Shen Zhiqi considered that since the husband caught the adulterous man and the woman on the spot, the evidence was very clear. Further, such killing was committed out of righteous frustration, so the husband should be clear of any punishment (Shen 1715/2000, p. 664).

In the same article *tiaoli* 1, the provision specified that if the adulterous affair was not caught by the husband at the place where the adultery had taken place, but the wife or concubine died after interrogation, and if it was discovered by the magistrate that no adultery had happened, the husband would be punished under the offence of beating a wife to death in accordance with Article 293 (*Da Qing Lü Li* 1993, pp. 441–442). Article 293 specified that, if the adulterous affair was not caught at the place of adultery, or caught after some days, and that the adulterous woman died and the adulterous man pleaded guilty of the affair, the husband would be punished by 100 strokes of heavy bamboo and sentenced to penal servitude for 3 years, based on the law that "the accused had been caught but was killed afterwards without authority" (*yijuzhi ershansha*).[19] The adulterous man would be punished by 100 strokes of heavy bamboo and penal servitude for 3 years (Jones 1994, p. 279; *Da Qing Lü Li* 1993, p. 463). The Qing scholar Xue Yunsheng commented that Article 293 was unfair to the husband, since the husband would not be punished if he killed the adulterous man and wife at the place of committing adultery, but he would be punished if he just killed the adulterous wife. Xue Yunsheng commented that since the provisions (Articles 285 and 293) had given the right of the husband

[19] See Article 277 of GQC on the punishment related to the offence of *yijuzhi ershansha* (Jones 1994, p. 263; Da Qing Lü Li 1993, p. 482).

to kill the adulterous man and woman, the laws should not on the other hand punish the husband if he did not kill both (Xue 1970, pp. 784–785).

However, these provisions did not address this issue: what was the level of punishment if the husband arrested the adulterous man and killed the concubine at the place of committing the adultery? Would there be any difference in the penalty if the adulterous woman was the wife or concubine in this circumstance?

In the Liu Shanjue case at Sichuan in 1824 ("Xin an hui lan" 2006, p. 1394), the defendant Liu Shanjue killed his concubine, nee Li, after the defendant's mother learnt of the adulterous affair of his concubine with another man, Xu Yuan. The Board of Punishments agreed that Xu Yuan would be sentenced to 100 strokes with heavy bamboo and penal servitude for 3 years. But on the killing of Liu Shanjue's concubine, the Board of Punishments ordered that his penalty should take reference to Article 314 and sentenced him to 100 strokes of heavy bamboo.[20] In effect, the penalty would be the same for the husband who beat the wife or concubine to death, that is, 100 strokes of heavy bamboo.

What, then, was the level of punishment given to the adulterous man if the husband killed his adulterous wife or concubine? Would there be any differentiation to the level of punishment to the adulterous man if the victim was the adulterous wife or concubine of the husband?

In other parts of Article 285, *tiaoli* 1 provided that if the husband killed the adulterous woman at the place of the adulterous affair, but arrested the adulterous man and brought him to the magistrate, the husband would receive 80 strokes of heavy bamboo, but the adulterous man would be punished by strangulation (by delay). In this part, the *tiaoli* used "woman" but did not specify the wife or concubine, so would there be any differentiation in penalty if the victim was the wife or concubine?

In the Yang Youli case at Yunan in 1798 ("Xin an hui lan" 2006, pp. 1394–1396), the Board of Punishments had to decide the proper punishments of the defendants—the adulterous man Yang Youli and the husband Yin Zongtang. In this case, Yang Youli had an adulterous affair with the concubine of Yin Zongtang, nee Gao. The husband, Yin Zongtang, killed nee Gao at the place where Yang Youli and Gao committed adultery, but Yin Xongting did not kill Yang Youli on the spot. Instead, Yin Zongtang tied up Yang Youli and took him to the magistrate. However, Article 285 and its *tiaoli* did not clearly specify the punishments for the husband who killed his adulterous concubine, though *tiaoli* 1 suggested that the penalty would be the same. The Board of Punishments considered that there was no difference in the punishment of the husband if he killed the adulterous wife or adulterous concubine under the same circumstance. This was because the Board of Punishments considered that the husband's killing of the wife or concubine was committed out of "righteous frustration" (*yifen*). The Board of Punishments finally ruled that Yang Youli should

[20] Article 314 of GQC: "If a slave is guilty of an offence (whether fornication or theft-this includes all violations of the law), if the head of the household, or a relative in the second degree of the head of the household or his maternal grandparent does not inform the official having jurisdiction, (but privately himself) strikes and kills [the slave], the penalty is 100 strokes of the heavy bamboo" Jones, 298; (Jones 1994, p. 298; *Da Qing Lü Li* 1993, p. 484).

be punished by strangulation (by delay) and Yin Zongtang would be punished by strokes of heavy bamboo.[21] This case shows that there should be no differentiation of punishment for an adulterous man, if the husband killed the adulterous wife or concubine.[22]

2.4.4 The Second Wife or Concubine in Kim Tiu

There was a special marriage in Chinese customary practice called *Kim Tiu* (*Jian Tiao*). It was a very special arrangement between at least two households within the same family. In a family where a man had no son but his brother had an only son, the man with no son might, upon the agreement or instruction of the senior members of the family, adopt his brother's only son to become his heir and then arrange a marriage for him. Consequently, this only son might have two wives: one from the marriage arranged by his natural parents and another from the marriage arranged by his adoptive parents. For example, in 1813, a *Kim Tiu* contract was signed between two families of the *Yi* (an ethnic group) at Wuting County in Yunan, Mrs. Na nee Li agreed to have his only son, Na Zhenxing, appointed as an heir to her brother-in-law family. Mrs. Na nee Li considered that since her brother-in-law was the clan's head but had died without an heir, it was important to have an heir to continue the patrilineal lineage. In this connection, she agreed to have his son, Na Zhengxing, be an heir to her brother-in-law's family, and after the conclusion of this contract, Na Zhengxing would be under the guidance of the wife and concubines of the brother-in-law (Zhang 2014, pp. 1792–1793). This contract showed that even in ethnic minorities, *Kim Tiu* marriage could be regarded as a practical way to resolve the question of patrilineal lineage.

However, this customary practice was not legally recognised until 1775. At this time, because such practice was so popular, the emperor decided to add a new *tiaoli* in the GQC under Article 78 legalising the practice: "if there is no son to appoint an heir…, the proposed man to inherit is the only son from the brothers of the same father, and if both families agreed, with the consent and evidenced by the whole clan, the laws also allowed that man to inherit these two households (*zong tiao*)".[23]

---

[21] The Board of Punishments did not specify the number of strokes.

[22] One very important element of this decision was the application of the principle of "proper status" (*mingfen*) in determining the penalty. On the offences relating to differentiation of the penalty of wife and concubine when they committed offences against their senior relatives, or the offences of the senior relatives committed offence against the wife and concubine, there was a differentiation in the level of punishments for the wife and concubine. The purpose of this was to respect a strict family order. But on the offence relating to the adultery in Article 285, there was no such differentiation on the level of punishment to the husband and adulterous man if the victim of the homicide was the wife or concubine.

[23] This was added in the 42nd year of Qianlong reign (*Da Qing Lü Li Gen Yuan* 1871/2012, p. 411; *Da Qing Lü Li* 1993, pp. 196–197).

In this provision, there were four legal requirements for a valid *Kim Tiu* marriage. Firstly, there must be no son in one family. Secondly, the brothers of the father's family must have an only son. Thirdly, both families must agree with the arrangement, and fourthly, the whole clan must agree to this arrangement. Consequentially, this only son would have two marriages: one arranged by his natural parents and another one arranged by his adoptive parents.

The problem was that, as mentioned earlier, Article 103 of the GQC only allowed for a one husband and one wife relationship. So, there was a legal question on whether the married woman in a *Kim Tiu* marriage (in other words, the second marriage) could be regarded as a legal "wife". In the Yu Dusheng case at Henan in 1814, the Board of Rites was asked by the Board of Punishments on the proper title of the "wife" in Yu Dusheng's second marriage, in other words, his *Kim Tiu* marriage. The Board of Rites replied that, the woman in the first marriage of Yu Dusheng should be the wife, and the woman in his second marriage should be the concubine. Consequently, Yu Dusheng did not commit the offence of Article 103 for bigamy (*Xin An Hui Lan* 1840/1968, p. 2518). In another case, the Peng Zili case in 1820, the defendant killed his daughter-in-law who was the second "wife" in a *Kim Tiu* marriage. The Board of Punishments considered that the "wife" of the second marriage should be regarded a concubine. Therefore, in determining the nature of the offence, the Board of Punishments considered that the defendant should be punished by the offence of killing the concubine of his son, but not killing the wife of his son (*Xin An Hui Lan* 1840/1968, pp. 2519–2520). From the above cases, the Board of Punishments disapproved the customary practice of "equal wife" and upheld the principle of the monogamous nature of the marriage, in other words, one man and one woman. In the latter case, the Board of Punishments considered that the "proper order" was paramount in the Chinese family. The Board of Punishments criticised that some "foolish" people mistakenly believed that the women in the *Kim Tiu* marriage could be regarded as principal wives and allowed such marriages to be arranged for their daughters. By doing this, the Board of Punishments considered that one must not make any confusion in the family order of *Di* and *Shu*. To conclude, the Board of Punishments took the family order seriously. The woman in the first marriage should be the principal wife. The woman in the second marriage should be the concubine.[24]

[24] In another case, the 1851 Wang Zongmin case (*Xin An Hui Lan* 2006, pp. 262–263) in Zhili, Wang Zongmin attempted to fornicate with his son's wife, nee Zhang, of a *Kim Tiu* marriage. Later, nee Zhang had a quarrel with her husband and committed suicide. The issue was, whether nee Zhang should be regarded as the "wife" in determining the offence of Wang Zongmin, since the magistrate considered that nee Zhang was a concubine. If so, Wang Zongmin would only have a penalty of 100 strokes of heavy bamboo and 3 years of penal servitude. The Board of Punishments decided that the rules as established in the Yu Dusheng case (1814) were distinguished. The Board of Punishments argued that in Yu's case, the Board of Rite's decision would only be applied to the situation of wearing the mourning clothes by the father's sons and daughters. In other words, the sons and daughters would wear the different clothes in regard to the "wife" of the *Kim Tiu* marriage, where the wife of the second marriage was regarded as a concubine. The Board of Punishments considered that since this case was related to the life of a human being (in other

Despite the negative attitude of the Board of Punishments in the *Kim Tiu* marriage, such practice was common in many provinces in China. In an investigative report conducted in early Republican China, the provinces which still retained *Kim Tiu* arrangements were Heilongjiang (Judicial Administration Department of the Former Nanjing Nationalist Government (JADFNNG) 2005, pp. 625, 627, 631, 633, 635, 637), Henan (JADFNNG 2005, p. 659), Shandong (JADFNNG 2005, p. 659), Shanxi (JADFNNG 2005, pp. 669, 676, 681), Anhui (JADFNNG 2005, pp. 697, 702–703), Fujian (JADFNNG 2005, p. 749), Hubei (JADFNNG 2005, pp. 767, 774, 780), Hunan (JADFNNG 2005, p. 791), Shanxi (JADFNNG 2005, pp. 801, 822), Gansu (JADFNNG 2005, pp. 834, 836, 839), Rehe (JADFNNG 2005, p. 847)[25] and Suiyuan (JADFNNG 2005, p. 851).[26]

2.4.5 *Dissolution of the Institution of Concubinage*

The GQC did not specify the ways and means to dissolve the institution of concubinage, though there were provisions specifying the dissolution of marriage. In sum, there were three ways a husband and wife could divorce. These were specified in Article 116. Firstly, this article recognised the mutual right to dissolve a marriage: "If the two spouses do not get along together, but wish to divorce, there is no punishment" (Jones 1994, p. 134; *Da Qing Lü Li* 1993, p. 225). Secondly, a husband could divorce his wife if she committed one of the seven acts that constitute grounds of repudiation: "she has no son; she is wanton; she does not serve her parents-in-law; she talks too much; she steals; she is jealous and envious; she has a malignant disease" (Jones 1994, p. 134; *Da Qing Lü Li* 1993, p. 225). However, there were three impediments to repudiation—in other words, the husband could not dissolve the marriage based on these three situations: "she has carried on three years of mourning [for the husband's parents]; the husband had previously been poor and they have become rich; the home from which she was married no longer exists" (Jones 1994, p. 134; *Da Qing Lü Li* 1993, p. 225). Thirdly, if the wife has committed an act "that

words, the death of nee Zhang), then in this case nee Zhang should not be regarded as a "concubine", but as a wife, following to the analogy from Article 103 of the GQC. The Board of Punishments asked the Governor of Zhili to re-examine the case. A scholar, Su Yigong (2007, pp. 201–202) argued that this case showed that there was indeterminacy in treating the second wife as a concubine. And, the Board of Punishment's decision in this case should be paramount, and the rules of the Board of Rites had to be overruled. However, it is important to note that, firstly, the Board of Punishments did not revoke but instead uphold the general rule as laid down by the Board of Rites—that the woman in the second marriage (*Kim Tiu* marriage) was a concubine. Secondly, the Board of Punishments only disagreed with applying this rule in relation to the case of homicide as exemplified in the present case. In this situation, the rule established by the Board of Rites should be regarded as paramount. This rule was also upheld in a case adjudicated in the *Da Li Yuan* as seen in Chapter 3, note 29.

[25] Rehe province was revoked in 1955.

[26] Suiyuan province was revoked in 1954.

extinguishes the duty that binds them" (*yijue*), the husband should ask for divorce (Jones 1994, p. 134; *Da Qing Lü Li* 1993, p. 225). Since the GQC did not specify that these rules on dissolution of marriage applied to the institution of concubinage, the husband could dissolve the union of concubinage unilaterally. Furthermore, since there were mutual rights to dissolve a formal marriage, some scholars suggested that if the husband and the concubine decided to put an end to the union of concubinage, such a relationship would be dissolved.

However, it is doubtful whether the concubine might unilaterally dissolve the union of concubinage, because the GQC punished the act of remarriage of a concubine without authorisation by the court. In Article 116, the GQC prohibited certain acts of remarriage by the wife. Two notable offences are, firstly, if the husband abandoned his wife and ran away, and within a 3-year period the wife deserted without notifying the authorities, she would receive 80 strokes of heavy bamboo. Secondly, if she remarried without authorisation from the court, the wife would receive 100 strokes of heavy bamboo (Jones 1994, p. 134; Da Qing Lü Li 1993, p. 225). If a concubine committed the above offences, each punishment would be reduced two degrees (Jones 1994, p. 134; *Da Qing Lü Li* 1993, p. 225). From the above provisions in the GQC, it could be inferred that a formal dissolution might be necessary for the concubine to remarry legally. But this issue remained inconclusive.

Nevertheless, the customary practice was that in Taiwan, the husband could dissolve the relationship if he wished. There was no requirement to provide any reason, so the rich and noble man might let the concubine leave, whereas some husbands from the middle class might sell their concubines (Provisional Taiwan Customs Investigation Committee 1993, p 611).

2.4.6 The Inheritance Right of the Children of a Concubine

The reason a man took a concubine was to ensure the continuation of the patrilineal lineage of a family. In an early edition of the Great Qing Code, published in 1646, there was an age limitation to a husband's taking a concubine. It was specified in Article 160 that a commoner could only take a concubine at the age of 40 and should have no son (*The Origins of Da Qing Lü Li* 1871/2012, p. 456).[27] But these limitations were repealed in the Great Qing Code of 1740. Despite the removal of this restriction, the legislative purpose of the original provision was clear that the husband could only take a concubine if his wife could not give birth to a son. Therefore, the husband could not institute a concubinage for other purposes, such as personal pleasure. Furthermore, the age limitation in the original provision was to ensure that the husband and wife had enough time for giving birth to a son.

---

[27] See also http://lsc.chineselegalculture.org/eC/DQLJJFL_1646/3.3.3.106. Accessed on 10 August 2018.

The GQC did not require that a valid institution of concubinage should be accepted by the wife or by the family members. A scholar, Yue Chunzhi (2006, p. 164), by studying the literary materials of the Tang dynasty, suggested that during that time, the consent of the family members was necessary for an institution of concubinage. Customary practices, such as "Enter into Palace" (Yap Kung), were not specified in the GQC as a precondition of the union of concubinage.[28] But recognition by the parents or grandparents of the man was necessary if they were still alive, at least according to Taiwan customary practice (Ministry of Law 2004, p. 111). If the concubine gave birth to a son, the principal wife was called principal mother, *dimu,* while the biological mother—the concubine—was called concubine mother, *shumu*. The son of the concubine had an equal share of the household estate if the parents decided to divide the family properties and estates, which was called "household division" (*fenjia*). It is specified in Article 88, *tiaoli* 1 that: "on the division of family properties and estates, there would be an equal division amongst the sons, no matter the sons were born by the wife, concubine or mistress" (*Da Qing Lü Li* 1993, p. 201).[29] In addition, the son of the concubine would have an equal share of the household estates if the husband died intestate.

If the concubine gave birth to the only son in a family, as mentioned earlier the son should call the principal wife his principal mother (*dimu*), and his mother concubine mother (*shumu*). The only son was regarded as heir (*dizi*) for the succession of the family line and the estates after the deceased father. This succession was recognised in the case at Tamshui in 1876. In 1875, a family dispute occurred between Zheng Yi and his concubine mother (*shumu*) Mrs. Zheng nee Chen. Mrs. Zheng nee Chen was the concubine to the husband Zheng Bi, who had taken her as concubine after the death of his wife. The husband, Zheng Bi, adopted Zheng Yi as his son since his principal wife had not given birth to any offspring. After the death of Zheng Bi, Mrs. Zheng nee Chen, as concubine, refused to divide the household estates with Zheng Yi, because Zheng Yi had not abided with his parents' orders and the father, Zheng Bi, had expelled him from the family. Nevertheless, after reviewing the submissions from both parties, in 1876, the magistrate decided that Zheng Yi could have one third of the land assets of Zheng Bi. The magistrate further ordered that Zheng Yi should receive 100 dollars (*yuans*) from the land interests to end the dispute, and thereafter all lands of Zheng Bi should be given to the son of Mrs. Zheng nee Chen. However, the decision of the magistrate obviously did not follow the rules and practices as given in the GQC (Case number 21402, Tan-Hsin Archive 2009a v17, p. 107). Firstly, since the magistrate accepted the fact that Zheng Yi had been expelled from the family by his father Zheng Bi and had returned to the original clan, Zheng Yi's status as adopted son of Zheng Bi was in doubt. Secondly, it is also doubtful how the magistrate determined the level of the portion received by Zheng Yi on his adopted father's land interests.

---

[28] For a discussion of *Yap Kung*, please see the next chapter.

[29] One scholar argued that the "equal division amongst the sons" might be interpreted as the equal division of family properties and estates to the sons' households (Lu 2012, pp. 40–46).

2.4.7 Maintenance and the Appointment of a Posthumous Heir

The provision of maintenance to the concubine was not specified in the GQC. It was provided by customary practice. In Qing law, the provision concerning maintenance to the widow was a mixture of law and customary practice. The word *shan*, referring to the maintenance and support of widows, was used in the GQC in some provisions. Generally, if the husband died intestate, the widow had the right to be supported by the son. Or, if she had no son, she had the right to manage the estates until an heir was appointed. These are negatively provided in the *tiaoli* of Article 78. In *tiaoli* 2 of Article 78, the law provided that if the woman had no son but decided to remain chaste (*shouzhi*) after the death of her husband, the woman could succeed her husband's estates, and she had to accept an heir selected by the head of clan (*Da Qing Lü Li* 1993, p. 195). On the selection of heir, Article 78 *tiaoli* 1 required the family to appoint the son of the man's brother or, in the absence of this option, other family members with the same rank in accordance with the *wufu* order (*Da Qing Lü Li* 1993, p. 195).[30]

It is important to note that in this article, the word "woman" (*furen*) was used, not "wife" or "concubine". So, this article in effect gave certain rights to the concubine (provided that the wife was deceased) to succeed the husband's estates, until the appointment of a posthumous heir. To a certain extent, the concubine had the right of not accepting an heir as recommended by the head of clan (Bernhardt 1999, pp. 59–72). This explanation was further supported by the Qing legal scholar Shen Jiaben (1985, pp. 2204–2205). Shen Jiaben first considered that this provision was used to specify the process of the appointment of an heir, not the succession of her deceased husband's estates. Shen Jiaben considered that the only difference between the wife and concubine was the title, but in mourning obligations to the husband, the wife and concubine were the same. The principal wife would manage the family after the husband's decease. But if the principal wife died with no lower relatives in the second degree, the concubine's right should not be neglected. In addition, Shen Jiaben stated that it would be unreasonable for the concubine to simply watch the end of the patrilineal lineage and let the family assets be dissolved. Therefore, to Shen Jiaben, the concubine should have the right to succeed the deceased husband's estates and be involved in the selection of a posthumous heir.

In the same *tiaoli* 2, if the concubine decided to remarry, all the husband's properties and her wedding presents should be returned to the former husband's family (*Da Qing Lü Li* 1993, p. 195). The GQC had some provisions to protect the widow who wanted to remain chaste from pressure of the husband's family members to remarry. Article 105 of the GQC provided that: "If the mourning for her husband is over and (a wife or concubine) wishes to remain chaste, if her paternal grandparents

[30] The magistrate, Wang Huizi, in his memoir argued that *tiaoli* 1 used the words "(the family) allowed to appoint (xuling) an heir" which denoted that the family could have the right to or not to appoint an heir. It is because the Chinese word *xu* also carried a meaning of "perhaps". So the family had the discretion of not appointing an heir (Wang 2012, p. 24).

or parents, or her husband's paternal grandparents or parents force her to marry, they will be punished with 80 strokes of the heavy bamboo" (Jones 1994, p. 127; *Da Qing Lü Li* 1993, p. 219). In the same provision, if such an act was committed by the relatives in the second degree, one degree was added to the above punishment. And, if such act was committed by a relative of the third degree or below, one more degree was added to the above punishment (Jones 1994, p. 127; *Da Qing Lü Li* 1993, p. 219). The purpose of Article 105 was to protect the chastity of the widow from forced remarriage. Remarriage, if successful, would mean that the widow must return the former husband's estate to husband's family members.

2.5 Conclusion

The Qing law on the concubine was a mixture of statutory law and local custom. Since most provisions on the status of the concubine fell under the jurisdiction of local magistrates, the application of such law in the GQC depended upon the judicial approach taken by the local magistrates, in addition to precedents from the Board of Punishments. It is notable that most local magistrates relied upon mediation and local customs to settle family disputes so as to avoid litigation as much as possible. Nevertheless, the Qing laws on the concubine were not ambiguous. From the above analysis, several legal principles had been developed. Firstly, a concubine was inferior to a wife. Secondly, a concubine could have maintenance if there was a division of family households or after the death of her husband. Thirdly, a concubine could have certain rights to manage the estate of her deceased husband. Fourthly, a concubine had the right, upon the selection of the head the clan, to appoint an heir for the family.

However, even if Qing authorities had clear laws on the concubine, there were difficulties in applying the laws in other jurisdictions such as Hong Kong. The reason is that the laws on a concubine were knitted into traditional Chinese law and custom, some of which dated back to the Tang dynasty. Hong Kong colonial courts that applied common law could find it difficult to implement such laws because of the big gap between the two systems. Also, the role of the local magistrate in the Qing judicial system was totally different from the British magistrate in Hong Kong. The Qing magistrate had a high level of discretion—to maintain social harmony, he could even judge outside the boundaries of the GQC in family disputes. The magistrate in the Hong Kong colonial legal system could only strictly apply and interpret the rules within the remit of laws (such as GQC). The discretionary power of Hong Kong judges was limited, not to mention that they did not have to shoulder the social function of maintaining harmony in the community.

Furthermore, given the fundamental differences between the Qing and Hong Kong legal systems, plus a lack of understanding of the principles and rules of the Qing laws, the judges in Hong Kong mostly relied upon the analysis of experts, often from references and readings from Western scholars. Consequently, most of the rules and principles on Qing law were based upon Chinese law through Western lens, and not from an understanding of the law through the eyes of Chinese traditional legal values. Therefore, when the Hong Kong courts were required to apply Chinese law and custom, there was some misunderstanding of the Great Qing Code. This resulted in the Hong Kong courts (even in the common law courts in South East Asia) arriving at different interpretations of the rules and principles of the GQC than the Qing authorities, which will be dealt with in the next chapter.

References

Ban, G. (1949). *Po hu t'ung, the comprehensive discussions in the white tiger hall* (Tjan, T., Trans.). Leiden: E.J. Brill.

Bernhardt, K. (1999). *Women and property in China 960–1949*. Stanford: Stanford University Press.

Bo'an xinbian [A new edition of rejected cases]. (1968). (juan 21). Taipei: Cheng Wen. (Original work published 1781).

Board of Punishments. (1886). *Da Qing Huidian Shili* [Laws relating to Board of Revenue]. http://lsc.chineselegalculture.org/Asset/Source/lscDocument_ID-575_No-03.pdf. Accessed on 3 Mar 2019.

Bodde, D., & Morris, C. (1971). *Law in imperial China*. Philadelphia: University of Pennsylvania Press.

Chen, G. (1992). *Zhongguo hunyin shi* [The history of marriage in China]. Taiwan Commercial Press. (Original work published 1936).

Chen, H. S. (2017). *Xiang Qing fagui huigui zhi Qingdai faxue yanyiu* [The study of legal system in Qing dynasty–perspective on legal norms]. Taipei: Angle Publishing.

Cheng, Y. (2006). *Qing zhi minguo xuqie zisu zhi bianqian* [The evolution of the customs of the institution of concubinage from Qing to Republican China]. Shanghai: Shanghai Guji Chubanshe.

Chiu, V. (1966). *Marriage laws and customs in China*. Hong Kong: Institute of Advanced Chinese Studies and Research, New Asia College.

Chu, T. (1961). *Law and society in traditional China*. Paris: Mouton & Co La Haye.

Contract of selling daughter as concubine by nee Peng Cheng. (1996). The selection of archives of Ba County on Qianlong, Jiaqing and Daoguang reigns of Qing Dynasty. In Sichuan da xue li shi xi, Sichuan sheng dang an guan (Eds.), *Archive Bureau of Sichuan Province and History Department of Sichuan University*, (Vol. 2). Chengdu: Sichuan da xue chu ban she.

Da Qing lü li. (1993). (Zhang R., Liu Y. & Jin M, Punctuators). Tianjin: Tianjin Guji Chubenshe.

Da Qing Lü Li gen yuan [*The Origins of Da Qing Lü Li*]. (2012). Shanghai: Shanghai Cishu Chubanshe. (Original work published 1871).

Despatches. (1898). *Despatches and other papers relating to the extension of the Colony of Hong Kong, 1898*, (CO129/290). The National Archives, Kew.

Despatches. (1899). *Despatches and other papers relating to the extension of the Colony of Hong Kong: Laid before the legislative council by command of his excellency the Governor, 1899, SP 1899*. Hong Kong: Noronha and Co. http://sunzi.lib.hku.hk/hkgro/view/s1899/1610.pdf. Accessed on 10 Aug 2018.

Du, J. (Ed.). (2008). *Qing Jiaqingchao xingke tiben shehui shiliaon jikan* [A collection of the Board of Punishments on social history during Jiaqing reign of Qing dynasty]. Tianjin: Tianjin Guji chubenshe.

Endacott, G. B. (1973). *A history of Hong Kong* (2nd ed.). Hong Kong: Oxford University Press.

Evans, D. M. E. (1971). Common law in a Chinese setting—The kernel or the nut? *Hong Kong Law Journal, 1*, 9.

Fan, Z. (2007). *Fanshan zhengshu* [Administrative writings of Fan Zengxiang] (Vol. 19). Beijing: Chung hwa.

Haydon, E. S. (1962). The choices of Chinese customary law in Hong Kong. *The International and Comparative Law Quarterly, 11*, 231–250.

Hsieh, B. H. (2014). *Concubinage and Servitude in late imperial China*. Lanham: Lexington Books.

Huang, L. (1984). *A complete book concerning happiness and benevolence* [Fuhui chuanshu]. Tucson: The University of Arizona Press.

Jamieson, G. (1921). *Chinese family and commercial law*. Hong Kong: Kelly & Walsh.

Jernigan, T. R. (1905). *China in law and commerce*. New York: Macmillan.

Johneson, W. (1997). *The Tang Code, volume II, specific articles*. Princeton: Princeton University Press.

Jones, W. C. (1994). *The Great Qing Code*. Oxford: Clarendon Press.

Judicial Administration Department of the Former Nanjing Nationalist Government. (2005). *Minshi xiguan diaocha baogaolu* [The investigative report of the civil customary practices]. Beijing: CUPL Press.

Legge, J. (1885). *The sacred books of China: The texts of Confucianism, Part III, The Li Ki, I-X*. Oxford: Clarendon Press.

Li, Z. (2012). *Wanqing zhouxian susong zhongdi shenduan wenti* [The questions on the judicial decisions made by the magistrates in late Qing period]. Beijing: Law Press.

Lu, J. C. (2012). *Qingmo minchujiachan zhidu de yanbian: Congfenjia xichan dao yichanjicheng* [The evolution of the family household property system in the late Qing and early Republican period]. Taipei: Angle.

Mantie nongcu diaocha [Manchurian Railway Rural Investigation Report]. (2016). *Customary report* (Vol. 1). Beijing: China Social Sciences Press.

Ministry of Law. (2004). *Taiwan minshi xiguan diaocha baogao* [Investigative report on Taiwan customary practices]. Taipei: Ministry of Law.

Möllendorff, P. G. von. (1878). The family law of the Chinese, and its comparative relations with that of other nations. In *Journal of the North China Branch of the Royal Asiatic Society*. Shanghai: The Celestial Empire Office.

Möllendorff, P. G. von. (1896). *The family law of the Chinese*. Shanghai: Kelly & Walsh.

Na, S. (1992). *Qingdai zhongyang sifa shenpan zhidu* [The judicial system of Qing dynasty in central level]. Taibei: Wenshizhe chubanshe.

Nie, Y. (2012). *Nie Yifeng xiansheng weizai gongdu* [The judgments of Nie Yifeng]. Nanchang: Jiangxi renmin chubanshe.

Norton-Kyshe, J. W. (1971). *The history of the laws and courts of Hong Kong: From the earliest period to 1898*. Hong Kong: Vetch & Lee Ltd..

Parker, E. H. (1879). Comparative Chinese family law. *The China Review, 8*, 67–107.

Petition of Li Hongfa. (1996). Petition of Li Hongfa and others on the end of dispute on 17 July at 24 years of Daoguang reign. In Sichuan da xue li shi xi, Sichuan sheng dang an guan (Eds.), *The selection of Archives of Ba County on Qianlong, Jiaqing and Daoguang reigns of Qing Dynasty. Archive Bureau of Sichuan Province and History Department of Sichuan University* (Vol. 2). Chengdu: Sichuan da xue chu ban she.

Petition of Wang Fusheng. (1996). Petition of Wang Fusheng on 30 June at 24 years of Daoguang reign. In Sichuan da xue li shi xi, Sichuan sheng dang an guan (Eds.), *The selection of Archives of Ba County on Qianlong, Jiaqing and Daoguang reigns of Qing Dynasty. Archive Bureau of Sichuan Province and History Department of Sichuan University* (Vol. 2). Chengdu: Sichuan da xue chu ban she.

Provisional Taiwan Traditional Customs Investigation Committee [Rinji Taiwan Kyukan Chosakai]. (1993). *Taiwan private law* [Taiwan Shiho] (Chen, J., Trans.) (Vol. 2). Taichung: Taiwan Historica.

Shen, J. (1985). *Li dai xing fa kao: fu Jiyi wen cun* [Study on the chronicles criminal law]. Beijing: Chung hwa.

Shen, Z. (1999). *Da Qinglü jizhu* [Compiled annotation on the Great Qing Code]. Beijing: Law Press. (Original work published 1715).

Shen, Z. (2000). *Da Qinglü jizhu* [Compiled annotation on the Great Qing Code]. Beijing: Law Press. (Original work published 1715).

Shiga, S. (1978). Family property and the law of inheritance in traditional China. In D. Buxhaum (Ed.), *Chinese family law and social change in historical and comparative perspective*. Seattle: University of Washington Press.

Shiga, S. (2003). *Chūgoku kazokuhō no genre* [The principles of the Chinese family law] (Zhang, J. & Li, L. Trans.). Beijing: Law Press.

Shih, F. (1987). *Zhongguo gudai hunyin yu jiating* [The marriage and family in ancient China]. Wuhan People's Press.

Song, B. (2009). *The origins of the provisions in Autumn Assizes* [Qiushen tiaokuan yuanliu kao] (pp. 322–323). Beijing: Social Sciences Academic Press.

Staunton, G. T. (2012). *Ta Tsing Leu Lee: Being the fundamental laws and a selection from the supplementary statutes of the Penal code of China*. Cambridge: Cambridge University Press. (Original work published 1810).

Su, Y. (2007). *Chinese law applied by westerners: Traditional Chinese law and custom in Hong Kong* (2nd ed.). Beijing: Social Sciences Academic Press.

Tan-Hsin Archive. (2009a). *Vol. 17*. Taipei: National Taiwan University Library.

Tan-Hsin Archive. (2009b). *Vol. 36*. Taipei: National Taiwan University Library.

Tian, T., Xu, C., & Wang, H. (2004). *Huangyan litigation archives and related research reports*. Beijing: Law Press.

Translation of the Chinese Proclamation. (1899, August 26). Translation of the Chinese proclamation issued by His Excellency Sir Henry A. Blake, G.C.M.G., Governor and Commander-in-Chief of the Colony of Hongkong and its Dependencies and Vice-Admiral of the same, 15 April 1899 (26 August, 1899). *The Hong Kong Government Gazette*. http://sunzi.lib.hku.hk/hkgro/view/g1899/630307.pdf. Accessed on 10 Aug 2018.

Wang, H. (2012). *Bingta menghen lu* [Records of the Ashes of Dreams from a Sick Bed]. Jiangxi: Jiangxi renmin chubanshe. (Original work published 1796).

Wang, Z. (2017). *Qingdai guojiafa douyuan chayi yu tongyi* [State law in the Qing dynasty: Heterogeneous plurality and power centralization]. Beijing: Social Sciences Academic Press.

Wei, S. (2013). *Qingdai Qianlongchao shengji shijian yanmjiu* [Study on the judicial application of laws in provincial level at Qing's Qianlong period]. Beijing: Renmin daxue chubanshe.

Wesley-Smith, P. (1994). *The sources of Hong Kong law*. Hong Kong: Hong Kong University Press.

Xin An Hui Lan. (1968). (Vols. 7–40). Taipei: Cheng Wen Publishing. (Original work published 1840).

Xin An Hui Lan. (2006). (Vols. 8–52). In *Xin An Hui Lan Quan Bian*. Beijing: The Law Press.

Xue, Y. (1970). *Duli cunyi* [The doubts of studying laws] (T. Huang, Ed. & Punctuator) (Part IV). Tsingchia/ETaipei: Cheng Wen Publishing.

Ying, X. (1873). *Qiushen shihuan bijiao chengan* [Leading cases on execution and deferment at the Autumn Assizes] (Vol. 2). http://shanben.ioc.u-tokyo.ac.jp/main_p?nu=B3861300&order=ti_no&no=02231

Yue, C. (2006). *Tangdai minshi falu zhidu lungao* [The discussion on the civil law system in Tang dynasty]. Beijing: People's Press.

Yue, C. (2015). *Tang lü shu yi* [The annotated notes of the Tang Code] (juan 14). Shanghai: Shanghai Gu Ji Chubanshe.

Zhang, C. (2014). *Zhonguo lidai qiyue* cuibian [Collection of chronicles of Chinese contracts] (Vol. 3). Beijing: Peking University Press.

Zheng, Q. (1988). *Qingdai sifa shenpan zhidu yanjiu* [A study on the judicial system in the Qing dynasty]. Hunan Jiaoyu Chubanshe.

Zhu, Y. (1828). *Yuedong chengan chubian* [A preliminary edition of leading cases from Guangdong East].

Cases

Chan Hing-cheung & others v R [1897] HKLR 197.
Leung May Ling and Others v Leung Sai Lun Robert and Others (1999) 2 HKCFAR 94.
Ng Ying Ho v Tam Suen Yu [1963] HKLR 923.
Re Wong Choi Ho & Another [1969] HKLR 391.
Suen Toi Lee v Yau Yee Ping [2001] 4 HKCFAR 474.
Tang Kai-chung v Tang Chik-sang [1970] HKLR 276.
Wong Kam Ying v Man Chi Tai [1967] HKLR 201.

Chapter 3
Judicial Construction of *T'sip* in Chinese Family Law in East Asia: A Comparative Perspective

Abstract This chapter discusses the application of the Great Qing Code (GQC) in East Asian jurisdictions: Taiwan in the Japanese occupation period and the judgments from *Da Li Yuan* in the Republic of China. The judges interpreted the legal status of concubine under the GQC with a view to expanding the rights of the concubine as much as possible, leading to differences in the understanding of the general principle of the institution of concubinage in different jurisdictions. This chapter focuses on the judicial response to the GQC in different jurisdictions and shows how judges adapted the provisions of the GQC to local contexts when delivering judgments.

Keywords Elements of concubinage · Secondary wife · Kim Tiu · Dissolution of concubinage · Maintenance · Division of household (fenjia)

3.1 Introduction

The previous chapter analysed the complexity of the legal definition of a concubine under traditional Chinese law. But starting from the beginning of the nineteenth century, during the Qing dynasty, legal reform saw a shift towards a more modern system of family law. In 1911, soon after the beginning of the Republic of China, there was a genuine call in the name of the equality of men and women to end the institution of concubinage. The year 1931 was important in the modern legal history of the Republic of China. The promulgation of the Civil Code, which marked the end of legal recognition of concubinage in China, was hailed as a bold move towards greater equality between men and women (Civil Law Research and Amendment Committee 1976, p. 590). Although the institution of concubinage was no longer recognised in positive law, a woman who became a concubine before 1931 could still be regarded as a family member under the legal protection of the Civil Code, based upon such provisions as the duty of family members to provide maintenance for a *t'sip* (concubine) if the husband died intestate. Although one might argue that the legal protection of women was still inadequate, at least the institution of

M. WL Wong, *Chinese Marriage and Social Change*,
https://doi.org/10.1007/978-981-15-1644-3_3

concubinage was abolished in the Civil Code in 1931. This was followed by the Marriage Law of the People's Republic of China in 1950, which only allowed monogamous marriage. Together, these two pieces of legislation marked the beginning of the legal recognition of the monogamous marriage in Mainland China.

Although the Government of the Republic of China put an end to the union of concubinage and customary marriage in 1931, no immediate corresponding changes were made in other jurisdictions which recognised Chinese customary marriage. Singapore only abolished the legal recognition of concubinage in the Women's Charter in 1961, 30 years after the Civil Code came into force in the Republic of China. Taiwan legally abolished concubinage after the end of Japanese rule in 1945 and the resumption of rule by the Republic of China in the same year. Hong Kong abolished concubinage in 1971, after the promulgation of the Marriage Reform Ordinance, which only recognised monogamous marriage. Nevertheless, even after the abolition of concubinage, all these jurisdictions faced a common question regarding the application of Chinese customary law: how to determine the status of *t'sip* and their rights under Chinese customary law in court?

This chapter probes the interpretations of *t'sip* in the Chinese communities of five jurisdictions and the judges' approaches to family disputes involving the status of *t'sip*. In addition, this chapter investigates how Western legal concepts of marriage and inheritance may have affected the various judicial approaches in making these interpretations.

For comparative purposes, this chapter will look at cases and judgments delivered by the *Da Li Yuan* (the Supreme Court in the early Republic of China) in Mainland China, the Review High Court in Taiwan during the Japanese occupation (Review High Court Judgments 1995) and the common law courts in Hong Kong, Burma and the Straits Settlements (including Singapore and Malaysia). The *Da Li Yuan* was chosen for three reasons. Firstly, as the Supreme Court in the Republic of China after the 1911 Revolution, its judgments (which were recently published in full) were binding on the lower courts. Secondly, the laws relating to concubinage at that time were very similar to the GQC—the Qing imperial laws that other East Asian jurisdictions relied on when adjudicating family disputes within their Chinese communities. Thirdly, as the main source of Chinese customary law and practice, the judgments of the *Da Li Yuan* can help to illustrate the evolution of the judicial approach to Chinese customary marriage, especially on the status of *t'sip* in Mainland China before the abolition of concubinage in 1931. This chapter also analyses the decisions of the Review High Court in Taiwan during the Japanese colonial period—the Supreme Court in Taiwan at that time. Although the Japanese government extended the application of its own Civil Code to Taiwan, it decided that Taiwanese customs would still apply in the Review High Court. Thus, we can observe the evolution of Chinese customary law and practice during the Japanese occupation of Taiwan in the decisions of the Review High Court. Finally, the judge-made laws on Chinese customary practices in the common law courts in Hong Kong, Singapore and Burma formed part of the binding authority on the lower courts. Most importantly, all the above-mentioned courts applied the family provisions in the GQC and Chinese customary practices in adjudicating family disputes when both parties were Chinese.

This chapter will discuss the judicial interpretations of *t'sip* in the selected East Asian jurisdictions and how changes in Chinese customs and the abolition of concubinage in the Republic of China in 1931 contributed to the different interpretations of the status of *t'sip* in different jurisdictions. It will conclude that, due to the unique legal environments in different jurisdictions, the status and rights of a *t'sip*—even though she had an inferior status to a wife in the Chinese family—were very different. The reason was that as Chinese emigrants settled in various East Asian countries, bringing their customs with them, these customary practices, once they had been transplanted, evolved and adapted to different local circumstances.

This chapter (and later chapters) uses the terms "*t'sip*" and "concubine" interchangeably to refer to the Chinese word 妾 (pinyin, *qie*; Cantonese pronunciation, *t'sip*).[1] This is because cases reported in Hong Kong and the Straits Settlements used *t'sip* and concubine without qualification—there was no distinction between them in common law courts. Even though judgments in the *Da Li Yuan* in Mainland China and the Review High Court in Taiwan used *qie*, only *t'sip* and concubine are used here to avoid confusion.

3.2 Judicial Approaches to *T'sip*

3.2.1 The Application of Chinese Customary Law

As discussed in Chapter 2, so far as the application of the Chinese laws in the colony of Hong Kong was concerned, that was the laws to be enforced as of 5 April 1843 (see Chap. 2, n. 2). In the Straits Settlements—which comprised the territories of Penang, Malacca and Singapore—the ways and means of the reception of English common law were very different from Hong Kong. Unlike Hong Kong, where the constitutional status was granted by the Crown through two constitutional instruments—Letters Patent and Royal Instructions—the initial legal status of the Straits Settlements was established by the so-called Three Charters. In the Second Charter of Justice granted by the Crown to the British East India Company, a new and formal legal system was established in the Straits Settlements. Cases relating to the interpretation of the Second Charter indicated that the law of England as it stood on 27 November 1826 was received in the Straits Settlements (Woon 1999, p. 236). In the same Charter, there was an opening for the courts to apply Chinese customary law in civil disputes regarding marriage, divorce, inheritance, succession and children. This was because the judicial courts established under the Charter had to administer the principles of common law and equity which were then in force in England "as far as local circumstances will admit"

[1] Another scholar, Lisa Tran, used "minor wife" as a synonym for *t'sip* or *qie* in the GQC and *Da Li Yuan* judgments (Tran 2009, p. 123). Minor wife is not a legal term commonly used in the English common law jurisdictions in East Asia, so the author has used *t'sip* or concubine in this paper to avoid confusion.

(The Second Charter of Justice 1826, p. 26; Teng 2014, p. 418). Therefore, in *R v Willan*, Maxwell R (as he then was) stated:

> Thus, if a Mohammedan or Hindoo, or Chinese marriage, celebrated here according to the religious ceremonies of the parties be valid, it is not because the Charter makes it so—for, as I have already observed, it makes no exception in favour of native contracts of any kind—but because the law of England recognises it. The general rule of that law is, that the validity of marriage is to be determined by the law of the place where it is celebrated. (*R v Wilian* 1858, p. 32)

In addition, in the same judgment, Maxwell R (*Chulas & Kachee v Kolson binte Seydoo Malim* 1867) ruled that previous cases in the Straits Settlements suggested that "it has been laid down as the doctrine of our law that its rules (English rules) are not applicable to such races when intolerable injustice and oppression would be the consequence of their application". Maxwell CJ stated in another case that "(I)n this Colony, so much of the law of England as was in existence when it was imported here, and as is of general (and not merely local) policy, and adapted to the condition and wants of the inhabitants, is the law of the land; and further, that law is subject, in its application to the various alien races established here, to such modifications as are necessary to prevent it from operating unjustly and oppressively on them" (Woods 1869/1911, pp. 30–31). The principles laid down by Maxwell CJ (*Yeap Cheah Neo v Ong Cheng Neo* 1875) were approved in the Privy Council, which held that "(in) applying this general principle it has been held that statutes relating to matters and exigencies peculiar to the local conditions of England, and which are not adapted to the circumstances of the colony, do not become a part of its law, although the general law of England may be introduced into it" (*Yeap Cheah Neo v Ong Cheng Neo* 1875, p. 394). The Charter and the cases above gave the green light to the courts in the Straits Settlements to apply Chinese customary law to matrimonial cases if the circumstances required.

In another common law jurisdiction, Burma, the reception of Chinese customary law in issues of family law such as marriage was arguably first made possible under the Burma Laws Act 1898. Although there were rules (in particular on domicile) which governed the way a foreign law or custom might affect the validity of a local marriage, Section 13(1) of this Act had created some controversy and confusion about the application of Chinese customary law in Burmese courts:

> 13. (1) Where in any suit or other proceeding in Burma it is necessary for the Court to decide any question regarding succession, inheritance, marriage or caste or any religious usage or institution, —
>
> (a) the Buddhist law in cases where the parties are Buddhists;
> (b) the Mahomedan law in cases where the parties are Mahomedans; and the Hindu law in cases where the parties are Hindus;
> (c) shall form the rule of decision, except in so far as such law has by enactment been altered or abolished or is opposed to any custom having the force of law.

This provision implied that the application of customary law was based on religious belief but not race, which created confusion in court. At least in one case, the judge had to first discuss the application of Chinese customary law to the Chinese ethnic group based on Buddhist, Confucian and Taoist religious beliefs (Maung 1963,

p. 33; Huxley 1988–89, pp. 23–24). Furthermore, the provision did not clearly specify the circumstances to which Chinese law must be applied in Burmese courts, which cast doubt on the appropriateness of using Chinese customary law in some judicial cases. Nevertheless, section 13(3) opened a small window to the possibility of applying Chinese customary law:

> (3) In cases not provided for by sub-section (1), or by any other enactment for the time being in force, the decision shall be according to justice, equity and good conscience.

However, this section again created confusion in courts. For example, in *Sein Kyi v Ma E* (1916, p. 401), Parlett J considered that the marriage was invalid according to Chinese customary law: "no negotiation between the parties' parents having taken place and the defendant's mother not having given her consent".[2] But, in the same case, Fox CJ held a different view as he found no strong reason to apply Chinese customary law: "(P)rima facie there is no strong reason why the customary law of the man (Chinese) should be applied, and the customary law of the woman utterly disregarded, at any rate up to and at the time of marriage. After marriage other considerations apply" (*Sein Kyi v Ma* E 1916, p. 403). And he criticised those court decisions that overlooked the principles on the application of the conflict of laws to matrimonial cases:

> The decisions in this Province which have held that in order to constitute a valid marriage between a Chinaman and a Burmese woman it must be shown that certain formalities and ceremonies enjoined by Chinese Customary Law were gone through, and that the consent of the parents of the parties must have been given to the marriage overlook the rule of British Courts stated in *Brook v Brook* and cases that the *lex loci contractus quoad solemnitatis* determines the validity of a marriage, and the *lex domicilii* the question of the capacity of the parties to marry. (*Sein Kyi v Ma E* 1916, p. 403)

The confusion over the application of Chinese customary law to marriage was finally resolved in *In Re Ma Yin Mya and one v Tan Yauk Pu and two* (1927) where the judge did in effect make it very difficult for the Burmese courts to apply Chinese customary law in later cases. The judge gave a three-point guideline on the application of Chinese customary law in Burmese courts:

> My answer to the question referred is that (a) Burmese Buddhist law regarding marriage is *prima facie* applicable to Chinese Buddhists as the *lex loci contractus* and (b) to escape from the application of Burmese Buddhist law regarding marriage a Chinese Buddhist must prove that he is subject to a custom having the force of law in Burma and that that custom is opposed to the provisions of Burmese Buddhist law applicable to the case; and (c) in case the matter in issue is the marriage of a Buddhist Chinaman with a Burmese Buddhist woman he must show that the application of the custom having the force of law will not work injustice to the Burmese Buddhist woman. (*In Re Ma Yin Mya and one v Tan Yauk Pu and two* 1927, p. 420)

This guideline obviously mandated that Burmese Buddhist law must be applied to Chinese Buddhists. In addition, the courts had to protect Burmese Buddhist

[2] Accordingly, the judge applied the case of *Pai Beng Teng v Ko Muang* (1904). See also Alabaster (1899, p. 172).

women, so where an application of Chinese customary laws might "work injustice to Burmese Buddhist women", those laws should not be applied. In effect, this guideline prohibited a Chinese Buddhist man from having a concubine after getting married to a Burmese Buddhist woman because Burmese Buddhist law only recognised monogamy. This judgment was followed by *Ma Kyin Mya v Maung Sit Han* (1937). In this case, the judge had to decide whether Chinese customary law might apply to a marriage between a Chinese Confucian man and a Burmese Buddhist woman. The court considered that Section 13(1) (a) of the Burma Laws Act did not apply in this situation because the parties were not both Buddhists and Section 2 of the Special Marriage Act[3] also did not apply because one party was a Confucian and the other was a Buddhist. There was a possibility that, under Section 13(3) of the Burma Laws Act, customary law (either Chinese or Burmese) might be applicable in this case as a matter of justice, equity and good conscience. But, in the end, the judge considered that, according to the principle of *lex loci contractus,* Burmese customary law—not Chinese—ought to be applied:

> What is required to establish a marriage under that law? It is that there (must) be mutual agreement that the parties become man and wife coupled with consummation...The ceremony is not necessary; it is no more if it takes place than evidence whereby the fact of this mutual agreement can be proved. Similarly open living together is not necessary but a cogent evidence to prove the central fact, the mutual agreement. (per Spargo J, *Ma Kyin Mya v Maung Sit Han* 1937, p. 107)

---

[3]The Special Marriage Act (India Act III of 1872) was to legalise marriage for persons who do not profess the Christian, Jewish, Hindu, Muslim, Parsi, Buddhist, Sikh or Jaina religion and for persons who profess the Hindu, Buddhist, Sikh or Jaina religion. Section 2 provided:

> 2. Marriages may be celebrated under this Act between persons neither of whom professes the Christian or the Jewish, or the Hindu or the Muslim or the Parsi or the Buddhist, or the Sikh or the Jaina religion, or between persons each of whom professes one or other of the following religions, that is to say, the Hindu, Buddhist, Sikh or Jaina religion upon the following conditions:

(1) neither party must, at the time of the marriage, have a husband or wife living;
(2) the man must have completed his age of eighteen years, and the woman her age of fourteen years, according to the Gregorian calendar;
(3) each party must, if he or she has not completed the age of twenty-one years, have obtained the consent of his or her father or guardian to the marriage;
(4) the parties must not be related to each other in any degree of consanguinity or affinity which would, according to any law to which either of them is subject, render a marriage between them illegal.

First Proviso – No such law or custom, other than one relating to consanguinity or affinity, shall prevent them from marrying.

Second Proviso – No law or custom as to consanguinity shall prevent them from marrying, unless a relationship can be traced between the parties through some common ancestor, who stands to each of them in a nearer relationship than that of great-great-grandfather or great-great-grandmother, or unless one of the parties is the lineal ancestor, or the brother or sister of some lineal ancestor, of the other.

After this case, the courts had established that Burmese customary law would apply to marriages between two Chinese Buddhists, and between a Chinese Confucian man and a Burmese Buddhist woman. Consequently, it would be impossible for any Chinese Buddhist or Chinese Confucian domiciled in Burma to seek the application of Chinese customary law in court.

The judges in the common law systems in East Asia were quite similar in their approach to adopting Chinese customary law. The reason for adopting Chinese laws in the colonial governments was not only due to the convenience of administering Chinese communities, but also the nature of the Chinese laws, which gave flexibility in adjudication. Freeman observed that the magistrates might have more discretion in the litigation: "(t)he nature of Chinese law was such that the codes embodied a set of models for ideal behaviour rather than a system of absolute rules, and in the performance of their duties local magistrate in China were able to exercise considerable discretion in the extent to which they might incorporate local custom into the law they were to administer" (Freeman 1979, p. 96).[4]

But, other non-common law systems had different approaches to applying Chinese customary law in their judicial systems. Other than giving discretion to the judges to apply the Chinese customs and practices, codification of Chinese customs and practices was one alternative way to incorporate Chinese customary law into the judicial system. In Macau, for example, the colonial government decided to codify Chinese customs and practices when the Portuguese government extended its Civil Law to Macau in 1909. Article 1 specified that some Chinese customary practices would be applied in Macau.[5] A list of Chinese customary practices was codified in the subsequent articles of the same legislation. For example, Article 10 provided that a husband could take a concubine after marriage or after divorce.[6]

Taiwan adopted a different approach during the Japanese occupation. When the Qing authorities ceded Taiwan to Japan in 1895, the colonial government of Taiwan decided to use Chinese customary law on civil affairs in litigation. In 1898, the Governor-General of Taiwan adopted this measure by a *ritsurei* (a decree which had the same effect as a Japanese statute law) that Taiwanese customs should be applied to cases involving only Taiwanese (and Chinese) people (Wang 2000, p. 141). Two elements were identified as Taiwanese customs which could be adjudicated in

---

[4] Freeman might not have observed that the discretion that the local magistrate enjoyed in adjudication in Mainland China was mainly due to the use of the principle of "mediation" rather than "litigation" in resolving disputes in local administration. The rate of litigation in the local level was one of the important elements to assess the governance and performance of a local magistrate. The application of the local customs might help to resolve disputes and to avoid formal litigation. See Chapter 2, note 5.

[5] Article 1 of the law reads: "Artigo 1. São mantidos e resalvados aos chins de Macau os seus usos e costumes especiaes e privativos revistos e codificados nas disposições seguintes. Unico. Não são applicaveis aos chins catholicos as disposiçõs as disposições d'este codigo contrarias ás leis que regem o casamento catholico" (Official Bulletin of the Government of Macau Province, 31 July 1909).

[6] Article 10 of the law reads: "Art. 10. O marido pode, tanto na constancia do casamento como apos a dissolução, tomar concubinas".

courts: the GQC and local customs. To the latter, a special survey commission was established to identify the local customs that existed in Taiwan (Wang 2000, p. 142). The report of this commission became the basis for adjudication in courts, though the findings in the report were not binding (Wang 2000, p. 143). In 1908, the Taiwanese government wanted to codify Taiwanese customs in a civil law which applied to Taiwan only (Wang 2000, p. 145). However, this approach was not approved by the Japanese government. Instead, the Japanese government decided to extend the application of the Japanese Civil Code to Taiwan, except in family and succession matters, where Taiwanese customs were still applied in courts (Wang 2000, p. 145; Shen 2015, p. 83; Asano 2012, p. 139). Consequently, the application of Taiwanese customs in court was made possible under the umbrella of a Westernised Japanese Civil Code.

During the reception of Chinese customary law in the above jurisdictions, domicile was an issue of interest. In most cases, the judge had to consider the question of domicile to decide whether Chinese customary law should be applied to determine the matrimonial status of a relationship. The meaning of "domicile" was explained in the judgment of *Whicker v Hume* (1858), in which the learned judge Lord Cranworth determined that:

> By domicile we mean home, the permanent home; and if you do not understand your permanent home, I am afraid that no illustration drawn from foreign writers or foreign languages will very much help you to it.

In civil proceedings regarding marriage, this may refer to the legal capacity of marriage, which is governed by the laws of each party's antenuptial domicile (*Brook v Brook* 1858; *Mette v Mette* 1859). A marriage can be regarded as valid if both man and woman have the legal capacity to marry under the laws of each other's antenuptial domicile (e.g. in the case of age limitations, a minor must obtain the permission of a guardian). In divorce proceedings in Hong Kong, for example, the court has jurisdiction in proceedings for divorce and nullity if either party to the marriage is domiciled in Hong Kong at the date of the petition or if either party is habitually resident in Hong Kong for a period of three years before that date (Matrimonial Causes Ordinance, Sect. 3, 4).

For a Chinese inhabitant of Hong Kong seeking the application of Chinese customary law to a matrimonial relationship, proof of domicile was essential. In other words, the personal laws of ethnic Chinese were not automatically recognised by the courts. In *In Re Wong Wong* (1998), the court had to decide whether a man who entered into a monogamous marriage in China in 1944 could later, in 1958, enter into a union of concubinage in Hong Kong, in accordance with Chinese customary law in Hong Kong. The judge dismissed that Chinese customary law could be applied in this case and determined that there was not a valid union of concubinage. He considered that only when the first marriage was a polygamous one according to Chinese customary law would a husband have the right to take a concubine. The judge stated clearly that "(A)ccordingly, the personal law in Hong Kong was not available to the deceased to enable him to enter into a concubinage union when his original marriage was a monogamous one".[7] In the case of *Suen Toi Lee v Yau Yee Ping* (2001, 2002), the court had to decide whether a husband who had a monogamous marriage in Mainland China could institute a polygamous marriage under Chinese customary law in Hong Kong when he moved from Mainland China to Hong Kong. Having examined the two Proclamations by Captain Elliot when Hong Kong was ceded to Britain (see Chap. 2, n. 2), the judge agreed that both Proclamations in effect led to the dual nature of Hong Kong domestic law, part of which applied exclusively to persons of Chinese ethnic origin. Nevertheless, the judge considered that this did not affect the application of a foreign law when that was the applicable law under the rules of private international law in Hong Kong (*Suen Toi Lee v Yau Yee Ping* 2002, p. 223). The judge further held that:

> Before a Chinese inhabitant of Hong Kong could claim the benefit of Chinese customary law, he would have to establish that the question in issue fell to be decided in accordance with the domestic law of Hong Kong. If it fell to be decided by reference to a foreign law, the dual nature of our domestic law was irrelevant. (*Suen Toi Lee v Yau Yee Ping* 2002, p. 223)

The judge hereby held that since this case related to the succession to immovable property in Hong Kong, under the ordinary rules of private international law, it fell to be decided in accordance with the domestic law of Hong Kong.[8] He further held that:

> Chaos would ensue if the essential and formal validity of such a union were governed by different laws from those which would govern the essential and formal validity of a foreign marriage. Moreover, once a marriage has become monogamous by that law, it is treated as if it were monogamous from its inception. While such a marriage may become polygamous by a change in the husband's domicile, a mere change of his residence is not enough. (*Suen Toi Lee v Yau Yee Ping* 2002, p. 224)

In short, the court held that a monogamous matrimonial relationship could not become polygamous by the mere change of residence from China to Hong Kong.

---

[7] It was argued that, in this case, the judge only decided on the situation when the husband had a monogamous marriage in China but formed a union of concubinage in Hong Kong after he moved his domicile from China to Hong Kong. But, if there was a situation where a husband first entered a monogamous marriage in China after 1931, then later formed a union of concubinage in China, then finally brought his "concubine" to domicile in Hong Kong, could this union of concubinage be recognised in Hong Kong? The Court of First Instance in Hong Kong, after analysing the 1931 Civil Code of the Republic of China, concluded that the second marriage was not void but only voidable, and only if an interested party applied to set it aside. The second marriage in this case could be regarded as a second wife. See *Re Estate of Tse Chu* (2012, p. 348) and also *Wong Zhong Lan Xiang v. Frank Wong* (2003, p. 421, para. 40).

[8] It was held in the *Ho Tze Tsun* case that, on the distribution of an intestate's estates, the distribution of the movables was governed by the *lex domicilii* of the deceased (as such would be the law of the Republic of China). On the immovables, including leasehold properties, these were governed by the *lex loci*, which was meant to be the Chinese law and custom of inheritance as it existed in the neighbouring districts of China in q. This case decided that the Statute of Distribution did not apply to the devolution of the leasehold estate in Hong Kong of a Chinese intestate.

3.2.2 The Status of T'sip in the GQC

The second issue is how judges in different jurisdictions constructed the status of a *t'sip* (concubine) in the Chinese family. To begin with, it is very important to recap and give a brief introduction on the status of *t'sip*, generally, in the GQC, though a more thorough discussion of this issue has been made in the last chapter. The unique feature of the GQC was that its social function to promote social and moral order was emphasised in all its provisions. In short, the family provisions in the GQC served two functions. First, family laws were used to preserve family order through sanctions rather than by settling disputes in court. Secondly, although there were family law provisions in the GQC for magistrates to adjudicate family disputes, most of these disputes were settled by the magistrate through mediation. The preservation of family harmony was paramount. Family order, which in effect contributed significantly to social harmony in a family lineage, could be maintained by sanctions in the GQC when anyone attempted to disrupt it. Two provisions in the GQC relating to the position of *t'sip* in the family order should be highlighted: Articles 101 and 103. Article 101 specified that a marriage between a man and a woman had to be arranged by the parents. It implied a monogamous matrimonial relationship as the basis of the family (Jones 1994, p. 123). This provision could be regarded as the legal foundation of the principle of monogamy—a "one husband, one wife" relationship—in traditional Chinese law. Article 103 criminalised a husband who failed to observe the order between wife and concubines (see Chap. 2, n. 5; Jones 1994, p. 125). It provided that a man could have a *t'sip* in the family, but her status was inferior to that of the wife. In other words, the matrimonial relationship as specified in the GQC could be regarded as monogamous with an unlimited number of *t'sip* (if the husband so chose). However, an early Qing legal scholar, Staunton, described this institution of marriage as polygamous. He commented that the *t'sip* was the second wife in a family:

> The first or principal wife is usually chosen for the husband by his parents or senior relations, out of a family equal in point of rank and to the circumstances to his own, and is espoused with as much splendour and ceremony as the parties can afford…A Chinese may afterwards lawfully espouse other wives, agreeably to his own choice, and with fewer ceremonies, as well as without any regard to equality in point of family and connexions: these wives are subordinate to the first wife, but equal in rank among themselves. (Staunton 2012, p. 111)

Staunton's comments were partly correct—to the extent that a concubine was subordinate to the principal wife in the family order and that concubines were equal in rank among themselves. But his comments were partly incorrect because he considered that Chinese marriage as specified in the GQC was polygamous. Using "wives" to refer to *t'sip*—when the two were not equivalent in the GQC—was misleading. In the GQC, a concubine did not have the legal status of a principal wife. Staunton's comments showed that he might have misunderstood the nature of Chinese marriage. His distorted understanding of the "polygamous" nature of Chinese marriage had a profound impact on the way judges in the common law jurisdictions interpreted the form of marriage within the Chinese community.

In Hong Kong, the first reported case on the nature of Chinese marriage relating to the status of *t'sip* in the Chinese community was *Ho Tsz Tsun v Ho Au Shi and others* (1915) heard in the Full Court.[9] The President, Havilland de Sausmarez, agreed with the Chinese experts that marriage in the Chinese community was "polygamous". He held that:

> China is a polygamous country; that the first wife has precedence, but that the other wives are wives and not merely concubines; that the children of all are legitimate; that the children adopted into the family are in the same position as children by blood, that those adopted out of it lose their right to inherit, and this system of adoption is common; that males inherit to the exclusion of females, who also on their marriage cease to be members of the family; that wives principal and secondary are entitled as widow to maintenance so long as they behave themselves properly, but are not entitled to any share in the succession. (*Ho Tsz Tsun v Ho Au Shi and others* 1915, p. 73)

The judge and the experts were wrong in their understanding of the nature of Chinese marriage. In this case again, Rees-Davies CJ agreed that polygamous marriages were recognised in the Chinese community, but he was only required to consider the applicability of an English Act, the Statute of Distribution, to Chinese polygamous marriage (*Ho Tsz Tsun v Ho Au Shi and others* 1915, p. 81). In another case, *In the Estate of Chak Chiu Hang; Chan Chun Cho v Chak Hok Ping* (1925), Gollan CJ recognised that the form of matrimonial relationship in the Chinese community in Hong Kong was "polygamous" (*In the Estate of Chak Chiu Hang; Chan Chun Cho v Chak Hok* Ping 1925, p. 6). In this case, he first referred to the practice of the staff at the Probate Registry to grant administration to the *kit fat* (principal wife) or, if she was dead and the man had married again, to the *tin fong* (second wife, either a new wife or a *t'sip* elevated to the status of principal wife after the death of the *kit fat*) of a Chinese husband dying intestate (*In the Estate of Chak Chiu Hang; Chan Chun Cho v Chak Hok* Ping 1925, p. 3). Then, the judge ruled that "the Statute Law of the Colony…clearly recognises the position of a *Kit Fat* and *Tin Fong*", and *kit fat* and *tin fong* had a perfectly well-defined position according to the law of the colony (*In the Estate of Chak Chiu Hang; Chan Chun Cho v Chak Hok* Ping 1925, p. 18). However, this custom did not support the interpretation of Chinese marriage as polygamous; rather it suggested its monogamous nature. Interestingly, Gollan CJ considered that his views on Chinese laws and customs as they appeared in 1843 were formed by Western legal scholars such as Jamieson, Mollendorf, Alabaster and Parker, and no legal scholars from Mainland China were quoted in his judgment. Also, he set aside the judgments of the *Da Li Yuan* because he presumed it had "modernised Chinese law and custom as set forth in the *Tai Tsing Lut Lai* (ed. note: the GQC)" (*In the Estate of Chak Chiu Hang; Chan Chun Cho v Chak Hok* Ping 1925, p. 22). His supposition was clearly wrong because most of the

[9] Greenfield (1958, p. 444) stated that tsip came from a lower social order than the husband and tsai (principal wife). He agreed that there was no limit to the number of "tsip" a man could take, but, in addition to the economic factor, practical restraint was placed on excessive polygamy, by the rule that the concubine must be accepted by the wife. Greenfield stated that there was a formality the "tsip" must serve tea to the "tsai". He considered that to marry two "tsai" at the same time was bigamy in China. Lewis (1983, p. 360) considered that polygamy was a punishable offence under the GQC, except in the special case of a *Kim Tiu* marriage.

civil provisions in the GQC were retained in the Republic of China and used in adjudications by the *Da Li Yuan*.

The issue of polygamous marriage was discussed in other cases that related to the statutory definition of wife. In *Wong Kam Ying v Man Chi Tai* (1967), the court held that marriage contracted in Hong Kong under the Marriage Ordinance was monogamous and the husband could not contract a second marriage to another woman under Chinese customary law. Huggins J ruled that such an act was bigamous and void (*Wong Kam Ying v Man Chi Tai* 1967, p. 218). His decision was correct in this circumstance. The court did not, however, make any decision on what elements would constitute a valid form of Chinese marriage under Chinese customary law. But, interestingly, the judge did reach that conclusion based on judicial cases that referred to Chinese marriage as polygamy. In another case, *Kwan Chui Kwok Ying v Tao Wai Chun* (1995, p. 409), the judge ruled that a man who had a wife and had also taken a concubine was in a de facto polygamous marriage. The judge also held that if the man decided to keep the concubine after the death of the wife, he could not contract a valid monogamous marriage with another woman as his *tin fong* wife under the Marriage Ordinance. The judge, Chan J (as he then was), considered that:

> Chinese customary marriage may take a concubine but he need not do so. A concubine is not a spouse. Although she is sometimes described as a "secondary wife", she does not have the status of a wife according to Chinese customary law. However, she is still another woman of the man in the family apart from the wife. If the principal wife dies but the concubine is still living, I do not think the man can enter into a Christian marriage or its civil equivalent with a third woman. This is because he was already a party to a polygamous marriage and he cannot declare that his union to this third woman can be to the exclusion of all others. (*Kwan Chui Kwok Ying v Tao Wai Chun* 1995, p. 394)

This case was significant because the judge decided that a contract of marriage in Chinese customary law was potentially polygamous, not actually polygamous as previously decided in cases in Hong Kong. The contract of marriage would become de facto polygamous only after a husband decided to take a concubine. This approach was approved in *Suen Toi Lee v Yau Yee Ping* (2001). In this case, Bokhary PJ decided that the potential for the inclusion of a concubine rendered a marriage potentially polygamous and that the actual inclusion of a concubine would render a marriage actually polygamous (*Suen Toi Lee v Yau Yee* Ping 2001, p. 481). The judge considered that the use of the term "secondary wife" (to describe a *t'sip*) was not a term of art but merely a description (*Suen Toi Lee v Yau Yee* Ping 2001, p. 481). Would the new understanding of Bokhary PJ help to resolve the question of the nature of *t'sip* in a matrimonial relationship in Chinese customary law? The answer is negative, because other jurisdictions could have a different interpretation of this issue.

For example, the *Da Li Yuan* had a different understanding of the nature of Chinese customary marriage under the GQC and customary law. When the new Supreme Court was hastily established following the end of Qing rule after the 1911 Revolution, the new civil law code of the new Republic of China was not yet in place. The Government of the Republic of China decided to adopt the civil law provisions of the Criminal Law Code promulgated in 1910 for the courts to adjudicate civil cases. However, that Criminal Law Code did not have provisions on the institution of marriage. Consequently, the *Da Li Yuan* had to rely on customary practices and even the GQC's provisions in trials (Huang 2011, p. 200). In 1919, the *Da Li Yuan* decided that under the current law, the institution of marriage was monogamous—a husband and a wife.[10] Thus, at least in the Republic of China, the institution of Chinese marriage was conceived to be monogamous. The *Da Li Yuan* rejected the notion that a concubine could be regarded as a "formal house" or "principal house" (*zheng shi*)—in other words, a formal or principal wife—but only a "side house" or "secondary house" (*ce shi*), in other words, a concubine.[11]

Given that the interpretation of the form of matrimonial relationship in other Chinese communities was also based on an understanding of Chinese customary law in China, the decision of the *Da Li Yuan* was not shared by other jurisdictions. In *In Re Choo Eng Choon, deceased; Choo Ang Chee v Neo Chan Neo and others* (1908), the Court of Appeal in Singapore had to consider whether concubinage made the form of matrimonial relationship in Chinese customary law polygamous:

> I have already said that in the diversity of opinion before us we must decide the question of monogamy or polygamy mainly by a consideration of the position which the law assigns to these women; and it appears to me that when you find that concubinage is not only tolerated by the law but recognised as a legal institution, then concubinage ceases to be that which Western nations are accustomed to understand by that name and becomes polygamy. (per Hyndman-Jones CJ, *In Re Choo Eng Choon, deceased; Choo Ang Chee v Neo Chan Neo and* others 1908, p. 189)

In 1919, the Judicial Committee of the Privy Council in *Cheang Thye Phin v Tan Ah Loy* (1920) ruled that "(W)ith regard to Chinese settled in Penang, the Supreme Court recognizes and applies the Chinese law of marriage. It is not disputed that this law admits of polygamy" (per Viscount Finlay) (*Cheang Thye Phin v Tan Ah Loy* 1920, p. 373). In another case, the judge in the Straits Settlements refused to follow the changing customs in the Republic of China. Terrell JA's *obiter* in *Woon Ngee Yew and others v Ng Yoon Thai and others* in 1940 is worth noting:

> The customs of the Chinese in Malaya are not based on those of Republican China, and accordingly no question of proving a foreign custom arises. The present customs are no doubt derived from the customs prevailing in the time of the Manchus, but have been adopted in Malaya with considerable modifications, particularly with regard to the status of a secondary wife or *t'sip*. The customs of Imperial China have accordingly a certain historical interest but nothing more. (*Woon Ngee Yew and others v Ng Yoon Thai and others* 1941, p. 45)[12]

---

[10] Eighth Year Appeal Number 106 (Huang 2012, p. 134).

[11] Fifth Year Appeal Number 116 (Huang 2012, p. 283).

[12] A Hong Kong colonial judge also shared a similar view regarding the legal development of Mainland China in the late Qing and Republican period. Briggs J's *obiter* was that: "I think that the correct law to apply is the Ching law and custom as it existed in 1843 with such modifications in custom and in the interpretation in the law as have taken place in Hong Kong since that period. The Hong Kong legislature reserved Chinese law and custom to Hong Kong in 1843 and I do not see how changes in the law made in another country whether by legislation or interpretation of the code can affect Hong Kong…A great deal of the evidence of these witnesses concerned the

The line of judicial authorities in the Straits Settlements suggested that the customary practices of Chinese emigrants had been transformed by the courts, from the monogamous practices in the GQC to polygamous practices. It is important to note that such interpretation of Chinese customary marriage as polygamous also influenced the courts in Brunei (*Lim Siew Yun v Soong Ah Kaw* 1960–63).[13] On the other hand, in Perak at Malaya, the Perak Order in Council used "inferior wife" to denote the status of *t'sip*.[14] They were largely different from the provisions in the GQC and the rulings of the *Da Li Yuan*. A scholar, Carol Tan (1993, p. 150), therefore concluded that "(T)he wife/concubine dichotomy was replaced by that of the primary/secondary wife…The next step was to narrow the gap in the legal systems of the primary and secondary wife".[15] Indeed, the question of the nature of Chinese marriage—polygamous or monogamous—is important because this may help a court to decide whether a concubine can be determined as a "wife" in the laws regulating the adoption of the children, the maintenance of the widow, and the

development of Ching law in the Republic of China and modifications in Singapore and Malaya were not ignored. I am grateful to counsel and to the experts called for their industry but I do not think that that part of their evidence is relevant to the issue. We must in my view keep our eyes in the boat; and the boat is Hong Kong. *What happened outside Hong Kong must be ignored.* Developments and new interpretation of the Ching code undoubtedly took place but they were the result of pressures and conditions irrelevant to Hong Kong" (emphasis added). Briggs' remark followed the *obiter* of Huggins J in a previous case, *Wong Kam Ying and another v Man Chi Tai* (1967, p. 211): "(A)s I remarked in *Chan Wei-keung v Reg* (6 Cr. App. No. 386 of 1965), with reference to the common law of England one of the attributes of the English Common Law is that it does not change although it may develop to meet new circumstances. That remark appears to be equally applicable to the Chinese common law. Thus in 1843 the marriage law, although still theoretically based on the Six Rites, was very different from what it was a thousand years earlier. Accordingly, the words '*as it existed prior to the cession*' would not mean…that customary law was 'ossified' as at 5th April, 1843 any more than the common law of England, in so far as it applies in Hong Kong was ossified at that date: in many respects it will have developed and it lies within the jurisdiction of the courts in Hong Kong to decide how and to what extent it has developed and even to take a part in deciding the course of its development". But, given the geographical proximity and frequent mobility of people between Hong Kong and Mainland China, the severance of Hong Kong courts from the legal developments and customary practices in Mainland China would have created more difficulties in the domain of family law. Indeed, Hong Kong courts could not ignore the development of Chinese family law in Mainland China: they could not disregard the legislative and judicial decisions in the 1931 Civil Code of the Republic of China and the 1950 Marriage Law of the People's Republic of China to reform Chinese customary marriage practices by making registered monogamous marriage the only valid legal form of marriage.

[13] In this case Ainley C.J. *obiter* that: "I do not think that Chinese marriages celebrated by Chinese custom, for, though the matter has never been fully argued before this Court, I do not think that Chinese marriages celebrated by Chinese custom in these territories can be regarded as monogamous marriages". In another case, *Bon Sau Fei v Chong Chui Lien & Anor* (1986, p. 477), Roberts C. J. quoted the passage of Sir Ernest Williams C.J. in an unreported case of Brunei in 1957, *Ho v Liew*, on the nature of the Chinese customary marriages in Brunei: "Such a marriage, in my opinion, would be considered as a polygamous rather than a monogamous marriage in the State of Brunei".

[14] Perak Order in Council No. 23 of 1893, as amended by Order in Council No. 26 of 1895, Section 1(iv) "A Chinaman may espouse as many inferior wives as he pleases, provided that he supports them in a befitting manner" ("Straits Settlements Report" (1926), Appendix F).

[15] See also Leong (1985).

inheritance of the estate after the death of the husband. This will be dealt with later in this chapter.

3.2.3 The Elements of a Union of Concubinage

The third issue relating to the status of *t'sip* is the elements constituting a union of concubinage. In other words, how judges determined whether a union of concubinage was valid under Chinese customary law. The *Da Li Yuan* considered that the relationship between a husband and a concubine was a contractual relationship[16]—but a contract in which neither party could be named, which was totally different from a formal contract of marriage.[17] In this respect, the court ruled that those provisions regulating a formal contract of marriage could not be applied (Huang 2012, p. 134). The *Da Li Yuan* considered that there was no restriction on a husband taking a concubine, nor did the contract require any proper procedure for a husband to take a concubine. But the *Da Li Yuan* considered that a union of concubinage would only be valid if two conditions were satisfied: first, a woman intended to cohabit with a man and become a member of his family; and secondly, the woman intended to contract a relationship similar to that of a husband and a wife.[18] In another case, the *Da Li Yuan* further explained that, for a legally recognised union of concubinage, a man must confirm that a woman would be a "partner" other than the principal wife and become part of the family, and the woman must agree that she was willing to become a partner and accept that her status would be inferior to the principal wife.[19] So, to the *Da Li Yuan*, cohabitation between a man and a woman would not in itself constitute a valid union of concubinage.[20] In fact, cohabitation might not even be a necessary condition for such a union: if there was a dispute between a wife and a concubine, the *Da Li Yuan* ruled that the concubine might leave the house temporarily or try other solutions to resolve the dispute.[21] However, a domestic dispute between a wife and a concubine should not be regarded as a reason for a man to ask his wife to live separately from other family members.[22]

In 1935, a judge in Singapore held that three conditions must be satisfied for a woman to be legally recognised as a concubine or second wife. In *Re Lee Choon Guan, deceased; Lew Ah Lui (F) v Choa Eng Wan and others* (1935),[23] Terrell J

[16] Fourth Year Appeal Number 767 (Huang 2012, p. 76); Fifth Year Appeal Number 840 (Huang 2012, p. 94), Sixth Year Appeal Number 86 (Huang 2012, p. 106); Sixth Year Appeal Number 852 (Huang 2012, p. 180); Eighth Year Appeal Number 106 (Huang 2012, p. 134).

[17] Eighth Year Appeal Number 106 (Huang 2012, p. 134).

[18] Fifth Year Appeal Number 153 (Huang 2012, p. 105).

[19] Seventh Year Appeal Number 186 (Huang 2012, p. 114).

[20] Seventh Year Appeal Number 186 (Huang 2012, p. 114).

[21] Fifth Year Appeal Number 444 (Huang 2012, p. 551).

[22] Fifth Year Appeal Number 444 (Huang 2012, p. 553).

[23] Followed by *Tan Ah Bee v. Foo Thye and Another* (1947).

ruled that for a valid union of concubinage, a ceremony was not necessary, but three conditions were important: first, the evidence must establish an intention to effect a permanent union; second, there must be satisfactory evidence of the recognition of marriage (*Tan Ah Bee v Foo Thye and Another* 1947, p. 80); third, the union had to be proved as repute of marriage. Terrell J held that ceremonies only showed an intention to effect a permanent union and should not be the only proof of a valid union:

> If, for instance, it could be proved that the husband paid respect to the wife's parents and that the wife paid respect to the husband's parents and in particular to the husband's principal wife and that she was introduced to the male members of the husband's family such proof might well be conclusive, as there could be no better evidence of an intention to effect a permanent union and the ceremonies themselves would provide evidence of recognition. That would be the natural inference without any proof of what ceremonies were or were not necessary or usual according to Chinese custom. Ceremonies which are only partial and particularly ceremonies which are only on the wife's part are inconclusive and, particularly so far as the husband and his family are concerned, provide no evidence either of an intention that the union should be permanent or of recognition. (*Tan Ah Bee v Foo Thye and Another* 1947, p. 80)

In another case, the judge applied the above rules and held that recognition by the husband's family was strong evidence of a union of concubinage (*Khoo Guat Tee & others v Lim Kim Neo & others* 2016, p. 660). Compared with the elements of concubine status as decided by the *Da Li Yuan*, the most significant difference was the second requirement given by Terrell J—that a concubine had to be recognised by the man's family. The *Da Li Yuan* judgment did not have that requirement. This could be read together with another case from Hong Kong, *Kwan Chui Kwok Ying v Tao Wai Chun* (1995), which will be dealt with again later in this chapter.

However, the judgment by Terrell J was overruled in *Er Gek Cheng v Ho Ying Seng* in 1949—18 years after the legal abolition of concubinage in the Republic of China. In this case, Murray-Aynsley CJ began by stating that the court in any attempt to apply English law to Chinese custom made the *t'sip*, for purposes of inheritance, equivalent to the *t'sai* (principal wife), which gave her a position she had not enjoyed in China (*Er Gek Cheng v Ho Ying* Seng 1949, p. 171). In addition, on the legitimacy of a concubine, the court had made marriage an essential condition of a union of concubinage, which was very different from the customary practice in Mainland China (*Er Gek Cheng v Ho Ying* Seng 1949, p. 171). The judge held that:

> Chinese ideas of marriage do not correspond with those upon which the English conception of marriage is based; the *t'sip* in particular does not correspond exactly to a wife or to a concubine, and the decisions of the Courts in giving the children of a *t'sip* legitimacy and rights of inheritance have made that union equivalent to true marriage. (*Er Gek Cheng v Ho Ying* Seng 1949, p. 171)

In effect, the judge held that the legal requirements for marriage with a *t'sai* and a *t'sip* were the same. In other words, a consensual marriage—an agreement to form a relationship—was enough to constitute a valid union of concubinage. This judgment moved the definition of Chinese marriage closer to the definition of marriage in the English common law system (*Er Gek Cheng v Ho Ying* Seng 1949, p. 171).

And, Murray-Aynsley CJ ruled that "(i)t is no longer any part of that conception that such a relationship must be life-long. It merely means one of indefinite duration as distinct from one for a definite period as is allowed among Moslems" (*Er Gek Cheng v Ho Ying* Seng 1949, p. 171). The burden of proof was upon whoever claimed the status of *t'sip* to have existed (*Er Gek Cheng v Ho Ying* Seng 1949, p. 172).[24] This judgment has become an authority in deciding the status of *t'sip* in later cases. It is interesting to note that the judges did not refer to laws and cases in the Republic of China when delivering their judgments, nor did they refer to any evidence from Chinese legal experts during the proceedings (*Re Ho Phian Cheong* 1963, p. 317).[25] Instead, the court in Singapore based its decision on the evolution of Chinese customs in Singapore. This marked a complete severance from what had happened in Mainland China, previously the main source of Chinese laws and practices.

In Hong Kong, the judges never went so far as stating that a consensual marriage could be applied to both *t'sai* and *t'sip*. The Court of Final Appeal gave an authoritative judgment on the elements of a valid union of concubinage in the *Suen Toi Lee* case. Millett NPJ agreed with the Privy Council's judgment in *Cheang Thye Phin v Tan Ah Loy* (1920, p. 373) that no particular ceremony was required to enter into such a union. He gave three principles which formed the elements of a union of concubinage:

> All that was needed was (i) that the man should intend to take the woman into his family as a member of his household as his concubine (*t'sip*) and publicly hold her out as such; (ii) the woman's consent to become his concubine and to occupy a position inferior to that of the principal wife (*t'sai*); and (iii) acceptance of her status as his concubine by his principal wife (if any). (*Cheang Thye Phin v Tan Ah Loy* 1920, p. 373, para. 58)

Millett NPJ had the following observations on the characteristics of a union of concubinage. Firstly, such a relationship was an open one and was not adulterous. Secondly, a concubine was more than a mistress and less than a second wife. Thirdly, her legal status was inferior to that of the principal wife (*Cheang Thye Phin v Tan Ah Loy* 1920, p. 373, para. 60). One important feature of this judgment was the recognition of the definition of a "union of concubinage" in the Intestates' Estates Ordinance. In this ordinance, "'union of concubinage' means a union of concubinage, entered by a male partner and a female partner before the appointed day under the Marriage Reform Ordinance, under which union the female partner has, during the lifetime of the male partner, been accepted by his wife as his concubine and recognised as such by his family generally".[26] So, at least in the statutory provision, "acceptance by the wife and recognition by the family" was one element of the recognition of a concubine in the matrimonial relationship in law. In addition, the principle of acceptance of the concubine by the wife had become part of case law in

---

[24] See also *Tay Geok Yap v. Tan Lian Cheow* (1965) and *Yeap Leong Soon & Anor & another application* (1989).

[25] See also Buxbaum (1968).

[26] s13(2). This definition is also provided in other Hong Kong ordinances. See Chap. 6, note 18.

Hong Kong courts.[27] The form of acceptance—normally called the *yap kung* ceremony—included serving tea to the wife in a ceremony witnessed by family members and relatives. Further, such customary practice is at least regarded as strong evidence of the existence of a union of concubinage. In *Kwan Chui Kwok Ying v Tao Wai Chun* (1995), the trial judge, Chan J (as he then was), held that:

> I think it is important that the wife's acceptance must be present. This is because a concubine is supposed to be junior or subservient to the wife who has the status and authority as the female head of the family. The concubine must be secondary to her and must not usurp her position. Hence in almost all cases except where there is no principal wife, there would be a yap kung ceremony which includes the concubine serving tea to the wife. This is a symbol of subservience. In some cases, she would also be given a name by the wife. But that is not absolutely necessary. I would also think that the acceptance or at least recognition by the family generally is necessary. (*Kwan Chui Kwok Ying v Tao Wai* Chun 1995, p. 407)[28]

In an earlier case relating to the principle of acceptance by the wife, *In Re Wong Choi Ho, deceased v Wong Yuk-shu, deceased* (1969), Briggs J held that the first defendant entered the family as a concubine: "(A)gain when a concubine is taken it is usual to have some sort of a ceremony and the ceremonies deposed to by the first defendant when she entered the household would be sufficient for this" (*In Re Wong Choi Ho, deceased v Wong Yuk-shu, deceased* 1969, p. 399).

Recent cases suggest that the Court of First Instance in Hong Kong has adopted these three elements to determine a valid union of concubinage as developed in *Re Chan Cho Chak* (2005). Firstly, by applying the case of *Cheang Thye Phin v Tan Ah Loy* (1920), the judge held that a ceremony, though usual, was not essential to establish a union of concubinage; secondly, by applying the case of *Wong Kam Ying v Man Chi Tai* (1967), the judge held that a common intention among the parties to form a union of concubinage was necessary; thirdly, quoting Section 13 of the Intestates' Estates Ordinance (Cap. 73), the judge further held that acceptance of the concubine by the wife and recognition of the relationship by the family generally are required. Finally, by applying the case of *Suen Toi Lee v Yau Yee Ping* (2001), the judge held that the question of domicile was essential to determine the parties' legal right to form a union of concubinage (*Re Chan Cho Chak* 2005). These principles were applied in the case of *Ye Jin Xiang v Kam Pin Kwong* (2017, p. 197) in 2017. In establishing this line of authorities, the courts in Hong Kong relied on cases in the Straits Settlements and Hong Kong, and arguably the customary practices in both jurisdictions, to determine the status of *t'sip* in Chinese customary law. There was

---

[27] See, for example, *Wong Kam Ying v Man Chi Tai* (1967). Prior to this case, in *Ng Ying Ho v Tam Suen Yu* (1963), the Court accepted the expert's opinion and held that there were two elements of a recognised concubine in laws. The first was the intention of a man to take the woman as his concubine, and secondly, the public considered that this woman was a man's concubine.

[28] However, the recognition of the wife was not a necessary condition for the recognition of a t'sip in other jurisdictions which applied Chinese customary law. In Taiwan during Japanese occupation, for example, the wife could not reject a concubine instituted by the husband, though the husband might discuss the issue with his wife in order to preserve family harmony. See Temporary Investigation Committee on the Old Custom of Taiwan (1901, p. 607) and Cheng (2006, p. 177).

no mention of the GQC and judgments of the *Da Li Yuan* in these cases, which showed a clear departure from the practices in Mainland China.

The Review High Court in Taiwan during the Japanese occupation did not specify the elements determining the status of *t'sip*, but some cases showed that similar Chinese customary practices, as in other jurisdictions, were used to determine the status of *t'sip* in the Chinese family. In one case, for example, the Review High Court held that a *t'sip* was regarded as a secondary wife (*zhun qi* or *fu qi*), and in customary practice a man could only form a union of concubinage after a first marriage to a principal wife (Taisho 8 Prosecution Civil Number 758 1995, p. 279). This case indicated a recognition of a form of "one husband, one wife" relationship in court. In addition, if in contracting such a union the concubine's family had accepted gifts and money, the Review High Court held that the husband did not have the right to take them back even if the concubine left his family without giving any reason (Taisho 6 Prosecution Civil Number 506 1995, p. 279). This case also showed that in Taiwan, a ceremony resembling a formal marriage would be valid proof of a union of concubinage.

There was a special matrimonial relationship in Chinese customary practice called *Kim Tiu* marriage. It was a very special arrangement between at least two households within the same family. In a family where a man had no son but his brother had an only son, the man with no son might, upon the agreement or instruction of the senior members of the family, adopt his brother's only son to become his heir and then arrange a marriage for him. Consequently, this only son might have two wives: one from the marriage arranged by his natural parents and another from the marriage arranged by his adoptive parents (Committee on Chinese Law and Custom in Hong Kong 1953, p. 201; *Yau Tin Sung v Yau Wan Hoi* 1984, pp. 21–22; *Leung Sai Lun Robert & others v Leung May Ling & others* 1999, p. 657.). The purpose of the adoption was to continue the patrilineal lineage of a household that had no son. In Hong Kong courts, the concept of *ping t'sai* (equal wives) was used to describe women married to the same man under a *Kim Tiu* marriage in Qing law (*Re Estate of Tse Chu* 2012), though no such term called *ping t'sai* was seen in the GQC. In Hong Kong law, *Kim Tiu* wives enjoy equal standing (*Re Estate of Ng Shum (No 2)* 1990).

In contrast, in the *Da Li Yuan*, the judges considered that the wife of a *Kim Tiu* marriage should be considered as a concubine in law. If during the material time the woman did not know that the man had a wife, the court would allow her to ask for a divorce.[29] This ruling resembled that given by the Qing Board of Punishments.[30] Also, in the same case, the *Da Li Yuan* held that when the appellant received the proposal for marriage from the respondent, she had already been informed of the

[29] Eighth Year Appeal Number 177 (Huang 2012, p. 761).

[30] In 1808, the Board of Punishments sought the advice of the Board of Rites on the proper status of the second "wife" in a *Kim Tiu* marriage. The Board of Rites advised that this second "wife" should be regarded as t'sip but not wife ("Xin An Hui Lan" 2006, p. 2066). In another case, in 1833, the Board of Punishments held that the status of "wife" could be given to a *Kim Tiu* marriage with just one son, but not to other instances of *Kim Tiu* (*Xu Zeng Xin An Hui Lan* 2006, p. 550). See Chap. 2, Sect. 2.2.4.

existence of two wives. And, if the appellant still agreed to be the partner in a third household, she could not apply for the dissolution of the marriage in the name of bigamy ("Xin An Hui Lan" 2006, p. 763).[31] In other words, the status of wife or concubine in a *Kim Tiu* marriage could still be debatable when future cases come to court.

3.2.4 The Relationship Between the Principal Wife and the Concubine

The fourth issue is the relationship between the principal wife and the concubine. This relates to the status of a concubine in a family. In the GQC, Article 103 implied that the status of a concubine was inferior to the wife (see Chap. 2, Sect. 2.4.3; Staunton 2012, p. 111). That inferiority was recognised as early as the so-called Six Widows Case—*In Re Choo Eng Choon, deceased; Choo Ang Chee v Neo Chan Neo and others* (1908)—in which Law Ag CJ in the Court of Appeal opined: "I think that in regard to these secondary or inferior wives (or concubines, as they have been called), though socially their position is no doubt very inferior to that of a first wife, yet legally their position more nearly resembles that of a wife where polygamy is allowed than it resembles anything else" (*In Re Choo Eng Choon, deceased; Choo Ang Chee v Neo Chan Neo and others* 1908, p. 148). Law Ag CJ's approach suggested that the hierarchical order of a wife being superior to concubine might be recognised in customary practice but not in law. Since the court had taken that position, case law in the Straits Settlements had been evolving gradually to legally recognise the status of *t'sip*—at least in terms of succession upon intestacy—as the same as the principal wife.

Given their different status in the family, could a concubine be elevated to a principal wife if the latter was dead? This customary practice was called *fu ching*, as recognised in the case *In Re Wong Choi-ho, deceased and Wong Yuk-shu, deceased* (1969, pp. 397–398):

> There was a great deal of expert evidence that a concubine could, after the death of the Kit Fat wife, be elevated from the condition of a concubine to that of a Tin Fong wife. I was told that this is known as Fu Ching. And that as in all changes of status within a family it was usual at least in old times to effect this by some ceremony. When such a change in status is made there must be a degree of publicity. Some announcement by the husband that he will from henceforth consider his concubine to be his Tin Fong wife or some dinner to celebrate

[31] A late Qing scholar, Ji Tongjun (1910/2017, p. 129), who helped to draft the new Criminal Law in the late Qing period, commented that in *Kim Tiu* marriage, the husband—who was the only son in the two households—could only have one *di qi* (principal wife) according to Chinese ritual (*li*). The husband could not say that he had two "wives". Therefore, for the second marriage, the female partner could only be regarded as a t'sip. The Great Qing Criminal Law still preserved to a very large extent the provisions of the GQC, with only a few legal transplantations from western law codes. After the 1911 Revolution, the Great Qing Criminal Law was adopted in the Republic of China until the promulgation of a new Criminal Law Code in 1928.

> that event. The authorities are agreed that there was no established customary ceremony to achieve this, that it was up to the husband to devise his own method of effecting and making known the change. In China in later times it appears that no ceremony was required: mere tacit recognition by the husband being considered enough.[32]

Briggs J considered that the old customs quoted in this passage should prevail, which suggests that *fu ching* was recognised in Hong Kong as a way to become a *tin fong* wife. However, a *tin fong* wife was not a customary practice in all provinces in Mainland China, though *fu ching* was a customary practice recognised by the *Da Li Yuan*. According to the judgments of the *Da Li Yuan*, a woman must first be a concubine in the family before she could claim the status of wife by *fu ching*.[33] A concubine could only get *fu ching* when the family had no principal wife and the husband had expressed his will to take the concubine as principal wife.[34] No ceremony was required unless there were some special customary practices.[35]

Other than that, the *Da Li Yuan* took the hierarchical order of wife and concubine seriously. A concubine, like the wife, could retain her personal property.[36] But a concubine had to be supervised by the wife, though the ultimate right of supervision rested with the husband.[37] However, after the death of the husband, if a concubine had a quarrel with the principal wife and did not wish to live together and be supervised by the principal wife, the concubine might choose to live elsewhere.[38]

But in Taiwan during the Japanese occupation, the Review High Court held that the right of supervision by the wife over the concubine did not give the wife the right to expel the concubine to her original clan (Meiji prosecution 63 1995, p. 278). The court ruled that a concubine could not be the head of a family, even after the death of the husband.[39] The court also ruled that a woman could not have the status of wife if the union was made after a man had a principal wife, and if the concubine decided not to retain such a relationship, the union of concubinage had to be dissolved.[40]

---

[32] It is important to note, in at least one case, the opinion delivered by the Board of Punishments (which was later endorsed by the emperor in 1802) that *fu ching* could not be recognised because the GQC did not have any provision to validate such a relationship. In this case, the Board of Punishments had to consider the status of née Zhang, the *fu ching* "wife" of Yang Yujue, and whether she should be punished as a wife after she struck her servants. The Board of Punishments did not recognise *fu ching* and decided that née Zhang should be sentenced in the capacity of *t'sip*. The husband was punished by 80 strokes because of the *fu ching* and had to nullify the matrimonial relationship. See "Quarrelling and Fighting: Slaves Striking with Masters" (Xin An Hui Lan 2006, p. 2023) and Cheng (2006, p. 130).

[33] Third Year Appeal Number 610 (Huang 2012, p. 69).

[34] Eighth Year Appeal Number 389 (Huang 2012, p. 396).

[35] Eighth Year Appeal Number 389 (Huang 2012, p. 396).

[36] Fourth Year Appeal Number 2052 (Huang 2012, p. 87). See also Seventh Year Appeal Number 665 (Huang 2012, p. 567).

[37] Sixth Year Appeal Number 852 (Huang 2012, p. 108).

[38] Tenth Year Appeal Number 449 (Huang 2012, p. 153).

[39] Eighth Year Appeal Number 724 (Huang 2012, p. 147).

[40] Sixth Year Appeal Number 662 (Huang 2012, p. 714).

On the other hand, two cases in the *Da Li Yuan* related to article 103 of the GQC, "Failing to observe the order between wives and concubines" (see Chap. 2, Sect. 2.4.3) are worth noting. This article provided that if a woman during the material time mistakenly believed that by "marriage" she would become the principal wife (even though she had been informed that her husband had a principal wife), she would only have the status of concubine.[41] She could not rely on this provision to apply for the dissolution of such "marriage".[42] This rule also applied to the situation when a concubine did not during the material time have prior knowledge that her partner had a principal wife.[43]

The second part of the same article in the GQC provided that "(I)f, while he has a wife, he marries another wife, he will also receive 90 strokes of the heavy bamboo. (The woman who is married subsequently) will be divorced (and returned to her clan)" (see Chap. 2, Sect. 2.4.3; Jones 1994, p. 126). In one case, the *Da Li Yuan* held that, in accordance with this provision, the other "wife" (the woman of the second marriage) should be returned to her clan and the marriage should be null and void. But the *Da Li Yuan* held that if that "wife" had not dissolved the marriage and disagreed to be a concubine, she could become the principal wife immediately after the death of the original principal wife.[44] However, this case was unique because during the material time when the second marriage was instituted, the principal wife suddenly died.[45] Therefore, this case should be regarded as an exception to the rule rather than setting a precedent that could be applied in later cases.

3.2.5 *Dissolution of a Union of Concubinage*

The fifth issue is the elements of the dissolution of a union of concubinage. It would be important for a court to consider whether and how such a union could be dissolved, given that the GQC did not have any such provision. Rather, in the GQC, there were provisions on the dissolution of marriage between husband and wife. One important principle was that there was a consensual dissolution if both gave consent to dissolution. Another important principle could be summarised as "seven outs and three non-outs". This principle provided that there were seven reasons for a husband to initiate a divorce and that there were three situations in which the husband could not ask for the dissolution of a marriage.[46] A scholar, Chiu, has concluded that the "seven outs" are no son; lascivious conduct, which included laziness; failure to serve the parents-in-law; loquacity, which included mischief-making and

---

[41] Twelfth Year Appeal Number 1170 (Huang 2012, p. 821).

[42] Twelfth Year Appeal Number 1170 (Huang 2012, p. 821).

[43] Twelfth Year Appeal Number 1170 (Huang 2012, p. 821).

[44] Eighth Year Appeal Number 1036 (Huang 2012, pp. 494–495).

[45] Eighth Year Appeal Number 1036 (Huang 2012, p. 495).

[46] Article 116 Repudiating a Wife (Jones 1994, pp. 133–134).

quarrelsome conduct; larceny; jealousy; and incurable disease (Chiu 1950, p. 203). The "three non-outs" refer to three situations in which a husband could not ask for divorce: if the wife had completed three years of mourning for the husband's parents; if the husband's family was poor before the marriage but became rich after; and if after the divorce the wife had nowhere to go (Chiu 1950, pp. 203–204). All these reasons were strongly in favour of the husband, providing various grounds for divorcing the wife. In contrast, it was extremely difficult, if not impossible, for a wife to initiate a dissolution of marriage under the GQC. In other words, there was no mutual right to dissolve marriages in the GQC.

Considering how difficult it was for both husband and wife to initiate divorce proceedings, the question arises: did such harsh rules apply to the dissolution of a union between a husband and a concubine? This, in turn, leads to another question: did a concubine have the right to initiate a dissolution unilaterally in court under the GQC? A Qing scholar, Shen Zhiqi (1715/1999, p. 757), remarked that "*t'sip* has a lower and degraded status. The husband could decide to keep her if he wanted, or to expel her if he disliked her. There was nothing related to the seriousness of the cause. The principle directing to the dissolution between a husband and a concubine was not comparable with the dissolution between a husband and a principal wife". Therefore, a husband was free to initiate the dissolution of a union of concubinage as he wished. It is unknown whether a concubine in the late Qing period could initiate such a dissolution. Nevertheless, the *Da Li Yuan* had made some rules on the dissolution of a union between a husband and a concubine. The basic principle was that if a concubine did not give birth to a son, the husband and the concubine could dissolve the relationship any time they wished if there existed some serious causes. The *Da Li Yuan* also considered that if such dissolution was initiated by the husband and other family members, a concubine could ask for compensation. However, if the cause for such dissolution was some deliberate or negligent action by the concubine, the husband should not have to bear any responsibility. In addition, if such causes happened before the establishment of their contractual relationship, and if a concubine had committed fraudulent behaviour, she must return the wedding gifts to the husband. The judge ruled that if such serious causes happened before the conclusion of a contractual relationship, the claimant must show that he or she did not know that before the contractual relationship.[47] The court did not give examples of the causes, which made it very difficult for the lower courts to follow. But, according to the *Da Li Yuan*, it is important to note that both parties—husband and concubine—had almost the same right to initiate a dissolution. In another case, the court stated that since the relationship between a husband and a concubine was contractual, the rules governing divorce between husband and wife could not be applied. In any case, the husband and the concubine could dissolve the relationship any time they wished if there was a serious cause.[48] In another case, the court

[47] Third Year Appeal Number 610 (Huang 2012, p. 69). Followed by the case of the Eighth Year Appeal Number 106 (Huang 2012, p. 134).

[48] Fifth Year Appeal Number 840 (Huang 2012, p. 94).

affirmed the principle that a union of concubinage was a contractual relationship, so the husband could dissolve it unilaterally (e.g. if the husband had some serious cause to initiate dissolution).[49] In this case, the court considered fornication committed by the concubine to be the reason for dissolution.[50]

The biggest hurdle for judges outside Mainland China was that, since the GQC did not specify the rules for dissolving a union of concubinage, it was very difficult to identify the relevant Chinese customary practices to make such a dissolution. In the absence of statutory laws in Mainland China to refer to, it would be very important for the judge to make a decision when the relationship between a husband and concubine became difficult. In *In the Estate of Sim Siew Guan deceased Singapore Probate No 321 of 1923* (1932, 1933), Shaw CJ accepted the testimony of the Consul-General of China on this issue that the husband could make a divorce at will:

> it was at will of the husband, who was entitled to divorce his wife if she were disobedient to himself or his principal wife, if she did not conform to the household regulations, or was guilty of immoral conduct. The custom was that the husband should notify the dissolution either to his near relations or to his clansmen. It appeared that the dissolution was something like the inception of the union, that no actual ceremony was needed, and it depended upon the actual intention and notoriety given to the union or dissolution. (*In the Estate of Sim Siew Guan deceased Singapore Probate No 321 of 1923* 1932, p. 532)

In another case, *Khoo Hooi Leong v Khoo Chong Yeok* (1930),[51] the Privy Council held that a secondary wife (concubine) could not unilaterally be put away (divorced) by her husband if she had borne him a son during the marriage.[52] However, in *Woon Ngee Yew and others v Ng Yoon Thai and others*, the Appellate Court considered that the decision by the Privy Council was meant to be that such a "divorce" must be for cause and reasonable notoriety must be given to it. McElwaine CJ stated: "I gather that the principal points about a divorce are that there must be an intention to divorce and that it must not be kept secret—it must be published, and it appears to me that telling friends and relatives is just as much evidence that a divorce has taken place as it is a method of divorcing" (*Woon Ngee Yew and others v Ng Yoon Thai and others* 1941, p. 42).[53] Terrell JA considered that such a divorce could be justified by causes such as desertion or misconduct (*Woon Ngee Yew and others v Ng Yoon Thai and others* 1941, p. 46).

---

[49] Sixth Year Appeal Number 852 (Huang 2012, p. 108).

[50] Seventh Year Appeal Number 1372 (Huang 2012, p. 123).

[51] Their lordships stated that "a t'sip cannot be put away who has borne a son" and "in the Straits Settlements there is no divorce provided for by the laws for the Chinese" (per Lord Russell, *Khoo Hooi Leong v Khoo Chong Yeok* 1930, p. 353).

[52] The basic principle was similar to the rules established by the *Da Li Yuan*, see Fifth Year Appeal Number 840 (Huang 2012, p. 94).

[53] In the cases of *In the Estate of Sim Siew Guan deceased* (1932); *Re Lee Choon Guan, deceased, Lew Ah Lui (f) v Choa Eng Wan & Ors* (1935) and *Woon Ngee Yew & others v Ng Yoon Thai and others* (1941), the established rule on the divorce of the Chinese customary marriages was that, the husband could make a divorce at will. He had to inform the clansman or his relatives that he had divorced his wife.

In Taiwan during the Japanese occupation period, the right to dissolve a union of concubinage was mutual—in other words, both husband and concubine could dissolve the union if either party decided to discontinue it. In one case, the Review High Court considered that, according to local customs, the husband could dissolve the relationship without any restriction but a concubine did not have the same right to initiate such a dissolution. The court considered that such customary practices not only ignored the personal integrity of a concubine but also limited her freedom and were offensive to good public order. For this reason, the court held that such customary practices were not part of Taiwanese law (Taisho 8 prosecution civil number 853 1995, pp. 759–760).[54] In another case, the court expressly stated that this customary practice was modified by the theory of law (Taisho 11 appeal civil number 123 1995, pp. 48–51).[55] However, the need to provide education to young sons and daughters might be a bar for a concubine to initiate the dissolution. In another case, the court ruled that when a concubine decided to dissolve a relationship, unless there were reasons such as the education of the sons and daughters and other business that made the existence of the relationship necessary, the husband could not reject that request (Taisho 13 prosecution number 300 1995, p. 516). In other words, even though the Taiwan court recognised the mutual right of dissolution, a concubine did not have absolute freedom to make such a request in court if she was required to take care of her sons and daughters.

3.2.6 Financial Support for the Concubine from Family Members After the Death of the Husband

The sixth issue is financial support for the concubine after the death of the husband or after the distribution of the family assets. To the former, the issue was whether and how the heir in a family might support the life of the widows, including any concubines. To the latter, the issue was whether and how the wife and concubine(s) should be supported by the heir in the family after the "household division" (*fenjia*). The question of support for widows, such as the principal wife, was not specified in the GQC, but it was a customary practice in Mainland China that the heir of a family had to provide financial support to the widows after the death of the husband. In addition, Chinese customary practice also required that, after *fenjia*, some assets had to be kept specifically for the widows (including concubines) as long as they did not leave the family to remarry. This practice was derived from a principle called *yang shan*, sometimes called *yang lao fen*, which denoted the duty of the heir to support

[54] This case was followed by Taisho 11 appeal civil number 123 (1995, pp. 48–51) and Taisho 11 prosecution civil number 774 (1995, p. 510).

[55] See Aneha (1994, p. 391).

the elderly (including widows) for the rest of their life (Wakefield 1998, p. 88).[56] A provision in the GQC specified that if a son was too poor to support his parents and if this situation led to their suicide, the punishment for the son would be 100 strokes of bamboo and 3000 miles of exile.[57]

Since a wife or concubine (as widow) would receive financial support from the family members after the distribution of family assets (*fenjia*) or after the death of the husband, Chinese customary practice was to a certain extent similar to the common law system in which the surviving spouse could claim maintenance from the deceased spouse's estate. However, in Singapore, case law suggests that the judges did not follow Chinese customary practice, thus giving more rights and financial support to the wife or concubine. In *In the Estate of Yeow Kian Kee, deceased; Er Gek Cheng v Ho Ying Seng*, the courts gave the wife and concubine an equal share in the distribution of the deceased husband's estate, a treatment different from Chinese customary practice:

> To begin with, the Courts in an attempt to apply English law to Chinese custom made the *t'sip*, for purposes of inheritance, equivalent to the *t'sai*, which gave her a position which she had not enjoyed in China...According to Chinese ideas and custom neither a *t'sai* nor a *t'sip* would be entitled to a share of the husband's estate on a division. Both would be entitled to maintenance in the family house as long as, but only as long as, they chose to remain there. In this Colony both the *t'sai* and *t'sip* have an equal right to share in the distribution... The fact that the *t'sip* has become something different from what she was in China has given the Courts problems which would not have arisen if it were merely a question of applying Chinese custom. If the *t'sip* were being maintained at the time of the death of the man she would continue to be maintained, and such children of the man who had been recognized as such would share his estate whatever the status of their mothers might have been. (per Murray-Aynsley CJ, *In the Estate of Yeow Kian Kee, deceased*; *Er Gek Cheng v Ho Ying Seng* 1949, p. 171)

Whereas in Hong Kong it was suggested that a concubine could seek maintenance in accordance with Chinese customary practice (Hu and Chung 2009, p. 130).[58]

The Strickland Committee proposed a provision, to be put into law as part of the marriage reform package of 1950, whereby "suitable maintenance" for the life of a concubine could be ordered by the court upon intestacy (Committee on Chinese Law and Custom in Hong Kong 1953, p. 58).

---

[56] See also, Wakefield (1998, p. 123) on the local cases on granting *yang shan* to the concubine as shown in Bai Xian archives. Since there was no statutory provision under the GQC to provide *yang shan* to the widows, including t'sip, the local magistrate might use *yang shan* as a reason to require the family to support the remaining life of the widows. Another scholar, Cheng (2006, p. 154), considered that, at least in two local cases, the magistrates had decided to order the parties to provide *yang shan* to the concubine. It is also suggested that according to Taiwan customs, *yang shan* was the customary practice to support the grandparents and parents after the death of the husband (Temporary Investigation Committee on the Old Custom of Taiwan 1901/1993, p. 695).

[57] Article 338 *tiaoli* 1, GQC.

[58] The authors quoted the case of the *Da Li Yuan*'s decision of Eighth Year Appeal Number 575 to support this argument.

In Hong Kong, Hogan CJ stated as early as 1957 that a concubine was entitled to maintenance: "(U)nder Tsing law and custom which, as above-mentioned, is applicable to distribution, it is common ground that the estate is normally divisible between male descendants and that the females including the widow, concubine, if any, and daughters are entitled to maintenance only" (*Wong Yu Shi and others (No. 1) v Wong Ying Kuen* 1957, p. 432). Therefore, it would be important to investigate how the *Da Li Yuan* considered the provisions on the issue of maintenance and whether *yang shan* was really, as Hogan CJ said, part of the law and custom in Mainland China.

Maintenance as part of the concept of *yang shan* was recognised in the case law of the *Da Li Yuan*. The court recognised that, as a member of the family, an heir and the administrator had a duty to maintain the concubine when the husband died.[59] Also, a concubine had a right to receive maintenance.[60] Family members could not expel her from the family or force her to remarry.[61] But, that duty to maintain would be conditional upon her remaining a widow, in other words, chastity (*shouzhi*).[62] The court also held that in terms of calculation of living expenses, the family could make it a monthly lump sum payment (Huang 2012, p. 82). The heir could decide how much money he could afford, based upon the identity, financial situation and daily expenses of the widow.[63] Moreover, that duty could not be limited arbitrarily, or stopped by occasion.[64] On the ways of providing maintenance, the court held that the family members and the concubine had the freedom to make an agreement, or they could ask the court to decide.[65] Even if a concubine, for whatever reason, decided she could not live with the principal wife or the heir, the court could help to decide the ways and means to provide maintenance.[66] However, that duty would end when the relationship between the concubine and the family was severed,[67] for example, if the widow married again and left the family.

---

59 Third Year Appeal Number 348 (Huang 2012, p. 1067). See Third Year Appeal Number 5 (Huang 2012, p. 1055).

60 Third Year Appeal Number 385 (Huang 2012, p. 1074; p. 1086).

61 Fourth Year Appeal Number 1691 (Huang 2012, p. 82).

62 Eighth Year Appeal Number 575 (Huang 2012, p. 1192). However, the court stated that if the dissolution of such a relationship was due to the husband or other family members, they had to pay a certain amount of "comfort money" upon request by the concubine.

63 Third Year Appeal Number 5 (Huang 2012, p. 1055).

64 Third Year Appeal Number 5 (Huang 2012, p. 1055.) See also, Third Year Appeal Number 348 (Huang 2012, p. 1067).

65 Third Year Appeal Number 5 (Huang 2012, p. 1055). See also, Third Year Appeal Number 348 (Huang 2012, p. 1067) and Huang (2012, p. 1068).

66 Fourth Year Appeal Number 2294 (Huang 2012, p. 1135).

67 Seventh Year Appeal Number 1413 (Huang 2012, p. 1183).

3.2.7 Succession upon Intestacy

The seventh issue is the status of a concubine on succession upon intestacy. The concept of intestacy in the common law system was very different from the provisions in the GQC and Chinese customary practices. To begin with, it is important to note that the purpose of the institution of concubinage in the Chinese family was to produce a son (an heir for the husband) for the eternal continuation of the patrilineal lineage, in other words, so that the male line of the family would go uninterrupted for generation after generation. That institution (concubinage) would only happen if the wife could not give birth to a son, or was infertile. Therefore, it was specified, for example, that a divorce might be allowed if a wife did not give birth to a son.[68] Other than the right to maintenance, there were no other rights that a concubine could claim from the estate upon the death of her husband.

However, when this Chinese customary practice encountered English common law in other jurisdictions, the question was whether such practice should be maintained or be subject to the English laws or Acts which were applied in different jurisdictions. In the case of inheritance, in the Six Widows case, *Choo Ang Chee v Neo Chan Neo* (1911), the court in Singapore ruled that the secondary wives, or concubines, could share equally with the wife in the distribution of the estate of a Chinese husband who died intestate. In general, if there was one concubine and one wife, each would receive an equal share of the estate allotted under these circumstances. In the judgment, Hyndman-Jones CJ considered that the institution of concubinage denoted polygamy:

> I am of the opinion that, subject to divorce, the union with the *t'sip* is contemplated by the law to be of a permanent nature and the inference is that she is entitled to maintenance during her life time...it appears to me that when you find that concubinage is not only tolerated by the law but recognized as a legal institution, then concubinage ceases to be that what Western nations are accustomed to understand by that name and becomes polygamy. (*Choo Ang Chee v Neo Chan Neo* 1911, p. 189)

After analysing some judicial cases, the judge further considered that:

> if the Statute (of Distribution) was broad enough to cover the case of Hannah Piret[69] it is also broad enough to cover the unions we have been considering—unions which were entered into in accordance with the laws and usages of the contracting parties which the Courts have, in my opinion, rightly recognized, and that an apportionment among all the widows of the deceased of the share which in England would properly go to the wife was... not much an altering of the Statute as an application of it to existing circumstances. (*Choo Ang Chee v Neo Chan Neo* 1911, p. 194)

[68] Article 116 of the GQC (Jones 1994, p. 134; *Da Qing Lü Li* 1993, p. 225).

[69] The party of the appellant in the case of *In Re Goodman's Trust* (1881). In this case, the judge held that "the Statute of Distribution was not a Statute for Englishmen only...but applied universally to persons of all countries, races and religions whatsoever" (per Lush, *In Re Goodman's Trust* 1881, p. 300).

In the same case, Braddell J concluded that the principle of the Statute of Distribution was the "equality of division":

> it seems to me that our Courts have done more than to adopt that principle and object in directing, in a case when the deceased has left more than one widow whom the Court ought to recognize as lawful widows, that they shall take equally between the share which under the Statute is allotted to the widow. That is not in my opinion to alter the Statute but merely to being in aid of the Statute the equitable jurisdiction of the Court in declaring how that share ought to be divided, having regard to the rights of the persons claiming as widows of the intestate. (*Choo Ang Chee v Neo Chan Neo* 1911, pp. 222–223)

Given the experts' opinions that Chinese marriage was polygamous, the judges considered that a concubine could be regarded as a widow, and as such could have an equal division of the estate of a husband who died intestate. That was either a misunderstanding of the status of a concubine in Chinese marriage law and practice, or the judges were deliberately trying to protect the interests of the widows since they would not be in a better position if the Statute of Distribution was strictly followed. Such modification of Chinese customary practices into English common law was not uncommon, as Maurice Freedman commented, "(t)he chief concession to Chinese principles was to acknowledge that they were polygamous. But that polygamy so sanctioned was not in fact an institution that the Chinese could recognise as their own" (Freedman 1968, p. 51). Another example of this modification can be found in the issue of a letter of administration to a concubine after the death of her husband in the case of Hong Kong.

In Hong Kong, the case of *Ho Cheng Shi v Ho Sau Lam* (1920) was significant because the judge had to decide whether the status of the plaintiff as administratrix was lawful. The plaintiff was challenged by the defendant because the former was a concubine of the intestate, which under Chinese customary law did not entitle her to administer the estate. Having studied the different provisions relating to probate laws and procedures, Gompertz J considered that in the Probate Ordinance of 1897, "only part of the Chinese law which relates to distribution of assets has become the law of the Colony. If this is so, the Chinese custom that property on death vests directly in the successor, has no application to Hong Kong assets" (*Ho Cheng Shi v Ho Sau* Lam 1920, p. 39). In other words, the court rejected that such a rule in Chinese customary law was part of Hong Kong law. Their lordships were not convinced by the experts' view that the inferior status of concubines in Chinese customary practice was part of Hong Kong law, and concluded that a concubine was competent to be the administratrix of the estate:

> So much for the disabilities of a woman; especially a concubine in China. The answer is, I think, that the status of a woman is different in our law. She is competent to be administratrix, and as such to do anything that is necessary for the administration. In dealing with assets which are, *ex hypothesi*, Hong Kong assets, her status under the law of China is immaterial. In dealing with an estate in Hong Kong it cannot be material that the proper tribunal in China would be the elders of the clan, or that she must manage the property under their direction during the minority of the person entitled. (*Ho Cheng Shi v Ho Sau* Lam 1920, pp. 40–41)

In another case, *Chan Yeung v Chan Shew Shi* (1925), the Hong Kong court had to decide whether a concubine would obtain an ordinary grant in the letters of administration given by the Probate Office. It was, before this case, the usual practice that a concubine would only receive a letter of administration with limited grant for the use and benefit of the children. Gollan CJ held that the law of England was not applicable in this case as it recognised only one wife, so, in this situation, the law of China had to be used to find the person suitable to be the administrator of the intestate. The judge considered that the meaning of Article 38 of the GQC recognised that the "*Tsu Mo*" [*sic*] (in the judgment he called this the "Compassionate Mother", so the correct term should have been *ci mu*) was entitled to have the letter of administration, followed by a concubine or *t'sip*. After considering the experts' evidence in court and Section 38 of Staunton's translated texts of the GQC (*Chan Yeung v Chan Shew Shi* 1925, p. 42), the judge held that: "In my opinion, the widow of an intestate, if she was his *kit fat* or *tin fong*, is primarily entitled; if there is no such widow then a *Tsu Mo* (*ci mu*) comes next in order; and if there is no *Tsu Mo* then a concubine or concubines" (*Chan Yeung v Chan Shew Shi* 1925, p. 51).[70] He opined that under Chinese law and custom, such a grant was unlimited: "(A)pparently a practice has arisen in the Probate Registry of issuing limited grants to concubines, but I see no objection for this practice of limitation. On the facts that I have stated, it appears to me that if a concubine is entitled at all, she is entitled to a full grant; and I so hold" (*Chan Yeung v Chan Shew Shi* 1925, p. 51).[71]

In the above cases, the judges, by basing their decisions on the equality of men and women, and using the prevalence of English common law and legal provisions in the colonial law system, altered Chinese customary practices—an outcome of which was the codification of such rule in the Intestates' Estates Ordinance in Hong Kong (see Chap. 6, Sect. 6.6.10).

The above cases show that English common law in the Straits Settlements and Hong Kong had modified Chinese customary laws and practices to accommodate the requirements of the English common law system. But, for Chinese customary law and practice in Mainland China—before the enactment of the new Civil Code

---

[70] The right of *ci mu* to administer an estate for sons and daughters was also recognised by the *Da Li Yuan*. See n 90.

[71] The judge might have oversimplified the relationship in his judgment on the proper relationship of the eight types of mother, as established in the Southern Song dynasty and followed by the law codes of the Ming and Qing dynasties (Lau 2014, p. 646). In the present case, the defendant was the *shu mu* of three daughters and one son fathered by the intestate, and was appointed by the father as *ci mu* (foster mother) of two sons borne by another concubine of the intestate. The defendant claimed that her *ci mu* status—she was appointed by the father to take care of the two sons—gave her the right to be granted a letter of administration. But the judge used "*Tsu Mo*" instead of *tsi mo* to translate the modern pinyin of *ci mu*, which created confusion. (In fact, "*Tsu*" resembles neither the Cantonese "*tsi*" nor the Mandarin "*ci*", nor even "*t'zu*" in the Wade-Giles system.) Therefore, the improper translation created misunderstanding rather than clarity. The Strickland Report considered that the judge was referring not to *ci mu* but to *shu mu*. However, by reading through the judgment and comparing the English judgment with the Chinese text of the GQC, it is clear that the judge was in fact referring to *ci mu*. Nevertheless, because he used *Tsu Mo*, it confused the authors of the Strickland Report.

in 1931 and the Succession Laws in 1929—the *Da Li Yuan* also had to make judgments in response to the rising demands in society for equality between men and women. In the GQC, apart from the request for maintenance, a concubine had no other rights and interests in the estate if a husband died intestate. However, there was room for a concubine to be involved in the allotment of the estate and the appointment of an heir.

Firstly, the *Da Li Yuan* considered that the estate given to the minors born to a concubine had to be administered by the wife as *di mu* (proper or principal mother).[72] The judge held that the status of the *di mu* in this circumstance was equal in law to the natural mother. Moreover, the sequence of guardianship should strictly follow the order of *di mu* and *shu mu*, unless the *di mu* had a problem of mismanagement or was so biased in administration that it might harm the property of the issue, in which case the guardianship of the *di mu* would have to be abolished.[73] If the *di mu* was not capable of administering the estate, the court could appoint an administratrix for the benefit of the issue.[74]

Secondly, a concubine would lose her parental right to her natural son if she remarried after her husband died[75] or if she dissolved the union of concubinage with her husband.[76] She could retain her parental right to her son only if the principal mother agreed or if the father appointed her to be the guardian.[77] That said, the courts concluded that she could still be regarded as the natural mother.[78]

Thirdly, on the rights of a son born to a concubine, the *Da Li Yuan* held that the son was called *shu zi* and would be legitimated only if he was recognised by the father before the death of the father.[79] If a concubine gave birth to a son before marriage to her husband, the son would have the status of *shu zi* only after both parties formed a union of concubinage.[80]

Fourthly, the right of a *ci mu* to administer the estate of her son was recognised. In one case adjudicated by the *Da Li Yuan*, the appellant was the concubine of the respondent's father. The respondent was born to another concubine of his father, but was brought up by the appellant. The court held that the appellant was the *ci mu* of the respondent, and if she had a legitimate purpose to administer the estate of the respondent who was a minor, then such a decision could not be regarded as invalid.[81]

Finally, a concubine had the right of refusal on the appointment of an heir in a family meeting. The *Da Li Yuan* held that although a concubine did not have the

[72] Fourth Year Appeal Number 564 (Huang 2012, p. 845).

[73] Fifth Year Appeal Number 1209 (Huang 2012, p. 860).

[74] Tenth Year Appeal Number 449 (Huang 2012, p. 879).

[75] Seventh Year Appeal Number 1120 (Huang 2012, p. 889).

[76] Fifth Year Appeal Number 1209 (Huang 2012, p. 864).

[77] Fifth Year Appeal Number 1209 (Huang 2012, p. 864).

[78] Fifth Year Appeal Number 1209 (Huang 2012, p. 864).

[79] Third Year Appeal Number 729 (Huang 2012, p. 902).

[80] Eighth Year Appeal Number 1400 (Huang 2012, p. 894).

[81] Eighth Year Appeal Number 770 (Huang 2012, p. 1011).

right to appoint an heir, her position in the family meeting regarding the appointment of an heir was very important. If a concubine, with legitimate reasons, had a different view on the appointment of an heir, the family must seek her approval during or after the meeting. Without it, the appointment would be null and void. The court held, however, that if the family deemed the view of the concubine inappropriate, they should seek the decision of the court. Otherwise, a concubine had the right to revoke the decision of the family meeting.[82] In this situation, the *Da Li Yuan* had granted the right of appointment and the right of refusal of an heir to the concubine. This decision obviously deviated from the Chinese customary practice of reserving such rights for the principal wife.

3.3 Conclusion

The emigration of Chinese people from Mainland China brought Chinese customary law and practice overseas. The application of customary law and practice, as required under different jurisdictions in East Asia such as Hong Kong, led to their evolution in these new territories. This process ultimately led to "new" Chinese customary laws and practices that are totally different from the legal practices and developments in Mainland China. Seen in the light of case law in East Asian jurisdictions, one very important development emerges: the common goal of the courts and judges to gradually give more legal rights to concubines. Compared to concubines in Mainland China before 1911, the legal rights of concubines have been improved by the judgments in jurisdictions other than Mainland China. It is important to note that the legal entitlement of the *t'sip* was strictly limited under the GQC and Chinese customary practices due to her inferior status. But judges in East Asian jurisdictions tried to get rid of such restrictions and to give more rights to concubines in different ways.

For example, in the Six Widows case, the court gave the concubines the right to administer the deceased husband's estate. Under the GQC, even a wife could only in a limited circumstance to administer her husband's estate after his death. In Singapore, the right to administer the estate of a deceased husband was granted by statutory law by issuing a letter of administration to the wife. However, before the Six Widows case, it was doubtful whether a concubine had the same right because the Statute of Distribution did not contain such a right for a concubine. Nevertheless, the judges in the Six Widows case granted such a right to the concubines. Since this case, both wives and concubines have the right to administer the distribution of their husband's estate, but the right of the concubine can only be granted by the court if the wife predeceases the husband. It was a bold move, not only because this ruling deviated from the GQC but also because the judges tried to put the wife and the concubine on a more equal footing instead of treating the concubine as inferior in

[82] Seventh Year Appeal Number 386 (Huang 2012, p. 1044).

status and denying her the right to administer her husband's estate. Had the judge applied the GQC and Chinese customary practice, the concubines in the Six Widows case would have had no rights at all.

In another example, the court ruled that consensual marriage between a husband and wife could be applied to the union of concubinage. In this respect, the courts had indeed made significant changes to traditional Chinese laws and practices originating from the GQC and Mainland China, not to mention that these rulings redefined Chinese customary marriage from a monogamous to a polygamous one. Such recognition could help concubines because, if marriage was polygamous, a concubine could enjoy the same rights as a wife in some circumstances, such as inheritance of the husband's estate. Nevertheless, given the judicial limitations judges faced when trying to bring equality to women under Chinese customary law (some judges had expressed how distasteful they found the very institution of concubinage), the only way to give more rights to women was not by raising the status of *t'sip* in the family through laws but by abolishing concubinage in Chinese communities through legislation.

The diffusion of Chinese customary laws and practices had a significant impact on the development of Chinese customary law in the jurisdictions where Chinese immigrants settled. Firstly, even though the foreign judges had to rely on the GQC and expert evidence in legal proceedings, the social and moral functions behind the GQC were not their principal concerns when resolving matrimonial disputes. Secondly, in adjudicating many cases related to inheritance and succession issues upon the death of the husband, only a handful of the litigations had to apply the provisions in the GQC. Thirdly, given that the sources of other legal materials—such as the litigation reports published by the Board of Punishments under the Qing authorities—might not be readily available, the judges had to rely on the customary practices in the local communities rather than in Mainland China to adjudicate cases. Consequently, the development of local Chinese customary law gradually diverged from the legal developments in Mainland China. The sources of Chinese customary law in East Asian jurisdictions had been changing as well—from the reliance on Chinese customary law developed and evolved in Mainland China to the adoption of Chinese customary laws grown out of their own soil. The legal developments in Mainland China would no longer be the main source of Chinese customary law in other jurisdictions in East Asia. In sum, in jurisdictions other than Mainland China, Chinese customary laws and practices pertaining to *t'sip* had been undergoing a process of transformation: from legal transplantation from Mainland China, to evolvement and adaptation in different Chinese immigrant communities, to finally being grounded legally and locally after judicial interpretations in courts.

Following the 1911 Revolution and the new Civil Code of the Republic of China in 1931, which abolished the union of concubinage, there was a change in the development of case law in other jurisdictions that applied Chinese customary law. In fact, the abolition of concubinage and the judicial decision in Mainland China to recognise only registered monogamous marriage had made it very difficult for other jurisdictions to retain the (potentially) polygamous nature of Chinese customary marriage practices if the source of such custom and practice was itself changing.

Nonetheless, rather than referring to the legal developments in Mainland China, the courts in the Straits Settlements and Hong Kong relied more upon their own case law and local customs in making judgments. The case developments in overseas jurisdictions suggested that the judgments referred to the local Chinese customary practices in their own countries and regions but not the evolvement of such practices in Mainland China. Consequently, Chinese customary practices as envisaged in Mainland China were no longer the essential point of reference for family law cases in other jurisdictions. Finally, after the abolition of concubinage in Singapore in 1961, Hong Kong in 1971, and Taiwan after the end of the Japanese occupation and the reception of the Civil Code from the Republic of China in 1945—and following the Marriage Law in the People's Republic of China in 1950 which only allowed monogamous marriage—the decision on the status of *t'sip* in some jurisdictions has become one of historical more than legal significance.

References

Alabaster, E. (1899). *Notes and commentaries on Chinese criminal law*. London: Luzac & Co.

Aneha, S. (1994). *Jisi gongye yu Taiwan Twaian de teshu falü zhi yanjiu* [The study of ancestor worship guild and Taiwan special laws]. Taipei: Jong Wen Books.

Asano, T. (2012). Ume Kenjiro yu Goto Shinpei: chuqi Taiwan fazhi zhi fadian yu guan xi [Ume Kenjiro and Goto Shinpei: Law codes and customs in early Taiwan legal system]. In H. Hsueh (Ed.), *Modernisation and colonisation* (pp. 122–152). Taipei: National Taiwan University Press.

Buxbaum, D. C. (1968). Chinese family law in a common law setting. In D. C. Buxbaum (Ed.), *Family law and customary law in Asia: A contemporary legal perspective* (pp. 146–177). Hague: Martinus Nijhoff.

Cheng, Y. (2006). *Qing zhi Minguo xuqie zisu zhi bianqian* [The evolution of the customs of the Institution of Concubinage from Qing to Republican China]. Shanghai: Shanghai Guji Chubanshe.

Chiu, V. Y. (1950). Appendix 9. In Committee on Chinese Law and Custom in Hong Kong (1953) (Ed.), *Chinese law and custom in Hong Kong: Report of a committee appointed by the Governor in October, 1948*. Hong Kong: Government Printer.

Civil Law Research and Amendment Committee. (1976). *Historical materials of ROC civil law*. Taipei: Ministry of Judicial Administration (Chinese).

Committee on Chinese Law and Custom in Hong Kong. (1953). *Chinese law and custom in Hong Kong: Report of a committee appointed by the Governor in October, 1948*. Hong Kong: Government Printer.

Da Qing lü li (1993). (Zhang R., Liu Y. & Jin M, Punctuators). Tianjin: Tianjin Guji Chubenshe.

Freedman, M. (1968). Chinese family law in Singapore: The rout of custom. In J. N. D. Anderson (Ed.), *Family law in Asia and Africa*. London: George Allen and Unwin.

Freeman, M. (1979). Colonial law and Chinese society. In G. William Skinner (Ed.), *The study of Chinese society*. Stanford: Stanford University Press.

Greenfield, D. E. (1958). Marriage by Chinese law and Hong Kong. *The International and Comparative Law Quarterly, 7*(3), 437–451.

Hu, H. H., & Chung, C. (2009). *Xianggang de hun yin yu ji cheng fa* [The marriage and inheritance laws in Hong Kong]. Hong Kong: Red-Publish. (Original work published 1957).

Huang, Y. S. (2011). *Minchu dali yuan yu caipan* [The Supreme Court and its judgments in the early Republic of China (1912–1928)]. Taipei: Angle Press.

Huang, Y. S. (2012). *A compilation of the civil precedents of the Supreme Court in the Early Republic of China–Family*. Taipei: Li Zhai She.

Huxley, A. (1988–89). Burma: It works, but is it law? *Journal of Family Law, 27*, 23–24.

Ji, T. (2017). *Da Qing xiangxin xinglü jiangyi* [The lecture notes of the Great Qing criminal law]. Beijing: Tsinghua University Press. (Original work published in 1910).

Jones, W. C. (1994). *The Great Qing Code*. Oxford: Clarendon Press.

Lau, N. Y. (2014). Changes to women's legal rights in the family from the Song to the Ming. In J. Lagerwey & P. Marsone (Eds.), *Modern Chinese religion I* (pp. 643–721). Leiden: Brill.

Leong, W. K. (1985). Common law and Chinese marriage custom in Singapore. In A. J. Harding (Ed.), *The common law in Singapore and Malaysia* (pp. 175–194). Singapore: Butterworths.

Lewis, D. J. (1983). A requiem for Chinese customary law in Hong Kong. *The International and Comparative Law Quarterly, 32*(2), 347–379.

Maung, M. (1963). *Law and custom in Burma and the Burmese family*. Hague: Martinus Nijhoff.

Meiji prosecution 63. (1995). *Fukushin: Kōtō Hōin hanrei* [Review high court judgments] (Vol. 1). Tokyo: Bunsei Shoin.

Official Bulletin of the Government of Macau Province. (1909, July 31). *Bolitim Official do Governo da Provincia de Macau, Sábado, 31 De Julho De 1909* [Official bulletin of the Government of Macau Province] (Vol. IX). Macau: Imprensa Nacional de Macau.

Review High Court Judgments. (1995). *Fukushin: Kōtō Hōin hanrei (Vol. 1–3)*. Tokyo: Bunsei Shoin.

Shen, Z. (1999). *Da Qinglü jizhu* [Compiled annotation on the Great Qing Code]. Beijing: Law Press. (Original work published 1715).

Shen, C. P. (2015). *Duoyuan xiangqian de Taiwan rizhishiqi jiazu fa* [The diverse embedded Taiwanese family law under Japanese colonial rule]. Taipei: Angle Press.

Staunton, G. T. (2012). *Ta Tsing Leu Lee; Being the fundamental laws, and a selection from the supplementary statutes, of the Penal Code of China*. Cambridge: Cambridge University Press.

Straits Settlements Report. (1926). *Straits settlements Chinese Marriage Committee report*. Singapore: Government Printing Office.

Taisho 6 Prosecution Number 506. (1995). *Review high court judgments (Fukushin: Kōtō Hōin hanrei)* (Vol. 1). Tokyo: Bunsei Shoin.

Taisho 8 Prosecution Civil Number 758. (1995). *Review high court judgments (Fukushin: Kōtō Hōin hanrei)* (Vol. 1). Tokyo: Bunsei Shoin.

Taisho 8 Prosecution Civil Number 853. (1995). *Review high court judgments (Fukushin: Kōtō Hōin hanrei)* (Vol. 1). Tokyo: Bunsei Shoin.

Taisho 11 Appeal Civil Number 123. (1995). *Review high court judgments (Fukushin: Kōtō Hōin hanrei)* (Vol. 2). Tokyo: Bunsei Shoin.

Taisho 11 Prosecution Civil Number 774. (1995). *Review high court judgments (Fukushin: Kōtō Hōin hanrei)* (Vol. 2). Tokyo: Bunsei Shoin.

Taisho 13 Prosecution Number 300. (1995). *Review high court judgments (Fukushin: Kōtō Hōin hanrei)* (Vol. 3). Tokyo: Bunsei Shoin.

Tan, C. (1993). The twilight of Chinese customary law relating to marriage in Malaysia. *The International and Comparative Law Quarterly, 42*, 147–156.

Temporary Investigation Committee on the Old Custom of Taiwan. (1993). *Taiwan shifa* [Taiwan Private Law] (J. Chen, Trans.). Nantou: Taiwan Province Archive Committee. (Original work published in 1901).

Teng, H. B. (2014). Law, gongqin, and transnational polygamy: Family matters in Fujian and British Malaya, 1855–1942. In P. C. C. Huang & K. Bernhardt (Eds.), *Research from archival case records: Law, society and culture in China*. Leiden: Brill.

The Second Charter of Justice. (1826). In Braddell, J. (1982). *The law of the straits settlements: A commentary*. Oxford: Oxford University Press.

Tran, L. (2009). The concubinage in Republican China: Social perception and legal construction. *Études chinoises, XXVIII*, 120–149.

Wakefield, D. (1998). *Fenjia: Household division and inheritance in Qing and Republican China*. Honolulu: University of Hawai'i Press.

Wang, T. S. (2000). *Legal reform in Taiwan under Japanese colonial rule, 1895–1945: The reception of Western law*. Seattle: University of Washington Press.
Woods, R. C. (1911). *A selection of oriental cases decided in the Supreme Courts of the straits settlements (1835–1869)*. London: Sweet & Maxwell. (Original work published 1869).
Woon, W. (1999). The applicability of English law in Singapore. In K. Tan (Ed.), *The Singapore legal system* (2nd ed.). Singapore: Singapore University Press.
Xin An Hui Lan. (2006). (Vols. 8–52). In *Xin An Hui Lan Quan Bian*. Beijing: The Law Press.
Xu Zeng Xin An Hui Lan. (2006). (Vol. 11). In *Xin An Hui Lan Quan Bian*. Beijing: The Law Press.

Statutes

Burma Laws Act, 1898.
Intestates' Estates Ordinance (Cap. 73). http://oelawhk.lib.hku.hk/archive/files/6d5b44d0cd39f455aefa987db2e5cc9e.pdf
Marriage Ordinance (Cap. 181).
Marriage Reform Ordinance (Cap. 178).
Matrimonial Causes Ordinance (Cap. 179).
The Special Marriage Act (India Act III of 1872).

Cases

Bon Sau Fei v Chong Chui Lien & Anor [1986] 2 MLJ 475.
Brook v Brook (1858) 3 Sm & G 481.
Chan Yeung v Chan Shew Shi [1925] 20 HKLR 35.
Cheang Thye Phin v Tan Ah Loy (1920) AC 369.
Choa Choon Neoh v Spottiswoode (1868) 1 Ky 216.
Choo Ang Chee v Neo Chan Neo (1911) 12 SSLR 120.
Chulas & Kachee v Kolson binte Seydoo Malim (1867).
Er Gek Cheng v Ho Ying Seng [1949] 1 MLJ 171.
Ho Cheng Shi v Ho Sau Lam [1920] 15 HKLR 35.
Ho Tsz Tsun v Ho Au Shi and others (1915) HKLR 69.
In Re Choo Eng Choon, deceased; Choo Ang Chee v Neo Chan Neo and others (1908) SSLR 120.
In Re Goodman's Trust [1881] 17 Ch D 266.
In Re Ma Yin Mya and one v Tan Yauk Pu and two (1927) ILR 5 Ran 406.
In Re Wong Choi Ho, deceased v Wong Yuk-shu, deceased [1969] HKLR 391.
In Re Wong Wong [1998] 3 HKC 405.
In the Estate of Chak Chiu Hang; Chan Chun Cho v Chak Hok Ping (1925) HKLR 1.
In the Estate of Sim Siew Guan deceased Singapore Probate No 321 of 1923 (1932) 1 MLJ 95.
In the Estate of Sim Siew Guan deceased Singapore Probate No 321 of 1923 (1933) SSLR 539.
In the Estate of Yeow Kian Kee, deceased; Er Gek Cheng v Ho Ying Seng [1949] 1 MLJ 171.
Khoo Guat Tee & others v Lim Kim Neo & others (2016) 8 MLJ 639.
Khoo Hooi Leong v Khoo Chong Yeok [1930] AC 346.
Kwan Chui Kwok Ying v Tao Wai Chun [1995] 1 HKC 371.
Leung Sai Lun Robert & others v Leung May Ling & others [1999] 1 HKLRD 649.
Lew Ah Lui (f) v Choa Eng Wan & Ors [1935] 1 MLJ 78.
Lim Siew Yun v Soong Ah Kaw (1960–63) SCR105.
Ma Kyin Mya v Maung Sit Han (1937) RLR 103.
Meiji Prosecution 63 (RHCJ v1).

Mette v Mette (1859) 1 Sw & Tr 416 at 423.
Ng Ying Ho v Tam Suen Yu [1963] HKLR 923.
Pai Beng Teng v Ko Muang (1904) 2 LBR 261.
R v Willan (1858) 3 Ky 16.
Re Chan Cho Chak [2005] HKCU 1773.
Re Estate of Ng Shum (No 2) [1990] 1 HKLR 67.
Re Estate of Tse Chu [2012] 3 HKLRD 340.
Re Ho Phian Cheong (deceased) [1963] 29 MLJ 316 at 317.
Re Lee Choon Guan, deceased; Lew Ah Lui (F) v Choa Eng Wan and others [1935] 1 MLJ 78.
Sein Kyi v Ma E (1916) 8 LBR 399.
Suen Toi Lee v Yau Yee Ping (2001) 4 HKCFAR 474.
Suen Toi Lee v Yau Yee Ping [2002] 1 HKLRD 197.
Tan Ah Bee v Foo Thye and Another [1947] 1 MLJ 169.
Tay Geok Yap v Tan Lian Cheow [1965] 1 MLJ 102.
Whicker v Hume (1858) 7 H L Cas 124.
Woon Ngee Yew & others v Ng Yoon Thai and others [1941] 1 MLJ 37.
Wong Kam Ying and another v Man Chi Tai (1967) HKLR 201.
Wong Kam Ying v Man Chi Tai (1967) HKLR 201.
Wong Yu Shi and others (No. 1) v Wong Ying Kuen (1957) HKLR 421.
Wong Zhong Lan Xiang v Frank Wong [2003] HKEC 421.
Ye Jin Xiang v Kam Pin Kwong [2017] 2 HKC 195.
Yeap Leong Soon & Anor & another application (1989) 3 MLJ 157.
Yeap Cheah Neo v Ong Cheng Neo (1875) 6 LR (PC) 381.
Yau Tin Sung v Yau Wan Hoi (1984) HKLR 15.

Part III
Concubines and Colonialism

Chapter 4
The Origins of the Strickland Report and the Search for the Chinese Customary Law and Custom in Hong Kong

Abstract This chapter discusses the marriage reform proposed by the Strickland Committee. It investigates the origins of the committee and the discussions that led to its final report, published in 1951. It is important to note that because of the opposition from a senior political figure, Sir Man Kam Lo, the Hong Kong Government could not push forward the Strickland Report, even though the abolition of concubinage was championed by social organisations such as the Hong Kong Council of Women. The Executive Council of Hong Kong rejected the Strickland Report in 1956, frustrating the Colonial Office in London.

Keywords Strickland Report · Chinese customary law and practice · Chinese customary marriage · Civil Code Republic of China · Abolition of concubinage

4.1 Introduction

The legal reform of the Qing authorities before 1911 brought about fundamental changes in civil and criminal law. With the support of Japanese scholars and taking references from legal concepts in Western countries, new laws were developed that ceased to apply traditional Chinese law. 1911 put an end to the Qing government. The subsequent changes in civil law, particularly family law, were heavily driven by a strong social demand for the equality of men and women. This meant that family law reform, such as the abolition of concubinage, was considered the best way to achieve social equality through legal change. One of the focal points was the codification of such concepts into a new law governing the principle of the equality of men and women. Therefore, the abolition of concubinage and codification of monogamous marriage as exemplified in the Civil Code in 1931 in Republic of China was seen as a triumph for the social activists who had advocated for an equal and modern China.

Consequently, the legal changes introduced by the Civil Code in 1931 almost completely abandoned the traditional family provisions as provided for in the GQC and replaced them with a new Westernised marriage system. The new law

M. WL Wong, *Chinese Marriage and Social Change*,
https://doi.org/10.1007/978-981-15-1644-3_4

established a monogamous marriage system and no longer recognised traditional customary marriage. In other words, the law no longer legally recognised the status of concubine, although a concubine could still be regarded as a member of the household in law by which certain rights such as maintenance could still be claimed. In addition, the new Civil Code formally recognised the mutual right for the husband and wife to petition for divorce in court. The reasons and procedure for the dissolution of marriage were simplified, and, in comparison with the GQC, more rights were given to the wife to file the divorce.

These legal changes had profound impact on other jurisdictions that recognised Chinese customary marriage. For example, if a husband took a concubine after 1931 in China, this was illegal under the Civil Code. But if the couple came to Hong Kong, would this union become a legally recognised marriage? Another issue was: if a husband and a wife were married before 1931 by a traditional customary marriage and then successfully dissolved their marriage after 1931, could the divorce be recognised in other jurisdictions? But one issue stood out: should the other jurisdictions such as Hong Kong be brought in line with the Civil Code in China and propose similar legal reform of family laws regulating Chinese marriages?

The Strickland Report was the response of the Hong Kong Government to the legal changes in China soon after the Second World War. However, the "modernisation" approach as taken by the Strickland Report (notably the overhaul of the application of Chinese law and custom in Hong Kong) met with strong resistance from senior political figures in Hong Kong. This resulted in the retention of the institution of concubinage and Chinese customary marriage in the Hong Kong legal system following the report's release and its subsequent rejection by the Hong Kong Government in the 1950s. This chapter will uncover the missing pieces of the origins of the Strickland Report, and give reasons why the Hong Kong Government refused to implement the legal changes as proposed by the same report.

4.2 The Strickland Report

4.2.1 Origin

The origin of the establishment of a committee to investigate the laws applicable to the Chinese in Hong Kong came from the suggestion of Sir Man Kam Lo, a senior Chinese political figure and an unofficial member of the Executive Council. On 5 November 1947, a District Officer in the New Territories, John Barrow, asked the Colonial Secretary on the practice of the District Offices to witness and register a Letter of Separation (*fan shue*) at the District Offices in the New Territories. John Barrow disagreed with the continuance of this practice because, in his view, "if the legislature had intended its officials to give more or less official countenance to divorce, the legislature would have provided the machinery". Therefore, John Barrow asked the advice of the Chinese Unofficial members of the Executive and

Legislative Councils on this issue and whether the District Offices in the New Territories should continue with this practice (Minute to Hon C.S., 5 November 1947). This triggered some internal discussion in the government on the best way to deal with the application of Chinese customary laws in Hong Kong. Replying to the question asked by the Secretary for Chinese Affairs Ronald Ruskin Todd on the issue, the Executive Council member Sir Man Kam Lo stated that the issue of the recognition of divorce in China from the Hong Kong courts was very important and the whole position of the application of the Chinese law in Hong Kong was entirely unsatisfactory, because this might affect all aspect of Chinese life, such as the question of inheritance (Letter from Man Kam Lo, 21 November 1947, para. 2). Thus, Sir Man Kam Lo asked again for appointing a committee to look into the practice of the Chinese law in Hong Kong:

> I remember that as long ago as Halifax's time I urged in a memorandum, that the whole question of Hong Kong law as applicable to Chinese should be considered by a committee. After the British re-occupation, and on my suggestion, the Law Society wrote in to the then Acting Attorney-General, Mr Strickland, on the same subject. (Letter from Man Kam Lo, 21 November 1947, para. 3)

And again, in the end of his submission, Sir Man Kam Lo reiterated that: "[G]et Government to appoint a committee to consider the whole question of Hong Kong laws in relation to Chinese" (Letter from Man Kam Lo, 21 November 1947, para. 19). Another Chinese Unofficial member of the Executive Council, Sik Nin Chau, also concurred with Man Kam Lo: "I would like to support the suggestion of an appointed Committee to thrash out the question fully" (Letter from S.N. Chau, 24 November 1947).

Since the Chinese Unofficial members of the Executive and Legislative Councils were in support of the forming of a committee to deal with the issue of Chinese law as applicable to Hong Kong Chinese, the government considered that establishing a committee to review this issue was inevitable. The Solicitor General, George Strickland, prepared a long memo explaining the use of the Chinese law in Hong Kong after 1843. He considered that the non-Christian marriage (i.e. in this context, Chinese customary marriage) was recognised according to the personal law and religion of the parties preserved by Section 37 of the Marriage Ordinance and "it is precisely in this field of personal status that one expects the laws of England to be 'inapplicable to the local circumstances of the Colony, or of its inhabitants'" as specified in the Supreme Court Ordinance (Memo from Solicitor General, 10 March 1948, para. 10). Strickland considered that it was illogical to apply the English principles of divorce to marriage fundamentally different from a Christian marriage (Memo from Solicitor General, 10 March 1948, para. 11), and was illogical too to use the Letter of Separation for Chinese customary marriage in Hong Kong that could properly terminate the marriage (Memo from Solicitor General, 10 March 1948, para. 12).

Strickland was in support of "a review of this branch of the subject by a Committee", and he emphasised that:

> The longer we wait the more will Chinese law as applied in China differ from that in force in Hong Kong in 1843, and the more difficult will it for anyone to speak with authority as to what the latter was. I consider that inquiry should be undertaken now so far as regards those customs to which English law in considered inapplicable, principally personal status and inheritance. (Memo from Solicitor General, 10 March 1948, para. 14)

He then considered that after this enquiry, revision of the laws might be contemplated so as to adapt the laws to the present circumstances. However, he did not consider that the Legal Department could spare a member to serve on such a committee, and he proposed that "lawyers with more intimate knowledge of local law and custom would make a more valuable contribution" (Memo from Solicitor General, 10 March 1948, para. 14).

Nonetheless, senior government officials disagreed with his suggestion to ask other lawyers to head the Committee. The Secretary for Chinese Affairs, Todd, considered that "I doubt whether any member of the Law Society would be interested in this rather academic matter at the present time—they have other profitable business to attend to" (Minute from S.C.A., 16 March 1948b). The Deputy Colonial Secretary, Kenneth Myer Arthur Barnett, considered that the government had failed its duty to ensure that "the national and domestic status of its component people are adequately dealt with by law either of its own or of a larger unit to which it belong" (Minute from D.C.S., 19 April 1948a), when he minuted to the Colonial Secretary, David Mercer MacDougall. And Barnett considered that "[P]robably 50% of our people neither know nor care what nationality they are; and from this file it looks as if a large proportion of the people neither know or care whether they are legally married and if so, to whom" (Minute from D.C.S., 19 April 1948a). Barnett agreed with Todd that the government should not wait for the Law Society as "we shall wait till Doomsday", then he asked whether Strickland could make a push.

Strickland insisted on having a strong chairman, with government representatives forming the Committee (Minute from S.G., 12 May 1948a). This implied that he resisted to chair the Committee, as suggested by Barnett, and still favoured inviting the Law Society to lead the Committee. However, after a meeting with the Colonial Secretary MacDougall, his position was softened. The Colonial Secretary MacDougall asked him to write a minute to the Governor Mark Aitchison Young on the issues of appointing the Committee.

In this memorandum, Strickland gave two reasons for establishing such a Committee. First, he stated that in practice where Chinese law and custom prevailed in Hong Kong was in the field of family law, status and inheritance. And, he considered that there are some matters of considerable importance relating to the questions of legitimacy of marriage, divorce and of children and, finally, of sharing the succession (Minute from S.G., 28 May 1948, para. 4). Second, he argued that the Chinese law and custom which remained static from 1843 was "not only difficult to prove but is out of harmony with the development of the Colony and the present law and custom of China". Strickland agreed now that the "Government must to a large extent take the lead, as was once suggested, leave the matter to the Law Society" (Minute from S.G., 28 May 1948, para. 7), but he instead proposed to appoint the Deputy Colonial Secretary Barnett to chair the committee (Minute from S.G.,

28 May 1948, para. 8). He also proposed to have the following members: a representative of the Secretary for Chinese Affairs; the official representative of the Law Society, Mr C. Y. Kwan; Mr Hin Shing Lo (a temporary employee but one who could best represent the Legal and Judicial Departments because of his good knowledge of the subject); Mr M. W. Lo; Mr Y. H. Chan as Secretary, because his work was of legal nature and because he was a member of the firm of Tso and Hodgson; and, since Dr Tso Seen Wan had poor eyesight, so Mr Chan could be able to ask Dr Tso as an amanuensis (Minute from S.G., 28 May 1948, para. 8–9). On the terms of reference, he proposed the following:

> To consider and make recommendation as to how far Chinese law and custom as existing in 1843—
>
> (a) is now applicable to Chinese domiciled in Hong Kong or to other Chinese resorting here;
> (b) should with or without modification be incorporated into the law of the Colony;
> (c) should be superseded with or without modification by the law of the Colony applicable to whom such Chinese law and custom does not apply by other law
>
> and generally to consider and make recommendations as to what is the best course, legislative or otherwise, to adopt in relation to Chinese law and custom in force in Hong Kong. (Minute from S.G., 28 May 1948, para. 10)

The Colonial Secretary, MacDougall, submitted this minute to the Governor and later, sought the views from the Secretary for Chinese Affairs, Todd, on this minute as well. The Secretary for Chinese Affairs later minuted to the Colonial Secretary, after 4 months, that he generally agreed that the legal position of the Chinese domiciled or residing in Hong Kong required clarifications on the followings: marriage; divorce, including the custody of children; adoption of children; and inheritance (Minute from S.C.A., 14 September 1948a). In view of the complexities in identifying the "Chinese laws" (whether that referred to the old law of the Qing dynasty or the new Civil Code of the Republic of China), and "Chinese custom" (since Hong Kong had now consisted of different natives of other provinces in China), Todd considered that the government "should go ahead and enact commonsense enforceable law applicable to the Chinese resident in the Colony in respect of the matters mentioned …above". And, Todd considered that in enacting these new laws, the government should primarily look at the existing laws of the Colony as applicable to persons of non-Chinese race and only secondarily to Chinese custom. Todd further added that on the matter of "Chinese law", the government should "repudiate altogether the idea that it has or should have any legal validity in this Colony" (Minute from S.C.A., 14 September 1948a, para. 3–5). Furthermore, Todd disagreed with the terms of reference because that contained too many reference to Chinese law and custom: "I do not regard China as a 'modern state' and I would omit from the terms of reference any allusion to Chinese law and custom, ancient or modern, though the Committee will doubtless take them into consideration" (Minute from S.C.A., 14 September 1948a, para. 6). He still insisted on having a Chairman who was a senior law officer of the Crown, and he proposed to appoint the Attorney General to chair the Committee (Minute from S.C.A., 14 September 1948a, para. 7). Finally, he disagreed with appointing a nominee of the Council of Women because

"I feel that a nominee of the Council (of Women) would be quite useless as a member of the Committee", and he suggested that the delegates from the Council of Women could with "more advantage be invited to express its views either in writing or by sending a delegation to appear before the Committee."

The Governor agreed to establish the committee in October 1948. He decided to appoint the Solicitor General George Strickland to chair the Committee with the confirmation of the membership: J. Barrow (District Commissioner from the New Territories); M.W. Lo; C. Y. Kwan; Chung King-pui and Mrs Irene Ho Cheng; and Mr Y.H. Chan as Secretary (Minute from D.C.S., 6 October 1948b, para. 1). Also, the Governor ordered that "the terms of reference should be as wide as possible and should not exclude the possibility of adopting for any purpose the law of China" (Minute from D.C.S., 6 October 1948b, para. 2). After receiving this instruction, Strickland slightly changed the terms of reference by adding "by Ordinance" in (b) and by adding "whether already incorporated or not" after the word "should".[1] On 27 January 1949, Strickland issued a press release on the announcement of the Committee and its membership to the public (Minute from Solicitor General, 27 January, 1949).

In sum, it is clear that the abolition of concubinage was not on the agenda when government officials were discussing the possibility of setting up a Committee to reform Chinese law and custom in Hong Kong. One might argue that the terms of reference of the Committee were very wide, so, by reviewing Chinese customary marriage in Hong Kong, the discussion of the personal status of *t'sip* was inevitable. However, judging from the discussions of the above, one cannot escape the finding that the review of the status of *t'sip*, or even the abolition of *t'sip*, would become the focal point of the Committee. The leaf was turned by some members of the Committee with pressure from social organisations, which will be discussed later in this chapter.

4.2.2 Discussions

During the meetings of the Strickland Committee, two main issues were identified. First, the members had to identify the elements of the Chinese law and custom which were applicable to Hong Kong. The second was the abolition of concubinage.

---

[1] The final version of the terms of reference were: "To consider and make recommendation as to how far Chinese law and custom as existing in 1843—

(a) is now applicable to Chinese domiciled in Hong Kong or to other Chinese resorting here;
(b) should with or without modification be incorporated <u>by Ordinance</u> into the law of the Colony;
(c) should <u>whether already incorporated or not</u> be superseded with or without modification be incorporated by the law of the Colony applicable to whom such Chinese law and custom does not apply by other law

and generally to consider and make recommendations as to what is the best course, legislative or otherwise, to adopt in relation to Chinese law and custom in force in Hong Kong".

In the final stage of drafting the report, the abolition of concubinage became a point of friction between the conservative Chinese senior political figures and the supporters of the abolition of concubinage championed by women organisations.

The Committee had taken a lot of efforts to identify elements of Chinese law and custom as applicable to Hong Kong. The Committee relied upon two sources. First, the Committee asked the Secretary for Chinese Affairs to conduct a survey in the New Territories to gauge the Chinese customary practices that existed in the villages. Second, the Committee relied upon expert opinions, particularly Chinese legal experts, to give advice on Chinese law and custom in Hong Kong.

On 25 February 1949, the District Commissioner John Barrow wrote a memo to the DOO (which referred to all District Offices in the New Territories) about the application of the New Territories Regulation Ordinance—with this marginal note: "Supreme Court may enforce Chinese Customs". In reply, one District Officer drew attention to disputes regarding succession to property, "particularly in cases where succession is claimed by a woman (possibly wife, daughter or other relative)" (Memo from DC, 25 February 1949). A follow-up notice was written by Barrow, which asked for soliciting the opinion of the New Territories people on behalf of the "Government Committee on Chinese Law and Custom". In this notice, the Committee drew attention to the application of Section 25 of the New Territories Regulation Ordinance 1910, which stated that "[I]n any proceedings in the Supreme Court in relation to land in the New Territories, the court shall have power to recognise and enforce any Chinese custom or customary right affecting such land", and the Committee should consider that "it may now be possible to formulate and codify the main Chinese customs or customary rights affecting land in the New Territories" (Government Committee on Chinese Law and Custom, 25 March 1949). In the memo Barrow asked that the District Officers in the New Territories ("D.O.O.") distribute the notice and register their initial response (Government Committee on Chinese Law and Custom, 25 March 1949, para. 3). In reply, one District Officer stated that he had gathered some village leaders for a meeting to discuss the notice, including the issues on succession, adoption, provisions for the wife of a deceased, concubines, repossession of subleased land and registration of succession. He expected to have the replies in 2 weeks (Government Committee on Chinese Law and Custom, 25 March 1949, para. 3).

On 3 June 1949, a consolidated reply from the rural committees in the Southern Districts of the New Territories was given to Barrow. There were some observations on Chinese customary practices regarding the status of a concubine. On the right of succession, it was reported that in Cheung Chau, only if the deceased husband leaves no son or nephew, but was survived by widow or concubine, did his widow or concubine have the right of succession (Cheung Chau: Comments, 3 June 1949). In Ma Wan area, the widow, concubine or daughter of a deceased husband had the right of enjoyment of the benefit of property, but neither of them had the right of succession. Before the death of a widow or concubine, or before the marriage of a daughter of a deceased husband, the successor (son of the wife, or in the absence of son, a nephew, and if no nephew then the next closest relative) must not forcibly occupy or sell the property allotted to them for enjoyment of benefit, unless agreement had been made between them (Ma Wan: Comments, 3 June 1949). In Southern Lamma Island, it was reported that a widow, concubine, son or daughter could enjoy the right of succession. No maintenance could be claimed by the widow, concubine or daughter of the deceased after the remarriage of a widow or concubine or after the marriage of a daughter (Southern Lama Island: Comments, 3 June 1949). In Northern Lama Island, on the right of succession, the widow or concubine had the right to deal with the estate. A portion of the property was allocated for an unmarried daughter's dowry. On the maintenance of a widow, concubine and daughter, it is reported that they could live on the estate. If no estate was left, they should work for their living (Northern Lama Island: Comments, 3 June 1949). In Sai Kung, after the decease of a husband, "a portion of the estate was allotted to the concubine, amount to be fixed by the senior members of the community, for the purpose of maintenance during her lifetime and for burial expenses after her death" (Sai Kung: Comments, 3 June 1949). But, the allotted property would be registered as "Tso" property under the name of her deceased husband with the beneficiary (in other words the concubine) as trustee. After the death of the concubine, whether this property would become "Tsing Sheung" (*zheng chang*)[2] or be given back to the successor was a matter for individual consideration (Sai Kung: Comments, 3 June 1949). In Tsin Pit Tat of Tai O, the Hakka tradition was that the widow had no right of succession, and there was no provision for maintenance of mother and daughter, "Maintenance being in the nature of a moral obligation" (Tsin Pit Tat of Tai O: Comments, 3 June 1949). In Tsuen Wan, a concubine normally received the same treatment as the widow (Tsuen Wan: Comments, 3 June 1949). The amount for her maintenance had to be decided by senior members of the community. Similar to Sai Kung, the allotted property would be registered into "Tso" property under the name of the deceased husband, with the widow as trustee (Tsuen Wan: Comments, 3 June 1949). After a concubine died, the property would be given to the son. For the widow with no son, the estate would turn into "Tso" property under the name of the deceased husband with the widow to act a trustee (Tsuen Wan: Comments, 3 June 1949).

From the reports given by the districts (except Tai O), the Chinese customary practices in relation to the concubine and the right of succession and to receive maintenance were similar. Tai O was different. As mentioned by an anonymous writer contributing to the report on Tai O, the inhabitants of Tai O were Hakka who mostly came from Po On, Nam Tau and Tung Koon at Mainland China. Hakka usually observed the existing Hong Kong laws. This anonymous writer reported that, the customs of Hakka had always conflicted with human feelings and theories of law, because a female had no place in the Hakka family. He supported the view that the governing laws of the New Territories should be Hong Kong laws:

> Hakkas are found everywhere while their customs vary. If laws are based upon the opinion of a portion of the populace of N.T. (New Territories) much trouble may be expected. N.T. (New Territories) is a part of H.K. (Hong Kong) therefore the laws governing it should be

[2]Tsing Shueng refers to the common properties of the clan, normally the land assets. The income from these properties would normally be used for ancestor worship.

H.K. (Hong Kong) laws or laws partly borrowed from China with special regard to Chinese customs. Naturally it will not do if laws are based upon the customs of villages, which are contrary to human feelings. (Tsin Pit Tat of Tai O: Comments on Chinese customs and customary rights, 3 June 1949)

This comment points to the variations in Chinese customary practices found in different villages in Hong Kong. It must be noted that after the Second World War, the population in the New Territories were often a mix of migrants from different districts of Guangdong. Different clans living in the same districts would have different customary practices on issues such as succession. In comparison with similar surveys conducted in other jurisdictions such as Taiwan in the Japanese occupation period, this survey in Hong Kong was very simple and not very relevant to the work conducted by the Strickland Committee. In addition, most of the information gathered required further investigation and study. Finally, in the Strickland Report, the reports of this survey were not included. The Committee just picked one report from Tai O Residents Association as representative of the opinions of the New Territories inhabitants.

In response to the questionnaire sent by the Strickland Committee, the Tai O Residents' Association gave more specific answers that could be useful for the Committee (Views of Tai O Residents' Association, 3 November 1949).[3] In this report, firstly, the Tai O Residents' Association did not give a response to the question of recommending that the doctrine of monogamy be introduced for Chinese residents in Hong Kong, and did not give any opinion for providing additional protection nor advise on the concubine in the family. Secondly, they considered that the concubine should be entitled to maintenance, and could have the right to obtain the Letters of Administration from the court. Thirdly, they agreed that if the children left behind the deceased are minors, a trustee could be appointed by the Court to administer the estate (Views of Tai O Residents' Association, 3 November 1949).

In sum, it is important to note that this survey of the New Territories people was not in-depth. The scope was too broad and without focus. The answers were, then, also too broad and the information taken did not make any significant contributions to the understanding of the Chinese customary practices in the New Territories. In addition, there was no survey on the operation of Chinese customary law at the local level, in particular on issues such as marriage and succession in the New Territories. The village organisations of the New Territories, and especially the New Territories administrators in the government, were not well-informed of the positions and ideas behind the Strickland Committee before taking the survey. Therefore, it was foreseeable that they would strongly oppose to the report of the Strickland Committee especially on the issues such as marriage reform and the abolition of concubinage. This will be dealt with later in this chapter.

[3] Their replies were reproduced and consolidated with other respondents in the Appendix to the Strickland Report (Committee on Chinese Law and Custom in Hong Kong, 1953, pp. 237-254).

4.2.3 Experts

The Strickland Committee relied upon legal experts to provide the relevant rules and principles of the Chinese customary laws in Hong Kong. The most influential figures in this field were Dr Vermier Yantak Chiu (also a member of the Committee) and Mr Chung King-pui (a member of the Committee but an Assistant to the Secretary for Chinese Affairs). Dr F. M. Tung (formerly the judge of the District Court Shanghai) was invited to attend the meetings for discussion. In addition, another member of the Committee, Dr Irene Ho Cheng, though not an expert in legal field, wrote a powerful memo to the Committee pushing strongly for the abolition of concubinage. With the support of Chiu, Cheng's arguments on the abolition of concubinage were finally written into the Strickland report.

Chiu's opinions made a significant contribution to the final report, some being reproduced in Appendix 9. On the determination of the status of a concubine, Chiu and Cheung had held different opinions, but only Chiu's comments were accepted and published in the report. Chiu was appointed a member of the Strickland Committee on 8 March 1950 (Letter from Claude Burgess, 8 March, 1950). Approximately 2 weeks after the appointment, Strickland wrote a letter to Chiu seeking his comments on controversial matters upon which Dr F. M. Fung had been previously consulted but remained inconclusive (Letter from Strickland, 21 March, 1950a). One of these was the issue of the dissolution of the relationship between a husband and a concubine: could an institution of a concubinage be created before a man had taken a *kit fat* wife (principal wife)? On the issue of *Kim Tiu* marriage, Strickland asked Chiu about the meaning of *ping chai* (equal wife) and whether it was possible for a man to have two *kit fat* wives or two wives of equal standing? Strickland considered that *Kim Tiu* marriage was in force in Guangdong in 1843 and wanted to know whether *ping chai* was also in force in 1843.

In reply, Chiu considered that three qualifications must be satisfied to have a *Kim Tiu* marriage. Firstly, the man who undertook a *Kim Tiu* marriage must become the adopted son of another family. Secondly, he must become the adopted son of his paternal uncle, and thirdly, he must be an only son in his own family. Chiu considered that this man could marry two wives, and he could inherit the estates of both his own branch and another branch of family. And, he was also responsible for the propagation of the future generations of both families. Therefore, such a man had two wives, called *ping chai* or equal wives. Chiu mentioned that the law of *Kim Tiu* marriage was made by Qianlong emperor, and "was in force in 1843" (Letter from Dr Vermier Yantak Chiu, 13 April 1950). However, Chiu failed to mention that there was a case in the Board of Punishments that stated that the first wife in such a marriage was called the wife, whereas the second so-called wife could only be called *t'sip* (see Chap. 2, n. 24).

In reply to the enquiries from Strickland on the issue of *t'sip*, Chiu argued that there were two distinctive features of the Chinese custom of taking a concubine

(Memorandum from Dr Chiu, 23 July 1950).[4] First, the husband was required to make a public announcement of his intention to take the woman as his *t'sip* by holding a dinner party for his relatives and friends. Second, the *t'sip* must be "initiated" into the family of her husband by kowtowing and serving tea to the first wife, which Chiu described as the *yup kung* (*yap kung*, entering to the palace). Chiu quoted two judgments of the *Da Li Yuan* to support his positions. The first was the Appeal Number 1534 of the 5th Year which the *Da Li Yuan* decided that a concubine should have an intention to live permanently and continuously and to become a member of the family (see Chap. 3, n. 24). Secondly, Chiu quoted another case by *Da Li Yuan*—Appeal number 186 of the 7th Year—on the status of *t'sip*:

> there must be [an] intention on the part of the paterfamilias to acknowledge the woman as his spouse besides his wife and as a member of his family; on the part of the *t'sip*. [T]here must be [an] intention to enter the family of the paterfamilias to become a member of the paterfamilias family with a position second to that of his wife. (This is "yup king" (*yap kung*). [emphasis in original] (Memorandum from Dr Chiu, 23 July 1950)

Chiu concluded that first, a man must have an intention to take a woman as his *t'sip*, and secondly, the intention of a woman to become his *t'sip* must be expressed by performances. He argued that the former should be made by public announcement, while the latter must be done by *yap kung*.

It is important to note that there was a flaw in Chiu's interpretation of *yap kung* which he claimed to be part of the judgment in the *Da Li Yuan*. The original extract of this case did not give any reference to the process of *yap kung* as described by Chiu (Guo 1972, p. 210). The full text of this case, which might not have been available to Chiu at the time he prepared his memorandum, gives no indication of any ceremony of *yap kung* (Huang 2012, pp. 114–118). And, the translated version of the extract given by the Strickland Report stated that:

> According to the general principles of law the proper interpretation is that there should be on the part of the head of the house an intent to acknowledge the woman to be a spouse other than his principal wife and as a member of his house, and, on the part of the *t'sip*, the consent to enter into his house to be a member inferior to that of the principal wife, and only then can the woman be recognized as lawful *t'sip* of the head of the house. (Committee on Chinese Law and Custom in Hong Kong 1953, p.161)

Chiu's argument on *yap kung* was not agreeable to another member of the Committee. Chung King-pui, Assistant Secretary of the Secretary for Chinese Affairs, who submitted a letter to the Committee about the status of what he understood to be the Qing custom of a "kept woman" (*Ngoi Shut*, Outside the Room). The "kept woman" was also regarded as a concubine to the family even though the woman lived outside the family (Letter from Mr Chung King Pui, 21 July 1950). Chung stated that he wrote this submission in 1948 for the purpose of a hearing by a Magistrate in Hong Kong on the status of a girl who was regarded as a concubine. Chung stated in this submission that sometimes the wife might object to her husband

---

[4]This memorandum was reproduced in the Strickland Report (Committee on Chinese Law and Custom in Hong Kong, 1953, pp. 205–206).

taking a concubine. So, in this situation, the husband might keep a woman secretly, who was known as a "kept woman", "with or without the consent of his parents and without the knowledge of his wife." Chung then stated that after the husband and this concubine were living together for some time, or after the concubine had given birth to a child, "he tells his wife and with her approval he brings the concubine (and her child if there is one) home where she will reside as a member of the family and will have the status of concubine" after formalities had been performed". The formalities in Chung's submission included the performance of *kowtow* and offering of tea to the senior members of the man's family, including the man himself, his wife and all relatives and any guest who may be present. Most important of all, Chung stated that the objection of the wife to the concubine could be overruled: "[S]ometimes the wife may still object, but the man's parent can (with the assistance of elders if necessary) overrule her (wife)" (Letter from Mr Chung King Pui, 21 July 1950). Therefore, it was doubtful whether *yap kung* was a mandatory requirement for the institution of concubinage either in Qing law or custom in Hong Kong.

It is also important to note that, even in the Hong Kong Government's administrative survey on the local customs in Hong Kong, not all ethnic groups performed *yap kung* as confidently described by Chiu. In a paper prepared by the government official Kenneth M.A. Barnett between January 1956 and September 1957 (Memo from J.W. Hayes, 12 September, 1978a), it is reported that, regarding the institution of concubinage in the Tanka ethnic group, if a virgin was married to a man as a concubine, "there is no ceremony of Yap Kung but the principal wife must agree". And if the woman was a married woman (someone else's wife who has left the husband in the previous marriage) "the man just takes her to his boat and no ceremony is required". This latter customary practice also applied to the Hoklo ethnic group (Memo from J.W. Hayes, 12 September, 1978a). At this juncture, it was also doubtful in the eyes of the Hong Kong Government administrators whether *yap kung* was a necessary ceremony that must be performed when a man was going to institute a concubinage in Hong Kong.

The differences between Chiu and other government administrators on the understandings of *yap kung* further proved that it was very difficult to have consensus on Chinese customary practices in Hong Kong and on the kind of customary practices that should be recognised by the Committee. The problem of arriving at a consensus on agreeable customs had been the centre of discussions in the meetings of the Committee. On 16 November 1950, Chiu wrote a letter to Strickland about a remark made by Strickland in the last meeting in the Committee. Chiu was frustrated by the alleged comment that Chiu's experiences were taken from North China so he would not be competent to give his judgment on the customs existing in Guangdong.

Chiu responded that first, he was a Cantonese and brought up in a Cantonese family in Hong Kong, so he was familiar with all the customs and practices existing in Guangdong. Secondly, although he mostly worked in North China, he had spent 2 years as Attorney General for the Zhongshan district and 1 year as Chief Justice at Jieyang (near Shantou). Thirdly, Chiu considered that the customs and practices in Guangdong were not that different from North China. Chiu regarded himself as an expert on Guangdong customs (Letter from Vermier Y Chiu, 16 November 1950). In reply, Strickland expressed regret for his remark and stated that Chiu's Cantonese connections were not only by birth and upbringing but also professional. Strickland admitted that he was confused by the opinions of the experts on Chinese laws and customs: "I am still a little bewildered by the diversity of views held by experts on a number of matters, but this occurs also with other law as well as the Chinese Law and Custom" (Letter from Strickland, 17 November, 1950).

In another instance, Chiu possibly overlooked some legal provisions in the GQC on the issue of an illegitimate child, which might have guided the Committee to different thinking on the strategy of how to deal with the status of illegitimate children after the abolition of concubinage (Memorandum on the Status of Children, n.d).[5] In one Committee meeting, one member, M. W. Lo, asked about the status of children born from unlawful unions, should concubinage be abolished. Lo argued that the Chinese people "would be very averse to such children being declared or considered illegitimate" (Memorandum on the Status of Children, n.d). In reply, Chiu wrote a letter on 22 July 1950 first stating that there was a provision regulating fornication with consent (*hejian*) in the GQC.[6] This provision made "adultery" an offence, and "if any male or female child by the fruit of such connextion [sic] shall be born, it shall be supported at the expense of the father" (Letter from Vermier Y. Chiu, 22 July 1950). Therefore, to Chiu, the customary practice was that the women would either procure an abortion during pregnancy or kill the child after birth. Chiu stated that "[B]ut by customs and practices the natural father may acknowledge his illegitimate child before his clan and in so doing the child become legitimate". He considered that the man might marry the natural mother or take her as his *t'sip*, in which case the illegitimate child would become legitimate (Letter from Vermier Y. Chiu, 22 July 1950). To Strickland, such legitimation outside marriage was totally alien to English Law, because first, under English law, a father might acknowledge parentage, the effect of which was to make him responsible to a limited degree for maintenance of the child. Also, Strickland mentioned that in English law the reputed father of a child might adopt his offspring (with the consent of the wife), but in the ancient and modern Chinese law, illegitimate sons could not be adopted sons. Strickland, in a memorandum issued to the members of the Committee, raised the difficulties in accommodating English law and traditional Chinese law. There is no mention of these matters published in the final report.

However, during the discussions regarding this issue, Chiu might have overlooked the legal principles on the recognition of the status of the children born out of wedlock in the GQC. These children in the GQC were called "son born by fornication" (*jianshengzhi*), and their right of succession was provided by Article 88 of the GQC. In it, the *jianshengzhi* would have half the portion of the other sons in the division of the estate. Furthermore, if there were only *jianshengzhi* after the death

---

[5] The memorandum is undated. However, the archival file indicates the date to be after 22 July 1950.

[6] On the provision of *hejian*, see Wong (2018).

of a husband (without any *di* or *su* son), this son could have the succession of the whole estate (Lu 2012, p. 43). As stated above, the discussions on this particular issue are not evident in the final report. It is important to note that the Committee, if well-informed, might have reached a different conclusion on the issue raised by M. W. Lo on whether it would be necessary to legitimise children born out of wedlock after the abolition of concubinage by following the Chinese customary practices.

4.2.4 Membership

Perhaps the most powerful voice urging for the abolition of concubinage came from a member of the Committee, Dr Irene Cheng. Cheng (Letter from Chan Yinghui, 23 August 1949) who argued that since the UK government was going to introduce democracy into Hong Kong,[7] "the preservation of Ching dynasty legislation in Hongkong is not only a social and legal anachronism but is also a hindrance to the establishment of democracy". She considered that "the discrimination against Chinese women countenances an injustice that is a disgrace to a colony which has signed the United Nations Bill of Human Rights". She urged the abolition of concubinage based on three grounds. First, on moral and social grounds, she considered that "in the family with concubines, the petty jealousies, bickerings [sic] and intrigues" meant that the family had an "unwholesome effect on children who from infancy are exposed to an atmosphere of rivalry, subterfuge and sexual indulgence which warps their characters". And that the wife and concubine "are constantly tormented by their insecurity and frustration". The institution of concubinage only benefited the man "and the man is rarely in a position to know the full effects, on the household, of his introduction of a provocative element in the shape of a concubine". Secondly, on political grounds, Cheng argued that the institution of concubinage attacked the very roots of equal rights of men and women, who were also taxpayers and should have equal treatment from the state. Thirdly, on financial grounds, Cheng argued that concubinage imposed an additional burden on the man and lowered the standard of living of a family. She stated that since the Hong Kong Government was promoting democracy, family welfare and a higher standard of living, the government could not, "without self-contradiction, perpetuate the evils of concubinage".

Next, Cheng attacked the arguments of those who favoured the institution of concubinage. First, she disagreed with the excuse which stated that due to the failure of the wife to give birth a male heir within the certain period of time, so a man had to find a concubine. Cheng said that "a large number of concubines have been taken after the birth of male heirs by the *Kit Fat* wife" [emphasis in original].

---

[7] Cheng might be referring to the limited democratic reform introduced by Governor Young, which was regarded as the Young Plan in 1946. Governor Young proposed to establish a Municipal Council and elected Legislative Council members but was finally dropped in 1952.

She also commented that, regarding the ancient prejudice against female children, once they had the right of inheritance and the means to earn a living, there was no rational ground for upholding the concubine. She therefore proposed a registration system for concubines, before the new law on the abolition of concubinage was imposed. Under her proposed registration system, Cheng argued that the children of registered concubines should be regarded as legitimate and have the right to inherit, though not necessarily with equal right to the children of the *kit fat* wife. To Cheng, the reasons for proposing such a system were that first, concubines normally had more children and, second, these children should not assume priority in the claim to the husband's estates, as priority should be accorded to the *kit fat* wife according to Chinese custom. Cheng also proposed that registered concubines should be entitled to a share of the inheritance in cases of intestacy, though the share of the estate should be determined by the government. She opposed giving concubines the power of administrating the husband's estates (Letter from Chan Yinghui, 23 August 1949).

4.2.5 Other Comments

Although Cheng was the strongest voice in the Committee urging for the abolition of concubinage, not all government officials shared her views. The Chinese Advisory Committee, a consultative committee established by the Secretary for Chinese Affairs, was asked to comment on Chinese customary marriages. In a meeting held on 12 October 1950, the Chinese Advisory Committee agreed that Chinese customary marriages should continue to be recognised in Hong Kong. However, they argued that the law or custom in force in 1843 should now be disregarded in favour of those in force in China now, "and this should be so irrespective of whether the parties concerned were domiciled in China or in Hong Kong" (Minute from Acting S.C.A., 18 October 1950). These comments were self-contradictory: the institution of concubinage had not been given legal recognition in the Civil Code of 1931 in China, and nor was Chinese customary marriage legally recognised. Therefore, if the relevant laws had to be changed in favour of those in force in China, then the abolition of concubinage was inevitable. On the other hand, the Chinese Advisory Committee called for the retention of Chinese customary marriage in Hong Kong, requiring that the institution of the concubinage had to be maintained. In this regard, the comments from the Chinese Advisory Committee were clever in that they were ambivalent on the issue of the abolition of concubinage.

But according to the questionnaire sent by the Strickland Committee to some organisations and senior political figures of Hong Kong Chinese, the abolition of the concubinage was mostly welcomed (Committee on Chinese Law and Custom in Hong Kong 1953, p. 237). These included the Hong Kong Council of Women, Kowloon Chamber of Commerce, P. C. Woo (Member of Reform Club of Hong Kong) and S. N. Chau, the Executive Council member. Chau also proposed that the existing law should be amended in order to bring it in alignment with the existing law in China (Committee on Chinese Law and Custom in Hong Kong 1953, p. 237).

However, only Sir Man Kam Lo disagreed openly. Seen in this light, it was inevitable that abolition of concubinage would be proposed in the Strickland Report, as indeed it was.

The Hong Kong Council of Women submitted their opinions to the Committee on the questionnaire after their extraordinary executive committee meeting. They agreed to introduce monogamy. And, they agreed that there must be proper recognition given to concubines who had already been accepted by a family. They also agreed what the children of recognised concubines should be accepted as legitimate. However, it was important to note that they disagreed that a recognised concubine should be entitled to administer the husband's estates. In other words, they proposed that the letters of administration should be given to the wife and not the concubine, which was contrary to the court decision in *Chan Yeung v Chan Shew Shi* (1925) (Letter of the Hon. Secretary, Hong Kong Council of Women, 15 June, 1949).[8]

4.2.6 Publication of the Report

At the end of November 1950, Strickland had almost finished and informed the members of the Committee that the last meeting would take place on 6 December 1950 (Letter from Strickland, 25 November, 1950b). On 8 December 1950, Strickland submitted a memorandum to the Colonial Secretary that he had submitted a copy of the report of the Committee (Letter from Solicitor General, 8 December 1950). Firstly, Strickland recommended that the government publicly publish the report and gather public opinion. Strickland also suggested that the government should further edit the report. For example, the report could be expanded to cover those legal issues as recorded in the Appendices. And, he asked that the government rearrange the Appendices in the report. Secondly, he considered that the report should be paragraphed consecutively, and the report and Appendices should be paginated consecutively (Letter from Solicitor General, 8 December 1950). Because the report had to be approved and signed by the members of the Strickland Committee, it subsequently took the Attorney General more than a month to forward this memorandum to the Colonial Office (Memorandum from Attorney General, 18 January 1951).

In the signed copy of the report of the Committee, there was some discussion on the issue of concubines. The report first mentioned that there was no ceremony for taking a concubine into a family. Also, the report mentioned that in 1910 there was an imperial edict that abolished purchase and ordered that go-betweens should arrange the union of concubinage. Before that the taking of a concubine was "purely a matter of bargain and sale, red chair and music being [sic] not required nor even allowed". There was no reference to support the claim in the report that an imperial edict in 1910—presumably a reference to a decree by the Qing emperor—abolished

[8] On the case of *Chan Yeung v. Chan Shew Shi* (1925), see Chap. 3, n. 79.

the purchase of concubines.[9] In 1910, a new Criminal Code was promulgated by the Qing government which was supposed to regulate the criminal offences relating to the sale of woman for marriage. On the other hand, a draft Civil Code, including new family laws, was published for consultation by the National Assembly (*Ze Zheng Yuan*).[10] However, the provisions of this imperial edict were not included in the new Criminal Code. And the Civil Code had not been passed due to the end of Qing authorities in 1911. It is doubtful how this imperial edict had actually applied in Qing and the Republic of China. Seen in this light, it is also doubtful how the Committee could reach the conclusion that a go-between was required by law to arrange the taking of a concubine when such provisions were short-lived.

Moreover, in this report, a diversity of views on the status of a concubine were recorded in the copy, especially on the issue of whether the consent of a wife was necessary when the husband took a concubine (Original Signed Copy of Report, ca. 18 January 1951, p. 16). The report first stated that it was still undecided whether an expression of the intention of a concubine "to become a member of the family of the paterfamilias in a position second to that of the wife could be communicated otherwise by *Yap Kung*". And, the Committee also had to ascertain whether, if *Yap Kung* was necessary, how far the wife's consent was necessary (Original Signed Copy of Report, ca. 18 January 1951, p. 16). However, the Committee was inclined to consider that it was better for *yap kung* to be performed because this could resolve any allegation of bigamy and, secondly, because *yap kung* was a conclusive proof that a concubine had agreed to take a position inferior to that of the wife, it could help to defy any claim that she had been taken as a wife. Although the Committee considered that the consent of a wife was inconclusive, the following was added in a handwritten note:

> Nevertheless the Chinese members of the Committee from the experience in the Colony consider that one a man is married to a *tsai*, it is necessary to obtain her consent by yap kung to the taking of a *t'sip*. (Original Signed Copy of Report, ca. 18 January 1951, p. 17)

---

[9] The Strickland Committee report did not give any detail of the relevant laws. They might possibly refer to the imperial edict promulgated in January 1910 which prohibit all forms of human trafficking. In this imperial edict "Provisions Prohibiting All Forms of Human Trafficking" (Jinge mǎimài renkou tiaokuan), Article 6 stated that the institution of concubinage must be arranged by a go-between. It prohibited the sale of women by contract for instituting the concubinage between the man and the mother of the proposed "concubine". This provision also gave the right of the mother to visit her daughter after the institution (Da Qing Xin Fa Ling, 2010a, vol. 7, p. 124). In 1911, the Qing government urged those local officials to place those provisions especially relating to the prohibition of sale of women in public notice (Da Qing Xin Fa Ling, 2010b, vol. 8, p. 234). However, the provision relating to the use of go-between for the institution of concubinage fell short of moving towards the abolition of concubinage and did not give any additional right to concubine.

[10] The National Assembly was the parliament established in 1910 by the Qing government for the preparation of establishing a constitutional monarchy.

This further showed that the Committee was inclined to make *yap kung* a precondition of the husband taking a concubine, which was contrary to the GQC and other customary practices.[11]

Another controversy, though less likely litigated before the magistrate under the Qing administration, was the issue of the dissolution of concubinage. It is important to note that, while there was no special requirement for the husband to dissolve the institution of concubinage, a marriage between a husband and wife could only be dissolved in accordance with the rules as specified in Article 116 of the GQC.[12] However, the Committee reached the conclusion that the institution of concubinage was intended to be a permanent one because of the phrase in Article 116 that "[t]he above rules also apply to the case of *t'sip*s—the penalty in each case being reduced 2 degrees". This suggested that the rules of the dissolution of marriage with a wife also applied to a concubine. The Committee reported that this view was supported by the advice of Chiu and by another expert, Dr Tung. But, a careful reading of the whole Article 116 shows that such reading of the code was inconclusive. The phrase that the Committee quoted did not apply to the whole article, but only applied to the offence immediately preceding the phrase. The full text of the GQC as translated by Jones is:

> If, because the husband (abandoning the wife) has run away, and she does not, within the three-year period notify the authorities, but runs away, she will receive 80 strokes of the heavy bamboo. If, without authorization, she remarries (on her own), she will receive 100 strokes of the heavy bamboo. If she is a concubine, each [punishment] will be reduced two degrees. (Jone, 1994, pp. 133–134)

This shows that the phrase considered by the Committee in fact referred to cases in which a wife ran away without first notifying the authorities (in other words the local magistrate) about the disappearance of her husband within a 3-year period; an offence for which she would receive a penalty. It was very difficult to understand how the Committee, though not in full agreement with Chiu and Dr Tung's opinions, reached the conclusion that this phrase suggested that the institution of concubinage was intended to be permanent. There was no causal relationship between this offence and the conclusion reached by the committee (see Chap. 2, Sect. 2.4.5).

In sum, the findings of the Committee could only add more confusion rather than clarification to the understanding of the status of the concubine in Qing law.

---

[11] See Chap. 2, Sect. 2.4.6.

[12] Article 116 was read as "Whenever the wife has given no (cause) for repudiation (among the seven [causes] for repudiation), and where (as regards the husband) there are no circumstances that extinguish the duty [between them], and [the husband] without a valid reason) repudiates her, he will receive 80 strokes of the heavy bamboo. Even if she has committed one of the seven acts that constitute grounds for repudiation: (she has no son; she is wanton; she does not serve her parents-in-law; she talks too much; she steals; she is jealous and envious; she has a malignant disease), if there is one of the three impediments to repudiation: (she has carried on three years of mourning [for the husband's parents]; the husband was previously poor and they have become rich; the home from which she was married no longer exists), but he repudiates her, [the punishment] will be reduced two degrees, and he will be forced to take her back as his wife" (Jones 1994, pp. 133–134).

The reliance upon specific legal experts in this field was discernible since there was only about a year to write up the report. In addition, the archives show that there were only limited local legal experts available who were familiar with Chinese law and customary practice in both China and Hong Kong, which further reduced the opportunity for wider consultation. But since one of the duties of the Committee was to find out the laws and customs as practiced in Hong Kong, a comprehensive survey of Chinese customary practice would have made the findings more convincing and allowed the legal reform to absorb elements of Chinese customary law. In fact, some government officials had conducted their own investigations into local customs in the New Territories. Their findings, though not totally related to the practice of Qing law, reflected customary practices in the New Territories which could have been helpful for proposing legal changes to Chinese customary law. For example, as mentioned earlier, it was reported by the government local officials that for ethnic sub-groups such as the Tanka, the consent of a wife was not a precondition of the institution of concubinage (see Sect. 4.2.3).

4.2.7 Abolition of Concubinage

The Committee had some considerations in proposing changes to the Hong Kong laws relating to Chinese law and custom. These were later published in the final report as submitted by the Strickland Committee. First, because of the flow of migrants to and from China and Hong Kong, the Chinese community would consider that changes in China should also be made for the Chinese in Hong Kong in those spheres in which Chinese law and custom still prevailed. But, such changes, the Committee considered, would create legal uncertainty because change in China was unpredictable. They would also make litigation difficult because the courts would have to rely upon expert evidence in making judicial decisions. Secondly, the Committee must consider the need of the people in Hong Kong who were domiciled in Hong Kong under the rules of the private international law. In other words, they must be familiar with the principles of English law which governed their lives in Hong Kong, including those principles which governed those spheres in which Chinese law and custom prevailed (Committee on Chinese Law and Custom in Hong Kong 1953, pp. 36–37). It was the Committee's view that the needs of this part of the community had to be taken into account. Further, the Committee "must not lose sight of the influx of customs and ideas from China and the fact that persons not domiciled in Hong Kong may be resident here for considerable periods and may marry and acquire property here" (Committee on Chinese Law and Custom in Hong Kong 1953, p. 39).

The Committee reached a compromise on the legislative proposal—a blending of traditional Chinese and common laws that would create a workable new legal regime to regulate Chinese laws and customs in Hong Kong. The Committee hoped that by carefully crafting the above considerations in the report, the legislative proposals would be more readily understood by the courts when making interpretations.

On the other hand, on marriage reform including the abolition of concubinage, the Committee had some additional considerations. Firstly, they observed that in the Republic of China period *t'sip* did not have any status under the Civil Code of 1931, but were permitted to survive in the guise of a member of the household. Secondly, the People's Republic of China had been increasingly monogamous in practice as well as in theory. Thirdly, the government of the People's Republic of China had pledged to uphold the equality of the sexes, and so it would be doubtful whether the concubine could survive as a *t'sip* or a kept mistress. Fourthly, in Hong Kong, marriage had become increasingly monogamous. And, there were "quite a number of Chinese" in Hong Kong who had complied with the form of marriage as specified in the Civil Code 1931 of the Republic of China ("Chinese modern marriages") and did not follow the form of the traditional Chinese customary marriage Fifth, the Committee also noted that there were few *t'sips* in the New Territories and these occurred because the wife could not give birth to any child or look after the family (Committee on Chinese Law and Custom in Hong Kong 1953, pp. 39–41).

During the course of discussion, the Committee also noted that the institution of concubinage led to a lack of harmony and the affected women often felt frustrated. The concubine could be jealous because of her inferior status in the family. Further, the wife could feel that her position was a matter of form lacking substance because the husband had done little for matrimonial happiness. Another member of the Committee opined that his acquaintance who had taken *t'sip* bitterly regretted it because of the trouble caused by the jealousies and lack of harmony among the women (Committee on Chinese Law and Custom in Hong Kong 1953, pp. 41–42). In addition, the Committee noted that the institution of concubinage was inconsistent with the doctrine of sexual equality in China and the Hong Kong Council of Women had strongly urged them to uphold the principle of equality. The Committee also noted that the public opinion was so far agreed that concubinage should be abolished by legislation (though Sir Man Kam Lo disagreed with this).[13]

However, the Committee also had to face other considerations. Some argued that the end of the institution of concubinage could be achieved by public opinion or public education or, on the other hand, that there was overwhelming demand for prohibiting the institution. Further, some might have worried that the abolition of concubinage would lead to the extra-matrimonial unions if the wife was barren and that such unions would be even worse than the institution of concubinage (Committee on Chinese Law and Custom in Hong Kong 1953, p. 42). The Committee further considered that there was no legislative pressure to propose that the wife should be compelled to submit to the concubine, nor was any legislative proposal to relax the requirement of the consent of the wife in the institution of concubine.

Based on the above considerations, the Committee recommended the prohibition of any new union of concubinage and that any such new union would be deprived of legal effect. On existing concubines, the Committee proposed that the status should remain unchanged, because "such unions were lawfully created and should continue

[13] This will be dealt with later in this chapter.

unless severed by the means permissible under prevailing customs". And, the offspring of this union would still be legitimated, resulting in great hardship. Also, the Committee also recommended that, even in the case of a monogamous marriage where the wife died or the couple divorced, the husband could remarry a new wife and the husband did not have to dissolve the union of concubinage before remarriage (Committee on Chinese Law and Custom in Hong Kong 1953, p. 43).

Because of the introduction of monogamous marriage and the abolition of concubinage, other legislative changes would be inevitable. There were some major recommendations to change the Chinese marriage system. First, the Committee recommended the recognition of Chinese modern marriages that followed the legal rules under the Civil Code 1931 of the Republic of China, in other words, an open ceremony before at least two witnesses that should be validated with retrospective effect and should be permissible in the future.[14] Second, before the appointed day, Chinese customary or modern marriages with a wife and concubine should be registered at the Secretary for Chinese Affairs (Committee on Chinese Law and Custom in Hong Kong 1953, p. 72). Additionally, the Committee introduced a registration system at the Marriage Registry for monogamous Chinese customary or modern marriages, so that no Chinese marriage, customary or modern, would be complete without registration. Third, a bigamous marriage with another wife after the appointed day should be punishable as bigamy. The taking of *t'sip* was not to constitute a marriage or a form of marriage. There would be no legal effect in taking, or attempting to take, a *t'sip*. In other words, the *t'sip* was not recognised in law. Fourth, the dissolution of the union of concubinage was still to be governed by Chinese customary marriage. Fifth, in the case of posthumous adoption, the consent of the surviving widow (including the concubine) of the deceased husband was necessary. If the adopted person was *sui juris*, his consent for such relationship would be necessary; if not, then his parent or guardian's consent was required (Committee on Chinese Law and Custom in Hong Kong 1953, pp. 72–74). Sixth, the concubine would have suitable maintenance of the intestate when she was still in a lawful matrimonial relationship with the husband at his death. Seventh, on the letter of administration, the Court had decided, under the case of *Chan Yeung v Chan Shew Shi* (1925), to grant the letters of administration to the concubine (see Sect. 3.2.7). On this issue, the Committee recommended letting the Courts determine to whom, in view of the recommendations made by the Committee on the changes in the Chinese law and custom in Hong Kong. Eighth, on the issue of domicile, the Committee recommended following the English law, meaning that the laws to be applied in the case depended on the laws of the place where a person was considered to be domiciled. The proof of Hong Kong domicile could be raised in court. Finally, the Committee recommended establishing a Committee of experts to advise the possibility of codification of Chinese law and custom (Committee on Chinese Law and Custom in Hong Kong 1953, pp. 76–77).

[14] In the Marriage Reform Ordinance passed in 1971, it was decided that "Chinese modern marriages" would not to be recognised after the "appointed day".

Based on the above recommendations, the Committee attached five proposed legislative bills in the appendices (Committee on Chinese Law and Custom in Hong Kong 1953, p. 78). These are:

1. The Chinese Marriage (Regulation) Bill
2. The Divorce (Amendment) Bill
3. The Distribution of Estate (Instate Chinese) Bill
4. The Chinese Law and Custom (Miscellaneous Provisions) Bill
5. The New Territories Regulation (Amendment) Bill

The most important one was the Chinese Marriage (Regulation) Bill which set up the legislative framework on the abolition of concubinage (Committee on Chinese Law and Custom in Hong Kong 1953, p. 259). In this legislative proposal, the first part proposed the definition of some terms. In Clause 3, the "appointed day" means such day as the Governor may be by proclamation appoint for the commencement of this ordinance. "Chinese customary marriage" was defined as a marriage in accordance with Chinese law and custom. And "Chinese law and custom" was defined as the laws and customs of China as would have been valid immediately prior to the 5th day of April 1843 and as such applicable to Chinese inhabitants of the colony. Additionally, "tsai" and "*t'sip*" had the meanings attributed to them by Chinese law and custom (Clause 3). Next, Clause 4 proposed the abolition of concubinage. It stated that after the appointed day:

(a) No man may take any woman as his *t'sip* and any attempt to create such status shall be null and void; and
(b) sexual intercourse between a married man and any woman whom a man shall have taken or attempted to take a *t'sip* in contravention of this section shall be adultery.

But this clause did not propose to make adultery an offence.[15] Clause 5 protected the status of a *t'sip* and her children born before the appointed day.[16] In the explanation attached to this proposed bill, the act of adultery would not be an offence, and the remedies available to the wife would be going to the Divorce Court or other proceedings for maintenance or the custody of children (Committee on Chinese Law and Custom in Hong Kong 1953, p. 277). Clause 6 emphasised that after the appointed day Chinese customary marriage or Chinese modern marriage would be monogamous:

[15] There was a Chinese Marriage Preservation Ordinance enacted in 1912 to make Chinese men who committed adultery as an offence. This ordinance was repealed in 1971 by Marriage Reform Ordinance (Ord. No. 68/70).

[16] Clause 5: Nothing here in contained shall affect –

(a) the status or rights of a tsip lawfully taken before the appointed day or as the case may be before the husband of such tsip acquired a domicile in Hong Kong; or
(b) the status or rights of the children whether born before or after the appointed day, of a tsip lawfully taken, before the appointed day or before the husband of such tsip domicile in Hong Kong.

> Saving as thereafter provided the celebration after the appointed day of a Chinese customary marriage with a tsai and the celebration after such day of a Chinese modern marriage with a tsai shall imply a voluntary union for life of the husband and the tsai to the exclusion of others.

In the explanation attached to this proposed bill, *Kim Tiu* marriage would be abolished under this provision—because of the provision on monogamy—coupled with the Clause 11 that, after the appointed day, the husband had to register existing *t'sip* or children with the Secretary for Chinese Affairs before taking a new wife (Committee on Chinese Law and Custom in Hong Kong 1953, pp. 277, para, 5).[17]

Amendments were proposed to the Marriage Ordinance 1875 to make provisions that Chinese customary marriage and Chinese modern marriage must be registered under the charge of a Deputy Registrar of Marriages.[18] Another major change proposed was a new registration system that required husbands who had concubines to register with the Secretary for Chinese Affairs, along with details of any children from a Chinese customary or Chinese modern marriage.[19] If the husband were to celebrate a new marriage without making a registration, that marriage would still be valid but should constitute an offence for which the penalty would be a fine of one thousand dollars and imprisonment for six months.[20] Similarly, if the husband provided inaccurate information or omitted any materials on registration, the penalty for this offence would be one thousand dollars and imprisonment for 6 months.[21] Such a situation would make the marriage voidable, and the court could grant the wife a decree of annulment if the wife applied to the court within 6 months of the conviction of the husband. The court would not grant such a decree if the husband satisfied the court that the wife had prior knowledge of the facts that the husband

---

[17] In this context, there would never be any two wives in a matrimonial relationship after the appointed day.

[18] Clause 9 (1)(a) "2A (1) There shall be established for the registration of marriages to which section 6 of the Chinese Marriage Ordinance, 195, applies, such number of local registries as the Governor considers are required for the needs of the Chinese community, each of which shall be under the change of a Deputy of Marriages".

[19] Clause 10 (1) "No exempted Chinese marriage shall be celebrated prior to the registration by the husband of the intended marriage with the Secretary for Chinese Affairs of particulars of any tsip lawfully taken by the husband who is still his tsip at the date when such registration is effected, of all children of the previous customary marriage or Chinese modern marriage and of such other particulars as the Governor in Council may by regulation prescribe".

[20] Clause 10 (2) "Save as hereinafter provided failure to comply with subsection (1) shall not invalidate such marriage but shall constitute an offence: Penalty: a fine of one thousand dollars and imprisonment for six months".

[21] Clause 10(3) "If the husband of any exempted Chinese marriage contracted pursuant to subsection (1) shall have furnished any information required by virtue of subsection (1) and of any regulations made thereunder which he knew or had reason to believe to be inaccurate in any material particular or by reason of the omission of any material particular he shall be guilty of an offence: Penalty: a fine of one thousand dollars and imprisonment of six months".

had failed to disclose.[22] Another clause provided that such marriage would not be regarded as a bigamous marriage.[23]

There was a clause in the proposed legislation relating to the domicile of Chinese people in Hong Kong. Clause 13 specified a presumption of domicile for a person who had attained the age of 21 years old in Hong Kong, if any one of the following four situations could be proven. Firstly, they had lived in Hong Kong for a continuous period of 7 years after attaining the age of 21 years and prior to the date at, or before which, it was alleged that Hong Kong domicile had been acquired. Secondly, they had married in Hong Kong and lived there continuously for a period of 5 years after that marriage and prior to the date at, or before which, it was alleged that Hong Kong domicile had been acquired. Thirdly, they had acquired British nationality in Hong Kong and thereafter resided continuously in Hong Kong. Fourthly, they were born in Hong Kong and thereafter resided continuously in Hong Kong (Clause 13(1) a–d). This presumption could be rebuttable if there was evidence that the person had no intention to domicile in Hong Kong. But, evidence such as the fact that the person and their family had visited the tombs or resting places of ancestors outside of Hong Kong, or had registered births, marriages and deaths or other family matters in registers kept outside Hong Kong, or maintained some connection with clansmen outside Hong Kong, could not be used to rebut that presumption (Clause 13(3)).

Other amendments to law were proposed to give a husband and wife of Chinese race the right of dissolution of marriage by a joint petition to the Court. In the Divorce (Amendment) Bill, it was proposed that they could do so on the grounds of mutual consent (Committee on Chinese Law and Custom in Hong Kong 1953, p. 278).[24] Such a petition was to be filed at the Supreme Court, and the registrar would question the parties to ascertain that they had freely consented to the dissolution.[25] If there was some hope of reconciliation, or both parties did not understand the effect of the dissolution of marriage, or had not freely consented to, or wished to withdraw consent, the registrar might refer the parties to the Secretary for Chinese Affairs.[26] The Secretary for Chinese Affairs would inquire into the matter and issue a report to the registrar. If the registrar was satisfied with the report, then he would either put the case to the judge or dismiss the petition.[27] The judge would consider

[22] Clause 10(4) "If the husband of any exempted Chinese marriage shall be convicted of an offence under subsection (3) on the ground that he has failed to disclose the existence of any lawfully taken tsip or any child of the previous marriage, such marriage shall be voidable at the instance of the tsai and the Court may on the application of the tsai made by petition filed within six months of such conviction having become final grant the tsai a decree of annulment unless the husband shall satisfy the Court that the tsai had prior to the marriage full knowledge of the fact which he failed to disclose..."

[23] Clause 11(1) "An exempted Chinese marriage shall not be deemed to be a bigamous marriage by reason of the fact that at the time it is celebrated the husband was still in matrimonial relationship with one or more tsips".

[24] Clause 3, amendment to section 51(1).

[25] Amendment to section 51(2).

[26] Amendment to section 51(3).

[27] Amendment to section 51(5).

the case and grant a decree of dissolution of marriage. However, the judge might not grant the decree if he was dissatisfied with the provisions for custody maintenance and education of the minor children of the marriage, or the parties intimated that they were unwilling to conform with the judge's suggestions.[28]

The Committee also proposed the Distribution of Estate (Intestate Chinese) Bill. Clause 8 was a special provision in relation to the concubine. It specified that if a Chinese male died intestate, so long as the concubine remain chaste or unmarried, there would be a payment of an annuity to her. The annuity would be charged upon the shares of beneficiaries, but not upon the wife. This would ensure that the wife's share of the estate would not be affected, because under the legal changes proposed by this law, the residuary estates might devolve upon the wife. It is noted that the Committee intended that the wife's share should not be diminished simply because she had to pay the annuity of the concubine (Committee on Chinese Law and Custom in Hong Kong 1953, p. 292).[29]

One of the biggest challenges to these legislative bills was that the Committee failed to define Chinese customary marriage. First, the definition of Chinese customary marriage was too broad and therefore difficult to follow either by the public or the courts. In the legislative proposal, "Chinese customary marriage" was defined as "a marriage in accordance with Chinese law and custom", but Chinese law and custom was defined as "such of the laws and customs of China as would immediately prior to the 5th day of April 1843, have been applicable to Chinese inhabitants of the Colony". Such definitions did not map out the spaces nor the scope of the marriage laws in the Qing dynasty, not to mention that the rules and regulations might not be easy to find even with the support of Chinese law experts. It is also important to note that, considering the complexities of the Qing laws as exemplified in Chap. 2, different Chinese law experts might have different understandings of the application of Chinese laws and customs. To make things worse, even the Committee could not reach a conclusion on the proper definition of Chinese customary marriage, despite many rounds of meetings and discussions. Secondly, the Committee failed to define clearly the elements of determining the status of a concubine in the laws and customs immediately prior to the 5th day of April 1843. Failing to define the institution of concubinage in the proposed bills would create more problems than solutions. This would make the laws more litigious. For example, whether *yap kung* was a condition of the recognition of a concubine in a family was still an unresolved question. In the presence of such significant uncertainty, it would be practically impossible for the government officials to follow up the report.

[28] Clauses (6) (7) and (8) of the new section 51.

[29] Clause 8(1) "When a Chinese male dies intestate leaving tsip lawfully taken before the appointed day then, if by provisions of this Ordinance the whole of the residuary estate devolves upon the tsai, then the residuary estate, or, if that is not the case, such part of the residuary estate as does not devolve upon the tsai, shall stand charged with the payment to such tsip for so long as she remains chaste and unmarried..."

4.3 Post-strickland Report: Rejection of the Abolition of Concubinage in 1956

The biggest challenge for the government was to map out a strategy to follow up with the Strickland Report. The report proved to be very difficult to comprehend even for government officials who were familiar with the subject areas, such as the Secretary for Chinese Affairs. Furthermore, the key issue of the report, the abolition of concubinage, was proving too much for Chinese senior figures in the Executive and Legislative Councils and Chinese businessmen to swallow. Finally, after two meetings in the Executive Council, the Strickland Report was officially shelved in 1956.

4.3.1 Submission to the Executive Council in 1952

It took almost 2 years for government officials to compile, publish and submit the Strickland Report to the Executive Council for discussion. After Strickland submitted a signed copy of the report to the Colonial Secretary, in December 1950 (six months after the submission of the Strickland Report to government authorities), the Deputy Colonial Secretary minuted to the Clerk of Councils that he had retained the file to pursue but had discovered that the letters of thanks had not been issued to the members of the Strickland Committee, which he therefore decided to do. Furthermore, he questioned whether, since Strickland was back in Hong Kong, this copy would be amended before submission to the Executive Council for consideration (Minute of D.C.S., 30 July 1951). The letters were finally issued, but on 9 August 1951, the Acting Chief Secretary Ronald Ruskin Todd minuted to the Governor that the draft Strickland Report was not suitable in its present form for presentation to the Executive Council or anyone else (Minute of R.R.T., 9 August 1951b). On 25 August 1951, Todd minuted that since he did not have time to study the report as the Acting Colonial Secretary, he was requesting that the file should be sent to him when he resumed his duty as the Secretary for Chinese Affairs on 27 August 1951 (Minute of R.R.T., 25 August, 1951a). A further delay was caused by the transfer of the file to John Crichton McDouall (as Social Welfare Officer) 6 months later. McDouall minuted back to Todd that he agreed that the report had to be tackled by a piecemeal approach (Minute of McDouall, 4 June 1952). On 17 June 1952, when Brian Charles Keith Hawkins assumed position as Secretary for Chinese Affairs, the file remained in his hands. In a minute to the Colonial Secretary, he similarly agreed to a piecemeal approach (Minute of Hawkins, 16 June 1952). The file had been circulated among different senior government officials for 18 months but no further action had been taken by anyone.

On 18 June 1952, in a minute submitted by H. G. Richards to the Colonial Secretary, Richards summarised the development of the post-Strickland Report. He argued that this matter should not be let go by default, and he suggested the Colonial

Secretary to ask McDouall to deal with it as a matter of urgency and that the advice of the Secretary for Chinese Affairs should be sought as quickly as possible (Minute of D.C.S., 18 June). In a minute to the Governor, the Colonial Secretary recommended that the Secretary for Chinese Affairs follow up with some suggestions on the proposed piecemeal approach (Minute of C.S., 19 June 1952). Finally, the Colonial Secretary decided to submit the report to the Executive Council for discussion. On 2 July 1952, an Executive Council memorandum on the report was issued to the Executive Council members in which the government admitted that the subject was complex and no recommendation for action had yet been formulated. The paper proposed that after the meeting in the Executive Council the Legislative Council would then discuss the report and that the administration would consider what possible action would be taken on the various matters dealt with in the report separately (Memorandum for Executive Council, 2 July, 1952).

On 9 September 1952, the Executive Council decided that the report should be printed and published as soon as possible, together with Sir Man Kam Lo's memorandum commenting on the report (Memo of Colonial Secretariat, 9 September 1952; Committee on Chinese Law and Custom in Hong Kong, n. d.). Next, the Executive Council decided that Parts VI (relating to the summary of the recommendations of the report) and VII (relating to the methods of carrying the recommendations into effect) of the report should be published in Chinese, together with the Chinese version of Sir Man Kam Lo's memorandum. Finally, the Executive Council decided that publication should be accompanied by a brief official statement about the recommendations and that comments from the public were welcomed (Memo of Colonial Secretariat, 9 September 1952).

4.3.2 Sir Man Kam Lo's Comments and the Executive Council's Decision

After the Executive Council's meeting, government departments had to follow up with the decisions made at the meeting. The Secretary for Chinese Affairs was asked to make the necessary arrangements for the translation work with the assistance of the Attorney General. The Colonial Secretariat also suggested that the Secretary for Chinese Affairs consider whether an explanatory note or introduction to the report should be included in the abridged Chinese version. The memo also asked Strickland to settle the details of the report before he left Hong Kong (Memo of Colonial Secretariat, 9 September 1952, para. 4).

But the most serious attack upon the report came from this prominent and influential senior political figure: Sir Man Kam Lo. He was the one who had pressed for reform on Chinese law and custom in Hong Kong and the establishment of the Strickland Committee. Yet, now he stood in opposition, strongly disapproving of the efforts of the Committee and its report. Lo first argued against the approach to the legal reform proposed by the Committee. He considered that the proper approach, if any existing Hong Kong law was out of date, should be to bring it up to date. But if there was old law which was so "out-moded" that the consensus of opinion of those affected was for replacement or modification, "then legislate for such replacement or modification but in such a way as not to result in its total abolition" (Letter from Man Kam Lo, 21 July 1952, para. 20). After stating his views on legal changes, he argued strongly against the abolition of concubinage. He first disagreed that an adopted son could ease the desire for son in a family, because "[T]o most people an adopted child can never take the place of a child of one's own blood," in particular to the old-fashioned Chinese (Letter from Man Kam Lo, 21 July 1952, para. 29).

Lo also argued that personally he knew many a respected man of the old school who took a concubine at the express request of his wife, because a concubine could look after the husband during times of poor health or infirmity. He agreed that the institution of concubinage was gradually dying, "[i]f so let it die", and he agreed that one of the factors that would hasten this demise was the popularity of registry marriage. However, he insisted that mere legislation was never effective in dealing with the abolition of concubinage. Further, he considered that the report's proposal to leave the legitimacy of the issue (in other words, offspring) of a concubine dependant upon the conscience of the father, who could legitimise them either by adoption or by a court order, was unfair to the offspring. For the above reasons, he disagreed with the conclusion given by the report that public opinion in Hong Kong favoured legally abolishing concubinage, "though note is taken that this view is not so far shared by Sir Man Kam Lo". Lo reacted furiously against social calls for the abolition of concubinage and remarked, at the end of his comments: "if mine were the only voice in the wilderness to object to the proposed outlaw of this institution, I can only say that I am a little surprised, perhaps a little disappointed, but wholly unrepentant!" (Letter from Man Kam Lo, 21 July 1952, para. 28).

On the other hand, government officials also had the opportunity to render their views on the report after checking the text. Kenneth Barnett (during the time he was the Chairman of Urban Council) commented on the use of *Tsu Mo* or *Shu Mo* in the Strickland Report, where it was used to refer to a concubine who had to take care of the children born by other concubines. He also added a special note on the status of concubinage (Letter of Kenneth Barnett, 30 September 1952). He agreed with the Committee that *t'sip* is a kind of wife, and added that "in writing to her husband a 'Ts'ai' wife must refer to herself as 'Ts'ip'". He explained that in Chinese custom, when writing a letter, one had to "downgrade" oneself and "upgrade" the recipient. Therefore, in writing to a friend, one had to refer to oneself as "younger brother" even if the recipient was older, and in fact this did not mean that the recipient was an actual younger brother or cousin. Barnett concluded that "the difference between Ts'ai and Ts'ip is less than the difference between elder brother and younger brother, that is to say, they belong to the same class or stratum of relationship" (Letter of Kenneth Barnett, 30 September 1952, para. 14). On this part, in reply to Barnett, Strickland tried to tease Barnett by saying that he would be "considering stimulating [sic] a letter to the paper after the publication of the report" (Letter of Strickland, 7 October 1952).

4.3.3 Publication of the Report and Public Consultation

On 9 January 1953, the Colonial Secretary, R. W. Primrose, asked for support from the Secretary for Chinese Affairs on translating Parts VI and VII of the report into Chinese by arranging a translator from the Supreme Court to carry out this task. A draft press release was issued to the Secretary for Chinese Affairs commenting on the draft. In the same memo, Primrose sought advice from the Secretary for Chinese Affairs (a copy was sent to Attorney General as well for comments) on whether the focus would be on the abolition of concubinage because he had found it difficult to make the draft:

> I cannot help fearing that the press (including the Public Relations Officer!) may be inclined to seize the sensational question of concubinage, and I am not even certain that some of the Committee's recommendation could not be invested with a spurious political significance. Not that this is any argument against a covering statement, but it makes it more difficult to draft. (Memo from R. W. Primrose, 9 January 1953)

Also, in the same memo, Primrose asked the Secretary for Chinese Affairs to help ask Sir Man Kam Lo to arrange the translation of his own memorandum into Chinese (Memo from R. W. Primrose, 9 January 1953). But the Secretary for Chinese Affairs did not recall that he had promised to ask Lo for a translation and commented that "such as translation of that memorandum (of Lo), if could be done at all, would be quite useless ... without a translation of the whole Report, which is out of the question" (Memo from the Secretary for Chinese Affairs, 13 January 1953). Since the Secretary for Chinese Affairs was reluctant to help do any further work on Lo, the Colonial Secretariat had to ask Lo directly: he submitted the translated work of Parts VI and VII to Lo and asked him to deal with his own translation (Letter from Ronald Holmes, 23 January 1953a). Another letter written from Holmes to Lo on 29 January 1953 confirmed to Lo that a fairly free translation was acceptable, "especially of those parts which contain cross-reference to the full English text" (Letter from Ronald Holmes, 29 January 1953b). On 20 February 1953, the Chinese version of the foreword of the report was submitted to the Clerk of Councils, Ian MacDonald Lightbody (Memo from Chan Kwok Ying, 20 February, 1953). Lightbody estimated that the translation of the Parts VI and VII would be finished in mid-March 1953 (Memo from I. M. Lightbody, 20 February, 1953c). On 12 March 1953, Lo submitted the Chinese version of his memorandum to Lightbody (Letter from Man Kam Lo, 12 March 1953). On 13 March 1953, the translated work of Parts VI and VII of the report was completed, and a payment of $250 was arranged (Memo from I. M. Lightbody, 13 March 1953a). On 17 April 1953, it was agreed by the Financial Secretary that 750 copies were printed (Memo from I. M. Lightbody, 18th April 1953b). On 29 April 1953, the printed copy was submitted to the Legislative Council (Sessional Paper No. 18 of 1953, 29 April 1953).

The Hong Kong Government sent a copy of the report to the Secretary of States for the Colonies. In the savingram sent to the Secretaries of States for the Colonies at London, the memo from the Governor reported that since they were inviting public comment, so "it is not proposed to take any action on the recommendation which have been made" (Savingram from the Governor, 5th May 1953). In reply, an official from the Colonial Office stated that "I shall await your comments when public opinion on the Report has had time to make itself known" (Letter from Colonial Office, 4 July 1953). The Colonial Office did not pay too much attention on this issue, until the proposal of the abolition of concubinage as proposed in the Strickland Report was rejected by the Hong Kong government. This would be discussed later in the next chapter.

4.3.4 The Disapproval of the Report in Executive Council 1956

The public consultation began after the submission of the report to the Legislative Council on 29 April 1953, but the public response was very poor. In a letter sent by the Secretary for Chinese Affairs, Todd, to the Colonial Secretariat, Burgess, Todd mentioned that "I can say now that, as usual, the response has been very disappointing and that the comments are not helpful" (Letter from the Secretary for Chinese Affairs, 1 October 1954). The next step, as suggested by Todd, was either the government might have to appoint another committee to make recommendations on ways to implement the recommendations of the original Committee or, failing this, the government might instigate a round-table conference to study the four main subjects, namely, marriage, divorce, adoption and inheritance and succession, and the implementation of these areas one by one (Letter from the Secretary for Chinese Affairs, 1 October 1954). Todd considered that paragraph 34 of the comments of Lo were extremely helpful because in effect, this paragraph mentioned that if the government could not get much assistance from public opinion and that the government should make up its mind and go ahead. Todd considered that when the government published the legislative bill, or amended the ordinance, then at that time the government would come to know the real public opinion (Letter from the Secretary for Chinese Affairs, 1 October 1954).[30]

4.3.5 Opinions from Hong Kong Council of Women

The Hong Kong Council of Women was the main social organisation that pressed the government to implement the recommendations of the report, particularly the abolition of concubinage, as soon as possible. On 26 March 1954, the Hong Kong

[30] Paragraph 34 of Lo's memorandum was read as: "In view of the obvious necessity of ascertaining public opinion, and the difficulty of doing so, it is for consideration whether Government should not come to see early tentative views of the own not, indeed, in detail, but on broad lines—so that Government could publish such tentative views avowedly as tentative views, at the same time as the publication of the Report, it only to stimulate constructive views and reactions from the public".

Council of Women sent a letter to the Colonial Secretary, Robert Black. The Council of Women said that there was a strong impression that different classes of women were unanimously agreed to support the principle of monogamous marriage. The Council of Women further argued that the laws of Hong Kong should be brought up to date and in line with the modern Chinese Law of the Nationalist Government (in other words, the Civil Code 1931 of the Republic of China) now operative in Taiwan, the law of the People's Republic of China and the United Nation's Charter of Human Rights. The Council of Women also mentioned that they had received more than 30 letters, one of which bore 41 signatures, and all letters with one exception were in favour of the abolition of concubinage. They had also sent a copy of chapter VI of the Strickland Report to various organisations and all, except for the Chinese Chamber of Commerce, were in support of the abolition of concubinage (Letter of the Hong Kong Council of Women, 26 March, 1954). In the letter, the Council of Women enclosed a copy of the report of a sub-committee that had studied the recommendations of the Strickland Committee. In this report the sub-committee suggested that the definition of *t'sip* had to be confined to *yap kung* concubines only. This meant that a concubine had to be officially received into the family, offering tea to the legal wife and the Ancestors' Tablets and receiving a name from the legal wife (Comments on the Report, 26 March, 1954). Further, the Council of Women argued that the appointed day for the abolition of concubinage should be fixed at 6 months or a year after the adoption of the recommendations of the report. Regarding the registration system proposed by the Committee, they argued that any concubine who had not been registered within a year of the appointed day would not have legal status as a concubine. On adoption, the Council of Women argued that because of the principle of equality between men and women, it was unnecessary to adopt any other child posthumously. But if the widow would like to have a child, she should have a right to adopt either a male or female within the five degree of mourning. Moreover, they argued that the surviving spouse should be given at least one third of the residuary estate (on succession of intestacy) instead of one quarter as proposed by the Committee (Letter of the Hong Kong Council of Women, 26 March, 1954).

Given the little progress of the public consultation on the report, the government could only issue a letter of acknowledgement to the Hong Kong Council of Women, with a paragraph that "[y]our comments will be studied together with others received and it is possible that it will be some time before Government can reach a final decision on the recommendations made in the report" (Letter from the Colonial Secretary, D.C.C. Luddington, 29 March 1954). In reply, the Hong Kong Council of Women urged the government to take immediate steps to implement the report (Letter from the Council of Women, R.T. Eng, 12 April 1954).

4.3.6 Opposition from Secretary for Chinese Affairs

As mentioned by the Council of Hong Kong Women, one organisation—the Chinese Chamber of Commerce—stood out and reacted strongly against the abolition of concubinage. On 15 August 1953, they sent a letter to the Secretary for Chinese Affairs that they were "in favour of the opinion set out in the Hon. Sir Man Kam Lo's Memorandum on the subject" (Letter from the Chinese Chamber of Commerce, 15 August, 1953). Because Lo strongly disagreed with the recommendations given by the report, the Chinese Chamber of Commerce did not support the abolition of concubinage. The Chinese Chamber of Commerce represented the wealthiest Chinese businessmen in Hong Kong so their voices were influential. They disagreed with the recommendations of the report, which if implemented would lead to a drastic change of Chinese law and custom.

On 8 August 1954, the Secretary for Chinese Affairs, Todd, wrote a memo to the Colonial Secretary reporting his observations on the public consultation. First of all, he considered that the response of the public and the press was disappointing. He highlighted the letter given by the Chinese Chamber of Commerce to the Secretary for Chinese Affairs, in which the Chinese Chamber of Commerce did not support the abolition of concubinage (Memorandum of S.C.A., 8 October 1954). Similarly, a letter written by four prominent social leaders (they were Justices of the Peace) submitted a letter to the government was in support of Lo's memorandum: in other words, they too disagreed with the abolition of concubinage. One citizen wrote to Lo (which Lo then forwarded to the Secretary for Chinese Affairs) that he was in support of Lo's memorandum but the letter was far from clear. Todd further stated that the press was in support of the abolition of concubinage (Memorandum of S.C.A., 8 October 1954, paras. 4–5). To Todd, the only question was whether a measure of recognition should continue to be accorded to the institution of concubinage, but it was clear that public opinions had differed. Some groups were in support of the report but other social organisations pressed for the status quo.

Again, by quoting paragraph 34 of Lo's memorandum, Todd argued that, firstly, any constructive views could only be known when the public was made to realise that, "by the publication of the Bills of new or amended Ordinances, that the Government is going ahead"[emphasis in original] (Memorandum of S.C.A., 8 October 1954, para. 8). Secondly, Todd argued that since the government could state that the report was a monumental work, so the acceptance of the recommendations of the Strickland Report would not be in toto. The government would introduce the legislation (either by bill or amended ordinance) by piecemeal in four areas—marriage, divorce, adoption and inheritance and succession—due to the pressure of work on the Legal Department (Memorandum of S.C.A., 8 October 1954, para. 9).

Todd mentioned that he had discussed the opinions of the above with Lo. Both agreed that the next step might be to discuss the report again in the Executive Council. Todd proposed that by putting the opinions to the Executive Council, the members of the Executive Council would discuss whether to proceed with the "piecemeal" approach. Or, in other words, whether to make legislative changes in the four subject areas stated above, taking into account the recommendations of the Strickland Report. To this end, Todd's proposal implied that he did not intend to accept all recommendations of the report, and he did not intend to accept an immediate abolition of concubinage at this stage. In other words, he rejected the call from the Hong Kong Council of Women.

On 4 November 1954, the Colonial Secretariat Donald Collin Cumyn Luddington prepared a draft Executive Council memorandum for Todd to comment on (Memo from the Colonial Secretariat, 4 November, 1954a). In reply, Todd expressed clearly that he was in support of Lo's position to reject the abolition of concubinage. He mentioned that while the Executive Council was considering the report, "it might be as well grasp the nettle of the '*t'sip*' or concubine and take a decision on this subject", because that decision was important for the Attorney General to prepare for any legislation. Todd stated that his view was the same as Lo, that the government should not attempt to abolish concubinage in Hong Kong by legislation, because of the complications involving the registration of concubine and of their children, "but that we should allow the institution to die out as it is already, slowly but surely, dying out an account of the pressure of public opinion and the course of events in China" (Memo from the Secretary for Chinese Affairs, 12 November, 1954).

The Hong Kong Council of Women asked for the progress of the report on 8 June 1955 (Letter from the Hong Kong Council of Women, 8 June, 1955). But most important of all, the Colonial Office had made two enquiries on the development of the report on 11 November 1955 (Savingram from the Secretary of States for the Colonies, 11 November 1955) and 4 April 1956 (Savingram from the Secretary of States for the Colonies, 4 April 1956), respectively. In reply, though the Hong Kong Government stressed the importance of soliciting public opinion on the report, they put the blame squarely on the absence of the key Executive Council member, Sir Mam Kam Lo, since at the time the report was made Lo had held different views. They argued that the Lo's absence in the Executive Council's meetings caused the delay of the Executive Council in examining the report:

> The fact that Sir M.K. Lo had taken such an interests in this matter made it desirable that any discussion in Executive Council on the various recommendations should take place with his present and this is one of the reasons why further consideration has been deferred from time to time owing to his absence firstly for part of the time in 1954 and again last year. (Letter from E. B. David, 26 April 1956)

The Colonial Office acknowledged the letter without further comments. No political pressure was given from London at that time, so the Hong Kong Government had a free hand to disapprove the Strickland Report.

On the other hand, to facilitate the discussion for the Executive Council, the Legal Department had prepared a table summarising the recommendations and the relevant information for the Executive Council. On 11 June 1956, the Crown Counsel, John Pakenham-Walsh submitted a table to Attorney General on this matter. Pakenham-Walsh considered that one recommendation stood out—whether the institution of concubinage had to be abolished. He considered that most of the remaining recommendations in the report were based upon the assumption that all future marriage would be monogamous. So, he argued, before proceeding to examine the recommendations of the report in detail, the government must decide the issue of concubinage (Note from John Pakenham-Walsh, 11 June 1956).[31]

His view was echoed by the Attorney General. In a minute submitted to the Colonial Secretary, the Attorney General A. Ridehalgh considered that the fundamental issue was the abolition of concubinage and that the Executive Council should make decision on it. He stated that if the answer was "yes", the Legal Department would have to tackle the detailed examination of the rest of the recommendations of the report, but if the answer was no, the government had to rethink the issues again. Therefore, Ridehalgh proposed to amend the draft Executive Council memorandum "with a view to focussing[sic] attention, and inviting a decision, upon the question of the abolition of concubinage" (Minute from Attorney General, 2 August 1956). In another minute, the Secretary for Chinese Affairs agreed with this approach and amendments (Minute from Attorney General, 2 August 1956).

In the final version of the Memorandum Executive Council on 27 August 1956, the approach proposed by the Attorney General was to specifically ask the Executive Council members to decide on the abolition of concubinage:

> This question (of the abolition of concubinage) in any case have [sic] to be decided sooner or later on its own merits if the Report is to be followed up at all, and it is considered that an initial decision whether or not to accept the recommendation would clear the air considerably in dealing with the remainder of the Report. (Memorandum for Executive Council, 27 August 1956, para 5.)

Also, it was stated in the memorandum that if the recommendation of the abolition of concubinage was accepted by the Executive Council, the Legal Department "could tackle the detailed examination of the rest of the Report, including the legislative proposals given in the Report" (Memorandum for Executive Council, 27 August 1956, para 7.). But if the Executive Council rejected the abolition of concubinage, "considerable further study and thought will have to be given to the implementation of the rest of the Report, and as to how far other recommendations in the Report are affected by the concubinage" (Memorandum for Executive Council, 27 August 1956, para 8).

The outcome, however, was that on 11 September 1956, the Executive Council rejected the Committee's recommendations regarding the abolition of concubinage by legislation. In addition, the Executive Council asked the government further examine the report in order to assess how, in light of the above decision, other recommendations of the report could be implemented (Memorandum from Colonial Secretariat, 13 September 1956). So, in sum, after 7 years of discussion, the abolition of concubinage as suggested by the Strickland Committee was rejected, due mainly to the opposition from Sir Man Kam Lo and the Secretary for Chinese Affairs.

[31] The original note was filed in Chinese Customs and Law Committee: Chinese Law and Customs Correspondence (HKRS158-3-2(1)).

4.4 Conclusion

The Strickland Committee was established in 1948 due to the complexity and the confusions caused by the legal changes of the Chinese family laws in Mainland China. The Civil Code in 1931 in the Republic of China, and the new Marriage Law 1950 in the People's Republic of China had shown that marriage in China had become monogamous. Furthermore, the forms of Chinese marriage had changed from the traditional Chinese customs of "three books and six rites" to a simplified practice as stipulated and promoted in the Civil Code 1931 of the Republic of China. With the influx of the immigrants from Mainland China, such changes would cause confusion in the system of colonial Hong Kong, which still recognised traditional Chinese marriage with the institution of concubinage. During the time that Strickland was preparing the report, the Committee indeed had to decide whether Chinese marriage system in Hong Kong should be monogamous, following legal changes in the Republic of China and the People's Republic of China. If so, then the abolition of concubinage became the key issue at the heart of the report. With further influence from the Committee member Dr Irene Cheng, and the petition of the Hong Kong Council of Women, the Strickland Committee decided to propose to abolish concubinage in Hong Kong.

But the report failed to ignite a public debate in the wider community. For the general reader, this report was very difficult to read. For readers who had some understanding of Chinese law and custom, there were some inconsistencies in the report regarding the proper understanding of some key Chinese family law concepts. For example, the report failed to give a definite answer on whether *yap kung* was an essential element in the institution of concubinage. Another example was that, on the dissolution of the concubinage, the report failed to reach a conclusion on whether such dissolution could be freely made unilaterally, either by the husband or the concubine. And, as mentioned earlier, the legislative proposal as given by the report could only cause confusion because even the proposed bill did not define clearly the meaning of "Chinese customary marriage". Bearing in mind that the implementation of the Strickland Report might have created more confusion with far-reaching implications for family law in the Chinese community, and the opposition from senior Chinese political figures and businessmen, the Strickland Report was rejected in 1956.

It is very important to note the slight difference on the issue of abolition of concubinage taken by Lo and the Secretary for Chinese Affairs. To the former, there should be an outright rejection of the abolition of concubinage. To the latter, the Secretary for Chinese Affairs would have preferred to let the institution of concubinage die out naturally rather than abolish by legislation.[32] That did not mean that the

[32]As recorded in the Strickland Report, a simplified version of the questionnaire was sent to the various associations of residents in the New Territories. Their views, as confirmed by the District Commissioners, Mr Keen and Mr Barrow, that the concubinage was rare. And the New Territories representatives considered that the practice of concubinage was slowly becoming extinct but

Secretary for Chinese Affairs was in support of the system of concubinage. The government's position was ambivalent after the rejection of the Strickland Report. Then after 1957, when the Hong Kong Government was still hesitant to opt for the legislative abolition of concubinage, the Colonial Office stepped in and asked for the abolition of concubinage as quickly as possible. Under political pressure from the Colonial Office, the Hong Kong Government decided to go ahead with the abolition of concubinage. This will be discussed in the next chapter.

References

Abridged version in Chinese. (1952, September 15–1953, August 4). *Chinese law and custom Report–Publication of an abridged version in Chinese 15.09.1952 – 04.08.1953*, (HKRS 41-2-61). The Hong Kong Record Series, Hong Kong.

Cheung Chau: Comments. (1949, June 3). *Chinese custom 1949–1972, Cheung Chau: Comments on Chinese Customs and Customary Rights, 3 June 1949*, (HKMS178-1-69). The Hong Kong Record Series, Hong Kong.

Comments on the Report. (1954, March 26). *Chinese law and custom, letter of the Hong Kong Council of Women to the Colonial Secretary 26 March, 1954: Comments on the Report and Recommendation of the Committee on Chinese Law and Custom*, (HKRS 41-1-3106-5). The Hong Kong Record Series, Hong Kong.

Committee on Chinese Law and Custom in Hong Kong. (1953). *Chinese law and custom in Hong Kong: Report of a Committee Appointed by the Governor in October, 1948*. Government Printer: Hong Kong.

Committee on Chinese Law and Custom in Hong Kong. (n.d.). *Report of committee on Chinese law and custom*. Hong Kong: Government Printer, (File 2/3351/47 II) (X.C.S. 60).

Da Qing Xin Fa Ling 1901–1911. (2010a). Vol. 7, Beijing: The Commercial Press.

Da Qing Xin Fa Ling 1901–1911. (2010b). Vol. 8, Beijing: The Commercial Press.

Government Committee on Chinese Law and Custom. (1949, March 25). *Chinese custom 1949–1972, Government Committee on Chinese Law and Custom, 25 March 1949*, (HKMS178-1-69). The Hong Kong Record Series, Hong Kong.

Guo, W. (1972). *Da Li Yuan pan jue li quan shu (A Compilation of the Judgments of Da Li Yuan)*. Taipei: Chengwen. (Original work published in 1931).

Huang, Y. (2012). *A compilation of the Civil Precedents of the Supreme Court in the Early Republic of China: Family*. Taipei: Li Zhai She.

Letter from Chan Yinghui. (1949, August 23). *Customs and law committee: Chinese law and customs correspondence, letter from Chan Yinghui to Strickland: Memorandum in Favour of the Revision of Laws Affecting Chinese Women Resident in the Colony of Hong Kong, 23 August 1949*, (HKRS158-3-2(1)). The Hong Kong Record Series, Hong Kong.

Letter from Claude Burgess. (1950, March 8). *Chinese customs and law committee: Chinese law and customs correspondence, letter from Claude Burgess, Deputy Colonial Secretary to Vermier Yantak Chiu, 8 March, 1950*, (HKRS158-3-2(1)). The Hong Kong Record Series, Hong Kong.

favoured its being permitted to die a natural death rather than by legislative action to hasten its decease, Strickland Report (Committee on Chinese Law and Custom in Hong Kong, 1953, para. 61). Seen in this light, the Secretary for Chinese Affairs had indeed adopted the approach taken from the New Territories residents on the issue of concubinage.

Letter from Colonial Office. (1953, July 4). *chinese law and custom, letter from Colonial Office to the Governor of Hong Kong, 4 July 1953*, (HKRS 41-1-3106-5). The Hong Kong Record Series, Hong Kong.

Letter from Colonial Office. (1964, December 17). *Chinese law and custom: Letter from Colonial Office, J. D. Higham to Colonial Secretariat, E. B. Teesdale*, (HKRS 41-1-3106-10). The Hong Kong Record Series, Hong Kong.

Letter from Dr Vermier Yantak. (1950, April 13). *Chinese customs and law committee: Chinese Law and Customs Correspondence, Letter from Dr Vermier Yantak Chiu to Strickland, 13 April 1950*, (HKRS158-3-2(1)). The Hong Kong Record Series, Hong Kong.

Letter from E. B. David. (1956, April 26). *Chinese law and custom, letter from E. B. David to J. T. A. Howard-Drake, Far Eastern Department, Colonial Office, 26 April 1956*, (HKRS 41-1-3106-5). The Hong Kong Record Series, Hong Kong.

Letter from Man Kam Lo. (1947, November 21). *Chinese law and custom, letter from Man Kam Lo to Hon S.C.A., 21 November, 1947*, (HKRS 41-1-3106-1). The Hong Kong Record Series, Hong Kong.

Letter from Man Kam Lo. (1952, July 21). *Chinese law and custom, letter from Man Kam Lo to Clerk of Councils, 21 July 1952*, (HKRS 41-1-3106-5). The Hong Kong Record Series, Hong Kong.

Letter from Man Kam Lo. (1953, March 12). *Chinese law and custom report letter from Man Kam Lo to I. M. Lightbody, 12 March 1953*, (HKRS 41-2-61). The Hong Kong Record Series, Hong Kong.

Letter from Mr Chung King Pui. (1950, July 21). *Chinese custom and law committee: Chinese law and custom opinion, letter from Mr Chung King Pui with memorandum on old Chinese customs of marrying a concubine, 21 July 1950*, (HKRS158-3-3). The Hong Kong Record Series, Hong Kong.

Letter from Ronald Holmes. (1953a, January 23). *Chinese law and custom report letter from Ronald Holmes to Sir Man Kam Lo, 23 January 1953*, (HKRS 41-2-61). The Hong Kong Record Series, Hong Kong.

Letter from Ronald Holmes. (1953b, January 29). *Chinese law and custom report letter from Ronald Holmes to Sir Man Kam Lo, 29 January 1953*, (HKRS 41-2-61). The Hong Kong Record Series, Hong Kong.

Letter from S.N. Chau. (1947, November 24). *Chinese law and custom, letter from S.N. Chau to Hon S.C.A., 24 November, 1947*, (HKRS 41-1-3106-1). The Hong Kong Record Series, Hong Kong.

Letter from Solicitor General. (1950, December 8). *Chinese law and custom, letter from Solicitor General to Hon. CS, 8 December 1950*, (HKRS 41-1-3106-1). The Hong Kong Record Series, Hong Kong.

Letter from Strickland. (1950a, March 21). *Chinese customs and law committee: Chinese law and customs correspondence, letter from Strickland to Dr Vermier Yantak Chiu, 21 March, 1950*, (HKRS158-3-2(1)). The Hong Kong Record Series, Hong Kong.

Letter from Strickland. (1950b, November 25). *Chinese customs and law committee: Chinese law and customs correspondence, Letter from Strickland to the member of the Committee, 25 November, 1950*, (HKRS158-3-2(1)). The Hong Kong Record Series, Hong Kong.

Letter from the Chinese Chamber of Commerce. (1953, August 15) *Chinese law and custom, letter from the Chinese Chamber of Commerce, Pee Look Hui to the Acting Secretary for Chinese Affairs, 15 August, 1953*, (HKRS 41-1-3106-5). The Hong Kong Record Series, Hong Kong.

Letter from the Colonial Secretary. (1954, March 29). *Chinese law and custom, letter from the Colonial Secretary, D.C.C. Luddington, to the Council of Women, Mrs. Mathilde Ng, the Council of Women, 29 March 1954*, (HKRS 41-1-3106-5). The Hong Kong Record Series, Hong Kong.

Letter from the Council of Women, R.T. Eng. (1954, April 12). *Chinese law and custom, letter from the Council of Women, R.T. Eng to the Colonial Secretariat, D.C.C. Luddington, Colonial Secretariat, 12 April 1954*, (HKRS 41-1-3106-5). The Hong Kong Record Series, Hong Kong.

Letter from the Hong Kong Council of Women. (1955, June 8). *Chinese law and custom, letter from the Hong Kong Council of Women to D. C. C. Luddington, Colonial Secretariat, 8 June, 1955,* (HKRS 41-1-3106-5). The Hong Kong Record Series, Hong Kong.

Letter from the Secretary for Chinese Affairs. (1954, October 1). *Chinese law and custom, letter from the Secretary for Chinese Affairs to the Colonial Secretariat, 1 October 1954,* (HKRS 41-1-3106-5). The Hong Kong Record Series, Hong Kong.

Letter from Vermier Y Chiu. (1950, November 16). *Chinese customs and law committee: Chinese law and customs correspondence, letter from Vermier Y Chiu to Mr Strickland, 16 November 1950,* (HKRS158-3-2(1)). The Hong Kong Record Series, Hong Kong.

Letter from Vermier Y. Chiu. (1950, July 22). *Chinese custom and law committee: Chinese law and custom opinion, letter from Vermier Y. Chiu to Strickland, 22 July 1950: Illegitimate Children under Tsing Law and Custom, 22 July 1950,* (HKRS158-3-3). The Hong Kong Record Series, Hong Kong.

Letter of Kenneth Barnett. (1952, September 30). *Chinese law and custom, letter of Kenneth Barnett to George Strickland, 30 September 1952,* (HKRS 41-1-3106-5). The Hong Kong Record Series, Hong Kong.

Letter of Strickland. (1952, October 7). *Chinese law and custom, letter of Strickland to Barnett, 7 October 1952,* (HKRS 41-1-3106-5). The Hong Kong Record Series, Hong Kong.

Letter of the Hon. Secretary. (1949, June 15). *Chinese customs and law committee: Chinese law and customs correspondence, letter of the Hon. Secretary, Hong Kong Council of Women to the Committee, 15 June 1949,* (HKRS158-3-2(1)). The Hong Kong Record Series, Hong Kong.

Letter of the Hong Kong Council of Women. (1954, March 26). *Chinese law and custom, letter of the Hong Kong Council of Women to the Colonial Secretary, 26 March 1954,* (HKRS 41-1-3106-5). The Hong Kong Record Series, Hong Kong.

Lu, J. (2012). *Qingmo Minchujiachan zhidu de yanbian: Congfenjia xichan dao yichanjicheng* [*The Evolution of the Family Property System in Late Qing and Early Republican Period*] (p. 43). Taipei: Yuanzhao.

Ma Wan: Comments. (1949, June 3). *Chinese Custom 1949–1972, Ma Wan: Comments on Chinese Customs and Customary Rights, 3 June 1949*, (HKMS178-1-69). The Hong Kong Record Series, Hong Kong.

Memo from Chan Kwok Ying. (1953, February 20). *Chinese law and custom report memo from Chan Kwok Ying to Mr I. M. Lightbody, 20 February, 1953,* (HKRS 41-2-61). The Hong Kong Record Series, Hong Kong.

Memo from D.C. (1949, February 25). *Chinese custom 1949–1972, Memo from D.C. to D.O.O., 25 February 1949,* (HKMS178-1-69). The Hong Kong Record Series, Hong Kong.

Memo from I. M. Lightbody. (1953a, April 18). *Chinese law and custom report memo from I. M. Lightbody to the Registrar of the Supreme Court, 13 March 1953*, (HKRS 41-2-61). The Hong Kong Record Series, Hong Kong.

Memo from I. M. Lightbody. (1953b, April 18). *Chinese law and custom report, memo from I. M. Lightbody to Government Printer, 18 April 1953,* (HKRS 41-2-61). The Hong Kong Record Series, Hong Kong.

Memo from I. M. Lightbody. (1953c, February 20). *Chinese law and custom report memo from I. M. Lightbody to Government Printer, 20 February, 1953,* (HKRS 41-2-61). The Hong Kong Record Series, Hong Kong.

Memo from J.W. Hayes. (1978a, September 12). *Marriage reform ordinance, memo of Paper on Chinese Customary Marriages from J.W. Hayes (Town Manager & D.O. Tsuen Wan) to Thomas Chan (Secretary for the New Territories), 12 September, 1978,* (HKRS 927-1-21). The Hong Kong Record Series, Hong Kong.

Memo from J.W. Hayes. (1978b, July 3) *Marriage reform ordinance, memo of Paper on Chinese Customary Marriages from J. W. Hayes (Town Manager & District Officer, Tsuen Wan) to Secretary for the New Territories, 3 July 1978,* (HKRS 927-1-21). The Hong Kong Record Series, Hong Kong.

Memo from R. W. Primrose. (1953, January 9). *Chinese law and custom report, memo from R. W. Primrose to Hon. S. C. A., 9 January 1953,* (HKRS 41-1-3106-5). The Hong Kong Record Series, Hong Kong.

Memo from Solicitor General. (1948, March 10). *Chinese law and custom, memo from Solicitor General to Hon. C.S., 10 March 1948,* (HKRS 41-1-3106-1). The Hong Kong Record Series, Hong Kong.

Memo from the Colonial Secretariat. (1954a, November 4). *Chinese law and custom, memo from the Colonial Secretariat, D. C. C. Luddington to the Secretary for Chinese Affairs, 4 November, 1954,* (HKRS 41-1-3106-5). The Hong Kong Record Series, Hong Kong.

Memo from the Secretary for Chinese Affairs. (1953, January 13). *Chinese law and custom, memo from the Secretary for Chinese Affairs to Colonial Secretariat, 13 January 1953,* (HKRS 41-1-3106-5). The Hong Kong Record Series, Hong Kong.

Memo of Colonial Secretariat. (1952, September 9). *Chinese Law and Custom, Memo of Colonial Secretariat to Hon. Attorney General, Hon. Secretary for Chinese Affairs, 9 September 1952,* (HKRS 41-1-3106-5). The Hong Kong Record Series, Hong Kong.

Memo from the Colonial Secretariat. (1954b, November 4). *Chinese law and custom memo, from the Colonial Secretariat, D. C. C. Luddington to the Secretary for Chinese Affairs, 4 November, 1954,* (HKRS 41-1-3106-5). The Hong Kong Record Series, Hong Kong.

Memo from the Secretary for Chinese Affairs. (1954, November 12). *Chinese law and custom memo, from the Secretary for Chinese Affairs, R. R. Todd to the Colonial Secretary, 12 November, 1954,* (HKRS 41-1-3106-5). The Hong Kong Record Series, Hong Kong.

Memorandum for Executive Council. (1952, July 2). *Chinese law and custom, memorandum for Executive Council: Report of the Committee on Chinese Law and Custom, 2 July, 1952,* (HKRS 41-1-3106-1). The Hong Kong Record Series, Hong Kong.

Memorandum for Executive Council. (1956, August 27). *Chinese law and custom: Memorandum for Executive Council: Report of Committee on Chinese Law and Custom*, (HKRS 41-1-3106-5). The Hong Kong Record Series, Hong Kong.

Memorandum from Attorney General. (1951, January 18). *Chinese law and custom, memorandum from Attorney General to Hon. C.S. 18 January 1951,* (HKRS 41-1-3106-1). The Hong Kong Record Series, Hong Kong.

Memorandum from Colonial Secretariat. (1956, September 13). *Chinese law and custom, memorandum from Colonial Secretariat, D.C.C. Ludington to Attorney General, Report of the Committee on Chinese Law and Custom, 13 September 1956,* (HKRS 41-1-3106-5). The Hong Kong Record Series, Hong Kong.

Memorandum from Dr Chiu. (1950, July 23). *Chinese custom and law committee: Chinese law and custom opinion, memorandum from Dr Chiu to Strickland, 23 July 1950,* (HKRS158-3-3). The Hong Kong Record Series, Hong Kong.

Memorandum of S. C. A. (1954, October 8). *Chinese Law and Custom, Memorandum of SCA to the Colonial Secretary, 8 October 1954,* (HKRS 41-1-3106-5). The Hong Kong Record Series, Hong Kong.

Memorandum on the Status of Children. (ca. 1949) *Chinese customs and law committee, memorandum on the Status of Children Born Out of Wedlock after the Abolition of Concubinage, n.d.,* (HKRS 158-3-3). The Hong Kong Record Series, Hong Kong.

Minute from Acting S.C.A. (1950, October 18). *Chinese customs and law committee: Chinese law and customs correspondence, minute from Acting S.C.A. to Solicitor General: Extract from the Minutes of the Fourth Meeting of the Chinese Advisory Committee held on the 12th October 1950, 18 October 1950,* (HKRS158-3-2(1)). The Hong Kong Record Series, Hong Kong.

Minute from Attorney General. (1956, August 2). *Chinese law and custom, minute from Attorney General to Colonial Secretary, 2 August 1956,* (HKRS 41-1-3106-5). The Hong Kong Record Series, Hong Kong.

Minute from D.C.S. (1948a, April 19). *Chinese law and custom, minute from D.C.S. to Hon C.S., 19 April 1948,* (HKRS 41-1-3106-1). The Hong Kong Record Series, Hong Kong.

Minute from D.C.S. (1948b, October 6). *Chinese law and custom, minute from D.C.S. to Hon. A.G., 6 October 1948,* (HKRS 41-1-3106-1). The Hong Kong Record Series, Hong Kong.
Minute from S.C.A. (1948a, September 14). *Chinese law and custom, minute from S.C.A. to Hon. C.S., 14 September 1948,* (HKRS 41-1-3106-1). The Hong Kong Record Series, Hong Kong.
Minute from S.C.A. (1948b, March 16). *Chinese law and custom, minute from S.C.A. to Hon. C.S., 16 March 1948,* (HKRS 41-1-3106-1). The Hong Kong Record Series, Hong Kong.
Minute from S.G. (1948a, May 12). *Chinese law and custom, minute from S.G. to Hon C.S., 12 May 1948,* (HKRS 41-1-3106-1). The Hong Kong Record Series, Hong Kong.
Minute from S.G. (1948b, September 14). *Chinese law and custom, minute from S.G. to Hon. C.S., 28 May 1948,* (HKRS 41-1-3106-1). The Hong Kong Record Series, Hong Kong.
Minute from Secretary for Chinese Affairs. (1956, August 15). *Chinese law and custom, minute from Secretary for Chinese Affairs to Colonial Secretary, 15 August 1956,* (HKRS 41-1-3106-5). The Hong Kong Record Series, Hong Kong.
Minute from Solicitor General. (1949), January 27). *Chinese law and custom, minute from Solicitor General to P.R.O., 27 January, 1949,* (HKRS 41-1-3106-1). The Hong Kong Record Series, Hong Kong.
Minute of C.S. (1952, June 19). *Chinese law and custom, minute of CS to YE, 19 June 1952,* (HKRS 41-1-3106-1). The Hong Kong Record Series, Hong Kong.
Minute of D.C.S. (1951, July 30). *Chinese law and custom, minute of DCS to C of C, 30 July 1951,* (HKRS 41-1-3106-1). The Hong Kong Record Series, Hong Kong.
Minute of D.C.S. (1952, June 18). *Chinese law and custom, minute of DCS to CS, 18 June 1952,* (HKRS 41-1-3106-1). The Hong Kong Record Series, Hong Kong.
Minute of Hawkins. (1952, June 16). *Chinese law and custom, minute of Hawkins to CS, 16 June 1952.* (HKRS 41-1-3106-1). The Hong Kong Record Series, Hong Kong.
Minute of McDouall. (1952, June 4). *Chinese law and custom, minute of McDouall to Todd, 4 June 1952,* (HKRS 41-1-3106-1). The Hong Kong Record Series, Hong Kong.
Minute of R.R.T. (1951a, August 25). *Chinese law and custom, minute of RRT, 25 August, 1951,* (HKRS 41-1-3106-1). The Hong Kong Record Series, Hong Kong.
Minute of R.R.T. (1951b, August 9). *Chinese law and custom, Minute of RRT to YE, 9 August 1951,* (HKRS 41-1-3106-1). The Hong Kong Record Series, Hong Kong.
Minute to Hon C. S. (1947, November 5). *Chinese law and custom, minute to Hon C.S. from J. Barrow, 5 November 1947,* (HKRS 41-1-3106-1). The Hong Kong Record Series, Hong Kong.
Northern Lama Island: Comments. (1949, June 3). *Chinese custom 1949–1972, Northern Lama Island: Comments on Chinese Customs and Customary Rights, 3 June 1949,* (HKMS178-1-69). The Hong Kong Record Series, Hong Kong.
Note from John Pakenham-Walsh. (1956, June 11). *Chinese law and custom, note from John Pakenham-Walsh to Attorney General, 11 June 1956,* (HKRS 41-1-3106-5). The Hong Kong Record Series, Hong Kong.
Original Signed Copy of Report. (ca. 1951, January 18). *Chinese law and custom, Original Signed Copy of Report of the Chinese Law and Custom Committee,* (HKRS 41-1-3106-1). The Hong Kong Record Series, Hong Kong.
Sai Kung: Comments. (1949, June 3). *Chinese custom 1949–1972, Sai Kung: Comments on Chinese Customs and Customary Rights, 3 June 1949,* (HKMS178-1-69). The Hong Kong Record Series, Hong Kong.
Savingram from the Governor. (1953, May 5). *Chinese law and custom, savingram from the Governor to the Secretary of State for the Colonies, 5 May 1953,* (HKRS 41-1-3106-5). The Hong Kong Record Series, Hong Kong.
Savingram from the Secretary of States for the Colonies. (1955, November 11). *Chinese law and custom, savingram from the Secretary of States for the Colonies to the Officer Administering the Government of Hong Kong, 11 November 1955,* (HKRS 41-1-3106-5). The Hong Kong Record Series, Hong Kong.

Savingram from the Secretary of States for the Colonies. (1956, April 4). *Chinese law and custom, savingram from the Secretary of States for the Colonies to the Officer Administering the Government of Hong Kong, 4 April 1956,* (HKRS 41-1-3106-5). The Hong Kong Record Series, Hong Kong.

Sessional Paper No. 18. (1953, April 29). *Chinese law and custom report report tabled in Legislative Council on 29 April 1953 as Sessional Paper No. 18 of 1953, 29 April 1953,* (HKRS 41-2-61). The Hong Kong Record Series, Hong Kong.

Southern Lama Island: Comments. (1949, June 3). *Chinese custom 1949–1972, Southern Lama Island: Comments on Chinese Customs and Customary Rights, 3 June 1949,* (HKMS178-1-69). The Hong Kong Record Series, Hong Kong.

Tsin Pit Tat of Tai O: Comments. (1949, June 3). *Chinese Custom 1949–1972, Tsin Pit Tat of Tai O: Comments on Chinese Customs and Customary Rights, 3 June 1949,* (HKMS178-1-69). The Hong Kong Record Series, Hong Kong.

Tsuen Wan: Comments. (1949, June 3). *Chinese custom 1949–1972, Tsuen Wan: Comments on Chinese Customs and Customary Rights, 3 June 1949*, (HKMS178-1-69). The Hong Kong Record Series, Hong Kong.

Views of Tai O Residents' Association. (1949, November 3). *Chinese customs and law committee: Chinese law and custom opinion, views of Tai O Residents' Association re: Questionnaire from the Chinese Law and Customs Committee, 3 November 1949,* (HKRS 158-3-3). The Hong Kong Record Series, Hong Kong.

Wong, M. W. L. (2018). Chinese laws as fundamental, Western laws as assistance: The struggle for the retention of Hejian in the Qing Criminal Code. *Journal of Comparative Law, 13*(2), 208–341.

Chapter 5
The Colonial Office and the Abolition of Concubinage

Abstract This chapter discusses the follow-up action of the Hong Kong Government after the rejection of the Strickland Report leading to the abolition of concubinage in 1965. The determining factor was the attitude of the Colonial Office. The Colonial Office reacted furiously against the delay approach taken by the Hong Kong Government and disagreed with the Hong Kong Government's alternative proposals in the Ridehalgh/McDouall Report 1960. Faced with growing pressure from the Colonial Office, the Hong Kong Government finally decided to abolish the institution of concubinage in the draft McDouall/Heenan Report 1965. The draft report was welcomed by the Colonial Office and paved the way to the abolition of concubinage by local legislation.

Keywords Colonial Office · Hong Kong Council of Women · Ridehalgh/McDouall Report · McDouall/Heenan Report · Definition of concubine · Abolition of concubinage

5.1 Introduction

In 1956, the Hong Kong Government rejected the Strickland Report and decided not to abolish concubinage after public consultation. But this decision did not stop social organisations from advocating for the abolition of concubinage in Hong Kong. On the one hand, the Hong Kong Council of Women and other social organisations campaigned for the end of concubinage as soon as possible and collected signatures in a petition to this effect. On the other hand, social organisations tried to put more pressure on the colonial government through lobbying. The signature campaign helped to initiate and propagate the importance of the abolition of concubinage in Hong Kong society. The signature campaigns initiated by different social organisations had received overwhelming support from many secondary school teachers, lawyers and professionals, mostly the educated elites in Hong Kong, but not from the grassroots. However, such efforts were—in the eyes of the responsible

M. WL Wong, *Chinese Marriage and Social Change*,
https://doi.org/10.1007/978-981-15-1644-3_5

government officials—futile, since these campaigns could not put enough political pressure on the colonial government to propose legislation abolishing concubinage.

Perhaps the most pervasive political pressure came from the Colonial Office in the UK, which insisted upon the abolition of concubinage in Hong Kong as soon as possible. First, because of a bombardment of parliamentary questions relating to the institution of concubinage in Hong Kong, the Colonial Office did not wish to be regarded as supporting the Hong Kong Government in the retention of the institution of concubinage. Secondly, although the Colonial Office had expressed dissatisfaction with the institution in Hong Kong, progress to end concubinage was slow and ineffective after the rejection of the Strickland Report. Given that the Colonial Office felt the need to abolish the practice, it put pressure on the Hong Kong Government to reverse the decision of 1956 and introduce legislation for an immediate abolition of concubinage. The Hong Kong Government, after reviewing the legal issues and recommendations of two reports in 1960 and 1965, decided to reform the marriage system in Hong Kong and most importantly, in the 1965 report, proposed to abolish the institution of concubinage. This report was approved by the Colonial Office in 1965. Because of this, in 1969 the Hong Kong Government put forward a new legislative proposal to reform the marriage system by introducing the Marriage Reform Bill, resulting to the approval of the Marriage Reform Bill in 1970. In this new legislation, the Hong Kong Government decided to overhaul Chinese customary marriage by replacing it with a monogamous and registered marriage system. This new system would resemble marriage systems in other parts of the world.

This chapter will be divided into three parts. The first part discusses the petitions submitted by the social organisations such as the Hong Kong Council of Women and their demands for the abolition of concubinage. The second part focuses on the role of the Colonial Office in pushing the Hong Kong Government for the abolition of concubinage, drawing references from the government records in the Colonial Office. The records show that, due to the dissatisfaction of the officials in the Colonial Office with the institution of concubinage, a lot of pressure was put on the Hong Kong Government to firmly propose legislative changes abolishing the institution of concubinage. The third part will examine the legislative proposal made by the Hong Kong Government after 1965, which paved the way for the end of concubinage in Hong Kong.

5.2 Opposition from Hong Kong Council of Women and Other Organisations

After the decision of the Executive Council to reject the abolition of concubinage in September 1956 (see Chap. 4, Sect. 4.3.6), the response of some social organisations was outrage.

5.2.1 Six JPs

The first petition came in a letter from Dr Irene Cheng, member of the Strickland Committee. On 12 April 1957 she gave the draft petition to the Colonial Secretariat, E.B. David, to comment on and stated that Mrs Ellen Li and her "would be only too happy to wait on you for your advice" (Letter of Dr Irene Cheng, 12 April 1957a). In reply, E. B. David advised her to address the petition to the Governor. In addition, E. B. David directed her "to specify with as much particularity as you can exactly what measures it is that you are asking the Government to undertake". He also asked her to consider the measures that she would like to take and then "relate them to the recommendations made by the Committee on Chinese Law and Custom" (Letter of E. B. David to Dr Irene Cheng, 17 April 1957). Dr Irene Cheng, on 21 April 1957b, replied that "we are most grateful for your constructive comments and are adding a section embodying our comments on the Committee's Recommendations as listed in Chapter VI of their Report" (Letter of Dr Irene Cheng to E. B. David, 21 April 1957b). Finally, a petition was submitted to the government, which was signed by six leading female figures of the "Justice of the Peace" (JP) in Hong Kong pushing for the abolition of concubinage. These six JPs were Mrs Rose Helena Li Chow, Miss Alice Kwok, Mrs Ellen Tsao Li, Mrs Tseung Ts'o Lai-Ki, Mrs Yeoh Choy Wai-haan and Miss Shin Tak-Hing. Together with another 990 signatories, the petition argued that there was no right for a man to have a concubine. They argued that such right "was merely a custom whereby a man might try to beget sons to continue the family line", and they argued that "this problem could always be resolved by adoption of one's nephew or of other children". They stated that there was a feeling of insecurity shared by the secondary women (concubine) and their offspring, so, "when a system affects not only the person himself, are we right to allow him to indulge himself at the expense of the women and children?". The petition stated that:

> If we are truly concerned with the welfare and happiness of the Chinese residents of this Colony and wish to prevent for future generations some of the sufferings that have affected some members of our generation, now is the time to introduce positive legislation to put a stop to the evil." [emphasis in original] (Letter of the SCA to the Governor: Petition, 31 May 1957, p. 5)

In a supplement to this petition, the petitioners stated that they were in full agreement with the Committee's recommendations. On the issue of concubinage, they proposed that a registration system would be established for Chinese customary marriages and Chinese modern marriages. The registration system for a concubine would be established so that existing concubines, with the approval of the connivance of the wife, could be registered at the Secretary for Chinese Affairs after an "appointed day". Afterwards, the issues born by the concubine before or after the "appointed day" would still enjoy the privileges hitherto granted to them (Letter of the SCA to the Governor: Petition—supplement, 31 May 1957, para. 1–2).

The six JPs submitted the petition, but no follow-up action is recorded in the Hong Kong Government papers. Judging from the recommendations as stated in the government submission to the Executive Council in 1960 (the Ridehalgh/McDouall Report), their opinions were mostly ignored.

5.2.2 Hong Kong Council of Women

The Hong Kong Council of Women not only worked on the signature campaign; they also wrote additional letters to the government petitioning for the abolition of concubinage. On 25 May 1957, when the six JPs were preparing the petition for the abolition of concubinage, the Chairman of the Hong Kong Council of Women, Mrs R. T. Eng wrote a letter to E. B. David on this matter. Eng informed the Hong Kong Government that they might receive the petition of six JPs on this issue shortly. However, Eng clarified that the Hong Kong Council of Women did not initiate this campaign. Eng said that they were not in full agreement with the contents and recommendations of the six JPs and they would send their comments after reading the petition (R. T. Eng to E. B. David , 25 May 1957). But in the end, they did not make any comments on the petition made by the six JPs.

At the same time, the Hong Kong Council of Women, Mrs R. T. Eng wrote a letter to A. Ridehalgh, the Attorney General of the Hong Kong Government. In it, Eng asked Ridehalgh three questions regarding Chinese marriage law and custom in Hong Kong. Firstly, she asked what were the elements of the legal marriage for Chinese born in Hong Kong and other Chinese residing in the Hong Kong? Secondly, she asked on what basis did the Secretary for Chinese Affairs and the Courts decide the marital status of a man and woman who considered themselves married in accordance with Chinese customary marriage and Chinese modern marriage? Thirdly, she asked what were the elements of the capacity for marriage, and the forms and ceremonies of marriage, which would be recognised by the Secretary for Chinese Affairs and the Courts "in the course of their administrative duties" (R. T. Eng to A. Ridehalgh, 25 May 1957)? But Ridehalgh only gave a short reply that it was not permissible for him as the legal adviser to the Hong Kong Government to give legal advice to members of the public. He suggested that Eng should consult a solicitor (Letter from A. Ridehalgh, 27 May 1957).

This reply attracted further clarification from Mrs. R. T. Eng. In a letter to Ridehalgh on 8 June 1957, Eng stated that they were not seeking legal advice. She wanted to point out that there were native courts in other parts of the world which dealt with native law and the decisions of the court were known to the public. She considered that since there was no native court in Hong Kong, and the Secretary for Chinese Affairs was responsible for the personal problems of applicants under Chinese law and custom, she was requesting a general statement of the principles which he applied so that the Hong Kong Council of Women could advise its members of these matters (Letter from R. T. Eng, 8 June 1957).

The Attorney General passed the letter to the Secretary for Chinese Affairs for comments and reply (Memo from Attorney General, 12 June 1957). On 15 July 1957, the Secretary for Chinese Affairs J.C. McDouall replied to Eng. McDouall first arguing that marital or family problems were brought in to the Secretary for Chinese Affairs, or to one of his Assistants, "they are not 'dealt' with" even administratively. The Secretary for Chinese Affairs would only give advice and "that advice can however be taken or left, at the parties' discretion". The advice would be given "after careful consideration of all aspects of any apparently relevant Chinese Laws and Customs, and that that advice may be drawn both from departmental experience and external expert findings" (Letter from Secretary for Chinese Affairs, 15 July 1957, para. 3). He added that such advice do not have the authority of any Court decision. Secondly, McDouall emphasised that the Secretary for Chinese Affairs "could only operate under the Laws of Hong Kong and any consideration of past or present Chinese law or custom in so far as the Laws of Hong Kong permit and as internal or external expert evidence might be available" (Letter from Secretary for Chinese Affairs, 15 July 1957, para. 4). He denied that the Secretary for Chinese Affairs was the equivalent of the native courts of Hong Kong, as claimed by the Council of Hong Kong Women in the last letter, and stated that the services of the Secretary for Chinese Affairs only provided the services of a confidential adviser "and that such advice as it may be able to provide has to be and is drawn as required from the best sources available, whether within or outside the Department to meet each individual case" (Letter from Secretary for Chinese Affairs, 15 July 1957, para. 5). The Secretary for Chinese Affairs did not reply directly on the principles of the application of the Chinese laws and customs as practised in his department, but the Hong Kong Council of Women did not follow up with this issue.

Meanwhile, the Hong Kong Council of Women organised a signature campaign to push forward the abolition of concubinage. On 2 November 1957, Mrs. R. T. Eng sent a letter to E. B. David to mark the specific demands. The proposal, though not directly related to the abolition of concubinage, also formed part of a package to change the marriage system in Hong Kong. Firstly, Eng proposed a registered marriage system, which either took place in the Registry or Church. Secondly, Eng considered that after the registration system had been established, the Chinese customary practice of the divorce by mutual consent should be illegal. Thirdly, Eng proposed that all Chinese residents lived in Hong Kong for 7 years or longer, or who had lived more than 6 months in Hong Kong in each consecutive year, should be considered as domiciled in Hong Kong for the purpose of marriage and would come under the jurisdiction of the new marriage law (Letter from Chairman of the Hong Kong Council of Women, 2 November 1957). Eng concluded that this proposal aimed at the elimination of Chinese customary marriage through a mandatory registration marriage system. She hoped that this proposal could pave the way to a monogamous marriage system in the future. And, by giving a clear meaning to domicile, she considered that this new system could help to clarify the personal status of the Chinese in relation to matrimonial relationships in Hong Kong. Consequently, the court could more easily deal with situations such as whether a Chinese man who sought a divorce in Hong Kong could be regarded as domicile in Hong Kong. She argued that if a Chinese man could not be regarded as domicile in Hong Kong, then the courts in Hong Kong could not have the capacity to deal with the laws relating to his matrimonial relationship in Hong Kong.

The Hong Kong Council of Women made the petition to the Governor in a letter on 9 November 1957 (Letter from the Hong Kong Council of Women, 9 November 1957), though finally the Colonial Secretary replied that the Hong Kong Council of Women could send their petition through him to the Governor, or give the petition directly to the Colonial Secretary (Letter from E. B. David, 26 November 1957). With 21,000 signatures in support of this petition, the message of the Hong Kong Council of Women was clear: to amend the marriage and succession laws, by establishing monogamous marriage (one man and one woman), and to discontinue the recognition of concubine (*t'sips*) in Hong Kong, legal or otherwise (Letter from Irene Greenfield, 3 December 1957). One remark, however, made by the Colonial Secretary E. B David, was that the petition was mercifully brief and did not throw much more light on the matter (minute 113, n.d.). Another letter by the Hong Kong Council of Women on 7 April 1958 stated that in addition to their previous petition in December 1957, they had collected more than a thousand additional signatures to the petition and would like to submit these to the Governor (Letter from the Hong Kong Council of Women, 7 April 1958).

Apart from pressure applied through the petition and signature campaign, the Hong Kong Council of Women also asked the members of the Parliament in the UK to table some parliamentary questions, asking the Secretary of States for the Colonies to abolish the institution of concubinage in Hong Kong. This caused a lot of political pressure on the Colonial Office, which later forced the Hong Kong Government to adopt a more proactive approach in abolishing the institution of concubinage. This will be dealt with later in this chapter.

5.2.3 The YWCA in Hong Kong

The third petition from social organisations was a petition submitted to the government by the YWCA in Hong Kong. On 27 September 1957, the YWCA Hong Kong wrote a petition to the Governor supporting the Report and the abolition of concubinage. Their arguments were that, firstly, Qing laws had been replaced in China by the Civil Code in 1931 and as such had not been in existence for over 25 years. Secondly, they argued that the traditional Chinese family system had altered considerably in the past 100 years, so that old laws had to be amended and adapted to meet the needs and progress of the times. Thirdly, these old laws were against the United Nations Declaration of Human Rights. Finally, the institution of concubinage was greatly abused, resulting in confusion in the community and family troubles. In sum, they urged for express legislation to change the old Qing laws (Letter from the YWCA, 27 September 1957).

On the part relating to the abolition of concubinage, they proposed a clear definition of the term *t'sip*. Also, they proposed that a man should be allowed to marry a *t'sai* contracted prior to the appointed day while still living with a *t'sip* or *t'sips*, provided that the existence of the concubine was known to the prospective *t'sai* before the marriage. They agreed to establish a registration system for concubines.

Anyone who did not register should be prosecuted as perjury. Further, anyone who failed to register could be grounds for divorce or annulment with compensation.

On the grounds of divorce, they recommended that all marriages, including Chinese marriages and registry marriages, taking place in Hong Kong should have the protection of the laws of Hong Kong, notwithstanding the husband's status as a Hong Kong domicile. For marriages that had taken place outside Hong Kong, they proposed that the grounds for divorce should be the laws under the Civil Code 1931 of the Republic of China. Additionally, they proposed that divorce by mutual consent by Court decree could only be applicable to marriages that had taken place outside of Hong Kong. Finally, they proposed that adoption and posthumous adoption should not be limited to sex or blood relations (Suggestion for Modification, 27 September 1957).

This proposal was more radical than the other social organisations because they proposed to make it an offence if a husband did not register a concubine after the appointed day. And, they proposed to extend the meaning of "domicile" to cover all Chinese marriages. This might help to resolve the technical difficulties of the court in adjudicating the matrimonial relationships of the Chinese who were living in Hong Kong but remained domicile in China. The problem was that their idea of redefining the term "domicile" might contravene the international practices as provided in the private international law,[1] since domicile would usually be defined as the status of a person who considered himself to live, or legally reside permanently in that particular jurisdiction. Since, in the 1950s, many emigrants from China who lived in Hong Kong might still consider themselves domiciled in China, this proposal could well have created confusion rather than clarification. Nevertheless, it was important to note that the petition was signed by Mrs Ellen Tsao Li (i.e. Mrs. Ellen Li), the President of the YWCA Hong Kong, and Miss Shin Tak Hing, the General Secretary of the YWCA Hong Kong. Both were also signatories of the six JPs letter. Ellen Li was later appointed by the Hong Kong government as the Legislative Councillor in 1966 who fought very hard for the abolition of concubinage in the Legislative Council (Yip 2014, p. 155).

5.3 The Colonial Office

The Governor first sent the copies of the Strickland Report to the Colonial Office on 5 May 1953 (Savingram from the Governor of Hong Kong, 5 May 1953). The Colonial Office replied, on 4 July 1953, that they were waiting for the comments from the Governor when public opinion was heard (Letter from the Secretaries of State, 4 July 1953). However, the Colonial Office did not receive any reply, so they asked for an update on 22 November 1955 (Savingram from the Secretaries of State, 11 November 1955) and 4 April 1956 (Savingram from the Secretaries of State,

[1] See Chap. 3, Sect. 3.2.1, on the discussion of domicile.

4 April 1956). The reply finally came from the Hong Kong Government on 26 April 1956. A government official from the Colonial Secretariat, E. B. David, explained that the public in Hong Kong generally showed remarkably little interest in the issue and that opinions were by no mean unanimous. One significant cause of delay was that Sir Man Kam Lo was absent for part of 1954 and 1955. E. B. David proposed that the Executive Council would be discussing the issue in the near future and would keep Colonial Office informed (Letter from E. B. David, 26 April 1956a).

On 5 October 1956, after the decision of the Executive Council to reject the Strickland Report, the Hong Kong official C. B. Burgess reported to the Colonial Office about the decision. Burgess first informed the Colonial Office that the Executive Council had rejected the abolition of concubinage by legislation. Burgess then reported that the general feeling of the Executive Council was that the customary practice of concubinage "was dying a natural death and that any attempt to hasten this process by legislation was liable to cause individual hardship and to benefit no one in particular". Burgess also reported that the government would further examine the report to look for any other recommendations, other than the abolition of concubinage, which could be implemented (Letter from C. B. Burgess, 5th October 1956). This letter drew a furious reply from the Colonial Office. On 17 January 1957, K. G. Ashton from the Colonial Office replied to Burgess that, from the perspective of the United Kingdom, this rejection would invite "an adverse reaction from the Hong Kong Council of Women, the Reform Club, the Churches, and their friends in the United Kingdom and even in the United Nations". Ashton commented that the fact that the people and the interested organisations might not fully understand the institution of concubinage and all the issues involved could not save them from a good deal of trouble (Letter from K. G. Ashton, Colonial Office to C. B. Burgess, 17 January 1957).[2]

Ashton further commented that based on the information provided by the Hong Kong Government, it would be difficult for him to give a convincing brief to the Secretary of States for the Colonies if the Secretary for States for the Colonies might be called upon to defend this decision in parliament. Ashton considered that the reason for the rejection of the abolition of concubinage, which appeared to depend entirely on Sir Man Kam Lo's arguments, was not convincing. He also considered that the argument from the Hong Kong government's submission—that hardship might be caused to men if the men were no longer allowed to acquire a *t'sip*—would only arouse ridicule during the debate in parliament. Further, he argued that there was no evidence to suggest that "the legal abolition of concubinage would cause hardship to the tsips or prospective tsips, would cause popular discontent and unrest, or would intensify the problems of child care and protection". [emphasis in original] (Letter from K. G. Ashton, Colonial Office to C. B. Burgess, 17 January 1957, para. 3).

[2]This is a copy of the original letter, which was partially destroyed (Chinese Law and Custom, Letter from K. G. Ashton, 17 January 1957) as filed in HKRS 41-1-3106-5, *Chinese Law and Custom*.

Ashton asked the Hong Kong Government to send a note of arguments that would be used, or were proposed for use when necessary, to the Secretaries of States for the Colonies in order to defend their decision, answer Parliamentary questions and/or prepare answers to MP's letters or other correspondents. This, he reasoned, "would be a useful step to see how the arguments would stand up to the sorts of attack they would be likely to receive here". It was now clear that the Colonial Office refused to accept the decision and rejected the arguments provided by the Hong Kong Government entirely. In a note made by the Colonial Secretary, E. B. David, in the letter, he stated that "In the reply we might emphasise that this is a matter in which Chinese opinion should count for most" (Letter from K. G. Ashton, Colonial Office to C. B. Burgess, 17 January 1957, para. 3). The Hong Kong Government was preparing a reply to this letter but was frustrated by a parliamentary question on the abolition of concubinage

On 8 March 1957, a parliamentary question by Albert Roberts MP prompted an officer in Colonial Office to ask the Hong Kong Government for a reply. Albert Roberts asked what steps the Secretary of States for the Colonies proposed to take to make concubinage in Hong Kong illegal (Telegram from the Secretary of States, 8 March 1957)? In reply, on 11 March 1957, the Governor of Hong Kong, Sir Alexander Grantham, considered that the word "illegal" entailed two meanings. First, the fact that the government would withdraw the legal recognition of this institution. And secondly, the government would make the practice of concubinage an offence. Regarding the latter, neither the government nor the Strickland Committee had considered such an issue. Regarding the former, Grantham commented that "I believe the institution (of concubinage) can best be eliminated by the gradual pressure of education and public opinion rather than by legislative measures which would bring hardship to individuals" (Telegram from Hong Kong, 11th March 1957, para. 1). He stated that "[N]o local organisation has raised this question officially during the last two years and there has been little discussion of it. There is no certainty that public opinion would support enforcement of abolition". He provided additional information for the Colonial Office to answer this question which showed, he emphasised, that political opposition from the Chinese community complicated the issue of abolition: "concubinage is distasteful to British thought but Chinese opinion (99% of the population) must have weight. The Chinese Unofficial Members of the Executive Council were unanimously against legislation" (Telegram from Hong Kong, 11th March 1957, para. 3. Thus, to Grantham, "the best course is to leave well alone since it is clear that public opinion is already moving in the right direction and there is no clamour for action" (Telegram from Hong Kong, 11th March 1957, para. 4).

Mr Browning of the Colonial Office considered that the Governor's position was understandable, and sympathised with him on the political complexity in Hong Kong. Mr Browning minuted that:

> although I am wedded to the principle of monogamy, I have a good deal of sympathy with the Hong Kong govt [sic] in this matter. We very frequently take the line that customary and moral matters are best dealt with by education and not legislation and I do not think it would

> be difficult for the S of S (Secretary of States for the Colonies) to defend H.K. (Hong Kong) on this. (Minute by Mr Browning, 23 May, 1957)

Ultimately, the Colonial Office suggested a reply to this parliamentary question along the lines suggested by the Governor (Minute by Mr Browning, 23 May 1957). In the formal reply, on behalf of the Secretary of States for the Colonies, Mr Profumo replied that "[M]odern ideas are gradually doing away with concubinage and I think that may prove to be the best way to deal with it" (Reply from Mr Profumo, 25 March 1957).

A separate reply written by the Hong Kong Government official, Burgess, finally arrived at the Colonial Office on 17 April 1957 (Letter from Colonial Secretariat, 17 April 1957). In this letter, Burgess did not defend the decision to retain the system of concubinage. Burgess instead shifted the issue of the abolition of concubinage to, first, the fact that this decision might create hardship to women in the institution of concubinage, as claimed by the women organisations in Hong Kong because of the nature of the system, and secondly, the difficulty of defining what the Hong Kong Government was prepared to accept as a valid Chinese customary marriage.

After defining the issues above, Burgess replied that the Secretary for Chinese Affairs considered that he very seldom received complaints on the "ill-treatment or hardship suffered by concubines or hardship suffered by concubines or complaints in which a wife who has accepted a concubine into her husband's family later regrets having taken this step" (Letter from Colonial Secretariat, 17 April 1957). Burgess stated that on an average one case in several hundred cases heard at the Secretary for Chinese Affairs was related to concubinage. Most of the complaints brought by wives were related to mistresses taken by the husbands (Letter from Colonial Secretariat, 17 April 1957, para. 3).

Burgess argued that on the issue of the validity of the Chinese customary marriage, he emphasised that there had never been any serious suggestion to making the keeping of a concubine a criminal offence (following to the views given by the Governor to the Colonial Office in reply to the Parliamentary question on 11 March 1957). He suggested that the best the Hong Kong Government could do was to make the taking of a concubine an act of adultery, and one of the grounds for divorce. But Burgess considered that "it was difficult to see how any woman could bring an action for divorce who was unable to prove the validity of her own marriage". The root of the question, to Burgess, was that there was "considerable doubt as to exactly what constitutes a valid marriage according to Chinese custom in Hong Kong" (Letter from Colonial Secretariat, 17 April 1957, para. 4). Burgess attached a memo, written by the Secretary for Chinese Affairs on 14 February 1957, which clearly defined the views of the Hong Kong Government on the issue of the abolition of concubinage: "I simply do not see how any legislative steps could be taken to do away with the system of concubinage unless they were preceded by legislation to define what Hong Kong is prepared to accept as a valid customary Chinese marriage" (Memorandum from Secretary for Chinese Affairs, 14 February, 1957). In sum the Hong Kong Government did not try to relieve the Colonial Office's frustration, but tried to argue that the question of the abolition of concubinage was about the elements, forms, and finally the legal recognition of the Chinese customary marriage in Hong Kong. This reply obviously angered the Colonial Office, which will be discussed later in this chapter.

On 27 January 1958, prompted by the petition from the Hong Kong Council of Women, Albert Roberts MP asked the Colonial Office about the progress of the abolition of concubinage in Hong Kong. The Colonial Office asked the Hong Kong Government for materials to reply (Savingram from the Secretary of State for the Colonies, 27 January 1958). The Governor replied on 5 February 1958. This time, without making a firm commitment on a timetable to abolish concubinage, the Governor reported that he was considering approaching the question of concubinage from a different angle. Firstly, he suggested the promotion of monogamous marriage in Hong Kong "by expanding the number of marriage registries. Such a programme would also assist in encouraging the validation of any irregularly contracted Chinese monogamous unions" (Telegram from Hong Kong, 5th February 1958, para. 2). Secondly, he intended to appoint a new committee consisting of the Secretary for Chinese Affairs and the Attorney General to re-examine the question of introducing more practical legislation than that directed at the abolition of concubinage (Telegram from Hong Kong, 5th February, 1958, para. 3). The Governor opined that "any progress in these directions will not lead to the immediate abolition of concubinage" (Telegram from Hong Kong, 5th February, 1958, para. 5). In relation to the recommendations made by the Strickland Committee, the Governor stated that "[A]t present and at least until policy in regard to the major question of concubinage has been settled no further action is proposed on the other recommendations in the [Strickland] report apart from those dealt with in this telegram" (Telegram from Hong Kong, 5th February, 1958, para. 6). The Governor's response provided clues to the Hong Kong Government's strategy for resolving this issue, in other words, putting every effort into delaying the abolition of concubinage.

5.4 Decision of the Executive Council in 1958

A chance to abolish concubinage in Hong Kong surfaced in 1958. Unfortunately, this time, because of the opposition of government departments, the Executive Council did not proceed with the abolition of concubinage as pressed to by the Colonial Office. Further, it is important to note that those Chinese Unofficial members of the Executive Council who opposed the abolition of concubinage, such as Sir Man Kam Lo, were still serving as members of the Executive Council in 1958.

On 10 December 1957, a draft Executive Council paper was prepared by D. C. C. Luddington to the Registrar General and Secretary for Chinese Affairs for comments (Minute from D. C. C. Luddington, 10 December 1957). The official records did not contain the draft, but the comments from the Registrar General and the Secretary for Chinese Affairs suggested that the mere suggestion of a registration system for existing customary marriage would be denied due to administrative reasons, nor was any such suggestion welcomed by the Chinese Unofficial members of the Executive Council.

The Registrar General opposed establishing a registration system catering for Chinese customary marriages (Minute from the Registrar General, 14 January 1958). He considered that firstly, such a system was of little value and it was very difficult to check the facts or circumstances advanced by the parties in support of their claims. Secondly, he stated that such practices would only discourage or divert people from using the formal procedure of getting married in accordance with the Marriage Ordinance. Thirdly, he further stated that such a system required an effective date for Chinese customary marriages but that it would be impracticable for the registration date to be effective on the date of marriage, in accordance with the Chinese law and custom, because it would be very difficult to ascertain whether the couples really followed the formalities of marriage laid down in Chinese law and custom. He considered that the legal abolition of concubinage was inadvisable and impracticable:

> The customs and usages we are considering have been there for a very long time and are deeply ingrained as part of the way of life of a community which forms about 98% of the entire population of this Colony, and of all classes of that community. Direct interference with them is, in my opinion, likely to arouse considerable ill-feeling and resentment and might well have political repercussions. (Minute from the Registrar General, 14 January 1958, para. 4)

The Registrar General agreed to Paragraph 7 of the draft paper (Minute from the Registrar General, 14 January 1958). This paragraph proposed that the government should consider initiating a rapid expansion of the number of Marriage Registries, so that the Chinese residents could benefit from the Registry marriage in the Marriage Ordinance and have the protection of modern marriage and divorce laws.[3]

Indeed, the final draft Executive Council paper contained two proposals. Firstly, the government would establish a small Committee headed by the Secretary for Chinese Affairs and Attorney General (or his representative) to "re-examine the question of introducing legislation whereby after a certain date all marriages celebrated in Hong Kong would have to be registered with the Registrar of Marriages in order to be recognised as valid". Secondly, the government would increase the number of Marriage Registrars to facilitate legal marriages (Minute from Clerk of Councils, n.d.).[4]

The Secretary for Chinese Affairs endorsed the views of the Registrar General in another minute. Additionally, he took the draft and consulted the Chinese Unofficial members of the Executive Council, including Sir Man Kam Lo, who was strongly against the abolition of concubinage. The Chinese Unofficial members of the Executive Council were against any legislative proposal that would clearly and positively require all marriages in Hong Kong to be registered after a certain date,

---

[3] This was finally incorporated into the Memorandum of the Executive Council (22 May 1958, para. 7).

[4] The files show that the most likely date for this minute was from 21 February 1958 to 24 February 1958.

in order to be valid. Therefore, the Secretary for Chinese Affairs proposed a new Paragraph 10, which expressed the matter more indirectly: "[t]he legislation may well further provide that all 'customary marriages' celebrated in Hong Kong, in accordance with certain prescribed simple requirements, should be made valid, and that if such marriages were registered with the Registrar of Marriages, within a certain period, such registration should afford conclusive evidence of their validity" (Memorandum from Secretary for Chinese Affairs, 22 April 1958, para. 3).

This suggestion was finally included in the Executive Council paper which was discussed in the Executive Council meeting on 3 June 1958. In the Memorandum for Executive Council written on 22 May 1958 for the meeting on 3 June 1958, the government first admitted that the rejection of the abolition of concubinage made in the Executive Council meeting of 11 September 1957 "gave rise to some misgivings among officials of the Colonial Office who were concerned with probable Parliamentary questions on the subject" (Memorandum for Executive Council, 22 May 1958, para. 2). The government also received three petitions on this subject. The government concluded that part of the problem was that the law on Chinese customary marriage was in considerable confusion and "there is little doubt that there are unscrupulous persons who are able to take advantage of this position" (Memorandum for Executive Council, 22 May 1958, para. 6). Therefore, if the Hong Kong Government did not wish to be subjected to continuous criticism in the UK, some measures must be taken to protect the rights of women. The government then proposed to initiate "a programme for the rapid expansion of the number of the Marriage Registries which should be established in all parts of the Colony, particularly in the more densely populated and poorer areas of the Colony" (Memorandum for Executive Council, 22 May 1958, para. 7). And this might help to solve the problem of so-called customary marriages, so that the couples could go to the registry to "remarry" again (Memorandum for Executive Council, 22 May 1958, para. 8). Further, this measure could help to show that the government had done its best "to provide all legal facilities to enable women to insist upon their marriages receiving the full protection of modern marriage law" (Memorandum for Executive Council, 22 May 1958, para. 9).

The government also wanted to resolve the problem of the validity of Chinese customary marriage. But the problem here was that the validity of a marriage was governed by the "lex domicilii" of the parties, in other words, the issue of "domicile". To Hong Kong Chinese who were domiciled in Hong Kong, customary marriage would entail the application of the GQC. As a consequence, it should strictly comply with the elaborate ceremonies as prescribed by Qing law. But in reality, many persons had married according to Chinese modern marriage. So, the government considered that "there should be legislation by which customary marriages, as generally performed in Hong Kong, on the part of Chinese, whether domiciled or not in Hong Kong, shall be validated" (Memorandum for Executive Council, 22 May 1958, para. 11).

Finally, the government proposed appointing a small committee to consider this issue. The committee would consist of two government officials, the Secretary for Chinese Affairs and the Attorney General (or his representative).

After the Executive Council meeting, the policies mentioned in this paper were adopted. Firstly, it was agreed in the meeting that subject to the provisions of the necessary funds, steps must be taken to increase the number of Marriage Registries. Secondly, it was agreed that a committee be appointed "to consider the whole matter further and to consult any persons, including representatives of the three petitioners, whose views should be taken into account" (Minute: Executive Council Meeting, 4 June 1958). In sum, the Executive Council extended the scope of this two-man committee beyond what the government initially proposed, that is work on a legislative proposal for the validation of Chinese customary marriage, to a review of the "whole matter" relating to the issues of Chinese customary marriage.

After this meeting, the Hong Kong Government had identified four issues to follow up. Firstly, the government had to appoint the committee; Secondly, the government had to reply to the three petitioners of the decision made by the Executive Council. Thirdly, the government planned a press statement on the issue. Finally, the government had to reply to the Secretaries of State for the Colonies on the decision of the Executive Council (Minute from Clerk of Councils, 12 June 1958a). In a minute to the Colonial Secretary, the Deputy Colonial Secretary mentioned that, "it would be preferable not to supply the Colonial Office with all this detail, and better to keep the arguments on a more general plane" (Minute from the Deputy Colonial Secretary, 13 June 1958). The Colonial Secretary stated that he hoped to have a public statement that "should have the advantage of placing on record the whole history of this matter in our own words" (Minute from the Colonial Secretary, 16 June 1958). Clearly, then, the Colonial Secretary had this additional consideration in mind when they prepared a letter to the Colonial Office. On 19 June 1958, the Governor reported to the Colonial Office that the Executive Council in Hong Kong had approved his proposal. A committee was established with the ambit to consider just Chinese marriage reform and not wider reform of Chinese law and custom, as reviewed some years earlier by Strickland Committee:

> it will examine the introduction of legislation to legitimate the issue of couples married according to Chinese custom who remarry at a Registry; it will consider the possibility of legislative provision to validate 'customary marriages', and to facilitate their registration; and I will be permitted to go further and consider legislation to enforce the compulsory registration of all marriages after a certain date. (Savingram from the Governor, 19 June 1958)

However, officers in the Colonial Office were not impressed. They considered that this progress might not be sufficient to mollify the anger of members of parliament, because the issue of concubinage should have been resolved earlier. But, in the absence of any other policy option, they reluctantly agreed with the Governor's approach. Officers in the Colonial Office found the *t'sip* system distasteful. Mr Terrell taunted that "[A]s for the tsip system, it seems a good system to use. Perhaps it needs improvement rather than abolition. The committee seems [to be] a good idea" (Minute by Mr R Terrell, 29 August, 1958). His view was echoed by another officer, who stated that "So do I. I hope we shall not be asked for suggestion(s) for improving the tsip system!!" (Minute by Mr Chinn, 1 September, 1958). This teasing attitude recorded in the Colonial Office showed that the UK officials were dissatisfied with the progress made by the Hong Kong Government on the abolition of concubinage.

5.5 Ridehalgh/McDouall Report 1960

5.5.1 Social Organisations

After the decision of the Executive Council, the Hong Kong Government had to face political pressure from two fronts. First, the Colonial Office took parliamentary questions as an opportunity to press for the early abolition of concubinage. Second, social organisations such as the Hong Kong Council of Women did not stop their social campaigning and tried to garner as much social support as possible for the abolition of concubinage. Further, Hong Kong social organisations asked Members of Parliament in the UK to work together to inflict political pressure on the Colonial Office in London. This proved to be the most effective tool for pressing the Colonial Office into putting more pressure on the Hong Kong Government to change its delay approach.

Soon after the decision of the Executive Council, the Secretary for Chinese Affairs, McDouall, sent letters to invite the Hong Kong Council of Women, Young Women's Christian Association and Mrs Rose Helen Li Chow (representing the six JPs) to meetings, held in October 1950, to solicit their opinions (Chinese Marriages Validity Questions: Letters, 6 October 1958). Internally, McDouall also asked for the opinions of the District Commissioner of the New Territories, D. R. Holmes. In reply, on 6 October 1958, Holmes disagreed that Chinese customary marriage should be defined as those Chinese customs that prevailed in 1843. He considered that this approach was unrealistic because most of the departmental papers on the subject had somehow been lost. The papers relating to the Chinese marriage customs which were relevant—so far as the New Territories were concerned—were those which prevailed in 1899. He considered that the government should treat the Chinese customary usage in general, without specifying any particular date (Letter from District Commissioner New Territories, 6 October 1958, para. 4). He mentioned there were difficulties in defining Chinese customary marriage in the statutory provisions. For example, the essential elements which must be satisfied before any particular ceremony could be regarded as having complied with customary usage. He agreed that a more practical approach was to have the Secretary for Chinese Affairs or the District Commissioner of the New Territories certify the application for the validity of Chinese customary marriage that any marriage had satisfied those conditions.

At the end of his letter, he revealed a more general negative attitude to resolving the problem of the Chinese customary marriage:

> I cannot resist ending this memorandum with a quotation from a letter we have on record written by my predecessor on this general subject. It read as follows:- 'Attempts by a

foreign Government to legislate for Chinese marriages evoke the same sort of contemptuous amusement that we would feel if we were told that a committee of horses had decided that human being must have a Stud Book. The edict might be obeyed by jockeys, trainers and others whose livelihood depended on equine goodwill, but as for the rest …' (Letter from District Commissioner, New Territories, 6 October 1958, para. 5).

This paragraph shows what a Hong Kong expatriate administrator considered to be the proper limits of the colonial power to intervene in, or to attempt to change, Chinese customs. It suggests, moreover, that colonial administrators might have been concerned that such intervention in customs, by foreign hands, could lead to social instability and damage governance at the local level.

Before meeting with the social organisations, McDouall wrote a memo on 1 October 1958 to Attorney General, explaining the approach he was going to take in writing up the future report. Regarding the meeting with the petitioners, he considered that they could not give the representatives the majority of the "possible answers". In other words, McDouall did not want to clearly state the views of the social organisations. McDouall considered that these views were based on two assumptions: first, that marriages in Hong Kong contracted in accordance with the Civil Code 1931 of the Republic of China "were irregular and the children therefor[sic] bastard". Second, alleged concubines taken by men who contracted a marriage in accordance with the Civil Code of 1931 would have no lawful status of any kind. McDouall said that public disclosure of any views by government officials would be taken "willy nilly" as authoritative and that "could stir up a confused hornet's nest and make the already chaotic position worse confounded". He did not want to see, "Mrs. Matilda Wong, for instance, to go away and proclaim that the A.G. (Attorney General) and S.C.A. (Secretary for Chinese Affairs) had now ruled that 'all concubines are illegal'—which is the sort of thing that could too easily happen". So McDouall proposed that when they met with the petitioners, they could discuss "any points in their petitions which may seem obscure or which for other reasons may need further expansion of their points of view." Although, McDouall exclaimed, "I can't find any!". Finally, McDouall attached a letter written by Sir Man Kam Lo, who wrote in response to the letter given to him by Ellen Li (one of the JP who made the Six JPs petition). McDouall stated that he was "in complete agreement with Sir Man-Kam's masterly letter" (Memo from Secretary for Chinese Affairs, 1 October 1958, paras. 3–5).

The letter that McDouall referred in the preceding paragraph was written by Ellen Li in June 1957. On 17 June 1957, Ellen Li wrote a letter to Sir Man Kam Lo to persuade him to support the end of concubinage. Ellen mentioned that "[but] in the matter of concubines, we felt that you were perhaps a little more sympathetic towards the men, who imagined they had certain 'rights', whereas we felt it duty bound to consider the total effect on [S]ociety generally, and especially on the wives and children" (Letter from Ellen Li, 17 June 1957). Sir Man Kam Lo replied on 24 June 1957, though this mostly followed the arguments published in his memorandum in response to the Strickland Committee. On the matter relating to concubines, Lo did not promise to support the abolition of concubinage. He only stated that a man could not take a concubine if he contracted a marriage in Church or Marriage Registry:

> As regards the question of concubinage, it is, I think, generally conceded that a man who has gone through a marriage in Church in a licensed place of worship, or in the Marriage Registry cannot with immunity take a concubine, or a mistress, since the wife, if the husband were domiciled in Hong Kong, could obtain a divorce... (Letter of Man Kam Lo, 24 June 1957)[5]

It is important to note that the Secretary for Chinese Affairs was not convinced by the social organisations that an immediate abolition of concubinage could be easily implemented, but rather that it could only be achieved through gradual reform. Further, he considered that there were difficulties to start with such as how to properly define the system of Chinese customary marriage as it stood in 1843.

Subsequently, Ellen Li, representing the six JPs group and YWCA Hong Kong, met with the representatives of the Secretary for Chinese Affairs and Legal Department on 13 October 1958. Ellen Li argued that it was impossible to stamp out concubines and mistresses but that these women should not be allowed to acquire a position over and above that of the original wife. Li said that the system of concubinage was fast dying out. She suggested that a period of 5 years could be given to educate the New Territories' inhabitants to fight against concubinage, and thereafter "legal concubinage" should be abolished (Memo from Legal Department, 14 October 1958, para. 7).

On 17 October 1958, the Hong Kong Council of Women met with the representatives of the Secretary for Chinese Affairs and Legal Department. The representatives of the Hong Kong Council of Women argued that there were many examples in the New Territories that concubines were used as slave labour on the farms, and that concubinage had been made illegal by both Nationalist and PRC Governments in China. The Hong Kong Council of Women suggested that the Hong Kong Government should first consider legalising both customary and modern marriages up to a certain date and that existing concubines and their children should be protected. The Hong Kong Council of Women stated that the government should clearly define what was accepted as a registered concubine and only those concubines who were taken in accordance with the ceremony of *yap kung* should be recognised (Memo from the Legal Department, 21 October 1958). The Hong Kong Council of Women also proposed that after the death of the husband, a concubine should not be allowed to elevate their status to that of a *tin fong* wife by custom. They could only do so if the husband married them at the Registry (Memo from the Legal Department, 21 October 1958, para. 9).

In sum, the social organisations were in support of the abolition of concubinage during the meetings with government officials. The arguments from the social

[5] Letter from Ellen Li (17 June 1957) and Letter from Sir Man Kam Lo (28 June 1957) were originally recorded in the file *Chinese Marriages Reaction to Strickland Committee Report* (HKRS684-2-4). In a letter dated 29 June 1957, McDouall replied that "[m]ay I add how invaluable were the points made in hour latter to Mrs Lo in helping me grasp and re-assess the substance of the petition to which it referred." See Letter from J.C. McDouall (29 June 1957).

organisations were similar to the petitions they had sent to the government earlier. There was no sign that Sir Man Kam Lo was going to change his position to accept the abolition of concubinage. The Secretary for Chinese Affairs, the responsible officer for this policy, was not convinced by the social organisations and was inclined to support the views of Sir Man Kam Lo. Indeed, without strong political will from the very top to press for a change, the prominent Chinese senior figures and individual Hong Kong Government officials would still be the dominant voices in the Hong Kong Government.

5.5.2 *Pressure from Colonial Office, Again*

Social organisations in Hong Kong kept pressuring the Colonial Office for a change of policy in Hong Kong on the issue of the institution of concubinage. The Women Section of the United Nations Association of Hong Kong asked Barbara Castle MP, about the position taken by the Colonial Office to concubinage in the territory of Hong Kong. Consequently, the Colonial Office asked for an update from Hong Kong on this issue (Letter from Elsie Elliot, 6 June 1960). The Hong Kong Governor Sir Robert Black replied that "I regret that submission of the final conclusion has been unavoidably deferred due to the absence on leave until recently of both Attorney General and the Secretary for Chinese Affairs". No deadline nor time table was given by Sir Robert Black: "[I]t is hoped that their recommendations will be available for consideration in the near future" (Telegram from Hong Kong, 6 July 1960, para. 1). This answer disappointed the Colonial Office and contributed to their frustrated response following the later submission of the new report. This will be discussed later in this chapter.

5.5.3 *Submission of the 1960 Report to the Executive Council*

To recap, after some internal discussions, and meetings with social organisations, on 17 February 1960, the Secretary for Chinese Affairs, McDouall, gave a draft Executive Council paper to the Attorney General to comment on (Memo from Ag. Attorney General, 17 February, 1960). However, due to McDouall falling ill, and a long period away from Hong Kong on vacation leave, the submission of the draft paper was further delayed. In a letter to the Governor on 10 September 1960, the Attorney General and the Secretary for Chinese Affairs proposed to have 8 weeks for the members of the Chinese Unofficial members of the Executive Council to comment, with Chinese versions for those who had little or no command of English (Letter from A. Ridehalgh and McDouall, 10 September 1960). The Governor agreed that it would be helpful to consult the Chinese Unofficial members of the Executive Council (Letter from Governor, 12 September 1960). After consulting three Chinese Unofficial members of the Executive Council, some amendments were made to the issue of the recognition of Chinese modern marriage, the possible "re-registration" of the validity of the Chinese customary marriage and to how Secretary for Chinese Affairs and the District Commissioner of the New Territories could be empowered to give parties a "re-registration" in their offices (Memorandum from Secretary for Chinese Affairs, 3 November 1960). McDouall emphasised that such amendments did not commit those Chinese Unofficial members to agreeing to all the findings in the report. Further, there was an understanding between the members and the government that the members were free to suggest further amendments at later stage (Memorandum from Secretary for Chinese Affairs, 3 November 1960, para. 3).

On 22 November 1960, an Executive Council paper was finally submitted to the Executive Council for discussion in a meeting held on 13 December 1960. The members were asked to consider three issues. Firstly, whether any amendments to the report had to be made. Secondly, whether a Chinese version had to be prepared, and thirdly, whether the report had to be distributed to certain organisations (with the inclusion of Hong Kong Council of Social Service) for consultation (Memorandum for Executive Council, 22 November 1960, para. 5). After the meeting, the Executive Council decided that, firstly, some amendments should be made to the acceptance of modern marriages. Secondly, the Chinese modern marriage could be registered in the Marriage Registry and such arrangement must be given to the same spouse. The Executive Council also agreed to distribute the copies of the report for public consultation in accordance with the proposals suggested in the Executive Council paper (Memorandum from the Colonial Secretariat, 15 December 1960).

5.5.4 Commentaries on the Ridehalgh/McDouall Report 1960

The key issue, considering the pressure from the petitions of the social organisations and the Colonial Office, was that the report still did not propose to abolish the concubinage straight away. The government did not intend to resolve the issue of concubinage through this report. Instead, the report was drafted as if the issues originated from the validity of Chinese customary marriages and Chinese modern marriages in Hong Kong. Thus, this report was not drafted to resolve the issue of concubinage, let alone address the wider issues of Chinese law and custom.

The Daily Information Bulletin released by the Hong Kong Government on 14 March 1961 clearly stated the state of mind of the government officials. In it, it was stated that this report was a departure from the Strickland Committee: "It is not essential to read the Strickland Committee's 1953 Report on Chinese Law and Custom, nor the late Sir Man Kam Lo's comments thereon, in conjunction with the present Report on Chinese Marriages in Hong Kong" (Daily Information Bulletin,

14 March 1961).[6] However, the Ridehalgh/McDouall Report, the official title of which was "Chinese Marriages in Hong Kong", had adopted many of the legislative approaches suggested by the Strickland Committee, albeit with some deviation.

First the Ridehalgh/McDouall Report adopted the "appointed day" approach as proposed by the Strickland Committee to resolve the issue of legal recognition of the Chinese modern marriages, but they did not accept the Strickland Committee's recommendation to validate all Chinese modern marriage. The Ridehalgh/McDouall Report considered that Chinese modern marriage was an ill-defined institution which had "no roots in old Chinese custom and no affinity with British law" and that from the "Appointed Day" it should be ceased, after which couples must comply with one or other of the ceremonies in the Marriage Ordinance before their marriage could be regarded as valid in law (Daily Information Bulletin, 14 March 1961, para. 9(4)). In sum, the Ridehalgh/McDouall Report decided to put an end to the practice of Chinese modern marriage in Hong Kong.

Because of this decision, the Ridehalgh/McDouall Report did not adopt the Strickland Report's recommendation to legally recognise any concubine taken under the Chinese modern marriage. The Ridehalgh/McDouall Report considered that such a concubine was not lawfully wedded or taken and that in Hong Kong these unions were attached to a form of marriage which did not derive from any Chinese custom or GQC, "but which is a local imitation of an institution introduced into China during the time of the Nationalist Government". Moreover, in the Civil Code 1931 of the Republic of China, there was no provision for a man to have more than one living spouse, "and in no way recognized even the possibility of a lawfully taken ts'ip". Therefore, "[w]omen who in Hong Kong have been tricked by men, and those who have tricked men, into being taken on a[sic] alleged concubines attached to a Chinese modern marriage are legally, and often socially and economically, nothing more nor less than mistresses". Their children were also liable to be in a similar position, because at that time the Affiliation Ordinance did not offer much economic support for illegitimate children. The Ridehalgh/McDouall Report did offer changes to the law to protect the children's interests (Daily Information Bulletin, 14 March 1961, para. 12).

On Chinese customary marriage, the Ridehalgh/McDouall Report considered that there were strong representations from women's organisations to withdraw the recognition of Chinese customary marriages, but the opinions of Sir Man Kam Lo should not be overlooked. On balance, the Ridehalgh/McDouall Report did not recommend a total abolition of Chinese customary marriage, since they considered that there was a sturdy minority of Hong Kong residents who still wanted to continue

[6] The original texts in the Ridehalgh/McDouall Report 1960 did not give the impression to the readers that the present report was going to sever from the Strickland Committee: "At this stage we must make special acknowledgement of our indebtedness to the report on 'Chinese Law and Customs [sic] in Hong Kong' compiled by a Committee under the chairmanship of the late Mr. George Strickland, and the late Sir Man Kam Lo's Comments on that report. We have however thought it would be more convenient to present this report of ours in such a way that it will not be essential for any reader to have to keep on referring to the Strickland Committee's report, although we have indicated three cross-references by footnotes." See Ridehalgh & McDouall (1960, para. 4).

their marriages according to old Chinese custom (Daily Information Bulletin, 14 March 1961, para. 18). Rather, the Ridehalgh/McDouall Report recommended regulating the Chinese customary marriage so as to avoid any potential abuses of the system. The Ridehalgh/McDouall Report proposed that first, Chinese customary marriage "should be defined by legislation as meaning any marriage contracted as far as can be reasonably ascertained in accordance with the traditional customs of the parties' families". It argued that such definition was not rigid because even in 1843 there was no universally one fixed form of "Chinese Customary Marriage". An administrative mechanism would be devised by the government to determine "whether or not a particular ceremony or network of ceremonies wither was properly performed or was essential to a given Customary Marriage". The government should also encourage the additional carrying out of a civil ceremony (in other words, the remarriage of a couple married according to Chinese customary marriage) in accordance with the provisions of the Marriage Ordinance, in a marriage in which there was no concubine. And, if the couples did not want to "remarry" under the Marriage Ordinance, they could record their marriage in special registers kept by the Secretary for Chinese Affairs and the District Commissioner New Territories without going through any special ceremony. This record should be accepted as presumptive evidence of the original celebration of a lawful and valid Chinese customary marriage. The Ridehalgh/McDouall Report also recommended that a law should be drafted so that after the "Appointed Day", no marriage, either customary or otherwise, could be contracted in Hong Kong if either of the parties is under 16 years of age. This restriction also applied to *Sam Po Tsai*, but it was noted that this restriction would also apply to the final ceremony, and would not affect the betrothal part of marriages promised at early ages (although a *Sam Po Tsai* already had the freedom to break off her engagement).[7] The Ridehalgh/McDouall Report recommended not to recognise *Kim Tiu* marriages (Daily Information Bulletin, 14 March 1961, para. 20).[8]

Finally, this Report proposed that the government would review the whole position with regard to Chinese customary marriages in 5 years' time. The Ridehalgh/McDouall Report hoped that by doing so, they could achieve two objectives in connection with the reforms on concubines and divorce. Firstly, this approach remained sympathetic to social realities, rather than imposing an aggressive and impractical uprooting of age-old tradition. Secondly, it would ensure that those relatively small and decreasing number of genuine Chinese customary marriages would "steadily and by natural means approach vanishing form". The Ridehalgh/McDouall Report

[7]This refers to the Chinese customary practice of "child brides" (*Tongyangxi*). In Hong Kong it was called *Sam Po Tsai*, literally means "child daughter-in-law". In Hong Kong, an administrator in the New Territories refers this to a situation when a young girl who had been reared by a family not her own with the purpose of marrying her to one of the sons of that family. When this girl was up to an age of 15, she would only be working in the household just like a worker. Then when the girl and the son were both coming to an age of 16 to 18, the couple would then get married. See Notes on Some Chinese Customs in the New Territories (1955, pp. 5–6).

[8]But no reason was given.

considered that spreading "modern" ideas through the creation of more and more centres of education and entertainment, raising adult and juvenile literary, increasing facilities for the Registry of Marriage, and constantly improving communications could all help to eliminate the institution of Chinese customary marriage (Daily Information Bulletin, 14 March 1961, paras. 20–21).

In sum, the Ridehalgh/McDouall Report 1960 considered that the best way to deal with Chinese customary marriage was to let it vanish of its own accord rather than through outright abolition. By regulating Chinese customary marriage through legislation, the government intended to make the legal recognition of the institution more difficult, since such recognition would only be given with the "approval" of the new administrative mechanisms devised by the government. These recommendations, if accepted, would cause difficulties and indeterminacy for couples who wished to make an institution of Chinese customary marriage. Given such difficulties, the government hoped that this would encourage more couples to go for lawful marriage under the Marriage Ordinance, resulting, hopefully, in a gradual elimination of Chinese customary marriage in Hong Kong.

On the dissolution of marriage, to protect the right of concubinage, the Ridehalgh/McDouall Report proposed that after the "Appointed Day", the wife was entitled to dissolve the marriage if the husband took a concubine without her consent. That dissolution would have the wife entitled to maintenance until her death or remarriage. But the Ridehalgh/McDouall Report added that a subsequent withdrawal of consent by the wife should not constitute a valid reason for the dissolution of marriage. Further, the Ridehalgh/McDouall Report proposed that no such dissolution was valid unless both husband and wife had freely agreed to it. The Ridehalgh/McDouall Report also recommended that, subject to both husband and wife agreeing, the dissolution of Chinese customary marriage could rest upon the established and traditional customs of the families of the parties to the marriage (Daily Information Bulletin, 14 March 1961, para. 27). These recommendations significantly altered Chinese customary law and practice on divorce, contrasting with the reasons for divorce stipulated in the GQC. This is because in the GQC, the reception of a concubine into the family was not a reason for the wife to ask for a divorce. And, there was no right for the wife to request a unilateral dissolution of marriage under the GQC. Therefore, the Ridehalgh/McDouall Report was trying to give a statutory right of refusal to the wife on the taking of a concubine by her husband. But, given the inferior status of wife in a traditional Chinese family, it would be difficult for the wife to reject the reception of a concubine by her husband if he chose to do so.

On the issue of concubines, the Ridehalgh/McDouall Report considered that this had to be dealt with by civil but not criminal basis. Therefore, the report disagreed with the suggestion that all forms of concubinage could be stopped by making it a criminal offence. Before making recommendations on the status of concubine, the Ridehalgh/McDouall Report considered two factors. Firstly, in most Chinese customary marriages, the husband had the right to take a concubine with or without his wife's consent, if he thought he could afford it. Such practice had been recognised in Hong Kong for over a hundred years. Secondly, the concubine would find it very difficult to obtain a dissolution of concubinage if she had born a son. Consequently, the Ridehalgh/McDouall Report found it "impracticable to attempt to abolish by one stroke of the pen the institution of concubinage as a permissible though not apparently very widely practised part of the Chinese Customary Marriage system in Hong Kong". They considered that the local feeling was that the practice of concubinage was becoming extinct, and they felt that "a natural death was preferable to death hastened by legislative action".

Therefore, the Ridehalgh/McDouall Report recommended an accelerated policy of legislative attrition of the institution of concubinage in Chinese customary marriage. This policy comprised four elements. Firstly, they proposed the statutory right for a principal wife to ask for a dissolution of marriage if the husband wished to take a concubine against her wishes or without her knowledge. This did not apply to concubines who were lawfully taken before the "Appointed Day". Secondly, they proposed the statutory right for any concubine to dissolve her marriage whenever she might wish, with or without reason. The future custody of, and responsibility for, their children born by the concubines should be determined by mutual agreement or by a magistrate, with a right to appeal to a single judge in the Supreme Court. Thirdly, they proposed equal statutory rights for a principal wife, a concubine and their children to take legal action against the husband for maintenance. Fourthly, they proposed a review of the position after 5 years, to consider whether it would be practicable "to determine a date whereafter no husband would be allowed to take a concubine". In sum, the Ridehalgh/McDouall Report did not give extra rights to the concubine in a Chinese customary marriage. In Chinese law and custom there was no special requirement for a concubine to sever the relationship. Moreover, a concubine already had a right to maintenance if she decided to remain unmarried after the death of her husband. The Ridehalgh/McDouall Report only delayed the decision on the abolition of concubinage for another 5 years (Daily Information Bulletin, 14 March 1961, paras. 28–29).

The Ridehalgh/McDouall Report did, however, attempt to resolve the issue of the children born to a so-called concubine according to Chinese modern marriage (including Registry Marriage and Reputed Marriage). As mentioned earlier, the Ridehalgh/McDouall Report proposed to not validate Chinese modern marriage, or the so-called concubine (who was in fact a mistress) taken in such a marriage. The Ridehalgh/McDouall Report explained that they did not propose to recognise any institution of concubinage in the Chinese modern marriage for two reasons. First, it would extend rather than reduce the institution of concubinage. Second, it would be impracticable to make the laws which could distinguish between a woman who wanted to be a secondary wife to her husband and others who were trying to get married simply for the husband's money. Therefore, the report considered that it would inflict a gross injustice on the real wife if the law granted a mistress the lawful status and financial rights of a concubine. Nonetheless, the Ridehalgh/McDouall Report considered that the government should consider the interests and welfare of the children borne by mistresses carefully (Daily Information Bulletin, 14 March 1961, para. 30).

To this issue the Ridehalgh/McDouall Report proposed three solutions. Firstly, they proposed to enact legislation for the protection of a woman regarded as a so-called concubine under Chinese modern marriage. The Ridehalgh/McDouall Report proposed that if a so-called concubine did not break off the union on her own accord, or marry, then she might apply for maintenance in court, in addition to any court order made in respect of any of her children. Secondly, by proposing a new law, the wife and their children could seek for reasonable provisions to be taken out from his estate after the death of the husband in court. Finally, by amending the Affiliation Ordinance, the court might order a man to provide maintenance and education of a child born to him in wedlock (including a Chinese customary marriage) until the age of 16 years. In sum, these recommendations attempted to protect the interests of the so-called concubine and children and the interests of the wife in a Chinese modern marriage. These problems had to date remained unresolved due to the laissez-faire approach taken by the Hong Kong Government after the publication of the Strickland Report (Daily Information Bulletin, 14 March 1961, para. 30).

5.6 Final Decision: Abolition of Concubinage in 1965

The key issue facing the Ridehalgh/McDouall Report was that not only did it disappoint the social organisations which had been fighting for the abolition of concubinage since the 1950s, it also failed to meet the expectations of the Colonial Office, which also wanted abolition as early as possible. Soon after the publication of the Ridehalgh/McDouall Report, the Hong Kong Government had to face increasing pressure to end the institution of concubinage not from Hong Kong. This time, the Colonial Office pressed the Hong Kong Government to do this by pressuring the government to reform the Chinese marriage laws in compliance with various United Nations' conventions, thereby enforcing a minimum age for marriage, implementing monogamous marriage and protecting the interests of the wife and children. Finally, in 1965, the Hong Kong Government submitted a draft report to the Colonial Office in which it proposed to abolish the institution of concubinage. This draft was dispatched without prior submission to the Executive Council for approval, in order to mollify the frustration in the Colonial Office.

5.6.1 The District Commissioner of New Territories

Although the Executive Council approved the Ridehalgh/McDouall Report on 13 December 1960, the report was not officially released until 14 March 1961. Copies were sent to the relevant government departments, all members of the Executive Council and Legislative Council, professional organisations, social organisations such as the Hong Kong Council of Women, Y.W.C.A. of Hong Kong, Heung Yee Kuk and Rural Committees for comments (Memo from the Secretary for Chinese

Affairs, 11 March 1961a; Memo from District Commissioner New Territories, 22 March 1961; Letter from the Secretary for Chinese Affairs, 10 September 1960). Originally, the Secretary for Chinese Affairs had proposed an 8-week consultation period for these concerned groups and individuals to comment on the Ridehalgh/McDouall Report (Letter from the Secretary for Chinese Affairs, 10 September 1960). However, the District Commissioner of the New Territories, Holmes, asked for a delay to the consultation because of a delay in distribution and the fact that some leading officials in Heung Yee Kuk were out of town (Memo from District Commissioner New Territories, 22 March 1961). A special extension was granted by the Governor for the opinions of Heung Yee Kuk to be submitted up to the end of June 1961 (Memo from the Secretary for Chinese Affairs, 15 June 1961b).

Meanwhile, the Secretary for Chinese Affairs had arranged meetings with different organisations to discuss their views. The views from Heung Yee Kuk and the Rural Committees were taking longer than expected. Finally, Holmes the District Commissioner of the New Territories submitted a compilation of their views in a memo to the Secretary for Chinese Affairs on 12 September 1961. This memo was a mixture of comments from the Heung Yee Kuk and Rural Committees with some personal comments from Holmes. At first, Holmes complimented the Ridehalgh/McDouall Report for succeeding admirably in producing a simple and readable report. He was confident that all the recommendations could be safely implemented. But he reminded the Secretary for Chinese Affairs of the changes which might affect the laws on inheritances and succession: "there will undoubtedly be strong opposition from traditionalist opinion in the New Territories, though that should not necessarily deter us from making such changes as further examinations shows to be necessary?" (Memo from the District Commissioner New Territories, 12 September 1961, para. 2).

Having said that, Holmes criticised Heung Yee Kuk's reply as "no comments of real importance have emerged, except in the purely negative sense that they cannot now claim that they were never consulted". After that, Holmes made some personal comments on the Ridehalgh/McDouall Report. Regarding Chinese customary marriages, he was concerned about the administrative procedure, or mechanism of its implementation. In particular, he was concerned about the records of these marriages, which would require at the outset an investigation of each case, sight evidence, and perhaps calls for objections from the neighbourhood of each party to the marriage, before any such marriage could be recorded. He agreed with abolishing the practice of *Sam Po Tsai*, which he considered achievable by abolishing child betrothal. However, he concluded that the best way to enforce this was to make a prosecution when a case came to notice. He also agreed to end the recognition of *Kim Tiu* marriage (Memo from the District Commissioner New Territories, 12 September 1961, paras. 3–8).

On the recommendations relating to the dissolution of Chinese customary and modern marriages, Holmes said that these were eminently reasonable and had his support. He commented that these customary practices should be changed: "despite the probable objections from male traditionalists in the New Territories I agree with you that the time has come to over-ride Chinese custom to this limited extent".

Holmes also supported the recommendations on the issue of concubine and mistresses in the Ridehalgh/McDouall Report, though he considered that these recommendations would certainly be opposed by a considerable number of male traditionalists in the New Territories. In sum, after some considerable delay, the District Commissioner New Territories agreed entirely with what Ridehalgh/ McDouall Report had recommended. Holmes concluded that "[t]o my mind the best way of meeting the inevitable objections from male traditionalists will be to stress, in a carefully planned publicity campaign, not what is being changed but what is deliberately being retained" (Memo from the District Commissioner New Territories, 12 September 1961, paras. 11–12, 15).

5.6.2 *The United Nations Treaties*

The District Commissioner of the New Territories was the strongest supporter of the Ridehalgh/McDouall Report in the government. The comments outside the government did not favour the recommendations of the report. One of the biggest problems that the Secretary for Chinese Affairs encountered was the obligations of the Hong Kong Government in international treaties relating to marriage and other related matters, as signed by the UK in the United Nations (UN). The social organisations and the Colonial Office considered that such obligations should be observed by the Hong Kong Government so that the issues of the Chinese customary marriage and the institution of concubinage should be resolved following to the requirements of the international treaties.

The issue of the treaty obligations of Hong Kong under the UN treaties originated from the attendance of the Secretary for Chinese Affairs, McDouall, at a UN seminar in Tokyo, held on 8 to 12 May 1962 (United Nations 1962). In a personal memo sent by McDouall to the Attorney General, Heenan, McDouall mentioned that in the course of seminar a Pakistani observer read out a letter sent by the Hong Kong Council of Women and asked the question as to why the Hong Kong Government had done absolutely nothing for the last 10 years on the status of women in Hong Kong. McDouall expressed his dissatisfaction with what he considered as personal attacks from the Hong Kong Council of Women:

> I do not think it was meant to be as malicious as it sounded. Nor do I think that these good ladies were correctly described to me, in a recent confidential memo. [sic] from the Head of another Department, as a bunch of she-hyenas. Rightly or wrongly they are genuinely interested in what they feel is a need for drastic legislation and social reform, even if in some cases there may be strong personal reasons for those feelings. (Memo from Secretary for Chinese Affairs, 18 July 1962a, para. 1)

McDouall considered that the Council of Women had mistakenly presumed that the seminar would pass resolutions that might be binding on the representatives' respective governments. He decided to make an address to the Council of Women in a closed-door meeting, to spell out the positions of the government (Memo from Secretary for Chinese Affairs, 18 July 1962a, para. 2). A draft speech was attached for Heenan's comment. In the draft speech, McDouall first explained the background of the events leading to the Ridehalgh/McDouall Report. He stated that after the release of the Ridehalgh/McDouall Report on 14 March 1961, his files were "bulging with letters, reports, press cuttings and departmental memoranda" (Text of an Address by the Secretary for Chinese Affairs, 2 August 1962, p. 10). He explained that in November 1961, he had to take a leave for 4 months. Then while he returned to work in April 1962, he attended the UN seminar to Tokyo, which also brought him several extra kilograms of paper. He considered that there were some actions that the government should do after attending the seminar in Tokyo: firstly, he promised to study the effects of international conventions or resolutions on the status of women. Secondly, the government would also study all relevant information from the UN seminar, both in the report of the seminar and other papers brought back by McDouall. Thirdly, McDouall promised to study the stack of comments, criticisms and advice arising out of the Ridehalgh/McDouall Report (Text of an Address by the Secretary for Chinese Affairs, 2 August 1962, p. 16).

What McDouall referred to in the speech on the international conventions or resolutions were two publications: first, *Legal Status of Married Women (Reports submitted by the Secretary-General)*, published by the Commission on the Status of Women of the United Nations (New York, 1958), and second, *Report of the Fifteen Session of the Session of the Commission on the Status of Women (March 1961)* (Economic and Social Council; Official Records, 32nd session, supplement No. 7). These reports were requested by McDouall and were forward by the Governor to the Colonial Office in a Savingram on 24 July 1962. The Secretary for Chinese Affairs wished for them to be taken into consideration in the final recommendations on the UK's commitments under international conventions and resolutions (Savingram from the Governor, 24 July 1962, para. 2).

The international convention in question was the Convention on Consent to Marriage, Minimum Age for Marriage and Registration of Marriages, which was signed on 7 November 1962 but not ratified.[9] At the time that McDouall made his enquiry to the UK Government, the Colonial Office explained that the UK delegate at the UN regretted the omission of a suitable territorial applicable article, in other words, the omission of an article which would have granted the UK the right to make certain articles applicable or not applicable in overseas territories such as Hong Kong. As the Colonial Office put it, this omission "would frustrate the U.K.'s earnest desire to become a party to the Convention for a long time" (Savingram from the Secretary of State, 7 June 1963). For this reason, the UK Government was not considering ratifying the convention at the time this reply was given to McDouall on 7 June 1963. It had taken 11 months for the Colonial Office to make a reply. On the other hand, however, the Colonial Office was pressing very hard for the Hong Kong Government to make a decision on the Ridehalgh/McDouall Report, especially on the abolition of concubinage. This will be discussed later in this chapter.

[9] The UK government ratified it on 9 July 1970.

The Convention on Consent to Marriage, Minimum Age for Marriage and Registration of Marriages gave protection to children by setting the minimum age for marriage and promoting the freedom of marriage. It was seen as a manifestation of a recommendation adopted in 1956 by the Conference which introduced the Supplementary Convention on the Abolition of Slavery, the Slave Trade and Institutions and Practices similar to Slavery and the initiative of the Economic and Social Council, on the elimination of some customary practices which limited a spouse's freedom of choice (Schwelb 1963, p. 338). Article 1 stipulated that "No marriage shall be legally entered into without the full and free consent of both parties", and affirmed the principle of freedom of marriage. Article 2 specified that "States Parties to the present Convention shall take legislative action to specify a minimum age for marriage". But the minimum years of age was not specified in the Convention. Article 3 required that all marriages must be registered by the competent authority: "All marriages shall be registered in an appropriate official register by the competent authority"; no administrative procedure or mechanism was specified in the treaty so the State Parties could have the flexibility to enforce this article. In sum, this commission only specified certain principles on the freedom of marriage, the setting of minimum age and the registration of marriage. Other than that, this convention did not specify issues relating to the abolition of concubinage, which was the focal point of the social organisations in response to the marriage reform proposed by Ridehalgh/McDouall Report. International treaty obligations might not have been the main driving force for the abolition of concubinage, but with pressure from the Colonial Office, they were part of a last-ditch effort to change the state-of-mind of the Hong Kong Government.

5.6.3 The Colonial Office, Again and Again

In March 1961, the Hong Kong Government submitted a draft report for the Colonial Office's comment, upon request of an officer who spotted a paragraph on this issue from the daily information bulletin submitted by the Hong Kong Government.[10] Officers in the Colonial Office were angered by the slow progress of the Governor. For example, Freda Gwilliam, an officer who was responsible for advancing women's education rights in the colonies, commented that on the issues of equal pay of men and women and the abolition of concubinage in Hong Kong, "we are showing ourselves behind the thinking and practice of other areas for which we have responsibility or with which we have been in close association" (Minute, 5 May, 1961). On the matter of equal pay of men and women, she commented that "Hong Kong is a colony in a closer sense that almost any other territory for which we have responsibility and yet it is most retrogressive in its attitude of women. This comes at a time

[10]This report was subsequently published as the *Report on Chinese Marriage in Hong Kong* (Ridehalgh & McDouall, 1960) which was commonly referred as Ridehalgh/McDouall Report.

when internationally we are taking the lead in this field". Whereas on the issue of concubinage, she criticised the Colonial Office for having similar attitudes that "seem to be leaving the initiative to those who do not want to change". She considered that "we have a responsibility to be as progressive as possible in the advice we offer and continue to offer in order to stimulate a point of view more in keeping with the tenor of time". Admitting that the Colonial Office had a responsibility to press for change, she further commented that "I would hope that an expression of regret that a more humane and modern approach to these matters has not been adopted by the Chinese men could be made sorrowfully and frequently—the drip-drip method that the Chinese perfected in the literal sense!" (Minute, 5 May, 1961, paras. 1–2). Her comments, coupled with previous comments in the Colonial Office, showed firstly, the impatience of Colonial Office on the slow progress of the Hong Kong Government towards the abolition of concubinage. And secondly, in a broad sense, it showed the dissatisfaction of the Colonial Office with the Hong Kong Government's strategy to advance gender equality in the territory.

The long-awaited publication of the report "Chinese Marriage in Hong Kong" in 1961 (commonly known as the Ridehalgh/McDouall Report) seemed to mollify the Colonial Office on the progress of reform for the time being. The Colonial Office did not exert additional pressure on the Hong Kong Government to take further action. In addition, the Hong Kong Government had shown that they were undertaking preparatory work towards a comprehensive reform on Chinese customary marriage based on the recommendations of Ridehalgh/McDouall Report. For example, correspondence between Hong Kong and London showed that the Hong Kong Government asked for advice from the Colonial Office on the issue of the international obligations of Hong Kong concerning the equal protection of men and women. In May 1963, the Hong Kong Government asked the Colonial Office about the applicability of UN conventions such as the Convention on Consent on Marriage, Minimum Age for Marriage and Registration for Marriage to Hong Kong, as mentioned above. The Hong Kong Government argued that their recommendations on marriage reform had conformed to the conventions in the United Nations. Nevertheless, not much progress on Chinese customary marriage reform was recorded in the correspondence between London and Hong Kong. Yet, in response to a question raised by an MP on the inheritance law in Hong Kong in November 1964, the Hong Kong Governor Sir David Trench reiterated the complications of marriage reform:

> The variety of customary forms, including the modern style marriage contracted in supposed conformity with Articles 980–988 of the Nationalist Civil Code by very large number of people, and the complexity of legal problems of inheritance etc, make progress difficult, particularly as more urgent matters continue to demand prior attention. While we shall try to make headway I do not think any rapid progress is to be expected. (Telegram from Governor of Hong Kong, 18 November 1964, para. 2)

The reply surely annoyed an officer of the Colonial Office, Mr Higham, who was concerned about discriminatory practices in the law of succession and marriage (Minute by J. D. Higham, 9 February, 1965b). His view was echoed by Mrs Eriene White (Minute by L T Stapleton, 19 February, 1965), the Parliamentary

Under-Secretary of State for the Colonies, who had been advocating for the rights of women in the Labour Party for a long time.

The Colonial Office renewed its pressure on the Hong Kong Government. But the Hong Kong Government still refused to give any positive response on the progress of marriage reform. On 17 December 1964, Higham made an order that "I am afraid, therefore, that I must ask if you can let me have at greater length of your views on what further steps you propose to take before formulating final proposals and what sort of time you have in mind". Higham warned that "I am under directions from Ministers here to make this approach" (Letter from Colonial Office, 17 December 1964). Further, Higham asked the Colonial Secretariat in Hong Kong not only to consider the obligations under the UN Convention on Consent to Marriage, Minimum Age for Marriage and Registration of Marriages but also to take the Women's Charter of Singapore as a reference for reform. Higham dismissed any evolutionary approach to reform, as proposed by the Hong Kong Government, and warned again: "If you feel that it is going to be difficult to go for anything on the lines of the Women's Charter and, instead, you feel that a more evolutionary approach is called for, it would be helpful to know this soon, as I would expect there to be a certain reluctance here to accept the merits of gradualness except for the compelling reason" (Letter from Colonial Office, 17 December 1964, para. 3). It is important to note that the Women's Charter of Singapore abolished the institution of concubinage, so the Colonial Office was effectively instructing, even ordering, the Hong Kong Government to abolish concubinage. On 11 February 1965, the Colonial Secretary of Hong Kong Mr E. B. Teesdale foresaw dim prospects for marriage reform, stating: "I am afraid, however, that I still cannot give you any time-table for the introduction of new legislation to implement some of the recommendations in the Ridehalgh/McDouall Report" (Letter from E.B. Teesdale, 11th February). The Colonial Office was deeply disappointed. Mr Carter minuted that "we would be wrong, I think, to expect any startling changes to be made as a result of current deliberation". He further added that, if measures suggested by Ridehalgh/McDouall Report were substantially adopted, "there is a good prospect that a very useful start will be made in the regulation of Chinese marriages, in delivering the *coup de grâce* to concubinage and in meeting the requirements of the U.N. Convention on Marriages". He criticised the indecisiveness of the Hong Kong Government and suggested that they should "press Hong Kong to bring this to a conclusion in a reasonable speed" (Minute by W. S. Carter, 15 March, 1965, paras. 2–4). Shortly after the comments from Mr Carter, the Hong Kong Government released the long-awaited draft report in response to Ridehalgh/McDouall Report.

5.6.4 The Wind of Change in the Hong Kong Government

It took 4 years for the Secretary for Chinese Affairs to compile a report of the public response to the Ridehalgh/McDouall Report. One important issue was personal health problems of McDouall, who had to take long periods of leave from time to time. In addition, it required tremendous work and effort to compile and analyse the different views expressed by the social organisations and some key stakeholders. And, McDouall was, occasionally, frustrated by senior Chinese political figures in the Executive Council and Legislative Council and their lack of enthusiasm for the issues indicated in the Ridehalgh/McDouall Report.

Originally, McDouall thought that after 8 weeks of the release of the Ridehalgh/McDouall Report in 1961, he would only need a few extra months to compile a report in response. However, this plan was interrupted first by the longer than expected consultation exercise with Heung Yee Kuk and the Rural Committees (see Sect. 5.5.1). Also, his work was interrupted by long leave taken to deal with his personal health problems, and a lack of constructive opinions from senior Chinese political figures on how to resolve the pressure from the social organisations, who urged time and time again for the abolition of concubinage. The Colonial Secretariat had reminded McDouall to finish the task in timely fashion.

On 9 June 1961, the Secretary for Chinese Affairs, McDouall, mentioned in a minute that he would take at least 4 months to collate and analyse the materials, clear them with the principal government departments concerned and formulated the final views (Minute from the Secretary for Chinese Affairs, 9 June 1961). After 6 months, on 8 January 1962, the Colonial Secretary asked about the progress of the above (Memo from Colonial Secretary to Secretary for Chinese Affairs, 8 Jan 1962). And on 24 January 1962, the officer from the Secretary for Chinese Affairs, T.C. Cheng replied that any further action had to wait until the return of McDouall from vacation leave until mid-April 1962. Then, on 12 June 1962, the Colonial Secretary, again, asked about the progress of the report. McDouall this time, on 15 June 1962, mentioned that he had not been able to do additional work on this because after his participation into the UN seminar in Tokyo he had brought back several kilograms of papers and reports. McDouall stated that he would do the evaluation with the Attorney General and other government departments such as the Registrar-General, District Commissioner of the New Territories and Commissioner for the Co-operative Development and Fisheries then come back to the final recommendations. McDouall did not give any deadline on the report (Memo from Secretary for Chinese Affairs, 15 June 1962). After 8 months, on 22 February 1963, the Colonial Secretary asked for the present position of the report (Memo from Colonial Secretariat, 22 February 1963). McDouall replied in anger the very next day, 23 February 1963, with the words "please send no more hasteners" though he admitted that the progress was slower than he had hoped (Memo from Secretary for Chinese Affairs, 23 February 1963).

What McDouall did not state in the above memo was that, on 3 October 1962, he had sent a draft chapter (which presumably formed a chapter in a final report) relating to the analysis of the public opinions to three government departments for comment: the District Commissioner of the New Territories, the Commissioner for Co-operative Development and Fisheries and the Registrar General (Memo from Secretary for Chinese Affairs, 29 June 1962b). One notable part of this draft chapter was the public reactions on the gradual abolition of concubinage as recommended in the Ridehalgh/McDouall Report. To recap, this recommendation called for the restriction "but not at one stroke to attempt to abolish the genuinely traditional institution of Concubinage as a permissible though apparently comparatively rarely practised part of the Chinese Customary Marriage system" (see Sect. 5.5.4). In this draft chapter, McDouall mentioned that, of the 22 representations given by women or on behalf of women's organisations, 20 were opposed to the recommendation, and stood for the complete non-recognition, if not punishment, of any form of concubinage contracted after the "Appointed Day". Likewise, 28 men or male-dominated organisations, many of them with good standing in the community, took a similar view. However, 26 male-inspired representation, also well-informed and often westernised Chinese men, endorsed the government's recommendation. One typical view was that: "[C]oncubinage is an age-old system which cannot be run away with overnight. It involved too many women and children whose affairs are at stake, if this question is dealt with in a drastic manner". Another quote from a well-educated Chinese lady was that "[L]eave the question of concubinage alone and let it take the course of self-elimination". But the comments from the press were strongly against the recommendation, and five editorials advocated the immediate abolition of concubinage, or at least abolition after the Appointed Day (Memo from Secretary for Chinese Affairs, 29 June 1962b, paras. 86–87). Furthermore, this draft chapter stated clearly that the institution of concubinage, implying inferior status, might be in contravention with certain international treaties, such as the UN Charter and the Declaration of Human Rights. McDouall also remarked that the Tokyo Seminar which he attended had reacted against "the word"—that is, concubinage (Memo from Secretary for Chinese Affairs, 29 June 1962b, para. 88).

In their subsequent internal response to McDouall's request for comments on this draft chapter, the District Commissioner of the New Territories (Memo from District Commissioner New Territories, 9 October 1962) and the Registrar General did not touch upon the issue of concubinage. But, the Commissioner for Co-operative Development and Fisheries Department, Topley, warned of the rapid changes in this reform: "I do not think, however, that we should under-estimate the entire population aware of the implications of the new legal measures which are proposed and I fear, depending on what the real facts are, that we may find that our new laws are two steps ahead of the population as opposed to the half step which might be acceptable" (Memo from Co-operative Development and Fisheries Department, 13 October 1962).

Nonetheless, a letter sent by the Colonial Office on 17 December 1964 gave a final warning to McDouall and the instruction was clear: abolish concubinage now (Letter from Colonial Office, 17 December 1964). On 25 January 1965, the Secretary for Chinese Affairs sent a memo to the Deputy Colonial Secretary that he saw no difficulties with conforming to the UN resolutions and to producing a better outcome than the Singapore Women's Charter. He considered that the sole difficulty was the time needed to finish the task.

He stated that in March 1963, he had given the analyses, comments and revised recommendations of the issues relating to Chinese laws and customs to the

Chinese Unofficial members of the Executive and Legislative Councils for comment. Then, in June 1963, McDouall and the Attorney General met with the above members for a joint discussion. But the results—according to McDouall—were discouraging. McDouall commented that the approach of the members appeared to be ad hoc, and they seemed at times to have skipped much of what had been written in the original reports and the revised recommendations. Finally, McDouall was left with "a mangled draft on an exceeding complex matter, and with a peppering of unco-ordinated[sic] amendments that raised a host of new difficulties". McDouall stated that in June 1964, he had a long discussion with Mrs Ellen Li on the issue. Subsequently, McDouall considered that he would make a revised version of 12 recommendations and discussed with C. Y. Kwan (who was the only member of the Executive or Legislative Council and was a co-author of 1948 Strickland Report), before sending a new proposal to the Executive Council, with advice from the Attorney General and Registrar General. McDouall asked the Colonial Secretariat to conduct further checks on the UN Charter and resolutions. He then predicted that a minimum of 6 weeks was required, depending on the exigencies of other work (Memo from Secretary for Chinese Affairs, 25 January 1965, paras. 4–8). On 12 March 1965, the Colonial Office stated that they would like to see any proposals before the submission to the Executive Council (Letter from Colonial Office, 12 March 1965a).

In response to the pressures from the Colonial Office, on 25 January 1965, McDouall had provided a first set of consolidated recommendations to C. Y. Kwan for comments. McDouall wanted feedback from C. Y. Kwan due to the latter's strong views on the issue of inheritance laws in the Chinese community in the budget debate (Letter from Secretary for Chinese Affairs, 25 January 1965). In the enclosure to this letter, on the issue of concubine, the government revealed its intention to abolish concubinage. In it, the government stated that it would seek to enact legislation to provide that, after the Appointed Day, no woman could acquire legal status as a concubine. The status and rights of women as a concubine in the Chinese customary marriage before the Appointed Day would be affirmed. And, the government also proposed that the recognition of the legitimacy of their children should be ensured (Recommendations 1965, 9(1)). On the issue of maintenance of a concubine, it was recommended that a concubine in a Chinese customary marriage before the Appointed Day, or her minor children, might institute civil proceedings against the husband for maintenance (Recommendations 1965, 9(2)).

On 19 March 1965, McDouall gave his comments to the Colonial Secretary in a telegram to the Colonial Office sent on 17 March 1965. In it, McDouall said that after discussion with C. Y. Kwan, there would be no objections in principle from the Chinese Unofficial members of the Executive and Legislative Councils to introducing laws to conform with the UN Convention. McDouall still adhered to his promise that he was going to submit a paper to the Executive Council on the follow-up to the Ridehalgh/McDouall Report (Memo from the Secretary for Chinese Affairs, 19 March 1965). This intention had been made clear when C. Y. Kwan had spoken in the budget speech at the Legislative Council on 11 March 1965. In this speech

C. Y. Kwan discussed the issue of discrimination against female descendants in Chinese customary law and practice with regard to the distribution of the estate in cases of intestacy, after which he also asked for an update on the progress of the Ridehalgh/McDouall Report.[11] In reply, McDouall promised that, "with the advice and guidance which the Attorney-general and I will seek from the Chinese Unofficial members of this Council, it will shortly be possible to submit for Your Excellency-in-Council's consideration a firm set of what I hope will prove to be realistic recommendation" (Extract from Mr McDouall's Budget Speech, 26 March 1965). Accordingly, prior to this final submission, McDouall also sent a letter to another Chinese Unofficial member of the Legislative Council, P. C. Woo, to seek his views on the revised draft recommendations (Letter from J. C. McDouall, 29 March 1965a). In it, the recommendations on the abolition of concubinage were the same as those contained in the previous draft sent to C. Y. Kwan.

Finally, McDouall produced a comprehensive draft report to the Chinese Unofficial members of the Executive and Legislative Councils for comments on 3 May 1965. McDouall asked the members to attend a joint meeting to discuss this new paper (Letter from J. C. McDouall, 3 May 1965b). Additionally, a copy had been sent in advance to government departments for comment on 22 April 1965. On 7 May 1965, two copies of the draft report were sent to the Colonial Office (Letter from Colonial Secretariat, G. C. Hamilton, 7 May 1965). Upon receipt, the Colonial Office seemed to be satisfied with the recommendations of the Hong Kong Government. Consequently, shortly after receiving comments from a Mr Carter, the Hong Kong Government released the long-awaited draft report in response to the Ridehalgh/McDouall Report and sent a copy to the Colonial Office. After scrutinising the materials, Mr. Carter minuted that:

> if these proposals are finally accepted I do not think we could wish for more from Hong Kong. They meet in entirely the requirements of the U.N. Convention on marriages and are in line on all essential points with the Marriage and Divorce provisions of Singapore's Women Charter. Concubinage is abolished … Clearly there is still some way to go before we can be sure that they will be implemented in this form. (Minute by Mr. W. S. Carter, 24 June 1965)

Likewise, Mrs Eriene White minuted that she was encouraged by this report (Minute by Mrs. Eriene White, 25 June 1965).

Following this approval, the draft report became the backbone of the yet another formal report, McDouall/Heenan Report of 1965, which will be discussed in the next chapter.

[11] According to the traditional Chinese customary practices, only male descendants are entitled to succeed to the estate of the deceased paterfamilias. See Mr C.Y. Kwan's Budget Speech (11 March, 1965).

5.7 Conclusion

It took almost 5 years for the Hong Kong Government to change its mind, from a steady elimination of the institution of concubinage as proposed by Ridehalgh/McDouall Report in 1961, to the final decision to put an end to the institution of concubinage as proposed in the draft report prepared by the Secretary for Chinese Affairs in 1965.

It is important to note that according to government records, there was a sharp division in the community on the issue of the abolition of concubinage. Progressive social organisations urged for abolition, but conservative Chinese senior political figures kept resisting any such changes. Within government departments however there was no strong view urging for an immediate abolition. The government departments' opinions were understandable, because the institution of concubinage had become rare, and the traditionalists in the New Territories did not wish to end the institution very soon. In addition, some Chinese senior figures held strong views against the abolition of concubinage. On the other hand, social organisations, particularly women's organisations, were pressing very hard in both the UK (through parliamentary questions) and Hong Kong for an immediate abolition of concubinage. Given the issue of concubinage had been divisive since the Strickland Report, the steady approach taken by the government was discernible but arguably not a good solution in view of the rising demand of the equality of men and women from the social organisations.

But such an attitude of the Hong Kong Government was not appreciated by the Colonial Office in London. Because of the pressure of the parliamentary questions and the personal distaste of some officers for the institution of concubinage in Hong Kong, the Colonial Office pressed very hard for the Hong Kong Government to instigate an immediate abolition of concubinage. Given the sluggish approach adopted by the Hong Kong Government, the Colonial Office turned to the Women's Charter in Singapore and the UK's international obligations under UN conventions and resolutions as leverage to exert greater political pressure on the Hong Kong Government. Such political pressure finally forced the Hong Kong Government to back down and changed the course of the Ridehalgh/McDouall Report—from the steady and natural elimination of concubinage to an immediate abolition of concubinage. To this end, it is shown in the archival records that the Colonial Office did not have any master plan to destroy Chinese marriage customs, nor did they attempt to replace the Chinese family system with a new family order. The sole purpose of the Colonial Office was to abolish the institution of concubinage. They did not even comment on any of the recommendations in the Strickland Report and Ridehalgh/McDouall Report except for the institution of concubinage. It is also very important to note that the Hong Kong Government never revealed the political pressure from the Colonial Office to the public. Thus, without reading the records in the Colonial Office, one might reach the conclusion that the decision to abolish concubinage was made due to political pressure from the united action of social organisations in Hong Kong and not from the political drive of the Colonial Office.

References

Chinese Marriages Validity Questions: Letters. (1958, October 6). *Chinese Marriages Validity Questions and Appointment of AG-SCA Committee, Letters to the Hong Kong Council of Women, Young Women's Christian Association and Mrs Rose Helena Li Chow, 6 October 1958*, (HKRS 410-10-7). The Hong Kong Record Series, Hong Kong.

Chinese Law and Custom, Letter from K. G. Ashton. (1957, January 17). *Chinese law and custom, letter from K. G. Ashton Colonial Office to C. B. Burgess,17 January 1957*, (HKRS 41-1-3106-5). The Hong Kong Record Series, Hong Kong.

Extract from Mr McDouall's Budget Speech. (1965, March 26). *Chinese marriages in Hong Kong 1965 Developments SCA 172_65 1, Extract from Mr McDouall's Budget Speech on 26 March 1965*, (HKRS 410-10-27-1). The Hong Kong Record Series, Hong Kong.

Convention on Consent to Marriage, Minimum Age for Marriage and Registration of Marriages. https://treaties.un.org/pages/viewdetails.aspx?src=ind&mtdsg_no=xvi-3&chapter=16&lang=en. Accessed on 31 Oct 2018.

Letter from A. Ridehalgh. (1957, May 27). *chinese law and custom, letter from A. Ridehalgh to the Chairman of the Executive Committee, The Hong Kong Council of Women, 27 May 1957*, (HKRS 41-1-3106-5). The Hong Kong Record Series, Hong Kong.

Letter from A. Ridehalgh. (1960, September 10). *Chinese law and custom, letter from A. Ridehalgh and McDouall to His Excellency the Governor, 10 September 1960*, (HKRS 41-1-3106-10). The Hong Kong Record Series, Hong Kong.

Letter from Chairman of the Hong Kong Council of Women. (1957, November 2). *Chinese law and custom, letter from Chairman of the Hong Kong Council of Women to E. B. David, Colonial Secretary, 2 November 1957*, (HKRS 41-1-3106-5). The Hong Kong Record Series, Hong Kong.

Letter from Colonial Office. (1964, December 17). *Chinese law and custom, J. D. Higham to Colonial Secretariat, E. B. Teesdale, 17 December 1964*, (HKRS 41-1-3106-10). The Hong Kong Record Series, Hong Kong.

Letter from Colonial Office. (1965a, March 12). *Chinese law and custom, letter from Colonial Office, J. D. Higham to Colonial Secretariat E.B. Teesdale, 12 March 1965*, (HKRS 41-1-3106-10). The Hong Kong Record Series, Hong Kong.

Letter from Colonial Office. (1965b, April 22). *Chinese law and custom, letter from Colonial Office, W.S. Carter to Colonial Secretariat, G. C. Hamilton, Hong Kong, 22 April 1965*, (HKRS 41-1-3106-10). The Hong Kong Record Series, Hong Kong.

Letter from Colonial Secretariat. (1957, April 17). *Chinese laws and customs in Hong Kong, Letter from Colonial Secretariat, C. B. Burgess to Colonial Office, K. G. Ashton, 17 April 1957*, (CO1030/819). The Hong Kong Record Series, Hong Kong.

Letter from Colonial Secretariat. (1965, May 7). *chinese law and custom, letter from Colonial Secretariat, G. C. Hamilton to W. S. Carter, Colonial Office, 7 May 1965*, (HKRS 41-1-3106-10). The Hong Kong Record Series, Hong Kong.

Letter from District Commissioner. (1958, October 6). *Chinese marriages validity questions, letter from District Commissioner, New Territories to Hon. Secretary for Chinese Affairs, 6 October 1958*, (HKRS 410-10-7). The Hong Kong Record Series, Hong Kong.

Letter from E. B. David. (1957, November 26). *Chinese law and custom, letter from E. B. David, Colonial Secretary to the Chairman of the Hong Kong Council of Women, 26 November 1957*, (HKRS 41-1-3106-5). The Hong Kong Record Series, Hong Kong.

Letter from E.B. Teesdale. (1965, February 11). *Chinese law and custom, letter from E.B. Teesdale to J.D. Higham, Colonial Office, 11 February, 1965*, (HKRS 41-1-3106-10). The Hong Kong Record Series, Hong Kong.

Letter from Ellen Li. (1957, June 17). *Chinese marriages validity questions, letter from Ellen Li to Sir Man Kam Lo, 17 June 1957*, (HKRS 410-10-7). The Hong Kong Record Series, Hong Kong.

Letter from Elsie Elliot. (1960, June 6). *Chinese laws and customs in Hong Kong, Letter from Elsie Elliot, United Nations Association Hong Kong, Women Section to Barbara Castle M.P. 6 June 1960*, (CO 1030/1346). The National Archives, Kew.

Letter from Governor. (1960, September 12). *Chinese law and custom, letter from Governor to Attorney General and Secretary for Chinese Affairs, 12 September 1960*, (HKRS 41-1-3106-10). The Hong Kong Record Series, Hong Kong.

Letter from Irene Greenfield. (1957, December 3). *Chinese law and custom, letter from the Chairman of the Hong Kong Council of Women, Irene Greenfield to the Colonial Secretary with the Petition to the Governor, 3 December 1957*, (HKRS 41-1-3106-5). The Hong Kong Record Series, Hong Kong.

Letter from J. C. McDouall. (1965a, March 29). *Chinese marriages in Hong Kong 1965 Developments SCA 172_65 1, Letter from J. C. McDouall to P. C. Woo, 29 March 1965*, (HKRS 410-10-27-1). The Hong Kong Record Series, Hong Kong.

Letter from J. C. McDouall. (1965b, May 3). *Chinese marriages in Hong Kong 1965 Developments SCA 172_65 1, Letter from J. C. McDouall to the Chinese Members of the Councils, 3 May 1965*, (HKRS 410-10-27-1). The Hong Kong Record Series, Hong Kong.

Letter from J.C.McDouall. (1957, June 29). *Chinese marriage, reaction to Strickland Committee Report SCA 172_53, Letter from J.C.McDouall, Secretary for Chinese Affairs to Sir Man Kam Lo, 29 June 1957* (HKRS684-2-4). The Hong Kong Record Series, Hong Kong.

Letter from K. G. Ashton. (1957, January 17). *HKRS 684-2-4 Chinese marriages reaction to Strickland Committee SCA 172_53, Letter from K. G. Ashton, Colonial Office to C. B. Burgess,17 January 1957*, (HKRS 684-2-4). The Hong Kong Record Series, Hong Kong.

Letter from R. T. Eng. (1957, June 8). *Chinese law and custom, letter from the Chairman of the Hong Kong Council of Women, Mrs R. T. Eng to A. Ridehalgh, Attorney General, 8 June 1957*, (HKRS 41-1-3106-5). The Hong Kong Record Series, Hong Kong.

Letter from Secretary for Chinese Affairs. (1957, July 15). *Chinese law and custom, letter from Secretary for Chinese Affairs, J. C. McDouall to Chairman of the Council of Women, Mrs R. T. Eng, 15 July 1957*, (HKRS 41-1-3106-5). The Hong Kong Record Series, Hong Kong.

Letter from Secretary for Chinese Affairs. (1965, January 25). *Chinese marriages in Hong Kong 1965 Developments SCA 172_65 1, J.C. McDouall to The Hon. C. Y. Kwan, 25 January 1965*, (HKRS 410-10-27-1). The Hong Kong Record Series, Hong Kong.

Letter from the E. B. David. (1956a, April 26). *Chinese law and custom, letter from the E. B. David to J. T. A. Howard-Drake, Far Eastern Department, Colonial Office, 26 April 1956*, (HKRS 41-1-3106-5). The Hong Kong Record Series, Hong Kong.

Letter from the E. B. David. (1956b, October 5). *Chinese law and custom, letter from the E. B. David to Far Eastern Department, Colonial Office, K. G. Ashton, 5 October 1956*, (HKRS 41-1-3106-5). The Hong Kong Record Series, Hong Kong.

Letter from the Hong Kong Council of Women. (1957, November 9). *Chinese law and custom, letter from the Hong Kong Council of Women to the Colonial Secretary, E. B. David, 9 November 1957*, (HKRS 41-1-3106-5). The Hong Kong Record Series, Hong Kong.

Letter from the Hong Kong Council of Women. (1958, April 7). *Chinese law and custom, letter from the Hong Kong Council of Women to the Colonial Secretary, C. B. Burgess, 7 April 1958*, (HKRS 41-1-3106-5). The Hong Kong Record Series, Hong Kong.

Letter from the Secretaries of State. (1953, July 4). *Chinese law and custom, letters from the Secretaries of State for the Colonies to the Governor, 4 July 1953*, (HKRS 41-1-3106-5). The Hong Kong Record Series, Hong Kong.

Letter from the Secretary for Chinese Affairs. (1960, September 10). *Chinese law and custom, letter from the Secretary for Chinese Affairs to the Governor, 10 September 1960*, (HKRS 41-1-3106-10). The Hong Kong Record Series, Hong Kong.

Letter from the YWCA. (1957, September 27). *Chinese law and custom, letter from the YWCA Hong Kong to the Governor, 27 September 1957*, (HKRS 41-1-3106-5). The Hong Kong Record Series, Hong Kong.

Letter of Dr Irene Cheng. (1957a, April 12). *Chinese law and custom, letter of Dr Irene Cheng to E. B. David, 12 April 1957*, (HKRS 41-1-3106-5). The Hong Kong Record Series, Hong Kong.

Letter of Dr Irene Cheng. (1957b, April 21). *Chinese law and custom, letter of Dr Irene Cheng to E. B. David, 21 April 1957*, (HKRS 41-1-3106-5). The Hong Kong Record Series, Hong Kong.

Letter of E. B. David. (1957, April 17). *Chinese law and custom, letter of E. B. David to Dr Irene Cheng, 17 April 1957*, (HKRS 41-1-3106-5). The Hong Kong Record Series, Hong Kong.

Letter of Man Kam Lo. (1957, June 24). *Chinese marriages validity questions, letter of Man Kam Lo to Ellen Li, 24 June 1957*, (HKRS 410-10-7). The Hong Kong Record Series, Hong Kong.

Letter of the SCA. (1957, May 31). *Chinese law and custom, letter of the SCA to the Governor: Petition of Mrs Rose Helena Li Chow, Miss Alice Kwok, Mrs Ellen Tsao Li, Mrs Tseung Ts'o Lai-Ki, Mrs Yeoh Choy Wai-haan and Miss Shin Tak-Hing to the Governor, 31 May 1957*, (HKRS 41-1-3106-5). The Hong Kong Record Series, Hong Kong.

Letter of the SCA: Petition. (1957, May 31). *Chinese law and custom, letter of the SCA to the Governor: Petition of Mrs Rose Helena Li Chow, Miss Alice Kwok, Mrs Ellen Tsao Li, Mrs Tseung Ts'o Lai-Ki, Mrs Yeoh Choy Wai-haan and Miss Shin Tak-Hing to the Governor, 31 May 1957*, (HKRS 41-1-3106-5). The Hong Kong Record Series, Hong Kong.

Memo from Ag. Attorney General. (1960, February 17). *Chinese law and custom, memo from Ag. Attorney General to Hon. Colonial Secretary, 17 February, 1960*, (HKRS 41-1-3106-10). The Hong Kong Record Series, Hong Kong.

Memo from Attorney General. (1957, June 12). *Chinese law and custom, memo from Attorney General to Hon. C.S. and Hon. S. C. A., 12 June 1957*, (HKRS 41-1-3106-5). The Hong Kong Record Series, Hong Kong.

Memo from Colonial Secretariat. (1963, February 22). *Chinese law and custom, memo from Colonial Secretariat to Secretary for Chinese Affairs, 22 February 1963*, (HKRS 41-1-3106-10). The Hong Kong Record Series, Hong Kong.

Memo from Co-operative Development. (1962, October 13). *Chinese Customary Marriage NT 1_466_58 I, Memo from Co-operative Development and Fisheries Department, 13 October 1962*, (HKRS 634-1-21). The Hong Kong Record Series, Hong Kong.

Memo from District Commissioner New. (1961, March 22). *Chinese law and custom, memo from District Commissioner New Territories to the Secretary for Chinese Affairs, 22 March 1961*, (HKRS 41-1-3106-10). The Hong Kong Record Series, Hong Kong.

Memo from District Commissioner New Territories. (1962, October 9). *Chinese Customary Marriage NT 1_466_58 I, Memo from District Commissioner New Territories to Secretary for Chinese Affairs, 9 October 1962*. (HKRS 634-1-21). The Hong Kong Record Series, Hong Kong.

Memo from Legal Department. (1958, October 14). *Chinese marriages validity questions, memo from Legal Department, M. Merley-John to Secretary for Chinese Affairs, Notes of Meeting Between Ad Hoc Committee and Representatives from the Lady JPs and the Y.W.C.A., 14 October 1958*, (HKRS 410-10-7). The Hong Kong Record Series, Hong Kong.

Memo from Registrar General. (1962, October 13). *Chinese Customary Marriage NT 1_466_58 I, to Secretary for Chinese Affairs, 13 October 1962*, (HKRS 634-1-21). The Hong Kong Record Series, Hong Kong.

Memo from Secretary for Chinese Affairs. (1958, October 1). *Chinese marriages validity questions, memo from Secretary for Chinese Affairs to Hon. Attorney General, 1 October 1958*, (HKRS 410-10-7). The Hong Kong Record Series, Hong Kong.

Memo from Secretary for Chinese Affairs. (1962a, July 18). *Chinese law and custom, memo from Secretary for Chinese Affairs to Attorney General, 18 July 1962*, (HKRS 41-1-3106-10). The Hong Kong Record Series, Hong Kong.

Memo from Secretary for Chinese Affairs. (1962b, June 29). *Chinese Customary Marriage NT 1_466_58 I, Memo from Secretary for Chinese Affairs to District Commissioner New Territories, Commissioner for Co-operative Development & Fisheries and Registrar General, 29 June 1962*, (HKRS 634-1-21). The Hong Kong Record Series, Hong Kong.

Memo from Secretary for Chinese Affairs. (1963, February 23). *Chinese law and custom, memo from Secretary for Chinese Affairs to Colonial Secretariat, 23 February 1963*, (HKRS 41-1-31-6-10). The Hong Kong Record Series, Hong Kong.

Memo from Secretary for Chinese Affairs. (1965, January 25). *Chinese law and custom, memo from Secretary for Chinese Affairs to Deputy Colonial Secretary, 25 January 1965*, (HKRS 41-1-3106-10). The Hong Kong Record Series, Hong Kong.

Memo from the District Commissioner New Territories. (1961, September 12). *Chinese customary Marriage NT 1_466_58 I, Memo from the District Commissioner New Territories to Secretary for Chinese Affairs, 12 September 1961*, (HKRS 634-1-21). The Hong Kong Record Series, Hong Kong.

Memo from the Legal Department. (1958, October 21). *Chinese marriages validity questions, memo from the Legal Department, M. Morley-John to Secretary for Chinese Affairs, 21 October 1958: Notes of Meeting between the Ad Hoc Committee and Representatives from the Hong Kong Council of Women*, (HKRS 410-10-7). The Hong Kong Record Series, Hong Kong.

Memo from the Secretary for Chinese Affairs. (1961a, March 11). *Chinese law and custom, memo from the Secretary for Chinese Affairs to Deputy Colonial Secretary, 11 March 1961*. (HKRS 41-1-3106-10). The Hong Kong Record Series, Hong Kong.

Memo from the Secretary for Chinese Affairs. (1961b, June 15). *Chinese law and custom, Memo from the Secretary for Chinese Affairs to District Commissioner New Territories, 15 June 1961*, (HKRS 41-1-3106-10). The Hong Kong Record Series, Hong Kong.

Memo from the Secretary for Chinese Affairs. (1965, March 19). *Chinese marriages in Hong Kong 1965 Developments SCA 172_65 1, to Colonial Secretary, 19 March 1965*, (HKRS 410-10-27-1). The Hong Kong Record Series, Hong Kong.

Memorandum for Executive Council. (1958, May 22). *Chinese law and custom, Memorandum for Executive Council, 22 May 1958*, (HKRS 41-1-3106-5). The Hong Kong Record Series, Hong Kong.

Memorandum for Executive Council. (1960, November 22). *Chinese law and custom, Memorandum for Executive Council: Chinese Marriages, on 22 November 1960*, (HKRS 41-1-3106-10). The Hong Kong Record Series, Hong Kong.

Memorandum from Secretary for Chinese Affairs. (1957, February 14). *Chinese marriage, reaction to Strickland Committee Report SCA 172_53, Memorandum from Secretary for Chinese Affairs to Hon. Colonial Secretary, 14 February, 1957*, (HKRS 684-2-4). The Hong Kong Record Series, Hong Kong.

Memorandum from Secretary for Chinese Affairs. (1958, April 22). *Chinese law and custom, Memorandum from Secretary for Chinese Affairs, J. C. McDouall to Colonial Secretary, 22 April 1958*, (HKRS 41-1-3106-5). The Hong Kong Record Series, Hong Kong.

Memorandum from Secretary for Chinese Affairs. (1960, November 3). *Chinese law and custom, Memorandum from Secretary for Chinese Affairs to Colonial Secretary, 3 November 1960*, (HKRS 41-1-3106-10). The Hong Kong Record Series, Hong Kong.

Memorandum from the Colonial Secretariat. (1960, December 15). *Chinese law and custom, Memorandum from the Colonial Secretariat to the Secretary for Chinese Affairs, 15 December 1960*, (HKRS 41-1-3106-10). The Hong Kong Record Series, Hong Kong.

Memorandum from the Colonial Secretariat. (1961, March 14). *Chinese law and custom, Daily Information Bulletin: Chinese Marriages in Hong Kong, 14 March 1961*, (HKRS 41-1-3106-10). The Hong Kong Record Series, Hong Kong.

Minute 113. (n.d.). *Chinese law and custom, Minute 113, Re: Letter from the Chairman of the Hong Kong Council of Women, Irene Greenfield to the Colonial Secretary with the Petition to the Governor (n.d.)*, (HKRS 41-1-3106-5). The Hong Kong Record Series, Hong Kong.

Minute by J. D. Higham. (1965a, February 19). *Chinese laws and customs in Hong Kong, Minute by L T Stapleton, 19 February, 1965*, (CO1030/1704). The National Archives, Kew.

Minute by J. D. Higham. (1965b, February 9). *Chinese laws and customs in Hong Kong, Minute by J. D. Higham, 9 February, 1965*, (CO1030/1704). The National Archives, Kew.

Minute by Mr Browning. (1957, May 23). *chinese laws and customs in Hong Kong, Minute by Mr Browning to Mr Terrell, 23 May, 1957*, (CO1030/819). The Hong Kong Record Series, Hong Kong.

Minute by Mr Chinn. (1958, September 1). *Chinese laws and customs in Hong Kong, Minute by Mr Chinn, 1 September, 1958*, (CO 1030/819). The National Archives, Kew.

Minute by Mr R Terrell. (1958, August 29). *Chinese Laws and Customs in Hong Kong, Minute by Mr R Terrell, 29 August, 1958*, (CO 1030/819). The National Archives, Kew.

Minute by Mr. W. S. Carter. (1965, June 24). *Chinese law and custom, Minute by Mr. W. S. Carter to Mr. Stapleton, 24 June 1965*, (HKRS 41-1-3106-10). The Hong Kong Record Series, Hong Kong.

Minute by Mrs. Eriene White. (1965, June 25). *Chinese law and custom, Minute by Mrs. Eriene White to Mr. Carter, 25 June 1965*, (HKRS 41-1-3106-10). The Hong Kong Record Series, Hong Kong.

Minute by W. S. Carter. (1965, March 15). *Chinese law and custom, Minute by W. S. Carter to J. D. Higham, Colonial Office, 15 March, 1965*, (HKRS 41-1-3106-10). The Hong Kong Record Series, Hong Kong.

Minute from Clerk of Councils. (1958a, June 12). *Chinese law and custom, Minute from Clerk of Councils to D. C. S., 12 June 1958*, (HKRS 41-1-3106-5). The Hong Kong Record Series, Hong Kong.

Minute from Clerk of Councils. (1958b, May 22). *Chinese law and custom, Memorandum of the Executive Council, 22 May 1958*, (HKRS 41-1-3106-5). The Hong Kong Record Series, Hong Kong.

Minute from Clerk of Councils. (1958c, ca. February 21–24). *Chinese law and custom, Minute from Clerk of Councils to Deputy Colonial Secretary (n.d.)*, (HKRS 41-1-3106-5). The Hong Kong Record Series, Hong Kong.

Minute from D. C. C. Luddington. (1957, December 10). *Chinese law and custom, Minute from D. C. C. Luddington to Registrar General and Secretary for Chinese Affairs, 10 December 1957*, (HKRS 41-1-3106-5). The Hong Kong Record Series, Hong Kong.

Minute from the Colonial Secretary to the Governor. (1958, June 16). *Chinese law and custom, Minute from the Colonial Secretary to the Governor, 16 June 1958*, (HKRS 41-1-3106-5). The Hong Kong Record Series, Hong Kong.

Minute from the Deputy Colonial Secretary. (1958, June 13). *Chinese law and custom, Minute from the Deputy Colonial Secretary to Colonial Secretary, 13 June 1958*, (HKRS 41-1-3106-5). The Hong Kong Record Series, Hong Kong.

Minute from the Registrar General. (1958, January 14). *Chinese law and custom, Minute from the Registrar General to the Colonial Secretary, 14 January 1958*, (HKRS41-1-3106-5). The Hong Kong Record Series, Hong Kong.

Minute from the Secretary for Chinese Affairs. (1961, June 9). *Chinese law and custom, Minute from the Secretary for Chinese Affairs to Colonial Secretary, 9 June 1961*, (HKRS 41-1-3106-10). The Hong Kong Record Series, Hong Kong.

Minute from the Secretary for Chinese Affairs. (1962a, June 15). *Chinese law and custom, Memo from Secretary for Chinese Affairs to Colonial Secretary, 15 June 1962*, (HKRS 41-1-3106-10). The Hong Kong Record Series, Hong Kong.

Minute from the Secretary for Chinese Affairs. (ca. 1962b, Jan 8). *Chinese law and custom, Memo from Colonial Secretary to Secretary for Chinese Affairs, 8 Jan 1961 [sic]*, (HKRS 41-1-3106-10). The Hong Kong Record Series, Hong Kong.

Minute: Executive Council. (1958, June 4). *Chinese law and custom, minute: Executive Council Meeting of 3 June 1958, Clerk of Councils, 4 June 1958*, (HKRS 41-1-3106-5). The Hong Kong Record Series, Hong Kong.

Mr C.Y. Kwan's Budget Speech. (1965, March 11). *Chinese marriages in Hong Kong 1965 Developments SCA 172_65 1, Mr C.Y. Kwan's Budget Speech, 11 March 1965*, (HKRS 410-10-27-1). The Hong Kong Record Series, Hong Kong.

Notes on Some Chinese Customs in the New Territories. (1955). *General notes on Chinese custom, notes on some Chinese customs in the New Territories: Compiled by B. D. Wilson, M.A., District Officer*, (HKRS119-1-92). The Hong Kong Record Series, Hong Kong.
R. T. Eng to A. Ridehalgh. (1957, May 25). *Chinese law and custom, The Hong Kong Council of Women, Attorney General, 25 May 1957*, (HKRS 41-1-3106-5). The Hong Kong Record Series, Hong Kong.
R. T. Eng to E. B. David. (1957, May 25). *Chinese law and custom, The Hong Kong Council of Women, R. T. Eng to E. B. David, Colonial Secretary, 25 May 1957*, (HKRS 41-1-3106-5). The Hong Kong Record Series, Hong Kong.
Recommendations. (1965). *Chinese marriages in Hong Kong 1965 Developments SCA 172_65 1, Chinese marriages: Preliminary Draft of Revised Recommendations 1965*, (HKRS 410-10-27-1). The Hong Kong Record Series, Hong Kong.
Reply from Mr Profumo. (1957, March 25). *Chinese laws and customs in Hong Kong, to Albert Roberts MP, 25 March, 1957*, (CO1030/819). The Hong Kong Record Series, Hong Kong.
Ridehalgh, A., & McDouall, J. C. (1960). *Chinese marriages in Hong Kong*. Hong Kong: Government Printer.
Savingram from the Governor. (1953, May 5). *Chinese law and custom, Savingram from the Governor of Hong Kong to the Secretary of States for the Colonies, 5 May 1953*, (HKRS 41-1-3106-5). The Hong Kong Record Series, Hong Kong.
Savingram from the Governor. (1958, June 19). *Chinese laws and customs in Hong Kong, Savingram from the Governor, Hong Kong to the Secretary of State for the Colonies, 19 June 1958*, (CO 1030/819). The National Archives, Kew.
Savingram from the Governor. (1962, July 24). *Chinese law and custom, Savingram from the Governor, Hong Kong to the Secretary of State for the Colonies, 24 July 1962*, (HKRS 41-1-3106-10). The Hong Kong Record Series, Hong Kong.
Savingram from the Secretaries of State. (1955, November 11). *Chinese law and custom, Savingram from the Secretaries of State for the Colonies to the Officer Administering the Government of Hong Kong, 11 November 1955*, (HKRS 41-1-3106-5). The Hong Kong Record Series, Hong Kong.
Savingram from the Secretaries of State. (1956, April 4). *Chinese law and custom, Savingram from the Secretaries of State for the Colonies to the Officer Administering the Government of Hong Kong 4 April 1956*, (HKRS 41-1-3106-5). The Hong Kong Record Series, Hong Kong.
Savingram from the Secretary of State. (1958, January 27). *Chinese marriage reaction to Strickland Committee Report SCA 172_53, Savingram from the Secretary of State for the Colonies to the Officer Administering the Government of Hong Kong, 27 January 1958*, (HKRS 684-2-4). The Hong Kong Record Series, Hong Kong.
Savingram from the Secretary of State. (1963, June 7). *Chinese law and custom, Savingram from the Secretary of State for the Colonies to the Officer Administering the Government of Hong Kong, 7 June 1963*, (HKRS 41-1-3106-10). The Hong Kong Record Series, Hong Kong.
Schwelb, E. (1963). Marriage and human rights. *American Journal of Comparative Law, 3*, 337–383.
Suggestion for Modification. (1957, September 27). *Chinese law and custom, suggestion for modification or reconsideration of Chapter VI of the Report on Chinese Law and Custom in Hong Kong, 27 September 1957*, (HKRS 41-1-3106-5). The Hong Kong Record Series, Hong Kong.
Telegram from Governor of Hong Kong. (1964, November 18). *Chinese laws and customs in Hong Kong, telegram from Governor of Hong Kong (Sir D. Trench) to the Secretary of State for the Colonies, 18 November 1964*, (CO1030/1704). The National Archives, Kew.
Telegram from Hong Kong. (1957, March 11). *Chinese laws and customs in Hong Kong, telegram from Hong Kong (Sir A. Grantham) to the Secretary of State for the Colonies, 11 March 1957*, (CO1030/819). The Hong Kong Record Series, Hong Kong.
Telegram from Hong Kong. (1958, February 5). *Chinese Marriage Reaction to Strickland Committee Report SCA 172_53, Telegram from Hong Kong (Sir R. Black) to the Secretary of States for the Colonies, 5th February, 1958*, (HKRS 684-2-4). The Hong Kong Record Series, Hong Kong.

Telegram from Hong Kong. (1960, July 6). *Chinese laws and customs in Hong Kong, telegram from Hong Kong to Secretary of State for the Colonies, 6 July 1960*, (CO 1030/1346). The National Archives, Kew.

Telegram from the Secretary of States. (1957, March 8). *Chinese law and custom, telegram from the Secretary of States for the Colonies to the Governor of Hong Kong, No. 183, 8 March 1957*, (HKRS 31-1-3106-5). The Hong Kong Record Series, Hong Kong.

Text of an Address by the Secretary for Chinese Affairs. (1962, August 2). *Chinese law and custom, The Tokyo Seminar: Before and after: Text of an Address by the Secretary for Chinese Affairs to the Hong Kong Council of Women at a Closed Meeting on 2 August 1962*, (HKRS 41-1-3106-10). The Hong Kong Record Series, Hong Kong.

United Nations. (1962). *1962 Seminar on the status of women in family law: Tokyo, 8 to 21 May 1962, organized by the United Nations in Collaboration with the Government of Japan* (ST/TAO/HR/14), New York: United Nations, 1962.

Yip, K. (2014). *The abolishment of concubinage in Hong Kong: An analysis of its process and opinions on the issue (1948–1971)*. Ph.D. thesis, Chinese University of Hong Kong.

Chapter 6
The Marriage Reform Ordinance 1971 and Its Aftermath

Abstract This chapter discusses the aftermath of the initial proposal to abolish the institution of concubinage in Hong Kong as approved by the Colonial Office. Following the draft McDouall/Heenan Report 1965, the Hong Kong Government published a White Paper in 1967 to solicit public opinions on marriage reform, paving the way to ending the recognition of Chinese customary and modern marriages and, most importantly, the abolition of concubinage. At the same time, a new definition of the union of concubinage was strongly advocated by the Chinese Unofficial members of the Executive and Legislative Councils. This was ultimately accepted by the Hong Kong Government. Finally, the Marriage Reform Ordinance was approved in 1970 and promulgated in 1971 which abolished the institution of concubinage in Hong Kong.

Keywords Monogamous marriage · Marriage Reform Ordinance · Legitimacy Ordinance · Intestates' Estates Ordinance · Matrimonial Causes Ordinance

6.1 Introduction

On 4 December 1965, the Secretary for Chinese Affairs submitted an Executive Council paper asking for approval to abolish concubinage. This recommendation, together with other recommendations aimed at reforming Chinese customary marriage and Chinese modern marriage—especially with regard to issues such as the dissolution of marriage, inheritance and succession—would bring marriage and other related matters in line with the common law principles of the UK. The decision of the Executive Council, as approved and supported by the Secretary of State of Colonies in the UK, marked an end to the recognition of the Chinese marriage system in Hong Kong. In a package of marriage reform laws, it is hoped that after the implementation of the legislative proposals as approved by the Executive Council, there would be a registered monogamous marriage system which applied to all ethnic groups in Hong Kong.

M. WL Wong, *Chinese Marriage and Social Change*,
https://doi.org/10.1007/978-981-15-1644-3_6

It is important to note that the Executive Council's decision to abolish concubinage was made not because of social pressure from the masses but was made in accordance with the instruction given by the Secretary of State of Colonies from the UK. Given that this decision was a sudden twist in the attitude of the Hong Kong Government—from a gradual and natural elimination of the institution of concubinage to an immediate abolition of concubinage—resistance from the Chinese Unofficial members of the Executive and Legislative Councils was inevitable. The compromise reached by the Chinese Unofficial members of the Executive and Legislative Councils with the government was that a legal definition of concubine was added to the laws of Hong Kong which restricted the legal status of a concubine in a family. This legal definition of concubine represents a departure from the rules and practices in GQC and customary practices as given in the Qing laws.

This chapter will first discuss the resistance of the Chinese Unofficial members of the Executive and Legislative Councils to the abolition of concubinage in 1965. Next, this chapter will discuss how the Chinese Unofficial members of the Executive and Legislative Councils put forwards a definition of concubine during the internal debates on the Marriage Reform Bill between government officials and the Chinese Unofficial members. Then, after examining the passage of the relevant laws in Hong Kong—especially the promulgation of the Marriage Reform Ordinance in 1971—this chapter will discuss how subsequent amendments to Hong Kong statutory law gave more rights to wives and concubines in Chinese customary marriages than they would have had under Qing law.

6.2 Opposition from the Chinese Unofficial Members of the Executive and Legislative Councils in 1965

The Colonial Office gave the green light to the draft version of a new report in June 1965. This paper was written by the Secretary for Chinese Affairs, McDouall, and formed the backbone of the McDouall/Heenan Report. McDouall had in mind to finalise the proposal before the end of 1965 (Chap. 5, Sect. 5.5.4). But first, he had to secure the support from the Chinese Unofficial members of the Executive and Legislative Councils. At this juncture, he had met with the strongest disapproval from the Chinese Unofficial members of both Councils. As early as January 1965, the Secretary for Chinese Affairs, McDouall, had sent a letter to C. Y. Kwan, a member of the Executive and Legislative Councils. McDouall sought Kwan's comments on a draft paper which consolidated all responses taken after the release of the Ridehalgh/McDouall Report 1960. In this draft paper, McDouall was going to make new recommendations, which included the abolition of concubinage. In a letter dated 25 January 1965, McDouall attached this preliminary draft which contained his new recommendations. However, at that time, C. Y. Kwan was only concerned with customary practices of Chinese inheritance law; the issue of abolition of concubinage was left undiscussed (Chap. 5, Sect. 5.5.4).

After the submission of the draft recommendations to the Colonial Office on 7 May 1965, McDouall arranged a meeting with the Chinese Unofficial members of the Executive and Legislative Councils to solicit their views. The meeting was scheduled on 27 May 1965, based on the draft recommendations given to them in the letter dated 3 May 1965. A redraft of the recommendations was sent to them on 10 May 1965, and the recommendation on the abolition of concubinage remained intact (Letter from the Secretary for Chinese Affairs, 20 May 1965b).

However, this meeting became an avenue of confrontation between the Chinese Unofficial members of the Councils and the Secretary for Chinese Affairs. The key issue was not the abolition of concubinage but issues relating to the rights of a wife and concubine such as maintenance of a concubine. In the draft notes of the meeting, prepared by an attendee who represented the Legal Department, C. Y. Kwan seemed to accept the recommendation on the abolition of concubinage after the Appointed Date (Memo from Assistant to Law Officers, 28 May 1965). But the Chinese Unofficial members of the Councils strongly disapproved of one recommendation that gave existing concubines in Chinese customary marriages and their children the right to claim support from the concubine's husband. It was recorded that C. Y. Kwan spoke for all the Chinese Unofficial members when he stated that "they were unanimously opposed to it". C. Y. Kwan advanced two arguments. Firstly, the rights of the concubine being afforded were not in accordance with Chinese customary law. Secondly, he argued that any kind of the legislation which gave such rights to a concubine "would open the door to forms of blackmail through spurious claims" (Memo from Assistant to Law Officers, 28 May 1965, para. 5).

This draft record did not further elaborate the meaning of "spurious claims", but probably what worried C. Y. Kwan was that a mistress might claim herself to be a concubine, thus leading to "spurious claims" against the husband. Nevertheless, McDouall argued in the meeting that this recommendation was widely supported by the public. McDouall also said that the government might face criticism for abandoning existing concubines without such protection. But this argument failed to persuade other Chinese Unofficial members of the Councils. One member, P. C. Woo, stated that in the Civil Code 1931 of the Republic of China, "concubinage had been outlawed but the status and custom had been given legal recognition and protection in another guise". He further argued that this could be achieved as given in the Civil Code 1931 in the Republic of China, where the husband was responsible for the maintenance of all members of his family and household, and therefore, if another woman became part of that household, she could claim legal rights of maintenance. All in all, every Chinese Unofficial member held that "nothing should appear in the legislation on the subject of concubines" other than the abolition of concubinage after the Appointed Date. They further stated that the institution of concubinage should be permitted to wither away by the course of time. They also stated that even providing additional safeguards on claims relating to the rights of a concubine could make the recommendation acceptable (Memo from Assistant to Law Officers, 28 May 1965, p. 2).

Another draft note of meetings recorded by one attendee, the Assistant Secretary for Chinese Affairs, Patrick Wong Kwong-man, gave additional details on the meeting relating to arguments between McDouall and the Chinese Unofficial members of the Councils on the legal rights of the concubine. In this draft, C. Y. Kwan was recorded as saying that the concubines should not be given certain rights which they did not possess under Chinese custom. C. Y. Kwan further stated that concubines did not have a place in the family, so they should not be entitled to claim maintenance. Another member, Y. K. Kan, stated that in practice there was no difference in the status of a concubine under customary marriages and a "member" of a household, because they were all called *t'sip*. Y. K. Kan considered that *t'sip* knew that they had no legal protection and they would seek prior settlement (on the maintenance value) before entering the household. So even though McDouall stated that this special recommendation was done in response to the request made by "numerous responsible organisations", the Chinese Unofficial members of the Councils unanimously agreed to propose for the complete deletion of this recommendation (Notes by Mr Patrick Wong, 28 May 1965, p. 2). In other words, the Chinese Unofficial members of the Councils wished to give no maintenance to concubines.

The official notes of the meeting issued by McDouall watered down the heavy confrontation of the above issues in the meeting, by stating that "[t]he meeting reached unanimous agreement on the recommendation attached herewith as Enclosure I (of the notes of meeting)" (Letter from the Secretary for Chinese Affairs, 31 May 1965d). The notes of the meeting did not record any disagreements or opinions from the Chinese Unofficial members of the Councils. In "Enclosure I" attached to the notes of the meeting, the issue of the maintenance of a concubine was redrafted in a way which did not specifically give such rights to the concubine. This recommendation was drafted as: "[t]o provide for the making of affiliation and maintenance orders if a father refuses to take responsibility for the maintenance of a child born out of wedlock". Accordingly, any child who was born out of wedlock (that might include the child born by the concubine or mistress) might apply for a maintenance order. While the views of the Chinese Unofficial members of the Council had not been recorded in the official notes of meeting, they were finally included in the first draft of Appendix C to the final report submitted to the Executive Council on 4 June 1965 (Letter from the Secretary for Chinese Affairs, 4 June 1968, para. 53; para. 58). However, this draft met with some disagreements from C. Y. Kwan. On 17 June 1965a, McDouall mentioned in a letter that after telephone conversations he had proposed to make some changes to the draft Appendix C (Letter from the Secretary for Chinese Affairs, 17 June 1965a). One significant change signified the retraction of the previous strong objection of the Chinese Unofficial members of the Councils on the issue of giving the right of maintenance to the concubine. The original first draft relating to this issue was made at pages 11 to 12 of paragraph 58:

> They (the Chinese Unofficial Members of the Councils) stated that even the revised Recommendation would invite blackmailing attempts by gold-diggers, that all girls who became concubines nowadays saw to it first that they received adequate settlements in advance, and that where such a woman did become a genuinely permanent member of the

> household, all her children would be legitimate and entitled to maintenance by Custom. (Letter from the Secretary for Chinese Affairs, 17 June 1965a)

The opinions submitted by C. Y. Kwan led to the deletion of "maintenance by Custom" which was substituted with "maintenance if they appealed to Custom, failing that, Common Law" (Letter from the Secretary for Chinese Affairs, 17 June 1965a, p. 2).

It is important to note that such a change would open the door to the future possibility that a concubine could apply for the redress of a maintenance order in common law. Since the statutory law, broadly speaking, could be regarded as part of common law, such a change would mean that legislation which gave the concubine a right to apply for a maintenance order at court would be regarded as part of common law. Change in this form was something that the Chinese Unofficial members of the Councils might be able to accept, though reluctantly. This proposed amendment was not seen in the notes of the meeting of 31 May, and no reason was given in the letter for C. Y. Kwan's change of heart.

Although this might have resolved the disputes of the Chinese Unofficial members of the Councils and McDouall, the issue relating to the legal right of a concubine resurfaced when draft legislation was put to the Legislative Council. This will be dealt with later in this chapter.

6.3 The International Obligations of the Hong Kong Government

To recap, on 17 December 1964, Higham from the Colonial Office instructed the Hong Kong Government to deal with the issue of concubinage along two lines. Firstly, the Hong Kong Government should take reference to the provisions of the Women's Charter of Singapore on the abolition of concubinage. Secondly, Higham asked the Hong Kong Government to consider the provisions of UN Convention on Consent to Marriage, Minimum Age for Marriage and Registration of Marriages in dealing with the issue of marriage reform (Chap. 5, Sect. 5.5.4). However, this convention could not affirm that there was an international obligation of the Hong Kong Government, under international law, to abolish the institution of concubinage.

In the absence of an international treaty which mandated that the Hong Kong Government must directly abolish the institution of concubinage, the Hong Kong Government had to search for ways to show that the colonial government had an international obligation under international treaties to abolish concubinage. The strategy that the Hong Kong Government adopted was to include all possible international treaties which might be helpful in reaching this conclusion, such as all international treaties that contained provisions on the equality of men and women. The government hoped that by putting all these laws together, the Hong Kong Government would have to abolish the concubinage to fulfil their international treaty obligations. All these international legal obligations were put in Appendix B of the draft report later submitted to the government. On 3 May 1965c, Appendix B was attached by a letter given by the Secretary for Chinese Affairs to the Chinese Unofficial members of the Councils (Letter from the Secretary for Chinese Affair, 3 May 1965c).

In it, McDouall explained the binding and non-binding effects of the international treaties to Hong Kong. First, he stated that any UN or UN-sponsored recommendation in any convention "can be morally even when not legally binding on the Hong Kong Government" (Letter from the Secretary for Chinese Affair, 3 May 1965c, Appendix B, para. 1). Then, this paper noted the general rules of international law meant that the terms of conventions ratified by the UK were binding on the non-self-governing territories. The practice of the UK Government was that it would seek prior consultation and the consent of the territory before committing the territories to the international conventions. Finally, this paper also stated that the resolutions and recommendations of certain Councils or Commissions set up by the UN were not binding internationally on member states. The latter was obviously written in reply to the social organisations, who asked the Hong Kong Government to follow the recommendations as discussed in the Tokyo Seminar in 1962 (Letter from the Secretary for Chinese Affair, 3 May 1965c, Appendix B, para. 2).[1]

The paper then listed some UN documents that supported the equality of men and women. The first one was the Charter of the United Nation. The Preamble and Chapter I, Article 3, emphasises the importance of the equality of men and women and the fundamental freedoms for all without distinction as to race, sex, language or religion (Letter from the Secretary for Chinese Affair, 3 May 1965c, Appendix B, para. 3).[2] The second was the Universal Declaration of Human Rights in which Article 16 states that men and women of all age have the right to marry and to find a family and that they have equal rights to marriage, during marriage and at its dissolution. Article 16(2) supports the freedom of marriage which stated that "marriage shall be entered into with the full and free consent of the intending suppose". Article 16(3) states that the "family is the natural and fundamental group unite of society and is entitled to protection by society and the State". Article 25 states that all children, whether born in or out of wedlock, shall enjoy the same social protection (Letter from the Secretary for Chinese Affair, 3 May 1965c, Appendix B, para. 4).[3]

After that, the paper added that General Assembly Resolution 843(IX) urged all states where "ancient laws and practices exist" to do the following: ensure complete freedom in the choice of a spouse; guarantee the rights of widows to the custody of

[1] See Chap. 5, Sect. 5.6.2 for discussion of the Tokyo Seminar.

[2] The Preamble of the United Nations Charter states that "We the people of the United Nations determined…to affirm faith in …the equal rights of men and women". Chapter I Article 3 states that "The purposes of the United Nations are: to achieve international co-operation…in promoting and encouraging respect of human rights and for fundamental freedom for all without distinction as to race, sex, language, or religion". See http://www.un.org/en/charter-united-nations/. Accessed on 12 November 2018.

[3] See http://www.un.org/en/universal-declaration-human-rights/. Accessed on 12 November 2018.

their children; eliminate prepuberty marriages and betrothals; establish appropriate penalties and ensure the official registration of all marriages (Letter from the Secretary for Chinese Affair, 3 May 1965c, Appendix B, para. 5).[4] Then, the paper stated that on 4 September 1956, a Supplementary Convention on the Abolition of Slavery was adopted in the Conference of Plenipotentiaries. It was agreed in the conference to eradicate certain practices whereby a woman may be sold or given in marriage by her family, and anyone under the age of 18 was delivered by his parents to a third party for exploitation (Letter from the Secretary for Chinese Affair, 3 May 1965c, Appendix B, para. 6).[5] Next, the paper stated the importance of the Convention on Consent to Marriage, Minimum Age for Marriage and Registration of Marriages, signed on 7 November 1962 (see Chap. 5, Sect. 5.5.2; Letter from the Secretary for Chinese Affair, 3 May 1965c, Appendix B, para. 7), which required the contracting parties to ensure that a marriage should only be legally entered into with the full and free consent of the parties; to specify a minimum age for marriage and be registered in an appropriate official register by the competent authority.[6] Afterwards, the paper stated that the General Assembly had asked the United Nations Economic and Social Council (ECOSOC) to ask the Commission on the Status of Women to consider some draft recommendations on this Convention. In the revised draft, as quoted in draft Appendix B, one recommendation stood out. It recommended that member states must enact legislation or take other actions, at the earliest practicable moment, not later than 18 months after the adoption of the convention (Letter from the Secretary for Chinese Affair, 3 May 1965c, Appendix B, para. 8). Finally, draft Appendix B summarised the UN seminar on status of women in family law held in May 1962 at Tokyo, which McDouall had attended. It emphasised that the conclusions reached in the seminar "do not of course bind any participant's government; they can however carry persuasive authority, based as they are on practical instead of politically conducted discussions and findings" (Letter from the Secretary for Chinese Affair, 3 May 1965c, Appendix B, para. 9). It concluded that there were eight issues to be dealt with later: the age, consent and forms of marriage, the effect of marriage on the personal status of women, the effects of marriage on the property rights of women, the dissolution of marriage, parental authority, the legal status of unmarried women, the inheritance rights of women and the social

[4]This resolution, called the "Status of women in private law: customs, ancient laws and practices affecting the human dignity of women", was passed on 17 December 1954. See https://documents-dds-ny.un.org/doc/RESOLUTION/GEN/NR0/095/78/IMG/NR009578.pdf?OpenElement. Accessed on 12 November 2018. The resolution recommended that member states inform the public of the rights of women through fundamental education and through media of communications.

[5]See https://treaties.un.org/pages/ViewDetailsIII.aspx?src=TREATY&mtdsg_no=XVIII-4&chapter=18&Temp=mtdsg3&clang=_en Accessed on 12 November 2018.

[6]See https://treaties.un.org/pages/viewdetails.aspx?src=ind&mtdsg_no=xvi-3&chapter=16&lang=en Accessed on 12 November 1968. The UK Government only ratified it on 9 July 1970. Therefore, at the time when McDouall prepared for the report on Chinese marriages in 1965, this treaty had not been ratified by the UK Government.

factors affecting the status of women in family law (Letter from the Secretary for Chinese Affair, 3 May 1965c, Appendix B, para. 9).

In sum, the UN conventions or resolutions quoted in the draft Appendix could only be conclusive on one principle: that the laws should respect the freedom of marriage. These conventions or resolutions did not directly call for the establishment of a monogamous marriage, or the abolition of concubinage, and not even the nullity of customary marriage. From a practical point of view, these conventions and resolutions asked for the competent authority to establish a registered marriage system and offered some protection for children born out of wedlock. However, all in all, international law could not offer any particular support to the government arguing for the abolition of concubinage.

6.4 Executive Council Paper 1965

On 26 November 1965, in preparation for the Executive Council paper, the Secretary for Chinese Affairs, McDouall, in a memorandum to the Colonial Secretary mentioned that the covering memo of the Executive Council paper should spell out the difficulties of implementing the recommendations. He had in mind that this would be submitted to the Colonial Office:

> In anticipation of the possibility of the covering Ex. Co. (Executive Council) memo being forwarded in due course to the Secretary of State, it therefore seemed to the A.G. (Attorney General) and myself that it would be better to spell out these difficulties and their disposal somewhat fully, instead of leaving them all to be dealt with verbally in Executive Council. (Memo from Secretary for Chinese Affairs, 26 November 1965, para. 4)

In the same memo, McDouall mentioned that Mr Cater from the Colonial Office would be leaving Hong Kong on 20 December 1965 so that it would be better for the Executive Council to discuss the paper on or before 14 December 1965 (Memo from Secretary for Chinese Affairs, 26 November 1965, para. 5).

The Executive Council paper was issued on 29 November 1965 and discussed on 4 December 1965. On the issue of the abolition of concubinage, the paper stated that, practically speaking, some traditionally organised families might still continue the practice of concubinage (Memorandum for Executive Council, 29 November 1965, para. 4 (g)). Although such practice would not affect the legal position of the concubine after the abolition of concubinage, the paper recognised that they could be the cause of subsequent and bitter disputes within a family or between two families. The paper expressed that it would be reasonable to hope that "only a small number of any such disputes would not in the end be settled privately, as is also in accordance with tradition, instead of leading to attempted litigation or to feuds" (Memorandum for Executive Council, 29 November 1965, para. 4 (g)).

In the paper, the government also considered that to protect the lawful interests of a child born out of lawful wedlock, if the sixth recommendation was approved, such proposal would persuade the father to make a voluntary acknowledgement of paternity. The father might try to re-enforce it by making appropriate provisions in a will (Memorandum for Executive Council, 29 November 1965, para. 4 (g)).[7] In sum, if this recommendation was accepted, the lawful interests of a child born by a mistress after the abolition of concubinage would be protected. If the father did not want to take up paternal responsibility for a child born out of lawful wedlock, the seventh recommendation stipulated that the court could give affiliation and maintenance orders if a father refused to accept responsibility for maintenance of his child (Memorandum for Executive Council, 29 November 1965, Recommendation no. 7).

The Executive Council agreed to the recommendations after the meeting. McDouall made a handwritten note that the paper was "accepted, without amendment, at meeting on 14.12.65" (Memorandum for Executive Council, 29 November 1965, p. 6). In the minute written by McDouall, he mentioned in the note that government officials had a discussion with Mrs Eriene White, Under-Secretary of the Secretary of State from the Colonial Office, and had obtained her personal agreement to these recommendations on 6 January 1966:

> 1965 recommendations discussed with Mrs. Eriene White, Parliamentary Under-Secretary of State, this a.m. (morning) in C.S. (Colonial Secretary) Office—C. S. (Colonial Secretary), Mr Cater of Colonial Office also being present. She appeared to be in general agreement with the principal recommendations, personally, but was of course unable to commit the S. of S. (Secretary of State) at this stage. (Minute of McDouall, 6 January 1966)

So, from the response given by McDouall, it is assumed that the Colonial Office was satisfied with the deliberation of the Hong Kong Government. Final approval was given by the Colonial Office on 11 March 1965: "[T]he recommendations set out in Enclosure I of the 1965 Report on Chinese Marriage are approved" (Savingram from the Secretary of State, 11 March 1965). In a personal letter sent by W. S. Carter of the Colonial Office, he complimented the approval of Mrs. White on this matter: "I had, of course, to bring to Mrs. White's attention of the anomalies and difficulties which will have to be faced, as brought out in the Ex. Co. (Executive Council) paper. Her reaction was to regard these as a price well worth paying for the changes

[7] Recommendation no. 6 related to the "voluntary acknowledgement of paternity". It was attached in the Executive Council paper in Enclosure I. This recommendation stated that legislative provisions would be enacted, whereby a man might be able to declare by will or by a written document before a Justice of the Peace, Notary Public, Solicitor or any Public Officer designated for this purpose by the Governor of his intention to be responsible for the maintenance of any child of whom he admitted fatherhood. Such declaration should be admissible in court. The purpose of this provision was to give the father of a child born out of lawful wedlock to have the right to maintenance. It asked the father to accept the responsibilities of paternity voluntarily without recourse to the court. See Annex A (29 November 1965, Enclosure I, p. 4).

you will be introducing" (Letter from Colonial Office, 11 March 1966). Thereafter, the primary task of the Hong Kong Government was to implement the recommendations through legislation.

6.5 McDouall/Heenan Report 1965 and White Paper on Chinese Marriages 1967

The report submitted to Executive Council paper was edited and published as the "White Paper on Chinese Marriages in Hong Kong" in May 1967, with the addition of the whole Enclosure I to the Executive Council paper in full. But the appendixes as attached to the original Executive Council paper submitted in 1965 were omitted. This paper gave a clearer picture of the strategy in implementing the 1965 report.[8]

The whole reform was based on the decision of the government to abolish the institution of concubinage. Since the institution of concubinage was only allowed in Chinese customary marriage, if the government decided to legally abolish concubinage, then the government should also need to cease the recognition of Chinese customary marriage. In addition, some husbands married under the Chinese modern marriages (referring to the marriage in pursuant to the Civil Code 1931 of the Republic of China) also had an institution of so-called concubinage. On the issue relating to the so-called concubine in Chinese modern marriage contracted under the Civil Code 1931 of the Republic of China, it is noted in the White Paper 1967 that in principle Chinese modern marriages contracted in Hong Kong were strictly not legally recognised. And, since Chinese modern marriage was monogamous in nature, the so-called concubine was in effect a mistress. In addition, the Hong Kong Government had to deal with the issue of the validity and legality of Chinese modern marriages, which were very common in the Chinese community before and after the Second World War. Finally, the Hong Kong Government had to resolve whether a concubine and her children could apply in court for maintenance provided by the husband. Since the government decided to establish a monogamous and registered marriage system, so the next step of the government was to decide an "Appointed Date" after which all marriages in Hong Kong should be monogamous and registered.

The White Paper 1967 stated in brief the three principles behind the reform. Firstly, the Hong Kong Government recognised that the Chinese people in Hong Kong would marry according to the form of their choice. Secondly, legislation would provide that after an "Appointed Date", every marriage in Hong Kong would be a union between one man and one woman and that it should be registered. Thirdly, the rights of any concubines taken before the "Appointed Date", and their children, would continue to be recognised in law after the "Appointed Date": "[c]

[8] It is important to note that the whole McDouall/Heenan Report has never been published to the general public.

oncubines taken before the Appointed Date, and their children, should continue to be accorded such recognition in law as now exist, and no more" (Hong Kong Colonial Secretariat 1967).

On the Chinese customary marriages, the White Paper 1967 emphasised the importance of the standards as given in the international conventions and resolutions of the United Nations. The White Paper 1967 called it "United Nations standards". The White Paper 1967 considered that Chinese customary marriages were not registered or registrable, were not celebrated before an official and were not monogamous. Additionally, the White Paper 1967 stated that because the dissolution of Chinese customary marriages could be done unilaterally by a husband, they were not consistent with Article 16 of the United Nations Universal Declaration of Human Rights, which provided that men and women were entitled to equal rights to marriage, during marriage and at its dissolution (Hong Kong Colonial Secretariat 1967, para. 15).

The proposed solution as stated in the White Paper 1967 was to establish a new monogamous and registered system to replace the Chinese customary marriage. The White Paper 1967 proposed that the new conditions and procedure must be met in order to make Chinese customary marriages valid. These were, firstly, both man and woman must be free to marry. Secondly, both parties must agree to marry of their own free will. Thirdly, prior public notice of intention to marry must be given without valid objection being raised. Fourthly, the marriage must be celebrated within 3 months of the giving of notice and, finally, that the marriage must be registered at a marriage registry within 14 days of the celebration (Hong Kong Colonial Secretariat 1967, para. 16(b)). This procedure was in effect a registered system resembling existing practices of registered marriage in Hong Kong. The White Paper 1967 further proposed that the law would be changed to allow for the recognition and registration of "monogamous marriages celebrated elsewhere than in a licensed place of worship or in a marriage registry" (Hong Kong Colonial Secretariat 1967, para. 17). On the other hand, the White Paper 1967 proposed that legislation would be introduced after the Appointed Date so that no woman might newly acquire any legal status as a concubine. The White Paper 1967 stated that such new practices were intended to show that, after the Appointed Date, both parties could still enter into a monogamous marriage by means of a customary ceremony, provided that they complied with the above formalities (Hong Kong Colonial Secretariat 1967, para. 16(c)).

On Chinese modern marriage, the White Paper 1967 proposed that those marriages contracted before the Appointed Date could be validated by retrospective legislation, subject to certain conditions such as the age and status of the parties at the time of the marriage and "subject also to a proviso relating to marriage that have been dissolved in the meantime" (Hong Kong Colonial Secretariat 1967, para. 26(a)). Then, legislation would be introduced to allow the parties to such marriage validated as above to post-register their marriage on production of evidence to the registrar (Hong Kong Colonial Secretariat 1967, para. 26(b). Finally, both parties could use the "new" form of Chinese modern marriages after the "Appointed Date" but still follow the monogamous and registered system as proposed for Chinese customary marriages. This solution, as stated by the White Paper 1967, was "exactly the same solution should be applied to future Chinese Marriages and to future Modern Marriages". And ceremonies of both forms of marriages would remain the same but would only be valid in law provided that such marriages were monogamous and registered.

On the dissolution of Chinese customary marriages and Chinese modern marriages, the White Paper 1967 proposed that both forms of marriages should only be dissolved by mutual consent. They reached this recommendation because firstly, the dissolution of mutual consent was the practice of Chinese customary marriage in Hong Kong. Secondly, in Chinese modern marriages in Hong Kong, such a form of dissolution was regarded as an integral part of the marriage contract (Hong Kong Colonial Secretariat 1967, para. 31). The White Paper 1967 proposed that legislation should be introduced to validate dissolution by mutual consent, before the Appointed Date, of Chinese customary and retrospectively recognised Chinese modern marriages, on the condition that such written evidence must be signed by the parties and duly witnessed (Hong Kong Colonial Secretariat 1967, para. 34(1). Also, the same legislation should allow the dissolution by mutual consent, after the Appointed Date, of any Chinese customary marriages or modern marriages, whether contracted before or after the Appointed Date. The White Paper 1967 laid down the procedure that such dissolution required public notice of the intention to dissolve the marriage. And, the parties had to be interviewed by a government official who would confirm that such intention was genuinely mutual and voluntary on both sides. Such divorces would then be officially registered (Hong Kong Colonial Secretariat 1967, para. 34.(2)). Finally, the White Paper 1967 proposed that all other forms of dissolution of marriages, other than those specified in the Matrimonial Causes Ordinance should be declared invalid in law (Hong Kong Colonial Secretariat 1967, para. 34(3)). In sum, this proposal, if approved, would ensure that dissolution by mutual consent would be the one and only way for the dissolving Chinese customary or modern marriages. This had the potential to create some trouble, for example, if a husband refused to make a divorce, or a husband deserted and his whereabouts was unknown, thus making a divorce practically impossible. This would be dealt with by later amendments in law and will be discussed later in this chapter.

On the status of concubines in marriage, the White Paper 1967 reiterated that the rights of a concubine remained the same before and after the Appointed Date: "[i]t would follow that those who are already Concubines[9] or who become concubines before the Appointed Date, will continue to be accorded such recognition in law as now exists, and no more" (Hong Kong Colonial Secretariat 1967, para. 38). The White Paper 1967 considered that it would be important to safeguard the well-being and interests of the children of such unions. The focus was the responsibilities of a father for paternity of these children. The White Paper 1967 proposed two ways to regulate this. Firstly, the father must have a legal mean to accept the responsibilities of paternity voluntarily to any child born out of wedlock. Secondly, there should be

[9] "Concubines" refer to the concubines in the Chinese customary marriages in Hong Kong.

provision for any child born out of wedlock, or the mother of such a child, to apply to a court for an affiliation and maintenance order if the father did not wish to maintain the child up to the age of 16. The White Paper emphasised that these two were alternative approaches to the same objective—that the former approach would be regarded as a preferable and welcome alternative to the latter approach (Hong Kong Colonial Secretariat 1967, para. 39).

The White Paper 1967 concluded that, unlike the Strickland Report which attempted to deal comprehensively with the Chinese law and custom including questions related to marriage and succession, the government only wanted to deal with the issues relating to Chinese marriage. It followed the strategy as laid down in the White Paper 1960 that "after which at least some of the complexities and uncertainties in the field of succession will have been removed, whilst others will have been simplified". And, the government considered that the White Paper 1967 and its proposals should be paused at this final stage, even though there would still remain some elements of controversy, "before the introduction of changes in the law designed to cure or remove the anachronisms and defects of which the community has for so long been aware" (Hong Kong Colonial Secretariat 1967, para. 46-47). But after the White Paper 1967 and the subsequent legislation, the effects of the marriage reform were more far-reaching than the White Paper 1967 had originally intended. This will be discussed later in this chapter.

6.6 Executive Council Paper and Marriage Reform Bill 1969

The communist riot in Hong Kong disrupted the legislative programme. After the publication of the White Paper 1967, the Secretary for Chinese Affairs was going to prepare a legislative bill to put forwards the recommendations from the White Paper 1967. On 2 February 1968, the Legal Department passed a report written by a Sub-Committee of the Hong Kong Bar Association, commenting on the White Paper 1967 (Letter from Legal Department, 2 February 1968). This report called for a registered marriage system in Hong Kong, following which the legal recognition of all future marriage would depend on the fact of registration. Thus, no marriage would be regarded as legal unless it was registered (Chinese Marriages, 16 December 1968, p. 1). On the institution of concubinage, this report agreed with the recommendation to abolish concubinage but proposed that relationships existing before the Appointed Date ought to be "Post-Registrable" (Hong Kong Bar Association 1967, para. 51). This report also asked the government whether they should consider those less well-informed or well-educated woman who entered into secondary or unofficial matrimonial status. The report stated that, for example, in the Civil Code 1931 of the Republic of China, "despite the introduction of monogamy as the sole legal basis of marriage, protection was afforded to concubines who had already acquired the status of members of the household of a head of a family before the Code came into effect" (Hong Kong Bar Association 1967, para. 52). In such cases, the report stated that if the public opinion required, the government should also deem to "obviate undue harshness in the application of a rule that might not be understood, particularly by the women most concerned, for some time". The report did not suggest whether the government should consider the legislative model of the Civil Code 1931of the Republic of China (Hong Kong Bar Association 1967, para. 53). This report was submitted to the members for the Executive and Legislative Councils on 18 April 1968 (Note for Executive, 18 April 1968). Nevertheless, the legislative proposal as drafted by the government did not take any account of these recommendations.

During the course of discussion of the legislative proposal, the arguments within the administration were about, for example, the use of the term to define the new form of a statutory Chinese monogamous customary marriages—the government officials called it a new form of monogamous Chinese "modern" marriage internally—in accordance with the White Paper 1967 (Memorandum from the Secretary for Chinese Affairs, 12 August 1968, para. 2); whether the Registrar General was responsible for registering such new form of marriage (Memorandum from the Colonial Secretariat, 13 August 1968, para. 3); and the details of the new registration system (Hong Kong Bar Association 1967, para. 6). Such discussion on administrative details delayed the whole legislative process. In the meeting of 10 January 1969, the Secretary for Chinese Affairs reported that some issues had been raised with the Foreign and Commonwealth Office, and he was waiting for the reply. The Secretary for Chinese Affairs was confident that, given London's answer, the legislation could be finalised soon. The Governor clearly stated that this legislation was being delayed, and he wanted to get the new legislation passed in 1969 (Notes of Government House, 10 January 1969).

One key issue was that, since the White Paper 1967 proposed to have a new form of statutory monogamous Chinese "modern" marriage (to replace the Chinese customary marriages and to resolve the issue of the non-recognition of Chinese modern marriages) and to register marriage celebrated elsewhere other than in a licensed place of worship or in a marriage registry, the Attorney General had to put a new form of such marriage in the draft bill (Hong Kong Colonial Secretariat, 1967, para. 64). However, this kind of new registered marriage system was rejected by the Registrar General, who commented that this kind of "monogamous" Chinese "modern" marriage was outdated and that "the Chinese community in general would not be so foolish as to wish to perpetuate by legislation an out-moded custom that is already dying of its own accord" (Memorandum from Registrar General, 30 March 1969, para. 1). This view was shared by Paul Tsui of the Secretary for Home Affairs, who said that after his brief non-scientific survey by asking no more than six suppliers of bridal accessories shops in the urban part of Hong Kong, he considered that there were very few (if at all any) couples who would choose to celebrate their marriages other than in one of the marriage registries or in a church. He considered that if the government was not providing this new form of marriage in the legislation, "there will be no demand for facilities to register such marriages" (Memorandum from Secretary for Home Affairs, 12 March 1969a, para. 4).

With the release of the draft Marriage Reform Bill 1969 given by the Attorney General on 25 March 1969, a meeting of government officials, representatives from

Colonial Secretariat, Attorney General, Secretary for Home Affairs and Registrar General was held to discuss the issues relating to the draft bill on 23 April 1969. During the meeting, it was agreed that this new statutory form of the Chinese "modern" marriage had to be abandoned, because firstly, such a form of marriage was no longer popular. Secondly, local opinion would accept that, after a stipulated date, only marriage performed under the Marriage Ordinance would receive legal recognition, while at the same time formal recognition would be given to Chinese customary marriage and modern marriage entered into before that time. Thirdly, from a legal point of view, it was better not to put two alternative forms of marriage on the statute book. Fourthly, local opinion would not be upset if this was no provided in the new law. Finally, in the last two financial years, there were more than 2000 couples who had previously married under Chinese customary marriage who had come to make registration under the Marriage Ordinance, and "at present some 80 to 90% of marriages in the colony took place under the Ordinance" (Memorandum from the Colonial Secretariat, 5 May 1969, para. 1; Memorandum from Secretary for Home Affairs, 7 May 1969b). On the issue of concubinage, the meeting agreed that any attempt to codify the status and rights of concubines would be regarded by the public as consolidating the concubines' positions, which might attract opposition (Memorandum from the Colonial Secretariat, 5 May 1969, para. 3). Because of this consideration, the registration of concubines should be deleted in the draft bill. And, the Attorney General said that the reference to concubines in the Intestates' Estates Bill could be removed although he noted that if the bill was to make provision for concubines, "it would not be satisfactory for this provision to be in indefinite terms" (Memorandum from the Colonial Secretariat, 5 May 1969, para. 10). In other words, the issue of the definition of concubine would be surface if there was a discussion of the rights of concubine.

The Secretary for Home Affairs, Holmes, wanted to gauge the opinions from the Chinese Unofficial members of the Executive and Legislative Councils on the legislative details. In a letter sent to C. Y. Kwan, Holmes attached a note on the points raised in the above meeting, and the letter attached new bills which formed as a package of the whole Chinese marriages legislation (Letter from the Secretary for Home Affairs, 16 May 1967). These included the Intestates' Estate Bill, the Deceased's Family Maintenance Bill, the Legitimacy Bill and the Affiliation Proceedings Bill (Points Raised, 16 May 1967, para. 2). A meeting with the Chinese Unofficial members of the Executive and Legislative Councils was held on 9 June 1969.

During the course of discussion, C. Y. Kwan made the most of the opportunity to speak on behalf of other Chinese Unofficial members. In one of the notes of a meeting (which was a personal note rather than a formal note), it was recorded that C. Y. Kwan first proposed that at the present legislative proposals, only two bills would be introduced: the Marriage Reform Bill (the principal bill on the abolition of concubinage) and the Intestates' Estate Bill. His suggestion was agreed to at the meeting.

But subsequently the discussion centred on the definition of "concubine" in the draft bill.[10] C. Y. Kwan argued that the definition was meaningless because nobody knew the pre-1842 Chinese law and custom. He considered that "we should get away from this 'Chinese law and custom' (of a past era) influence and consider these matters in a purely present day Hong Kong context". He rejected a vague and loose definition and wanted something definite and even restrictive in order to avoid women who "could not really be regarded as concubines contriving to slip through the net under the cloak of the law". He emphasised that a mistress was not a concubine and therefore that distinct procedures were necessary leading up to the acceptance of a concubine into the family by the principal wife and the family. He considered that the welfare of the concubines' children was important since they were accepted as the proper children of the father (Notes of a Meeting, 9 June 1969, 11 June 1969, para. 3). And, in the formal note of meeting, it was stated that C. Y. Kwan also considered that there was a danger that a woman would appear and claim to have been his concubine after a man's death, which would lead to difficulty and embarrassment (Memorandum from Secretary for Chinese Affairs, 27 June 1969). In a record by a government official, C. Y. Kwan proposed to legally define "concubine" on the following lines:

> A Concubine or Tsip is the female partner in a union of concubinage who has been admitted into the male partner's family and accepted by his wife as a concubine during the lifetime of the male partner; and has also been recognised by the male partner's relatives generally. (Notes of a Meeting, 11 June 1969, para. 4)

In the formal notes of meeting, C. Y. Kwan's proposed definition was given on the following lines:

> [c]oncubine or tsip means a female partner of a union of concubinage, who has been admitted into the partner's family and accepted by his wife as such, and recognised by the body of the male part's family generally. (Notes of a Meeting, 11 June 1969)

This proposed definition raised some comments from government officials who thought it too restrictive. The Deputy Commissioner of the New Territories, D.S. Whitelegge, considered that this definition would be tougher than the present position. The Attorney General, D. T. E. Roberts, considered that there was very little case law as many families were reluctant to take the cases relating to a concubine to court. Even one Chinese Unofficial member, P. C. Woo, questioned whether it would be sufficient for a concubine to be accepted by the family generally and not necessarily specifically by the wife (Memorandum from Secretary for Chinese Affairs, 27 June 1969, pp. 1–2). In another notes of meeting, P. C. Woo further argued that there might be circumstances in which the principal wife would not give positive approval but merely acquiesce to the situation, and in this case the concubine was no less than a concubine for it. In the formal notes of a meeting, another Chinese Unofficial member, P. Y. Tang, mentioned that in Shanghai the male party's

---

[10] In this draft Marriage Reform Bill, Clause 2 defined "concubine" as "tsip in accordance with Chinese law and custom". This definition was finally dropped in the final version of the legislation (Memorandum from Attorney General's Chambers, 28 April 1969).

wishes always dominated regarding the status of the concubine in the family (Memorandum from Secretary for Chinese Affairs, 27 June 1969, p. 2). In another notes of meeting, it was revealed that C. Y. Kwan insisted on having a strict line for defining a concubine, because there were some rights being considered by the government under other pieces of legislation in which a concubine would have more rights than before. Accordingly, C. Y. Kwan wanted an initially tough definition and then to let the public judge (Notes of a Meeting, 11 June 1969, para. 5). Another government official, Deputy Secretary for Home Affairs, Paul K. C. Tsui, commented that the Secretary for Home Affairs, Holmes, had reservations about defining a concubine in the Marriage Reform Bill. Finally, the meeting agreed that a new definition of concubine would be drafted before the Marriage Reform Bill and Intestates' Estate Bill were submitted to the Executive Council (Memorandum from Secretary for Chinese Affairs, 27 June 1969, p. 2). The Deputy District Commissioner recorded in a minute that this definition would be put in the Intestates' Estate Bill rather than the Marriage Reform Bill because that involved practical entitlements and effects of the concubine (Minute of D.D.C., 23 June 1969). The meeting, when discussing the Intestate' Estates Bill, also noted that C. Y. Kwan considered that the Clause 14 had to be redrafted to take into account the changes of the Marriage Reform Bill (Memorandum from Secretary for Chinese Affairs, 27 June 1969, p. 3).

The Marriage Reform Bill was submitted to the Executive Council on 8 July 1969 for a consultation of 3 months. In the Executive Council paper, it was explained that the fundamental principle of this bill was that after the Appointed Date, valid marriage taken in Hong Kong must be celebrated in accordance with the Marriage Ordinance (Memorandum for Executive Council, 30 June 1969, para. 3). This was made in Clause 4:

> Marriage entered into in Hong Kong on and after the Appointed Date shall imply the voluntary union for life of one man with one woman to the exclusion of all others and may be contracted only in accordance with the Marriage Ordinance. (Annex to Memorandum for Executive Council, 30 June 1969)

This clause in effect forbids, after the Appointed Date, any forms of marriage in Hong Kong other than a marriage of a "union of one man with one woman to the exclusion of others". In other words, after the Appointed Date, only monogamous marriage would be legally recognised. Clause 5 prohibited the institution of concubinage after the Appointed Date and that the status or rights of a child legally taken before the Appointed Date, and the right of the child born before, on or after the Appointed Date of a concubine, would be protected:

> 5. (1) On or after the Appointed Date, no man may take a concubine and no woman may acquire the status of a concubine.
> (2) Subsection (i) shall not affect in any way –
> (a) the status or rights of a concubine lawfully taken before the Appointed Date; or
> (b) the status or rights of a child, whether born before, on or before the Appointed Date, of a concubine lawfully taken before the Appointed Date. (Annex to Memorandum for Executive Council, 30 June 1969)

The Executive Council paper stated that any additional form of marriage, based on traditional and modern Chinese marriages (as proposed in the White Paper in 1967 which referred to the statutory monogamous "modern" marriage as mentioned in Sect. 6.6 of this chapter), as an alternative to marriage under the Marriage Ordinance was dropped in this bill. It explained that, since there was an increase in public acceptance of marriage under the Marriage Ordinance, it was about time to expand the facilities of marriage registry, which made such proposal unnecessary. And, there was also an objection in principle that there were two forms of marriage in the statute book, which might produce more confusion (Memorandum for Executive Council, 30 June 1969, para. 4).

On Chinese customary marriage, the paper explained that since it had always been accepted as valid in Hong Kong, Clause 7(2) of the bill provided that such marriage was recognised if celebrated in accordance with the traditional Chinese customs for marriage pertaining in the part of Hong Kong where the marriage took place, or in the place of origin of the family party to the marriage (Memorandum for Executive Council, 30 June 1969, para. 6). Clause 8 specified that marriages celebrated in Hong Kong as "modern" or "open" had not been recognised as legal marriages. So, this clause validated every such marriage as from the date of its celebration (Memorandum for Executive Council, 30 June 1969, para. 7). A registration system was established so that the parties could go to register the customary or modern marriages, and in case of dispute, Clause 9(3) provided an appeal to the District Court for a declaratory order as to the existence of a registrable marriage (Memorandum for Executive Council, 30 June 1969, para. 8). Clauses 16–20 specified the procedure for the dissolution of mutual consent in the customary and modern marriages. It was important to note that a validated modern marriage (in other words, a celebrated modern marriage which had completed registration), would be capable of dissolution by the court in accordance with the Matrimonial Causes Ordinance (Memorandum for Executive Council, 30 June 1969, para. 10). Also, the bill proposed to "bypass" the strict requirement of "domicile" in private international law, whereby parties who wanted to dissolve their marriage must prove their domicile in Hong Kong. Clause 23 provided that the dissolution by consent of customary and validated modern marriages would exist where one of the parties had a substantial connection with Hong Kong as stipulated in amendments to Matrimonial Causes Ordinance (Memorandum for Executive Council, 30 June 1969, para. 15).

In sum, this proposed bill had reached the final stage of legislation. If the new law were passed by the Legislative Council, it would put an end to all recognition of Chinese law and custom relating to Chinese customary and modern marriages. Chinese marriage customs might still be celebrated in the community, but registered and monogamous marriage under the Marriage Ordinance would become the only way to contract a valid marriage in Hong Kong.

6.7 Delay in London

While domestically the Hong Kong Government was trying to put forwards the legislative bills and discussing the definition of concubinage as quickly as possible, the Attorney General was worried about the issue of domicile in the proposed reform. On 22 October 1968, in a savingram from the Acting Governor of Hong Kong to the Secretary of State for Foreign and Commonwealth Affairs, the Hong Kong Government sought advice after the House of Lords decision in *Indyka v Indyka* (1969).[11] The Hong Kong Government stated that, in the Executive Council paper, there was a risk that other countries might not recognise the dissolution of marriage by mutual consent as effected in Hong Kong, where the parties were not domicile in Hong Kong (Savingram from Acting Governor of Hong Kong, 22 October 1968). However, the Hong Kong Government also stated that, "to maintain domicile requirement as a pre-requisite to divorce in Hong Kong would be deprive the majority of the benefits which it is considered essential to confer". The Hong Kong Government submitted a report from its Legal Advisor on the impact of *Indyka v Indyka*, in which the Legal Advisor considered that the lordship in this case might lessen the requirement of domicile in divorce. The Solicitor General in Hong Kong, G. R. Sneath, mentioned in his legal advice that, so far as the Hong Kong Government was concerned, this case could help to establish that divorce effected in Hong Kong would be recognised as valid, "as long as one or both of the parties had a 'real and substantial' connection with Hong Kong" (Note: Recognition, 21 September 1968). The Hong Kong Government sought confirmation from the Foreign and Commonwealth Office along the above lines so that it could proceed in accordance with the rules established in this case.

On 26 November 1968, a legal advice paper was provided by I. H. Cruchley to I. R. Murray of the Foreign and Commonwealth Office. In it, Cruchley considered that in *Indyka v Indyka*, the House of Lords decided that recognition of the divorce decrees of foreign courts would be based on two conditions. Firstly, it would depend

[11] The issue of this case was whether the courts in the UK should recognise a divorce decree granted by a foreign court, as submitted by the petitioners. Lord Wilberforce ruled that "[I]n my opinion, it would be in accordance with the developments I have mentioned and with the trend of legislation—mainly our own but also that of other countries with similar social systems—to recognise divorces given to wives by the courts of their residence wherever a real and substantial connection is shown between the petitioner and the country, or territory, exercising jurisdiction. I use these expressions so as to enable the courts, who must decide each case, to consider both the length and quality of the residence and to take into account such other factors as nationality which may reinforce the connection. Equally they would enable the courts (as they habitually do without difficulty) to reject residence of passage or residence, to use the descriptive expression of the older cases, resorted to be persons who properly should seek relief here for the purpose of obtaining relief which our courts would not give" (*Indyka v Indyka*, 1969, p.727). See also *Angelo v Angelo* (1967).

upon the basis of nationality of the spouses. Secondly, this would perhaps when granted "on the basis of the nationality separately acquired by a wife, living apart from her husband, in which the wife had a real and substantial connection with the country pronouncing the decree" [emphasis in original]. Cruchley had no legal objection to Hong Kong's proposal (Minute from I. H. Cruchley, 26 November 1968).

However, the Foreign and Commonwealth Office did not give a reply on this issue, despite savingrams from the Governor of Hong Kong asking for a response on 9 January 1969 (Savingram from the Governor, 9 January 1969b), 6 February 1969 (Savingram from the Governor, 6 February 1969a)[12] and finally on 19 March 1969 (Letter from Attorney General's Chamber, 19 March 1969). In the last letter, the Attorney General of Hong Kong, D. T. E. Roberts, asked the Legal Adviser of the Foreign and Commonwealth Office for their response to the matter, since Roberts considered that "*Indyka v. Indyka* does, I think, give us some encouragement, and it would be helpful if we could be told that the S. of S. (Secretary of States) would have no objection to legislation on those lines". Ultimately, the Foreign and Commonwealth Office picked up the issue and replied on 16 April 1969, confirming its approval of the Hong Kong Government's proposal: "It is confirmed that you may proceed as proposed. The long delay since your proposals were put to us (and indeed since the legal advice was tendered) is greatly regretted" (Savingram from the Secretary of State, 16 April 1969, p. 2). This letter of confirmation gave the green light to the Hong Kong Government to submit and publish the Marriage Reform Bill in July 1969. The legislative programme in Hong Kong, however, was delayed by this piece of paper for 6 months.

6.8 Marriage Reform Bill 1970

After the publication of the Marriage Reform Bill 1969 in July 1969, the public response was "very poor" during the consultation period because the government only received 19 letters other than a few newspaper editorials (Memo from Secretariat, 16 December 1969, para. 9). But on the issue of the abolition of concubinage, opinions were still divided. One women's organisation considered that it must be clearly written in the legislation that existing concubines should only be recognised as lawful upon the consent of the principal wife and members of the family. They also commented that the legislation failed to give the definition of a concubine. Another women's organisation commented that a woman could acquire the status of concubine if she had been with a man for over 10 years and had children, even in the absence of the consent of the principal wife. An Urban Council member, Dr Danny Huang, doubted whether the new legislation could deter the practice of concubinage. And, the Kowloon Chamber of Commerce commented that

[12] In this savingram the Hong Kong Government stated that until the views of the Foreign and Commonwealth Office were known, "we are unable to proceed with what is a major piece of legislation which we wish to pass this year".

all concubines taken before the Appointed Date, and their children, should be registered at a marriage registry and issued certificates (Memo from Secretariat, 16 December 1969, para. 6). The Secretary for Chinese Affairs, J. N. Black, considered that there was no strong objection to the bill, so he recommended that "we [should] go ahead with the necessary procedure to enact the bill taking into account in doing so, the public comments received".

On 6 May 1970, the government submitted a memorandum of the Marriage Reform Bill to the Executive Council for the discussion on 12 May 1970. The government mentioned that though there was little public comment on the Marriage Reform Bill 1969, the public responses were favourable. The Heung Yee Kuk, representing the New Territories, had expressed general agreement with the provisions. No strong oppositions came from other New Territories inhabitants. This 1970 Bill was generally similar to the 1969 Bill with some changes. First, on the definition of the "parties to the customary marriage", it would be defined clearly that this would not refer to the relationship of the husband and concubine. Another was a minor amendment to the bill in which responsibility for the registration of the dissolution of validated and modern marriage was moved from the Registrar General to the Secretary for Home Affairs. Finally, some technical amendments were made to the Marriage Ordinance to remove some consequential inconsistency (Memorandum for Executive Council, 6 May 1970, paras. 1, 4, 6).

The Executive Council paper proposed that the Appointed Date of the new law should be 12 months after the date of enactment of the bill. This would help to give sufficient advance notice to the public and time for the administrative arrangement after the passage of the bill (Memorandum for Executive Council, 6 May 1970, para. 7). The Executive Council agreed generally to the bill with some minor amendments. Firstly, the Chinese characters for *Kim Tiu* would be inserted in Clause 6.[13] Secondly, a revised Section 38 of the Matrimonial Causes Ordinance (relating to the maintenance of the spouse) introduced by Clause 26(2) of the bill and, thirdly, an explanation of the above provision would be added in the explanatory memorandum. Finally, the Executive Council agreed that the Appointed Date should be 12 months after the enactment of the bill. The bill would then be submitted to the Legislative Council on 3 June 1970.

6.9 Passage in the Legislative Council

On the first and second reading of the Marriage Reforms Bill 1970 in the Legislative Council on 3 June 1970, the Secretary for Home Affairs, D. R. Holmes, introduced the bill. On the issue of the abolition of concubinage, he said that the purpose of the bill was to preserve the status and rights of the existing concubines and their

[13] Clause 6 of the bill abolished the *Kim Tiu* marriage: "(1) On or after the Appointed Date no person shall contract a *Kim Tiu* marriage." *Kim Tiu* marriage was discussed in Chap. 2, Sect. 2.2.4.

children and that in due course the institution would die out altogether (Speech by Secretary for Home Affairs, 3 June 1970; Hong Kong Legislative Council, 3 June 1970b, p. 679). He disagreed with the criticisms that firstly, the government's proposal did not have any procedure on the assumption of a concubine's status written in law and, secondly, the government did not establish a registration system for the existing concubines. Holmes stated that:

> since we have managed for nearly a century and a half without these definitions, and without any form of codification or registration, it would be quite incongruous to attempt to introduce them in the present Bill, of which the main purpose in this connection is to abolish the institution as soon as this can be done without causing distress or hardship. (Speech by Secretary for Home Affairs, 3 June 1970; Hong Kong Legislative Council, 3 June 1970b, p. 679)

In the resumption of the second reading in the Legislative Council held on 17 June 1970, the Legislative Councillor, P.C. Woo, supported that bill, and on the issue of concubinage, he stated that the abolition of concubinage was intended to bring the Hong Kong laws in line with Taiwan and Mainland China:

> The reforms proposed in this bill, Sir, are no more than to put the legal position of the Chinese spouses in the same status as in Taiwan or in Communist China. Complaints have been made about the delay in bringing up the Chinese law of marriages to suit the present condition in Hong Kong, but such a delay in my opinion is worthwhile as we now clearly see that we are heading at the right direction in this aspect of law reform. (Hong Kong Legislative Council, 17 June 1970a, p. 732)

Another legislator, Ellen Li, had been advocating for the abolition of concubinage and spoke in support of the Marriage Reform Bill. She criticised the fact that a few selfish males still wanted to retain their right to polygamy. In addition, she disagreed with setting up a registration system for concubines because that would "bring embarrassment to many self-respecting and self-righteous men who would prefer to keep their private affairs private". Then, she considered that a definition of concubine in the context of the Marriage Reform Bill was unnecessary because that was a family affair and could be dealt with between the man, his wife and the other woman or women. But in relation to the intestates' estate, she considered that the definition of concubine was necessary because it was done to "protect the man's good name, because he is not there to defend himself". She finally stated that this bill had her full support and she was glad "after all these years to see that this measure is about to become law" (Hong Kong Legislative Council, 17 June 1970a, p. 733).

But one legislator, Oswald Cheung, questioned whether a monogamous marriage was superior than the traditional Chinese institution of marriage and "that we should completely denied the right to people to opt out of it if they wish?" He further questioned whether the government had the right to force such institution upon people who did not believe in it. He was not persuaded that the experience of monogamous marriages in other countries would merit a change of law in Hong Kong:

> From time to time within the last two thousand years various Chinese emperors, with the cry of equality of the sexes, protection of women and the stoppage of abuse, have tried to abolish concubinage, with very little success...Even if all the evidence of the last fifteen or

twenty years points to the unqualified success of monogamy in those countries—and I have no evidence to suggest that monogamy has been a complete success—even if the evidence were so, in a matter like this, in tampering with an institution which has been held honourable for upwards of two thousand years, I am completely unpersuaded that ten, fifteen or twenty years experience obliges us to change our laws. (Hong Kong Legislative Council, 17 June 1970a, p. 733)

The Acting Colonial Secretary, Holmes, felt regret on hearing the views from Oswald Cheung. He considered that he would not attempt to characterise the views of Oswald Cheung "as being part of what Mrs Li (Ellen Li) called the 'dying struggle of the few selfish males' who would like to retain their right to polygamy". He further stated that after the publication of the Strickland Report, the government had to a large extent accept many thoughtful comments and views expressed by very respectable and worthy citizens which were accorded with the general spirit of Oswald Cheung's remarks. Holmes commented that in the intervening years from the Strickland Report to the Marriage Reform Bill, "there have been changes, positive and comparatively rapid changes in public attitudes, public thinking and public practice" where there was a very considerable force of public opinion in support of the government (Hong Kong Legislative Council, 17 June 1970a, pp. 738–739).

The bill was finally moved to third reading in the Legislative Council meeting on the meeting of 8 July 1970 (Hong Kong Legislative Council, 8 July 1970c, p. 783). After some internal discussion, especially as the government was considering to enact the laws in tandem with the enactment of the Intestates' Estates Bill, it was decided that the "Appointed Date" for the purpose of Marriage Reform Ordinance would be 7 October 1971 (Memo from Colonial Secretariat, 11 November 1970).

6.10 Other Legislative Changes Relating to the Abolition of Concubinage

One important piece of legislation relating to Marriage Reform Bill was the Intestates' Estate Bill 1970. The purpose of the bill was to abolish the application of the Chinese laws of succession in Hong Kong. This bill gave the children (whether male or female) of the intestate equal rights to share in his estate. This also applied to children born by a concubine. The Intestates' Estates Bill, which was subsequently passed and promulgated on 7 October 1971, provided the definition of concubinage in Section 13(2). It stipulated that the "union of concubinage" (夫妾關係) means "a union of concubinage, entered into by a male partner and a female partner before 7 October 1971, under which union the female partner has, during the lifetime of the male partner, been accepted by his wife as his concubine and recognized as such by his family generally."[14]

[14]This ordinance was enacted on the same day of the Marriage Reform Ordinance (Intestates' Estates Ordinance, Cap. 73). In an amendment to the Intestates' Estate Ordinance in 1993, a subsection was added, as Section 13(3), which gave stronger protection to the concubine: "Where in

Another piece of legislation was the Deceased's Family Maintenance Ordinance (Cap. 129) promulgated on the same day as the Marriage Reform Bill, in other words, 7 October 1971. This law was intended to provide for the maintenance of certain dependents out of the estates of the deceased. A concubine could also apply for a maintenance order. A definition of the "union of concubinage" was provided in Section 17(2), which was identical to Section 13(2) of the Intestates' Estates Ordinance.[15]

On the same day, 7 October 1971, the Legitimacy Ordinance (Cap. 184) was enacted. The purpose of this law was to legitimate the illegitimate offsprings by the subsequent marriage of their parents, on condition that the father of the offspring was domiciled in or has a substantial connection with Hong Kong at the time of the marriage.[16] Section 14 specified that the Ordinance applied to the union of concubinage. In Section 14(2), the "union of concubinage" was defined as "entered by a male partner and a female partner before the Appointed Date under the Marriage Reform Ordinance, under which union the female partner has, during the lifetime of the male partner, been accepted by his wife as his concubine and recognized as such by his family generally" (Legitimacy Ordinance, Cap. 184).[17]

Also on the 7 October 1971, the Affiliation Proceedings Ordinance (Cap. 183) was enacted.[18] This law gave the right of a single woman of an illegitimate child to apply to the court for an affiliation order to make the putative father maintain the child until the age of 16 years old (Sec. 8).[19] Or, if the child was engaged in a course of education or training after attaining the age of 16 years, or the child was suffering from a mental or physical disability, the court could order payments from the putative father for an additional period beyond the age of 16, though not exceeding 2 years from the date of the order (Sec. 9).

---

any proceedings a union of concubinage is proved to have been entered into by a male partner and a female partner before 7 October 1971, it shall be presumed until the contrary is proved that the female partner has, during the lifetime of the male partner, been accepted by his wife as his concubine and recognized as such by his family generally".

[15] This legislation was subsequently repealed in 1995 (Deceased's Family Maintenance Ordinance, Cap. 129).

[16] See section 3(1). In common law, the rule is that a child is illegitimate if his parents are not validly married to one another either when he was born or when he was conceived. The Legitimacy Ordinance would legitimate an illegitimate child where his parents subsequently marry. It is stated in Section 3 (1) that "...where the parents of an illegitimate person marry or have marry or have married one another, whether before or after the commencement of this Ordinance, the marriage shall, if the father of the illegitimate person was or is at the date of the marriage domiciled in Hong Kong or had or has at such a date a substantial connection with Hong Kong, render that person, if living, legitimate from the commencement of this Ordinance, or from the date of marriage, whichever last happens" (Legitimacy Ordinance, Cap. 184).

[17] Section 14 was subsequently amended in 1995, by adding Subsection (3): "Where in any proceedings a union of concubinage is proved to have been entered into by a male partner and a female partner before 7 October 1971, it shall be presumed until the contrary is proved that the female partner has, during the lifetime of the male partner, been accepted by his wife as his concubine and recognized as such by his family generally" (Legitimacy Ordinance, Cap. 184).

[18] This ordinance was repealed in 1997 by the Ordinance No. 80 of 1997 (Affiliation Proceedings Ordinance, Cap. 183).

[19] This law was repealed in 1995.

There were other pieces of legislation enacted on 7 October 1971 but not introduced due to the abolition of concubinage. They were made to reform family law. These were the Married Persons Status Ordinance 1971,[20] the Matrimonial Causes (Amendment) Ordinance 1971[21] and the Law Reform (Miscellaneous Provisions) Ordinance 1971.[22]

Perhaps the most important piece of legislation was the Marriage Reform (Amendment) Bill in 1971, proposed after the Marriage Reform Bill was passed in 1970. The amendments to the Marriage Reform Ordinance were submitted to the Executive Council after the Appointed Date of the first Marriage Reform Ordinance. The purpose of the amendments was to validate the dissolutions of marriage by consent obtained in Hong Kong, by persons who were married in the Republic of China under the Civil Code 1931 between 1931 and 1950 and at the time of the dissolutions either domiciled or had the substantial connection with Hong Kong (Memorandum for Executive Council, 4 November 1971). The submission stated that the Hong Kong Government had a practice until 1968, where couples who were married in the Republic of China between 1931 and 1950 under the Civil Code 1931 then moved to Hong Kong and dissolved their marriage by mutual consent in accordance with Articles 1049 and 1050 in accordance with the same Code. The paper stated that many of these dissolutions were made before officers at the Secretariat for Home Affairs. The paper further stated that legal advice considered that this practice was invalid, because both parties need to prove that they were domicile in Hong Kong. The paper further stated that despite this problem, the practice was generally accepted by the Hong Kong Government to the extent that after such dissolution, a person could then go to remarriage in accordance with the Registrar General under Marriage Ordinance. To complicate the situation, another legal advice in 1968 stated that even if the parties could establish a domicile in Hong Kong, this form of marriage could only be dissolved under the Matrimonial Causes Ordinance. The paper argued that there was a problem of this dissolution because if such dissolution was not recognised, the children born of that subsequent "remarriage" would be illegitimate. To protect the so-called "illegitimate" children, the government proposed some amendments to the Marriage Reform Ordinance. Firstly, the amendment was to validate the practice of dissolution by consent and, secondly, to validate the legitimacy of these children whether born before or after the purported declaration (Memorandum for Executive Council, 4 November 1971, paras. 4–7, 10). This bill was submitted to the Executive Council and was discussed on 16 November 1971. The law was subsequently passed on 15 December 1971 (Hong Kong Legislative Council, 15 December 1971, p. 291).

---

[20] This law gave the right of a married woman to alienate her property past, present and future (Section 4). This law also gave the right of either party to sue the other in tort (Section 5) (Married Persons Status Ordinance, Cap. 182).

[21] This law, Matrimonial (Amendment) Ordinance (Ord. No. 31 of 1971), amended the Matrimonial Causes Ordinance (Cap. 179), which simplified the procedure of giving matrimonial relief (Matrimonial (Amendment) Ordinance, Ord. 31 of 1971).

[22] This Law, Ord. No. 35 of 1971, abolished some old causes of actions relating to a married person, such as that the engagement ring was an absolute gift whether the marriage took place or not (Law Reform (Miscellaneous Provisions) Ordinance, Ord. 35 of 1971).

Finally, there was a legislative proposal submitted by the government to the Legislative Council in 1979, on whether provisions of the Matrimonial Causes Ordinance should be extended to the parties on the dissolution of the Chinese customary marriage. On 23 May 1977, a Legislative Councillor, T.S. Lo, argued that under Section 15(1) of the Marriage Reform Ordinance, a registered customary marriage could only be dissolved by mutual consent. But Section 15(2) of the same Ordinance stated that a registered validated marriage (Chinese modern marriage) could be dissolved whether by mutual consent or in accordance with the Matrimonial Causes Ordinance. Mr T. S. Lo considered that a person married in a customary marriage was in a less favourable position when obtaining divorce (Hong Kong Legislative Council, 15 December 1971, p. 291). He considered that the Qing laws on divorce were no longer the modern standards, and the basic purpose of divorce today was to free the spouses so that they could remarry again. He proposed that the right of the couples to obtain dissolution of marriage in accordance with Matrimonial Causes Ordinance should be extended to Chinese customary marriage (Hong Kong Legislative Council, 15 December 1971, p. 2). On 7 December 1977, a memo from the Director of Home Affairs, K. Fok, was in support of T.S. Lo's proposal because she argued that most people at that time would strongly oppose the discriminatory aspects of customary practices towards woman. She considered that the public would support any measures aimed at removing any remaining hardship suffered by these women (Memo from Director of Home Affairs, 7 December 1977). The Director of Legal Aid, Desmond Mayne, was in support of T.S. Lo based on a minute from his colleague, Miss Barbara Chan, who was in charge of litigation in the Family Law Section of the Litigation Unit. In it, Chan mentioned that she had come across cases where the marriages of the applicants clearly observed all the Chinese customs, but their proposed divorces were rejected. Hence, the applicants had no other legal recourse to obtain their divorces under the Marriage Reform Ordinance (Memo from Director of Legal Aid, 26 January 1978).

The legislative proposal, based on the above comments, was submitted to the Executive Council together with other legislative proposals on the family law. The government proposed to make some amendments to the Marriage Reform Ordinance. Firstly, it was proposed to allow applications for a declaration in court that a marriage subsists where the other party could not be traced or notified (Legal Report, 7 August 1979). Secondly, an amendment was proposed on the same ordinance to allow a registered customary marriage be dissolved either by dissolution by mutual consent or in accordance with the Matrimonial Causes Ordinance. In the same Executive Council paper, amendments were proposed to the Matrimonial Causes Ordinance, to disallow the former husband to make an application for maintenance in a registered modern or customary marriage. This amendment was introduced to make it in line with the same restriction given to a former wife under the same Ordinance. At the same time, a minor amendment was made to Matrimonial Proceedings and Property Ordinance. This amendment enabled a court hearing matrimonial petitions to revoke an existing maintenance order made by another course, so that parties are not compelled to go back to that other court (Amendments, 11 June 1979, paras. 3, 8, 9, 11). These bills were discussed in the Executive Council meeting on 26 June 1979 and were passed in the Legislative Council on 1 August 1979 (Hong Kong Legislative Council, 1 August 1979, p. 1047).

6.11 Conclusion

This chapter traced the legislative development of the abolition of concubinage from the year of 1965 to the date of promulgation in 1971. These 6 years were significant because firstly, under the pressure of the Chinese Unofficial members of the Executive and Legislative Councils, the Hong Kong Government defined "concubine", a definition that was clearly drafted in consideration of the Hong Kong context but not in mind of any Qing law or the applicable laws in China in 1843. Moreover, if compared with the Qing laws as discussed in Chap. 2, this definition of the "union of concubinage" was a departure from the traditional meaning, especially on the requirements of such a union to have the consent of the principal wife and the acceptance of the family members. These new requirements had become the interpretation of the administrative departments in Hong Kong on the meaning of concubine and appeared in the administrative manual of the government. In the papers distributed to the enquiry counters of the District Offices in Hong Kong, an internal government paper stated that to substantiate a woman's claim as a lawful concubine, three conditions must be satisfied: "(1) her husband's first marriage is a polygamous one (2) she has been accepted into the family, and (3) she has performed some rites such as tea pouring to the principal wife and the parents-in-law, and ancestor worship". Such an administrative interpretation of concubine was even broader than the statutory provisions, in which the rites such as *yap kung* was accepted as a proof of the status of a concubine (Memo from O/C Information Division, 20 May 1970, p. 2).

Secondly, given the decision on the abolition of concubinage, the gate was further opened for reform of Chinese customary marriages and modern marriages as practised in Hong Kong. The legislative proposals following to the Marriage Reform Ordinance in Hong Kong were made to achieve a dual purpose. Firstly, more rights were given to the women in Chinese customary marriages and modern marriages on the laws of succession, adoption and the right to apply for maintenance in court. Secondly, the introduction of the monogamous and registered marriage system put an end to the Chinese modern marriage and transformed the Chinese customary marriage to a set of rites that the man and woman conducted before making a formal registration at the marriage registry. The abolition of concubinage was the last intrusion of the colonial government into the private sphere of the Chinese community and successfully transformed the customary practices of the Chinese community by legislation. Although there were no archival records which showed that the Colonial Office had a plan to mastermind such drastic changes in the Chinese family order in Hong Kong, without much social resistance from the community, after 1971, the family relationship in Hong Kong has been mostly governed by the common law system transplanted by the colonial government.

References

Amendments. (1979, 11 June). *Matrimonial Causes (Amendment) Bill 1979, Matrimonial Proceedings and Property (Amendment) Bill 1979, Marriage Reform (Amendment) Bill 1979, Memorandum for Executive Council: Marriage Reform (Amendment) Bill 1979; Matrimonial Causes (Amendment) Bill 1979; Matrimonial Proceedings and Property (Amendment) Bill 1979, 11 June 1979* (HKRS 618-1-249). The Hong Kong Record Series, Hong Kong.

Annex A. (1965, 29 November). *Chinese Customary Marriages NT 1_466_58 II, Annex A to the Memorandum of the Executive Council: Chinese Marriages in Hong Kong, 29 November 1965* (HKRS 634-1-22). The Hong Kong Record Series, Hong Kong.

Annex to Memorandum for Executive Council. (1969, 30 June). *Chinese Customary Marriages Part I, Annex to Memorandum for Executive Council: Marriage Reform Bill 1969, 30 June 1969* (HKRS 634-1-23). The Hong Kong Record Series, Hong Kong.

Chinese Marriages. (1968, 16 December). *Chinese Customary Marriages Part I, Summary: Annex to Note for Executive/Legislative Councils: Chinese Marriages, 16 December 1968* HKRS 634-1-23. The Hong Kong Record Series, Hong Kong.

Hong Kong Bar Association. (1967). *Chinese Marriages in Hong Kong: A Report by the Sub-Committee of the Hong Kong Bar Association on Chinese Marriages*. Hong Kong Bar Association Hong Kong.

Hong Kong Colonial Secretariat. (1967, May). *Chinese Customary Marriages Part I, White Paper on Chinese Marriages in Hong Kong, May 1967* (HKRS 634-1-23). The Hong Kong Record Series, Hong Kong.

Hong Kong Legislative Council. (1970a, 17 June). *Official Report of Proceedings, 17 June 1970*. Hong Kong: Government Printer.

Hong Kong Legislative Council. (1970b, 3 June). *Official Report of Proceedings*. Hong Kong: Government Printer.

Hong Kong Legislative Council. (1970c, 8 July). *Official Report of Proceedings, 8 July 1970*. Hong Kong: Government Printer.

Hong Kong Legislative Council. (1971, 15 December). *Official Report of Proceedings, 15 December 1971*. Hong Kong: Government Printer.

Hong Kong Legislative Council. (1979, 1 August). *Official Report of Proceedings of Hong Kong Legislative Council, 1 August 1979*. Hong Kong: Government Printer. https://www.legco.gov.hk/yr78-79/english/lc_sitg/hansard/h790801.pdf. Accessed on 23 Nov 2018.

Legal Report. (1979, 7 August). *Legislation for Marriage in Hong Kong, Legal Report: The Matrimonial Proceedings and Property (Amendment) Ordinance 1979* (FCO 40/1085). Kew: The National Archives.

Letter from Attorney General's Chamber. (1969, 19 March). *Hong Kong Legal Affairs Chinese Laws and Customs, Letter from Attorney General's Chamber, D. T. E. Roberts to Foreign and Commonwealth Offices, James McPetrie, 19 March 1969* (FCO 40/225). The National Archives, Kew.

Letter from Colonial Office. (1966, 11 March). *Chinese Marriage–1965 Development SCA 172_65 II, Letter from Colonial Office, W. S. Carter to Secretary for Chinese Affairs, J. C. McDouall, 11 March 1966* (HKRS 410-10-27-2). The Hong Kong Record Series, Hong Kong.

Letter from Legal Department. (1968, 2 February). *Chinese Customary Marriages Part I, Letter from Legal Department, G. R. Sneath to Secretary for Chinese Affairs D. R. Holmes, 2 February 1968* (HKRS 634-1-23). The Hong Kong Record Series, Hong Kong.

Letter from the Secretary for Chinese Affairs. (1965a, 17 June). *Chinese Marriages in Hong Kong 1965 Development SCA 172_65 I, Letter from the Secretary for Chinese Affairs to C. Y. Kwan, 17 June 1965* (HKRS 410-10-27-1). The Hong Kong Record Series, Hong Kong.

Letter from the Secretary for Chinese Affairs. (1965b, 20 May). *Chinese Marriages in Hong Kong 1965 Development SCA 172_65 I, Letter from the Secretary for Chinese Affairs to C. Y. Kwan and others, 20 May 1965* (HKRS 410-10-27-1). The Hong Kong Record Series, Hong Kong.

Letter from the Secretary for Chinese Affairs. (1965c, 3 May). *Chinese Marriages in Hong Kong 1965 Development SCA 172_65 I, Letter from the Secretary for Chinese Affair to R. C. Lee and others, 3 May 1965* (HKRS 410-10-27-1). The Hong Kong Record Series, Hong Kong.

Letter from the Secretary for Chinese Affairs. (1965d, 31 May). *Chinese Marriages in Hong Kong 1965 Development SCA 172_65 I, Letter from the Secretary for Chinese Affairs to Attorney General and others, 31 May 1965* (HKRS 410-10-27-1). The Hong Kong Record Series, Hong Kong.

Letter from the Secretary for Chinese Affairs. (1968, 4 June). *Chinese Marriages in Hong Kong 1965 Development SCA 172_65 I, Letter from the Secretary for Chinese Affairs to Attorney General and others, 4 June 1968: Attachment* (HKRS 410-10-27-1). The Hong Kong Record Series, Hong Kong.

Letter from the Secretary for Home Affairs. (1967, 16 May). *Chinese Customary Marriages Part I, Letter from the Secretary for Home Affairs to C. Y. Kwan, 16 May 1967* (HKRS 634-1-23). The Hong Kong Record Series, Hong Kong.

Memo from Assistant to Law Officers. (1965, 28 May). *Chinese Marriages in Hong Kong 1965 Development SCA 172_65 I, Memo from Assistant to Law Officers, G. R. Sneath to Secretary for Chinese Affairs, 28 May 1965* (HKRS 410-10-27-1). The Hong Kong Record Series, Hong Kong.

Memo from Colonial Secretariat. (1970, 11 November). *Marriage Reform Ordinance, Memo from Colonial Secretariat to Director of Information Services, 11 November 1970* (HKRS 927-1-20). The Hong Kong Record Series, Hong Kong.

Memo from Director of Home Affairs. (1977, 7 December). *Marriage Reform Ordinance, Memo from Director of Home Affairs to Attorney General, 7 December 1977* (HKRS 927-1-21). The Hong Kong Record Series, Hong Kong.

Memo from Director of Legal Aid. (1978, 26 January). *Marriage Reform Ordinance, Memo from Director of Legal Aid to Attorney General and others, 26 January 1978* (HKRS 927-1-21). The Hong Kong Record Series, Hong Kong.

Memo from O/C Information Division. (1970, 20 May). *Marriage 08.02.1969 – 27.05.1974, Memo from O/C Information Division to O/C C.D.O. Enquiry Counters, 20 May 1970* (HKRS 582-1-1). The Hong Kong Record Series, Hong Kong.

Memo from Secretariat for Home Affairs. (1969, 16 December). *Marriage Reform Ordinance, Memo from Secretariat for Home Affairs to Colonial Secretary, 16 December 1969* (HKRS 927-1-20). The Hong Kong Record Series, Hong Kong.

Memo from the Secretary for Chinese Affairs. (1965, 26 November). *Chinese Marriage–1965 Development SCA 172_65 II, Memo from Secretary for Chinese Affairs to Colonial Secretary, 26 November 1965* (HKRS 410-10-27-2). The Hong Kong Record Series, Hong Kong.

Memorandum for Executive Council. (1965, 29 November). *Chinese Marriage–1965 Development SCA 172_65 II, Memorandum for Executive Council: Chinese Marriages in Hong Kong, 29 November 1965* (HKRS 410-10-27-2). The Hong Kong Record Series, Hong Kong.

Memorandum for Executive Council. (1970, 6 May). *Marriage Reform Ordinance, Memorandum for Executive Council: Marriage Reform Bill 1970, 6 May 1970* (HKRS 927-1-20). The Hong Kong Record Series, Hong Kong.

Memorandum for Executive Council. (1971, 4 November). *Marriage Reform Ordinance, Memorandum for Executive Council: Marriage Reform (Amendment) Bill 1971, 4 November 1971* (HKRS 927-1-21). The Hong Kong Record Series, Hong Kong.

Memorandum for Executive Council: Marriage. (1969, 30 June). *Chinese Customary Marriages Part I, Memorandum for Executive Council: Marriage Reform Bill 1969, 30 June 1969* (HKRS 634-1-23). The Hong Kong Record Series, Hong Kong.

Memorandum from Attorney General's Chambers. (1969, 28 April). *Chinese Customary Marriages Part I, Memorandum from Attorney General's Chambers to Colonial Secretary, 28 April 1969* (HKRS 634-1-23). The Hong Kong Record Series, Hong Kong.

Memorandum from Registrar General. (1969, 30 March). *Chinese Customary Marriages Part I, Memorandum from Registrar General to Colonial Secretary, 30 March 1969,* (HKRS 634-1-23). The Hong Kong Record Series, Hong Kong.
Memorandum from Secretary for Chinese Affairs. (1969, 27 June). *Chinese Customary Marriages Part I, Memorandum from Secretary for Chinese Affairs to Colonial Secretary and others: Note of a Meeting held in the Executive Council Chamber 9 June, 1969 to Discuss the Marriage Reform Bill and the Intestate's Estates Bill, 27 June 1969* (HKRS 634-1-23). The Hong Kong Record Series, Hong Kong.
Memorandum from Secretary for Home Affairs. (1969a, 12 March). *Chinese Customary Marriages Part I, Memorandum from Secretary for Home Affairs to Colonial Secretary, 12 March 1969* (HKRS 634-1-23). The Hong Kong Record Series, Hong Kong.
Memorandum from Secretary for Home Affairs. (1969b, 7 May). *Chinese Customary Marriages Part I, Memorandum from to the Colonial Secretary, 7 May 1969* (HKRS 634-1-23). The Hong Kong Record Series, Hong Kong.
Memorandum from the Colonial Secretariat. (1968, 13 August). *Chinese Customary Marriages Part I, Memorandum from the Colonial Secretariat to District Commissioner for New Territories and others, 13 August 1968,* (HKRS 634-1-23). The Hong Kong Record Series, Hong Kong.
Memorandum from the Colonial Secretariat. (1969, 5 May. *Chinese Customary Marriages Part I, Memorandum from The Colonial Secretariat to the Secretary for Home Affairs and others: Draft Notes of a Meeting Held on Wednesday 23 April 1969 to Consider Draft Legislation on Chinese Marriage, 5 May 1969* (HKRS 634-1-23). The Hong Kong Record Series, Hong Kong.
Memorandum from the Secretary for Chinese Affairs. (1968, 12 August). *Chinese Customary Marriages Part I, Memorandum from the Secretary for Chinese Affairs to Attorney General, 12 August 1968* (HKRS 634-1-23). The Hong Kong Record Series, Hong Kong.
Minute from I. H. Cruchley. (1968, 26 November). *Hong Kong Legal Affairs Chinese Laws and Customs, Minute from I. H. Cruchley to I. R. Murray, 26 November 1968* (FCO40/225). The National Archives, Kew.
Minute of D.D.C. (1969, 23 June). *Chinese Customary Marriages Part I, Note: Minute of D.D.C., 23 June 1969* (HKRS 634-1-23). The Hong Kong Record Series, Hong Kong.
Minute of McDouall. (1966, 6 January). *Chinese Marriage–1965 Development SCA 172_65 II, Minute of McDouall, 6 January 1966* (HKRS 410-10-27-2). The Hong Kong Record Series, Hong Kong.
Note for Executive. (1968, 18 April). *Chinese Customary Marriages, Note for Executive/Legislative Council: Chinese Marriage* (HKRS 634-1-23). The Hong Kong Record Series, Hong Kong.
Note: Recognition. (1968, 21 September). *Hong Kong Legal Affairs: Chinese Laws and Customs, Note: Recognition in Courts Abroad of Dissolutions of Marriage by Mutual Consent as Proposed in the White Paper by Solicitor General Hong Kong, 21 September 1968* (FOC40/225). The National Archives, Kew.
Notes by Mr Patrick Wong. (1965, 28 May). *Chinese Marriages in Hong Kong 1965 Development SCA 172_65 I, Notes by Mr Patrick Wong, Meeting with Chinese Unofficial Members on "Chinese Marriages in Hong Kong", 28 May 1965* (HKRS 410-10-27-1). The Hong Kong Record Series, Hong Kong.
Notes of a Meeting. (1969, 11 June). *Chinese Customary Marriages Part I, Notes of a Meeting on Chinese Marriages held on 9 June 1969, 11 June 1969* (HKRS 634-1-23). The Hong Kong Record Series, Hong Kong.
Notes of Government House. (1969, 10 January). *Chinese Customary Marriages Part I, Notes of Government House and Governor's Committee Meetings held on 10 January 1969,* (HKRS 634-1-23). The Hong Kong Record Series, Hong Kong.
Points Raised. (1967, 16 May). *Chinese Customary Marriages Part I, Points Raised from an Official Discussion of Proposed Marriage Reform Legislation and Connected Matters, 16 May 1967,* (HKRS 634-1-23). The Hong Kong Record Series, Hong Kong.
Savingram from Acting Governor of Hong Kong. (1968, 22 October). *Hong Kong Legal Affairs: Chinese Laws and Customs, Savingram from Acting Governor of Hong Kong to the Secretary*

of States for Foreign and Commonwealth Affairs, 22 October 1968, (FOC40/225). The National Archives, Kew.
Savingram from the Governor. (1969a, 6 February). *Hong Kong Legal Affairs Chinese Laws and Customs, Savingram from the Governor of Hong Kong to the Secretary of State for Foreign and Commonwealth Affairs, 6 February 1969* (FCO 40/225). The National Archives, Kew.
Savingram from the Governor. (1969b, 9 January). *Hong Kong Legal Affairs Chinese Laws and Customs, Savingram from the Governor of Hong Kong to the Secretary of State for Foreign and Commonwealth Affairs, 9 January 1969* (FCO40/225). The National Archives, Kew.
Savingram from the Secretary of State. (1965, 11 March). *Chinese Marriage–1965 Development SCA 172_65 II, Savingram from the Secretary of State for the Colonies to the Officer Administering the Government of Hong Kong, 11 March 1965,* (HKRS 410-10-27-2). The Hong Kong Record Series, Hong Kong.
Savingram from the Secretary of State. (1969, 16 April). *Hong Kong Legal Affairs Chinese Laws and Customs, Savingram from the Secretary of State for Foreign and Commonwealth Affairs to the Governor of Hong Kong, 16 April 1969* (FCO 40/225).
Speech by Secretary for Home Affairs. (1970, 3 June). *Marriage Reform Ordinance, Legislative Council: Speech by Secretary for Home Affairs: Proposed Second Reading of the Marriage Reform Bill 1970, Wednesday, 3 June 1970* (HKRS 927-1-20). The Hong Kong Record Series, Hong Kong.

Statutes

Legitimacy Ordinance (Cap. 184). http://oelawhk.lib.hku.hk/archive/files/9d65b97f803a9571ff973579fc7e0fbd.pdf. Accessed on 21 November 2018.
Affiliation Proceedings Ordinance (Cap. 183). http://oelawhk.lib.hku.hk/archive/files/2aecc6f92c87745624827d0b699519de.pdf. Accessed on 21 November 2018.
Deceased's Family Maintenance Ordinance (Cap. 129). http://oelawhk.lib.hku.hk/archive/files/02bbca938e4d9b7076249af9ac2cc55a.pdf. Accessed on 22 November 2018.
Intestates' Estates Ordinance (Cap. 73). http://oelawhk.lib.hku.hk/archive/files/6d5b44d0cd39f455aefa987db2e5cc9e.pdf.
Law Reform (Miscellaneous Provisions) Ordinance, Ord. No. 35 of 1971.
Married Persons Status Ordinance (Cap. 182). http://oelawhk.lib.hku.hk/archive/files/d7ae5d4506742194248bf1e251c83758.pdf.
Matrimonial (Amendment) Ordinance, Ord. No. 31 of 1971.

Cases

Angelo v Angelo [1967] 3 All ER 314.
Indyka v Indyka [1969] 7 All ER 689.

Part IV
Reflections

Chapter 7
Conclusion

Abstract This chapter concludes the book by examining the historical and social development leading to the abolition of concubinage in 1971. Concubinage had become illegal in the Republic of China in 1931 and the People's Republic of China in 1950. The continued existence of this Chinese custom (and its reinterpretation in Hong Kong by colonial courts) had been regarded as an obstacle to modernity, so its final eradication was unavoidable. The judicial response to the legal changes is demonstrated in the judgments of two cases decided by the Court of Final Appeal. Both cases show that the Marriage Reform Ordinance was adopted by the judges without difficulty in interpretation and that the new rules altering Chinese customary marriage remain intact to the present day.

Keywords Marriage Reform Ordinance · Monogamous marriage · Court of Final Appeal · Reception of Chinese customary law

7.1 Conclusion

After the Hong Kong Government decided to abolish concubinage in 1965, it took 5 years for the government to pass the Marriage Reform Ordinance, which was promulgated in 1971, to legally abolish the institution of concubinage in Hong Kong. The government also took this opportunity to propose and pass legislative changes to closely associated laws such as marriage, succession, inheritance and adoption laws. These legislative changes were passed without any controversy. All in all, since 1971, a registered monogamous marriage system on par with the common law has been practised in Hong Kong by the Chinese community.

As shown in Chap. 2, the retention of Chinese laws and customs was made possible by Captain Elliot's Proclamation and the Supreme Court Ordinance. The Chinese laws that were applied in Hong Kong were the Chinese laws and customs in force on 5 April 1843. The biggest challenge to the colonial government—so far as the Chinese marriage laws were concerned—was to ascertain the relevant Qing laws as enforced on 5 April 1843. The problem was that the laws promulgated by

M. WL Wong, *Chinese Marriage and Social Change*,
https://doi.org/10.1007/978-981-15-1644-3_7

the Qing government could not be directly applied in Hong Kong due to material differences between the colonial common law system in Hong Kong and the system of traditional Chinese law under Qing rule. Although the key legal principles of the marriage laws were provided in the Great Qing Code, as shown in Chap. 2, there were different laws and customary practices which might lead to different interpretations of Chinese laws and custom regarding concubinage under the Qing. In sum, such indeterminacy in the interpretation of the Chinese law and custom gave rise to many difficulties in interpreting such law in Hong Kong. Other jurisdictions also faced the same problems when court systems had to interpret Chinese law and custom, especially the provisions relating to the status and rights of the concubine.

Given the migration of the Chinese to other places in Asia, different jurisdictions had to adjudicate cases relating to Chinese communities. The biggest challenge was cases relating to the status and rights of a concubine. As shown in Chap. 3, different jurisdictions adopted similar approaches to the interpretation of concubinage in the name of Chinese law and custom. This chapter concluded that, in common with each other, when adjudicating cases the courts in these jurisdictions, while acknowledging the discriminatory nature of the traditional Chinese marriage system, attempted to give more rights to the concubine. For example, in the Strait Settlements, the court affirmed the right of a concubine to unilaterally dissolve the union of concubinage. In Hong Kong, meanwhile, a concubine could obtain an ordinary grant in a letter of administration issued by the Probate Office—a right that a wife enjoyed under statutory law. In sum, the discriminatory nature of Chinese law and custom did not prevent the courts from giving more rights to the concubines and their children—a deviation from the laws and practices under Qing law.

The successive reports released by the government on the reform of Chinese law and custom since the Strickland Report 1952 revealed that the Hong Kong Government did not initially intend to abolish concubinage. The reason was that the issue of abolition was not acceptable to the Chinese Unofficial members of the Executive and Legislative Councils. As seen in Chap. 3, Sir Man Kam Lo's comments to the Strickland Report showed that they were not prepared to accept any changes to Chinese law and custom relating to the marriage system. In the name of protecting Chinese customary practices, they intended to retain this system to their own benefit, since such a system was widely practised in their own community. Given that the Chinese senior political figures were key collaborators in colonial rule, who could help to sustain the social stability of Hong Kong, the government did not wish to break such an alliance.

It is important to note that the final impetus to stop the practice of concubinage in Hong Kong did not come from social pressure generated by local social organisations, but from the Colonial Office in London. As shown in Chap. 4, the Colonial Office, out of support for the equality of men and women, and a dislike of the system of concubinage of Hong Kong, did not support the approach taken by the Hong Kong Government, which was to let the institution of concubinage die a natural death. After the publication of the Ridehalgh/McDouall Report 1960, the Colonial Office reacted furiously to the "steady" approach taken by the Hong Kong

Government on abolition. Under repeated pressure from the Colonial Office, the Hong Kong Government decided to issue the McDouall/Heenan Report 1965, and its preliminary draft was sent to the Colonial Office for early approval of the decision to abolish concubinage. As shown in Chap. 5, after the Colonial Office was satisfied with the decision to wipe out the institution of concubinage, the Hong Kong Government then decided to publish a White Paper to formally announce this decision to the public, with an excerpt from the McDouall/Heenan Report. However, what the Hong Kong Government did not reveal, either in government records or to the public, was that the decision to abolish concubinage originated from the Colonial Office. The decision was not the result of the public consultation exercise conducted by the Hong Kong Government, nor did government officials decide to make concessions due to social pressure.

Afterwards, the Hong Kong Government had to introduce legislation to legally abolish concubinage. As shown in Chap. 6, dissatisfied with such decision, the Chinese Unofficial members of the Executive and Legislative Council put forward a last-ditch attempt to limit the rights of a concubine by proposing a legal definition of "concubine" in the legislation. Given the insistence of the Chinese Unofficial members of the Executive and Legislative Councils, a restrictive definition of concubine was specified in the Intestates' Estate Ordinance, which required that a concubine should be accepted by the principal wife or recognised by family members generally. Such restrictions limited the rights of a concubine who might give birth to a son and heir to a family, but who was denied equal rights if she was not accepted by the principal wife or the family members. This statutory requirement, which might possibly refer to *yap kung*, was not a requirement for valid status as a concubine in the GQC. Nor was it a legal requirement in other jurisdictions. Nevertheless, this redefinition of "concubine" is now generally part of Hong Kong law and applied generally in cases and administration.

This study shed lights on the use of Chinese law and custom as applied in many jurisdictions. Firstly, under colonial rule in Hong Kong, the abolition of the old customs required strong political will if the government was to resist pressures from traditionalists in the community. It is important to note that during the colonial development of Hong Kong, there were two major changes to family law in Hong Kong, which directly altered Chinese customary practices in Hong Kong. Before the Second World War, the abolition of the *Mui Tsai* system directly challenged Chinese customs, and finally, under pressure from London, the Hong Kong Government had to enforce laws to abolish this practice.[1] After the Second World War, the Marriage Reform Ordinance was the biggest intrusion of the imperial government of London, completely altering the Chinese family system in Hong Kong through the abolition of concubinage. Such drastic changes undoubtedly met with fierce opposition from the Chinese wealthy class, who were traditionally

[1] "Mui Tsai" was the name given to the female servants working in the Chinese family and was often regarded as an exploitive child slavery. See Miners (2003) and Jaschok (1988, pp. 133–144).

collaborators of colonial rule. Again, the insistence of the Colonial Office, under the principle of the equality of men and women, finally made such social changes a success through the Marriage Reform Ordinance.

Secondly, a successful case of legal transplantation such as the Marriage Reform Ordinance in Hong Kong not only required a strong political will to enforce the changes but also required the preparation of the community to receive the new laws voluntarily. The abolition of concubinage would not have been a success without community values being receptive to the concept of equality between men and women. In this context, social organisations played a pivotal role in popularising the importance of gender equality in the community and the abolition of concubinage. The campaigns of social organisations helped to expose the hardship of women in the institution of concubinage, leading to a social consensus in the community advocating for its earliest abolition. Thus, when the colonial government conceded to the demand for the abolition of concubinage, the social resistance (except in the Chinese wealthy class) to the changes was very small, and the reception of the new laws was completed without social unrest. Subsequent changes to the laws of succession, inheritance and adoption following the abolition of concubinage brought Hong Kong law in lines with the common law in the UK and were also received without opposition. It is important to note that some legal changes such as the extension of the Matrimonial Causes Ordinance to Chinese customary marriages originated from the Chinese member of the Legislative Council, T. S. Lo, and not from social organisations. This example shows that after the Pandora's box of legal change to Chinese custom was finally opened in Hong Kong, other social changes related to the marriage reform became unstoppable.

Thirdly, the judicial approach also played a pivotal role in facilitating social changes relating to the rights of a concubine in the Chinese marriage system. The judges in many jurisdictions had attempted to give more rights to concubines than they would have enjoyed if the judges had strictly followed traditional Chinese law and custom as enshrined in the GQC. The judges in some jurisdictions, taking the advantages of the common law system which gave flexibility in applying the rules in the liberal fashion, helped the concubine escape the cage of the GQC. The courts gave more rights to concubines, such as maintenance, and helped to rectify the inequality of men and women in the Chinese family system. In the absence of the legal abolition of concubinage, judges could provide judicial protection for ill-treated women, hopefully paving the way for legal abolition in the statute book. Even after the passage of the Marriage Reform Ordinance, judges played a significant role in giving more protection to women who were married under Chinese customary marriage. In this regard, it is important to investigate the reception of the Marriage Reform Ordinance in courts and how effective it could be in protecting wronged women in Chinese customary marriage.

7.2 Judicial Approach: Two Cases in the Court of Final Appeal

Two cases in the Court of Final Appeal help to illustrate the reception of Chinese customary marriages and the abolition of concubinage in the judicial system in Hong Kong. The first case is *Leung May Ling and Others v Leung Sai Lun Robert and Others* ([1999] 2 HKCFAR 94). In this case, the husband had married his first wife in 1951. The first wife died in 1963 with four children. Then the husband went through a Chinese customary marriage with his second wife in 1966. The second marriage produced three children. In 1985, the husband and second wife contracted their marriage under Section 38 of the Marriage Ordinance (Cap. 181).[2] The husband died in 1996. The children of the first marriage presented a will allegedly made in 1967, claiming that in this document the husband had named them his executors and only beneficiaries of the estate. The second wife and the children of the second marriage disputed, citing the Marriage Ordinance. However, there was no other testamentary document. The issue of this case was whether the 1985 marriage was valid, and if so, whether that marriage would have the effect of revoking the 1967 will produced by the children of the first marriage, assuming the will was genuine.

Much discussion in the judgment related to the interpretation of Section 13 of the Wills Ordinance. The appellants' (in other words, the children of the first marriage) appeal was dismissed. Litton PJ in the judgment stated that Section 38 of the Marriage Ordinance was not a mere ceremony. This marriage carried with it all the legal incidents attaching to a marriage:

> Once contracted, a 's. 38 marriage' carries with it all the legal incidents attaching to a *marriage*: Having been contracted before the Registrar under s. 21 of the Marriage Ordinance (Cap. 181) it is the 'civil equivalent of a Christian marriage': see s. 40(1) of the Marriage Ordinance (Cap. 181). Section 38 of the Marriage Ordinance (Cap. 181) may be compared with s. 39 of the same Ordinance dealing with persons living in 'unlawful concubinage' one of whom is dying: If a marriage between such persons is celebrated under s. 39 of the Marriage Ordinance (Cap. 181), sub-s.(2) expressly provides that such marriage shall not revoke any will previously made. It follows that, but for sub-s.(2), a s. 39 marriage *would* revoke a previous will. It would be odd if a 's.38 marriage' did not have the same effect in law. (*Leung Sai Lun Robert and others v Leung May Ling and Others* (1999) 2 HKCFAR 94; [1999] 1 HKLRD 649, per Litton PJ, pp. 99–100)

The judge, Litton PJ, agreed with the judgments of the courts below and held that this appeal had to be dismissed. In the High Court (*Leung May Ling & others v Leung Sai Lun & others* [1997] HKLRD 712), Patrick Chan J. stated that prior to the "Appointed Day" in 1971, as specified in the Marriage Reform Ordinance, the parties to a Chinese customary marriage could invoke Section 38 of the Marriage

---

[2] Section 38 specifies that "The parties to any non-Christian customary marriage duly celebrated according to the personal law and religion of the parties before the appointed day under the Marriage Reform Ordinance (Cap. 178) may, unless the husband has any other wife, contract with each other a marriage under this Ordinance; and such a marriage shall not invalidate the previous customary marriage".

Ordinance by voluntarily going through a registry marriage. The judge held that by doing this, the status of the husband and wife under Chinese customary marriage was subsumed in the registry marriage, which is monogamous in nature (Per Patrick Chan J., p. 716).[3] So this provision was an express statutory provision that allows the parties to an already valid marriage to marry again (Per Patrick Chan J., p. 717). The judge further explained that, if a husband had a concubine, the parties to the Chinese customary marriage could not go through a Section 38 of the Marriage Ordinance. Chan stated that this was because if the concubine was living, the husband and wife of the Chinese customary marriage could not say that their registry marriage under Section 38 of the Marriage Ordinance was a union for life between a man and a woman to the exclusion of others. To the judge, this section "is only a de facto monogamous status which can be subsumed in the monogamous status conferred under the registry marriage". In sum, the interpretation of the Chinese customary marriage by the judge followed precisely the rules and principles of the marriage reform laws as given in the Marriage Reform Ordinance: that a monogamous Chinese customary marriage would have the effect of the registered marriage under the Marriage Ordinance if the parties either registered under the Marriage Reform Ordinance (if under the Chinese customary marriage the husband had no other wife) or registered under Section 38 of the Marriage Ordinance (Per Patrick Chan J., p. 718).

Another case is *Suen Toi Lee v Yau Yee Ping* (2001). In this case, the husband, Mr Sung married his principal wife, in 1929. He then had instituted unions of concubinage with two women, Madam Sung in 1933 and Madam Chu in 1945. Then the husband Mr Sung moved to Hong Kong in 1951, and his second concubine Madam Chu joined him in the following year. His principal wife and his first concubine both remained in China. Madam Sung, the first concubine, died in 1983. Then the wife died in 2000. The husband died in 1985, and his second concubine Madam Chu died in 1987. It is important to note that all four of them were domiciled in China throughout. Subsequently, there were disputes on the entitlement of Madam Chu's estates. One claimant was the appellant, who was the daughter of the first concubine Madam Sung, and was born in Shanghai in 1940. The issue was whether her claim to a share in the second concubine Madam Chu's estate was good. This depended upon whether she, as the daughter of the first concubine Madam Sung, was an "issue" of the second concubine, Madam Chu for the purpose of the Intestates' Estate Ordinance. In other words, the court had to explain the meaning of "union of concubinage", for the purpose of Intestates' Estate Ordinance and, therefore, whether Madam Sung and Madam Chu, for the purpose of that Ordinance, were the concubines of Mr Sung.

The judge, Bokhary PJ, first had to decide the principle of domicile in relation to the application of the Chinese laws and customs in Mainland China and Hong Kong. He considered that the general principle was that there was scope for the Hong Kong court to apply Chinese laws and customs in the Mainland, but that it could

[3] The judge refers this rule to the case of *Yeung Yeu Kong v Yeung Fung Lai Mui* (1971).

only be applied indirectly via the rules of private international law (*Suen Toi Lee v Yau Yee Ping* 2001, p. 488). So, if such laws and customs were abrogated, this scope would naturally disappear. The judge explained that Hong Kong courts have proceeded on the view that a concubine's status was that of a "wife", but only a second wife. Her status was a matrimonial one, and unions of concubinage were therefore matrimonial unions. The judge explained that, under the rules of private international law applicable in Hong Kong, the capacity to enter into a matrimonial union (such as unions of concubinage), and therefore to acquire a matrimonial status, was determined by reference to the law of each party's place of antenuptial domicile. The judge considered that the laws of Hong Kong never conferred on the Chinese persons' capacity to enter into matrimonial unions, whether concubinage of any other type, if they had no such capacity under the law of their place of antenuptial domicile outside Hong Kong (*Suen Toi Lee v Yau Yee Ping* 2001, p. 488). In sum, the judge considered that if the parties' unions of concubinage were not recognised in the laws of China, then such unions would not be valid in Hong Kong.

The judge then held that, firstly, both Madam Chu and Madam Sung had never been domiciled in Hong Kong. However, Hong Kong law would have operated to give them capacity to enter into unions of concubinage under the Chinese laws and customs if they had been domiciled in Hong Kong at the time they entered into such unions. Secondly, when they were domiciled in Mainland China, unions of concubinage had been abolished in that jurisdiction. Therefore, under their domiciliary laws, Madam Sung and Madam Chu did not have the capacity to enter into a union of concubinage. The judge held that "[i]n the eyes of Hong Kong law therefore neither Madam Sung nor Madam Chu ever became Mr Sung's concubines under Chinese law and custom" (*Suen Toi Lee v Yau Yee Ping* 2001, p. 489).

The appeal from the appellant was dismissed. But the interpretation of the union of concubinage is worth mentioning here. The judge in obiter considered that there might be a possibility that a union of concubinage could exist for an unmarried man:

> Moreover, it should be pointed out that the description of a concubine a secondary wife should not be understood to imply that the taking of concubines was confined to married men. The writings on the subject suggest that although highly unusual it was not known for unmarried men to take concubines. It is well established that the valid taking of a concubine depended on open acceptance by the wife and open recognition by the man's family generally. But it would appear that this meant the acceptance by the wife *if any*. [emphasis in original] (*Suen Toi Lee v Yau Yee Ping* 2001, p. 481)

Another judge, Millet NPJ, considered that the laws of Hong Kong recognised unions of concubinage validly entered into abroad, just as it recognised marriages validly entered into abroad. He held that "once a marriage has become monogamous by that law, it is treated as if it were monogamous from its reception". So, he considered that if such a marriage might become polygamous by a change in a man's domicile, a mere change of residence was not enough. Millet NPJ held that Mr Sung's two unions of concubinage were contracted after 1931 (the year when the Civil Code 1931 of the Republic of China abolished the institution of concubinage) while he was still domiciled in Mainland China. Millet NPJ held that "Mr Sung remained domiciled on the Mainland of China throughout his life, and he could not change Mandam Sung's status or the marriage merely by coming to reside in Hong Kong". Millet NPJ further stated that even if he had entered into a fresh union of concubinage prior to the appointed day, such validity of the union would depend on his domicile (*Suen Toi Lee v Yau Yee Ping* 2001, p. 503).

This case showed the importance of domicile in determining the validity of the union of concubinage contracted outside Hong Kong before the appointed day of the Marriage Reform Ordinance. This case did not question the validity of the definition of the union of concubinage in the Intestates' Estate Ordinance. Seen in this light, the modified version of the definition of concubine, as suggested in 1969, subsequent to pressure from the Chinese Unofficial members of the Executive and Legislative Councils has been widely accepted as part of the Chinese customary law. This interpretation remains intact even in the twenty-first century.

References

Jaschok, M. (1988). *Concubines and bond servants: The social history of a Chinese customs*. Hong Kong: Oxford University Press.

McDouall/Heenan Report 1965, in Memorandum for Executive Council (1965, November 29). *Chinese Marriage–1965 Development SCA 172_65 II, Memorandum for Executive Council: Chinese marriages in Hong Kong, 29 November 1965*, (HKRS 410-10-27-2). The Hong Kong Record Series, Hong Kong.

Miners, N. (2003). The attempts to abolish the Mui tsai system in Hong Kong, 1917–1941. In D. Faure (Ed.), *Hong Kong: A reader in social history*. Hong Kong: Oxford University Press.

Ridehalgh, A., & McDouall, J. C. (1960). *Chinese marriages in Hong Kong*. Hong Kong: Government Printer.

Statutes

Intestates' Estates Ordinance (Cap. 73). http://oelawhk.lib.hku.hk/archive/files/6d5b44d0cd39f455aefa987db2e5cc9e.pdf

Marriage Ordinance (Cap. 181).

Marriage Reform Ordinance (Cap. 178).

Cases

Leung May Ling & others v Leung Sai Lun & others [1997] HKLRD 712 (High Court).

Leung Sai Lun & others v Leung May Ling & others [1999] 1 HKLRD 649, (1999) 2 HKCFAR 94.

Suen Toi Lee v Yau Yee Ping (2001) 4 HKCFAR 474, [2002] 1 HKLRD 197.

Yeung Yeu Kong v Yeung Fung Lai Mui [1971] HKLR 13.

Glossary

Terms marked (c) are in Cantonese, (p) are in Pinyin, and (w) are in Wade-Giles.

Ce shi (p)	側室
Chi (p)	笞
Ch'i (w)	妻
Da Li Yuan (p)	大理院
Da Qing Lu Li (p)	大清律例
Dagong (p)	大功
Di (p)	嫡
Di mu (p)	嫡母
Di qi (p)	嫡妻
Fen jia (p)	分家
Fen shu (p)	分書
Fu ching (c)	扶正
Fu qi (p)	副妻
Fuji (p)	服制
Furen (p)	婦人
Gusha (p)	故殺
Hakka (c)	客家
Hejian (p)	和姦
Heti (p)	合體
Hoklo (c)	鶴佬
Huajiao (p)	花轎
Hunshu (p)	婚書
Jiahao (p)	枷號
Jiazang (p)	家長
Jian sheng zhi (p)	姦生子
Kim Tiu (c) jian tiao (p)	兼祧
Kit fat (c)	結髮
Kwo men (w)	過門

M. WL Wong, *Chinese Marriage and Social Change*,
https://doi.org/10.1007/978-981-15-1644-3

Li (p)	例
Li Ji (p)	禮記
Lüshedafa lishunrenqing (p)	律設大法 禮順人情
Màixiu (p)	賣休
Mǎixiu (p)	買休
Mingfen (p)	名份
Mui Tsai (c)	妹仔
Nacai (p)	納采
Naji (p)	納吉
Nazheng (p)	納徵
Ngoi Shut (c)	外室
Ping t'sai (c)	平妻
Qingqi (p)	請期
Qiqin beiyou (p)	期親卑幼
Qiqin zunzhang (p)	期親尊長
Sam Po Tsai (c)	新抱仔
Shou zhi (p)	守志
Shengzheng (p)	升正
Shu (p)	庶
Shu mu (c)	庶母
Shu zi (p)	庶子
Shuitia (p)	說帖
Sima (p)	緦麻
Tanka (c)	蜑家
Tongpan (p)	通判
Tongyangxi (p)	童養媳
Tsing Sheung (c); Zheng chang (p)	蒸嘗
T'sip, tsip (c); qie (p); ch'ieh (w)	妾
Tiaoli (p)	條例
Tin fong (c)	填房
Tsi mu (c); ci mu (p); tz'u mu (w)	慈母
Wangmao (p)	妄冒
Wen (p)	文
Wenming (p)	問名
Wufu (p)	五服
Xiaogong (p)	小功
Xiefenniekong (p)	挾忿捏控
Xisong (p)	息訟
Xue guan (p)	學官
Yang lao fen (p)	養老分
Yang shan (p)	養贍
Yap kung (c)	入宮
Yayi (p)	衙役
Yi (p)	彝
Yifen (p)	義忿

Yijue (p)	義絕
Yijuzhiershansha (p)	已拘執而擅殺
Ying (p)	媵
Yiti (p)	一體
Ze Zheng Yuan (p)	資政院
Zhanchui (p)	斬衰
Zhang (p)	杖
Zheng shi (p)	正室
Zhouxianzili (p)	州縣自理
Zhun qi (p)	準妻
Zicui (p)	齊衰
Zouling (p)	佐領

The manufacturer's authorised representative in the EU is Springer Nature Customer Service Centre GmbH, Europaplatz 3, 69115 Heidelberg, Germany. If you have any concerns regarding our products, please contact ProductSafety@springernature.com

Printed and bound by CPI Group (UK) Ltd, Croydon, CR0 4YY
30/09/2026
02225234-0005